STUDYING
MEDIEVAL
WOMEN

A *SPECULUM* BOOK

STUDYING MEDIEVAL WOMEN

Sex, Gender, Feminism

edited by

Nancy F. Partner

The Medieval Academy of America

Cambridge, Massachusetts

1993

Contents

Foreword

This collection of articles first appeared as a special issue of *Speculum: A Journal of Medieval Studies*, published in the April 1993 issue.

The articles have for the most part not been revised, although a few minor corrections and additions have been made. New in this printing are an addendum to the Introduction and annotated bibliographies, which were commissioned by the editor to inspire further reading and study. The authors were asked to report on the literature that helped to shape their thinking about women's studies, with special emphasis on works outside the confines of medieval studies.

Nancy Partner, editor of this book as of the special issue of *Speculum* that preceded it, has earned my gratitude many times over. I am also grateful to the members of the Editorial Board of *Speculum* who read and criticized the articles before publication. They are John W. Baldwin, Roberta Frank, Ralph Hanna III, W. Eugene Kleinbauer, and Edith Dudley Sylla.

This first *Speculum* Book is intended as an invitation to medievalists and their students to explore important issues in the study of the Middle Ages.

LUKE WENGER
Editor of *Speculum*

Introduction

By Nancy F. Partner

It strikes me as mildly surprising to find myself able to contemplate with that certain tolerance we reserve for things safely dead, those times, so near and yet so far, when medieval history really was what so repelled Catherine Morland in Jane Austen's *Northanger Abbey*:

> The quarrels of popes and kings, with wars and pestilences in every page; the men all so good for nothing, and hardly any women at all—it is very tiresome.

And yet, the alteration has been so recent that only now can I reply, across some 193 years, to Catherine Morland—yes, and the "hardly any women at all" part *was* pretty tiresome.

The reasons which account for the recorded history of the political, social, religious, and aesthetic strivings of our mammalian species being so overwhelmingly dominated by only one of its two sexes have turned out, on repeated examination, to be so shamelessly thin and brittle that there is almost something comical about it, in a nasty bad-joke sort of way. Now that women medievalists and medieval women are visibly and permanently part of the scene, there remain some major disagreements over how centrally the results of more than two decades of scholarship on women have been incorporated into the main body of medieval studies: as Judith Bennett sees it, "although *women* are better assimilated into medieval studies in the 1990s, *feminist scholarship* is not," while in Allen Frantzen's view, "feminist scholarship today pervades the disciplines of art, history, law, literature, and religion." I myself cannot attempt to reconcile their views or side with one against the other; I am not sure. Intellectual influence and disciplinary centrality are tricky things to measure. What is beyond dispute, however, is that feminist scholarship (using the term in the inclusive sense proposed by Judith Bennett) has restored to the Middle Ages the substantial reality that human societies consist of *two* sexes.

Stated so baldly, it does seem a rather curious thing for so many people (albeit males) to have absentmindedly forgotten for so long. Like many profoundly important true things, this one, that human society consists of *two* sexes, can be stated so simply that it is faintly embarrassing to say or write it. But it is important almost beyond the power of expression to medieval studies. To a field of the historical past so poignantly vulnerable to desuetude and the offhand death by neglect we inflict on the nontrendy (and academics are fully implicated in this), the restoration of women to the historical scene is life itself. Medievalists mercifully forget just how easily the imagined medieval world virtually parodies itself into the tedious grinding of smallish power struggles over matters of incomprehensible advantage to opaquely obsessed belligerents, while somewhere in the cultural background celibate nonbelligerents think disembodied thoughts directed vaguely to sustaining an abstract worldview by thinking it over

1

and over again in ever more abstruse versions. The "one-sex model" (to misuse a current phrase) of medieval society gives all the "body" to one part of society and all the "mind" to another, which is a notably corpselike arrangement.

The restoration of women to the scene, to every locale and activity, restores a human world where body and mind are inextricably united, and where women and men struggle through their lives pursuing human wishes by human means, inevitably and always together (however inharmoniously), together in their emotions, thoughts, and imaginations, even when separate in their outward circumstances. This "together and against" conjuncture of both sexes carried even to the furthest precincts of single-sex exclusivity is a fundamental fact of human life, and will be until each sex masters parthenogenesis. If feminism, in its quite specialized role in medieval scholarship, is the energy behind this effort, then it is not only doing justice to medieval women, it is restoring their full humanity to medieval men. Far from radicalizing medieval studies, feminist scholarship is, in this respect, normalizing the discipline.

In one way or another, all the essays in this collection address the question of the distinctness of women in their historical experience, but with no monolith ideology or diversity-stifling agenda. No two of these essays formulates its questions in the same way; none of them use exactly the same method or consult the same sources or scholarship; they all reach for nonmedieval concepts and to nonmedieval disciplines but in nonidentical directions. Yet all the essays interestingly pursue answers and ideas which return men and women to the same world, not very happily always, but inexorably. If there is any theme deeply uniting this collection, which otherwise freely displays the unusual scope and variety of women-focused medieval studies, it is the multiform demonstration of the fact that medieval men and women were always on one another's minds.

The subjects covered in this issue of *Speculum* are simply what the title promises: sex, gender, feminism, but in some not-obvious combinations and permutations. If all the essays are marked by the note of both-sex inclusiveness, they are also notable for the range of nonmedieval disciplines and concepts brought to bear on medieval topics in the essentially traditional areas of literature, history, art history, and religion the writers address.

Studying Medieval Women opens with Judith Bennett's historical survey and assessment of the status of women scholars in academe and the Medieval Academy, and of feminist scholarship in the medieval fields. The *Speculum* that once stood for "Latinity, antimodernity, and masculinity" now is in a complicated state of transition. Medieval studies are generally open to women scholars, but feminist scholarship has yet to find its way to unquestioned acceptance in mainstream thought. Bennett argues that this lingering uneasiness is unfounded and unnecessary: "Feminist politics have . . . not undermined the fundamental disinterestedness of medieval research"; rather, feminism is invigorating the field and extending its audience.

In her analysis of the iconographic and expressive intentions in the illuminations to a prayer book created expressly for a young royal bride, Madeline Caviness shows how the traditional rigorous techniques of art history can be awakened to new interpretations when the viewer-scholar's deep responses are brought forward for conscious inspection and use. Reading the disturbing semi-explicit interplay between pious pages and lewd margins as a specifically *woman* scholar, Caviness opens the prayer book's subtext of gendered passivity and sexual threat.

The concept of gender, indicating the extrabiologic qualities regarded as masculine or feminine, has been producing some surprising results when applied to long-distant societies. Carol Clover examines early Scandinavian laws and sagas for evidence of the precise nature of their unstated assumptions about sex and gender; she finds that gender, organized around an exacting ideal of masculinity, was a system of values only loosely connected to maleness or femaleness: ". . . the principle of sex is not so final or absolute that it could not be overridden by greater interests." At times, the evidence disconcertingly suggests: "Better a son who is your daughter than no son at all."

Kathleen Biddick offers a complex and reflective analysis of the structural principles informing Caroline Walker Bynum's *Holy Feast and Holy Fast*, regarded as a book very much about the "problems concerning the production of gendered knowledge in history today." The intention of this essay is antistructuralist in the uncompromising sense that Biddick rejects the validity of models of explanation which appeal to coherence, completeness, or organic form for their persuasive force. Such appeals, she argues, are merely aesthetic and are too culturally embedded in our traditional value systems to be offered as objective or disinterested. Therefore Biddick deliberately sets out to undermine and disorient the very idea of any coherent picture of medieval culture because coherence as an effect is always and only purchased by means of exclusions, hierarchies, and doctrinal notions of what is natural, essential, and fundamental to reality.

My own contribution is an essay organized around a few medieval vignettes seen in relation to a new and forceful view of human sexuality-in-society known as social constructionist theory. I argue that this approach depersonalizes and dehumanizes its historical subjects, ignores the need for some explanation of human diversity and intransigence, and is built on an inadequate conceptual framework. The women of medieval and other deeply misogynist societies cannot be recognized with this approach. My opinion is that a psychoanalytically informed psychology addressed to the human "self" offers the most adequate corrective to this currently fashionable view of socially constructed beings.

An essay subtly and amicably addressing the various ways in which "women aren't enough" is the end-frame for this collection. Allen Frantzen, who claims here the title of "the token man," sees feminist studies in art, history, law, literature, and religion as so pervasive that, "if not the norm, [they] are now so regular an exception to it that they have redefined the norm." The time has come for men to be welcomed back. Specifically, the conceptual instrument of gender, so central to feminist analysis, cannot sensibly be limited to females and femininity: "Now that the study of the 'masculine' has become as crucial as the study of the 'feminine,' we find that gender . . . severs the supposedly 'natural' connection between the subject of sex and women. . . ." In short, the stage must now be shared.

At least the stage of this small collection is shared among several, not always perfectly compatible, points of view. This evident lack of any monolithic quality in a single-subject issue of *Speculum* should, I think, be reassuring to its readers; and it is with particular pleasure that I note the multitude of intriguing ways in which the footnotes, alone, to this issue make it worth, as they say, the price of admission.

*   *   *

It was precisely the unusually interesting quality of those footnotes tracing the routes the several writers have taken away from and back to medieval texts and images that started the idea of adding a special bibliographical appendix to the collection for its publication in book form. The title of this volume, *Studying Medieval Women*, places rather more stress on the process-verb than the object-noun because our organizing purpose was to open up the theoretical-interpretive premises of women-focused medieval studies to the readers of *Speculum* and as many others as we can attract. There is, after all, no longer anything very new or especially provocative about the subject of women or even gender or sexuality, considered simply as objects of scholarly attention. It is the quality and exact nature of that *attention* that deserves close inspection and even, we admit, some suspicion these days. Medievalists who are erasing old disciplinary boundaries ought therefore to be very candid, generously self-explanatory, and open, especially when their work is informed by concepts and language that are not part of the traditional training in medieval studies.

Even at the undergraduate level, courses in the Middle Ages remain some of the few occasions on which students are asked to learn things they don't already know; graduate students of the various medieval disciplines serve a time-absorbing apprenticeship mastering unfamiliar knowledge and technical skills. The prospect of critical reading and perhaps writing to a professional standard on medieval subjects with an added flourish of exotica imported from gender theory, feminist theory, psychoanalysis, deconstruction, semiotics, poststructuralist anthropology, postcolonialist queer theory, post-postmodernist theory . . . well, it can easily seem a bit much to ask of people. No theory enthusiast has any business demanding that medieval prosopographers drop their exacting tasks and instantly immerse themselves in anti-essentialist gender performance theory or risk . . . what? Any such venture has to seem intrinsically interesting and useful to the inquiring mind. Life is short; books are long.

It is the view of the writers of this anthology that at the very least, readers have a right to ask for a few credentials or some reasonable informal equivalent; and that prospective theory-informed medievalists should be offered practical advice and unmysterious explanations. The basis of the short, annotated bibliographies assembled at the end of this volume is to offer readers "what works," at least for each of us—that is, what books, essays, and journals have, in our quite various experiences, really helped us to think through some very old subjects in persuasive new ways and can be seriously recommended to others. The bibliographies are neither medieval nor comprehensive, but personal and draw frankly on elements of intellectual autobiography. Should this book be used in seminars, students can see plainly what sort of ideas helped to construct the intellectual frame of reference each article occupies, and this information can then be used as anyone's taste and inclination dictate.[1]

[1] This special issue of *Speculum* was, from first conception to finish, truly a Medieval Academy project and enjoyed the support and assistance of the journal's editorial staff. The entire collection was read in manuscript by the members of the Editorial Board, all of whom offered detailed and helpful responses. Each of the essays benefited from Jacqueline Brown's fastidious erudition and tactful, tireless attention to detail; and my special thanks to Luke Wenger, who apparently is immune to panic, for urbane and open-minded encouragement through every phase and crisis in the process that resulted in this book.

Medievalism and Feminism

By Judith M. Bennett

"What is this journal *Speculum?*" the prospective graduate student asked me. "Is it some sort of radical feminist journal? I saw copies of it in Professor So-and-So's office, and I can't imagine that *he* would subscribe to a feminist publication. . . . So, what is *Speculum?*" To understand this question, I had to remember myself at twenty-two years of age, educated but not professionalized, more familiar with speculum as an instrument used in gynecological examinations than with *Speculum*, the premier journal for medievalists. Vaguely recalling my own puzzlement at first encountering a journal for medievalists called *Speculum*, I explained to the student the Latin derivation of the title, the importance of the journal in medieval studies, and the absolute absence of a connection between the title of the journal and anything gynecological. We chuckled a bit—in female solidarity—about the naïveté of *Speculum*'s founders (all male, we correctly assumed), who had chosen to title their journal with a name that resonated so strongly (and so misleadingly) for modern women.

But were the founders of *Speculum* really naive, really unaware of the other meanings of their chosen title? In the months since that student and I so blithely assumed their ignorance of the gynecological speculum, I have begun to doubt it. The records of the formation of the journal in the 1920s tell us only that a few other titles were considered (e.g., *The Middle Ages* and *Mediaeval Studies*) and that E. K. Rand (who, as it turned out, became the first editor of the journal) especially advocated the choice of *Speculum* because it suggested to him "the multitudinous mirrors in which the people of the Middle Ages liked to gaze at themselves and other folk."[1] This sounds quite innocent of any gynecological reflection. Nevertheless, it now seems possible to me that Rand and his associates knew the gynecological meaning of "speculum."

In a rare moment for a medievalist, I have been able to conduct oral history on this point. My maternal grandfather, who in the 1920s was practicing obstetrics and gynecology in New Jersey, has assured me that the speculum was in regular use at the time, that his patients almost certainly knew the name of this instrument, and that "although most men at that time might have never seen a speculum, they probably knew of its gynecological use."[2] What he remembers so clearly can be confirmed in written sources. At the time that *Speculum* received its title, the most common meaning of "speculum" was its medical meaning; the gynecological speculum was regularly used by physicians; and it

---

[1] E. K. Rand in *Speculum* 1 (1926), 4. Luke Wenger provided me with photocopies of documents describing the early history of the journal (as well as his own reconstruction of that history). I would like to thank him not only for these materials but also for information about the membership, officers, and annual meetings of the Medieval Academy.

[2] Telephone interview with Robert Abbe MacKenzie, M.D., 4 November 1991.

had even been a subject of considerable public discussion and debate.[3] Perhaps
Rand and his associates were peculiarly insulated from all this, but perhaps not.
It seems quite possible that, rather than being ignorant of the term's gynecological usage, they were very aware of this modern meaning and happy (either
consciously or unconsciously) to counter speculum-as-a-gynecological-instru-
ment with a *Speculum* that asserted Latinity, antimodernity, and masculinity.

Whatever their intentions, the founders of *Speculum* gave their journal a title
whose double entendre has grown much louder in the last few decades. Since
the 1960s activists in the feminist health movement have focused even more
public attention on the speculum—urging doctors to exercise more care in its
use and urging women to use it on our own for self-examination.[4] Indeed, the
speculum became by the early 1970s a critical symbol of women's control of
our own bodies; in 1973, for example, one feminist newsletter published a
cartoon showing Wonder Woman swinging a speculum at an intimidated male
physician and shouting, "With my *speculum*, I *am* strong! I *can* fight!" (at her
feet lay already vanquished representatives of such groups as Planned Parent-
hood, the American Medical Association, the Pro-Life movement, and Zero
Population Growth).[5] More recently, Luce Irigaray's *Speculum of the Other Woman*
has become the center of intense debate among feminist theorists—about her
depiction of woman as a mirrored "otherness" or "absence," about her seemingly essentialist link between women's bodies and women's voices, about the
very (im)possibility of a truly free female speech.[6] For feminists in the 1990s,
then, the speculum is a powerful representation, speaking not only to women's
knowledge of our own bodies but also to women's cultural and social positioning
in a patriarchal world.[7] As a result of this ongoing feminist speculation, the title

---

[3] *A New English Dictionary*, 9/1 (Oxford, 1919), p. 560, gave as its first definition for "speculum"
"A surgical instrument of various forms, used for dilating orifices of the body so as to facilitate
examination or operations." It also reported that in English usage the medical meaning of "speculum" antedated its meaning as a mirror by about a half century. *The Oxford English Dictionary*
(Oxford, 1933) repeated this information without change. As this definition indicates, there are
many medical uses of the term "speculum," but the gynecological speculum has been and remains
the predominant use of the medical instrument. For public debates about the gynecological speculum, see especially Judith R. Walkowitz, *Prostitution and Victorian Society: Women, Class and the
State* (Cambridge, Eng., 1980).

[4] See, for example, Boston Women's Health Collective, *Our Bodies, Ourselves* (New York, 1971),
esp. pp. 270–71. Interestingly, both sorts of speculum are used in a gynecological self-examination:
a speculum to open the walls of the vagina *and* a mirror to reflect the images back to the subject.

[5] See the illustration on p. 9. I would like to thank Etta Breit for bringing this cartoon to my
attention. It was reproduced in Barbara Ehrenreich and Deirdre English, *Complaints and Disorders:
The Sexual Politics of Sickness* (Old Westbury, N.Y., 1973).

[6] Although published in French in 1974, this book was not widely read in the United States until
its translation in 1985: Luce Irigaray, *Speculum of the Other Woman*, trans. Gillian G. Gill (Ithaca,
N.Y., 1985). In seeking to understand Irigaray and her influence on modern feminist theory, I have
relied on four texts: Janet Todd, *Feminist Literary History* (Cambridge, Eng., 1988); Toril Moi, *Sexual/
Textual Politics: Feminist Literary Theory* (London, 1985); Margaret Whitford, "Rereading Irigaray,"
in *Between Feminism and Psychoanalysis*, ed. Teresa Brennan (London, 1989), pp. 106–26; Carolyn
Burke, "Irigaray through the Looking Glass," *Feminist Studies* 7 (1981), 288–306.

[7] I would like to emphasize that the speculum is not an unambivalently positive representation
for feminists, for it has often been seen as an instrument of male control over women. For example,

Cartoon by C. Clement, front cover of *Sister* (July 1973),
published by the Los Angeles Women's Center

Speculum can suggest—especially for the hundreds of medievalists today who
are also feminists—both medievalism *and* feminism.

Of course, *Speculum* rarely carries this double meaning. For most medievalists
Speculum is a modern echo of a popular medieval title, evoking reflection and
perspective, not gynecology and certainly not feminism.[8] *Speculum* resonates so
narrowly for us because we have accepted a narrow perception of our field, a
perception that usually treats the combination of feminist studies and medieval
studies as curious or anomalous or even appalling. Medievalism and feminism:
an odd and unwelcomed couple. I think this perception is wrong, for as I wish
to argue in this essay, the separation of medievalism and feminism is both
artificial and counterproductive. Feminist work in medieval studies is a thriving

---

in the late nineteenth century, Josephine Butler, campaigning against the use of the speculum in
forced examinations of prostitutes by police physicians, condemned it as a form of "instrumental
rape"; see Walkowitz, *Prostitution and Victorian Society*. For another example, its use in early-modern
Germany has recently been associated with "the intrusion of early modern male practitioners into
the birthing room"; see Lynne Tatlock, "Speculum Feminarum: Gendered Perspectives on Obstetrics
and Gynecology in Early Modern Germany," *Signs* 17 (1992), 725–60 (quotation from p. 757).

[8] See especially Ritamary Bradley, "Backgrounds of the Title *Speculum* in Mediaeval Literature,"
Speculum 29 (1954), 100–115.

enterprise with a distinguished past and a promising future. Although the medieval-studies community is often indifferent and sometimes hostile to this feminist scholarship, the blending of medievalism and feminism works to the mutual benefit of both feminist studies and medieval studies. In short, the founders of *Speculum* might have been either naive or unconcerned about the gynecological speculum of their own day, but they were prescient about the development of medieval studies. The title they chose in 1925 means even more today, speaking not only to what medieval studies has been but also to what medieval studies is becoming.

It is difficult to assess the rich, varied, and as yet, unwritten history of women in the development of medieval studies.[9] On the one hand, women have always been active in medieval studies, and indeed, women today are more active in medieval scholarship than in most other branches of academia. As David Herlihy reported in his presidential address ten years ago, women constitute more than one-third of the members of the Medieval Academy. This is not parity, but it is much better than most other academic disciplines.[10] On the other hand, although medieval studies has always accommodated women with more alacrity than other fields, the accommodation has been a restricted one. For example, women were part of the Medieval Academy from its beginning, but only a small part. Of the 33 fellows elected in 1926, only one was a woman (Nellie Neilson of Mount Holyoke). No women served on the original editorial board for *Speculum*, but one woman was included among 19 scholars on the advisory board (Cornelia Catlin Coulter of Vassar and then Mount Holyoke). The place of women in the Medieval Academy remained quite restricted for many decades: a few female fellows, a few female officers, and no female presidents until Ruth Dean in 1973–74.[11] Moreover, even this restricted place for women long relied on sex-segregated training and employment, especially at Bryn Mawr and Mount Holyoke, where generations of young women were inspired to take up careers in medieval studies.[12]

---

[9] Although some of my comments in this section pertain also to medieval studies in Europe, I shall focus on North American relationships between medievalists, female scholars, and feminist scholarship.

[10] David Herlihy, "The American Medievalist: A Social and Professional Profile," *Speculum* 58 (1983), 885. For comparison, women constituted less than 25 percent of the membership of the American Historical Association in the early 1980s (I am grateful to Noralee Frankel for providing me with this information).

[11] In addition to Ruth Dean, the following women have served as presidents: Eleanor Searle (1985–86), Katherine Fischer Drew (1986–87), Marcia L. Colish (1991–92). I would like to emphasize the accuracy of this list, for two women (Helen Wieruszowski and Nellie Neilson) have recently been misidentified as past presidents of the Medieval Academy. For Wieruszowski, see Susan Mosher Stuard, *Women in Medieval History and Historiography* (Philadelphia, 1987), p. 88. For Neilson, see Jacqueline Goggin, "Challenging Sexual Discrimination in the Historical Profession: Women Historians and the American Historical Association, 1890–1940," *American Historical Review* 97 (1992), 796.

[12] This sex-segregated training and employment severely limited the professional opportunities of early female medievalists. As Neilson herself complained in 1939, "Women scholars do not have access as a rule to the research professorships that are the Mecca of men scholars"; quoted in Margaret Hastings and Elisabeth G. Kimball, "Two Distinguished Medievalists—Nellie Neilson and Bertha Putnam," *Journal of British Studies* 18 (1979), 146.

To be sure, these early female medievalists were respected by their male colleagues. Eileen Power was remembered in *Speculum* as a scholar of "great distinction"; Nellie Neilson, noted for her "thorough and penetrating" work, was the first woman elected president of the American Historical Association (in 1943); Bertha Putnam was remembered as one of the earliest "feminist pioneers," with a "fine character" and "tough mind"; Hope Emily Allen was memorialized as "quick and ardent in research, bold in interpretation, meticulous in verification."[13] Nevertheless, these early female medievalists did not and have not found a place among the founders of medieval studies. In 1950 F. N. Robinson included in his presidential address an extended discussion of the scholars who helped form medieval studies in late-nineteenth-century and early-twentieth-century America. He mentioned not a single female scholar. More recent histories by S. Harrison Thomson, William J. Courtenay, and Norman Cantor do much the same.[14] In both its development and its own history, then, medieval studies has adopted a pluralistic model: men have tolerated women in the field, but women have been kept segregated from and subordinated to the mainstream. Perhaps "separate but equal" in conceptualization; certainly "separate and unequal" in actual practice.[15]

Today, of course, women are more numerous and more prominent in me-

[13] See memoirs published in *Speculum* as follows: Power, 16 (1941), 381–82; Neilson, 25 (1950), 417–18; Putnam, 35 (1960), 522–23; Allen, 36 (1961), 535. For other memoirs of early female medievalists (all either fellows or corresponding fellows of the Medieval Academy), see Belle Da Costa Greene, 32 (1957), 642–44; Lis Jacobsen, 37 (1962), 489–90; Helen Jane Waddell, 41 (1966), 600–601; Dorothy Waley Singer, 42 (1967), 593; Helen Maud Cam, 43 (1968), 572–73. See also Hastings and Kimball, "Two Distinguished Medievalists"; Susan Mosher Stuard, "A New Dimension? North American Scholars Contribute Their Perspective," in her edited volume *Women in Medieval History and Historiography*, pp. 81–99; John C. Hirsh, *Hope Emily Allen: Medieval Scholarship and Feminism* (Norman, Okla., 1988); Goggin, "Challenging Sexual Discrimination"; Maxine Berg, "The First Women Economic Historians," *Economic History Review*, 2nd ser., 45 (1992), 308–29.

[14] F. N. Robinson, "Anniversary Reflections," *Speculum* 25 (1950), 491–501, esp. pp. 493–95. S. Harrison Thomson, "The Growth of a Discipline: Medieval Studies in America," in *Perspectives in Medieval History*, ed. Katherine Fischer Drew and Floyd Seyward Lear (Chicago, 1963), pp. 1–18. William J. Courtenay, "The Virgin and the Dynamo: The Growth of Medieval Studies in America (1870–1930)," in *Medieval Studies in North America, Past, Present, and Future*, ed. Francis G. Gentry and Christopher Kleinhenz (Kalamazoo, 1982), pp. 5–22. Thomson briefly mentions two female scholars (Neilson and Edith Rickert) in an essay that details the work of dozens of male medievalists. Courtenay does note that honors bestowed upon Neilson and Coulter by the Medieval Academy recognized women's "importance and contribution to medieval studies" (p. 19), but beyond this token recognition, he says nothing about either the nature of women's importance or the extent of their contributions to the field. Norman F. Cantor, in his *Inventing the Middle Ages* (New York, 1991), includes only one woman (Eileen Power) in his discussion, and she is treated in a section on "the dissenters, the eccentrics, the nonconformists" (quotation from p. 376).

[15] I am building here on Alice Rossi's three models for talking about equality: the pluralist model, which seeks to retain differences among groups while hoping (unrealistically, in Rossi's view) for equality; the assimilation model, which seeks to eliminate inequality by erasing the differences that distinguish subordinate groups from the superordinate mainstream; and the hybrid model, which seeks to change all groups (superordinate as well as subordinate) in the search for equality. See Alice S. Rossi, "Sex Equality: The Beginnings of Ideology," *The Humanist* 29/5 (Sept.–Oct. 1969), 3–16. These models will be familiar to many readers as those used by Natalie Davis to assess the effect of the Reformation on women in her "City Women and Religious Change," in *Society and Culture in Early Modern France* (Stanford, 1975), pp. 65–96.

dieval studies. In the Medieval Academy alone many women are now active as advisers for *Speculum*, councillors, fellows, even presidents.[16] Yet although *women* are better assimilated into medieval studies in the 1990s, *feminist scholarship* is not. No direct equation links all women to all feminist scholars, but certainly feminist scholarship is a type of work particularly associated with women and particularly important to us. As a result, as women have grown more influential in medieval studies, we have promoted feminist scholarship on the Middle Ages. What exactly defines this scholarship as *feminist*? This question is not easy to answer. On the one hand, many would define all research on women as ipso facto feminist, whether explicitly informed by feminism or not. This broad definition is particularly pertinent to medieval studies since the antipathy of some medievalists towards the study of women has created a recursive link between "the study of medieval women" and "feminist medieval studies." In other words, since any study of medieval women is condemned by many medievalists as feminist, most scholars who undertake such projects have probably developed some feminist consciousness.[17] On the other hand, this ecumenical definition poses two problems: first, all studies of women are not informed by feminism (indeed, some scholars working on medieval women would almost certainly eschew the label "feminist"); and second, some feminist scholars focus not on women but instead on such topics as gender, masculinity, and sexuality.[18] In this essay I have tried to balance these competing definitions by recognizing the possibility that all work on medieval women might be feminist but focusing particularly on explicitly feminist research.

This year might mark the centennial of feminist research on the Middle Ages: in 1893, Florence Buckstaff published an article exploring the legal rights of married women in medieval England. Buckstaff explicitly eschewed any discussion of the status of women in her own time, but she did offer some feminist criticisms of contemporary circumstances (she noted, for example, that even in the liberal state of California "the sexes are not equal"). In subsequent years, other medievalists (mostly women) began investigating the history of women in the Middle Ages: Elizabeth Dixon looking at craftswomen in Paris in 1895; Lina Eckenstein investigating female monasticism in 1896; Mary Bateson discussing women in English towns in 1904; Annie Abram writing about working women in London in 1916; Eileen Power examining English nunneries in 1922.[19] In

[16] For modern participation of women in the Medieval Academy, see this issue of *Speculum*, which reports that two of eight associate editors are women, two of five members of the editorial board are women, and five women are among the twelve councillors.

[17] This broad definition of feminist scholarship is perhaps the most common. It is the definition used not only by the editors of the *Medieval Feminist Newsletter* (as reported to me by E. Jane Burns) but also by Ellen DuBois and her coauthors of *Feminist Scholarship: Kindling in the Groves of Academe* (Urbana, Ill., 1987).

[18] For discussions of the difference between women's history and feminist history, see Adrienne Rich, "Resisting Amnesia: History and Personal Life," in *Blood, Bread, and Poetry: Selected Prose, 1979–1985* (New York, 1986), pp. 136–55, and my "Feminism and History," *Gender and History* 1 (1989), 251–72.

[19] Florence Griswold Buckstaff, "Married Women's Property in Anglo-Saxon and Anglo-Norman Law," *Annals of the American Academy of Political and Social Sciences* 4 (1893–94), 233–64, quotation

the 1990s feminist medievalists have greatly expanded on this early tradition. Whereas Buckstaff and other early scholars usually studied medieval women as a sideline to their work on more traditional subjects, many feminist medievalists today focus primarily on the study of women and gender. Whereas Buckstaff and her colleagues were few in number, more than 350 scholars today belong to the Society for Medieval Feminist Scholarship.[20] And whereas the study of medieval women was a relatively isolated pursuit for Buckstaff and others, feminist medieval studies today generates not only dozens of sessions at the annual international congress at Kalamazoo but also such long-term research projects as the Barnard study on "Women's Religious Life and Communities, 500–1500."[21] Indeed, perhaps as many as one in every ten medievalists today in North America considers herself or himself to be a feminist.[22]

In short, a fine tradition has given birth to a distinguished and flourishing field. Yet just as female medievalists were once appreciated but marginalized within the institutions of medieval studies, so today feminist scholarship on the Middle Ages flourishes but only within a largely indifferent and sometimes hostile community of medievalists. Antipathy of this sort is hard to prove (and I do not wish to dwell upon it), but let me support this accusation with two types of evidence: collegial and institutional.

Collegiality is, of course, vitally important to every medievalist. Like all academics we derive a great deal of our professional positioning from discussions in hallways and at conferences, from recommendations and referrals, from the help of mentors and friends. On this person-to-person level most feminist medievalists endure at least occasionally the insults and denigrations (joking or serious) of colleagues. If you doubt this, ask us. Or for just one example, listen

---

from p. 263; E. Dixon, "Craftswomen in the Livre des Métiers," *Economic Journal* 5 (1895), 209–28; Lina Eckenstein, *Women under Monasticism: Chapters on Saint-Lore and Convent Life between A.D. 500 and A.D. 1500* (Cambridge, Eng., 1896); Mary Bateson, ed., *Borough Customs*, Selden Society 18 and 21 (London, 1904 and 1906), 1:222–30, 2:c–cxv and 102–29; Annie Abram, "Women Traders in Medieval London," *Economic Journal* 26/2 (1916), 276–85; Eileen Power, *Medieval English Nunneries* (Cambridge, Eng., 1922), and "The Position of Women," in C. G. Crump and E. F. Jacobs, eds., *The Legacy of the Middle Ages* (Oxford, 1926), pp. 401–33. It is worth emphasizing that other female medievalists who did not publish on women, such as Bertha Putnam, were nevertheless deemed feminists by their contemporaries. See her memoir in *Speculum* as cited above, n. 13.

[20] Subscriptions to the publication of this society, the *Medieval Feminist Newsletter*, can be secured by writing to Regina Psaki, Department of Romance Languages, University of Oregon, Eugene, OR 97403 ($15 for a two-year subscription in the U.S., $12 for students).

[21] For example, the call for papers for the Twenty-Seventh International Congress on Medieval Studies at Kalamazoo included some three dozen sessions of special interest to feminist scholars. For further information about the Barnard project, see Mary M. McLaughlin, "Looking for Medieval Women: An Interim Report on the Project 'Women's Religious Life and Communities, A.D. 500–1500,' " *Medieval Prosopography* 8 (1987), 61–91, and her "Creating and Recreating Communities of Women: The Case of Corpus Domini, Ferrara, 1406–1452," *Signs* 14 (1989), 293–320.

[22] I have derived this estimate by comparing the membership of the Society for Medieval Feminist Scholarship (about 350 members in 1990) to enrollments in the Medieval Academy (3,748 members in 1990). I would like to thank E. Jane Burns and Luke Wenger for providing me with information about those two societies. Of course, membership in the two organizations does not always overlap, but I think that the numbers nevertheless suggest that a significant minority of medievalists are also self-identified feminists.

to the testimony of graduate students who reported in 1989 that their professors derisively told them that "[f]eminism has no place in medieval studies" and urged them to avoid classes offered by a colleague whom they described as a "crazy medieval feminist woman."[23]

On an institutional level this sort of marginalization and even disparagement of feminist medieval studies is easier to trace. First, consider scholarly journals. In the twenty years from 1971 to 1990 *Speculum* published less than one article per year on a topic even remotely connected to women. The publishing records of *Mediaeval Studies* and *Medium Aevum* are even less satisfactory, with about one such article every two years. In this regard, we are doing much worse than our colleagues in other disciplines. *PMLA* (*Publications of the Modern Language Association*) has averaged three to four articles per year on topics related to women and feminism; the *American Historical Review* has published about three every two years.[24] Second, consider how the specialties of medievalists are described. In the 1990–91 *Directory of History Departments*, nearly 50 medievalists are listed among the top faculties in North America. These listings describe many medievalists as interested in political or constitutional or economic or intellectual history, but only one suggests a specialty in the history of medieval women. In contrast, the *Directory* abounds with historians in other fields—particularly the United States, but also modern Europe and the Third World—identified by a specialty in women's history.[25] Third, consider employment. Be-

[23] *Medieval Feminist Newsletter* 8 (1989), 5. Since I am quoting here from a "Report from Chapel Hill" by Merrimon Crawford and Alison Smith, I would like to note two things. First, I do not believe that problems such as these are unique to my own campus (and indeed, I am proud that feminist medievalists at UNC-CH are at the forefront of those willing to articulate these problems). Second, I am not, in fact, the "crazy medieval feminist woman" whom these students were encouraged to avoid. In short, I cite this report as symptomatic of a general trend, not as a specific event in my own life.

[24] The best medieval journal I found for the publication of feminist scholarship is the *Journal of Medieval History*, a relatively new journal (begun in 1975) which has published about two such articles every year. Of course, every editor can only accept what has been submitted, and it is possible that *Speculum* and other medieval journals have suffered from the perception of feminist medievalists that our articles will not be treated fairly by these journals. Yet editors, of course, can alter these perceptions—by including feminist scholars among editors and advisers, by soliciting more articles by feminist scholars, and by publishing special issues of interest to feminists (as *Speculum* is doing in this instance). Every editor has had to use strategies such as these to encourage publication by feminist scholars. My survey suggests that editors of medieval journals have accomplished this incorporation much less effectively than editors of journals in other disciplines.

[25] I examined the faculty of twenty-one departments, including all universities that reported graduate-level training in medieval studies to George Hardin Brown and Phyllis Rugg Brown in their survey "Medieval Studies Programs in North America," in *Medieval Studies in North America*, ed. Gentry and Kleinhenz, pp. 57–80. The following universities were considered in my survey: Boston College; Brown University; Catholic University; Cornell University; Columbia University; University of Connecticut; Duke University; University of California, Berkeley; University of California, Los Angeles; University of California, Santa Barbara; Harvard University; University of Michigan; Université de Montréal; Princeton University; University of Notre Dame; University of Pennsylvania; Stanford University; University of Toronto; Western Michigan University; University of Wisconsin, Madison; and Yale University. Monica Green, an assistant professor at Duke, identified her interests as "medieval, medicine, women." See *Directory of History Departments and Organizations in the United States and Canada, 1990–91*, ed. John Barnett (Washington, D.C., 1990), p. 132. It is interesting to

tween 1989 and 1991, students completing their doctorates in medieval history have pursued almost three dozen employment opportunities. In advertisements for these positions, many preferences were stated (e.g., expertise in textual editing, historiography, English history), but only one position gave a special edge to candidates interested in the history of medieval women. At the same time, literally dozens upon dozens of advertisements were running for specialists in the history of women in the United States or modern Europe or the Third World.[26]

For these institutional indices of the state of feminist research in medieval studies, I have relied particularly on information about medieval studies within my own discipline of history, but nothing suggests that medieval history is any worse in its treatment of feminist scholarship than medieval literature or medieval art history or any other branch of medieval studies. As medievalists, all of us share a curious state: our field has an exceptionally distinguished record of accommodating women, but it also is now (un)distinguished from other scholarly fields in its failure to incorporate the new feminist scholarship of the last few decades. How have we reached this impasse?

At least part of the answer lies, I believe, in our own history, for our distinguished past has shaped our less distinguished present. The key can be found in the old model of pluralist marginalization of female medievalists. As we have seen, long before other fields opened to women, medieval studies welcomed female scholars but accommodated us marginally: women were in the field but kept separate from and unequal to men. This tradition has, it seems, shaped the ways in which medieval studies has more recently treated feminist scholarship. While other disciplines, without a strong tradition of female scholarship, have integrated both women *and* feminist scholarship into their ranks since the 1970s, medieval studies has lagged behind by extending to *feminist* medievalists only the marginalized acceptance that so long served for *female* medievalists. If my surmise is accurate, we have committed an understandable error, but an

---

note that several scholars who have published in women's history—Caroline Bynum, Sharon Farmer, and Ruth Karras—are not identified with this specialty in this edition of the *Directory*. My own identification ("European women") errs in the other direction, asserting my feminist scholarship but not my expertise in medieval studies. As with my survey of journals, these data on the specializations of medievalists are suggestive, not definitive. Attributions in the *Directory* are not carved in stone but instead derive from several sources—self-identification, to be sure, but also directives from departmental chairs or determinations of secretaries. I would argue, however, that all attributions in the *Directory* are determined in these idiosyncratic ways and that the overall comparison of medieval historians with other historians is particularly telling: in the *Directory*, medieval history stands out from other fields of history as particularly untouched by feminist scholarship.

[26] I extracted these data from the "Employment Information Bulletin" published in the A.H.A.'s newsletter, *Perspectives*, between May/June 1989 and May/June 1991 inclusive (vols. 27/5 through 29/5). In December 1989 Queen's University in Kingston, Ontario, sought a medievalist in an advertisement that included the following exceptionally tentative statement of desired specialty: "While candidates from all fields of medieval history are strongly encouraged to apply, an interest or teaching competence in some area of women's history would, in specific circumstances, be considered an asset." I am happy to report that a historian of medieval women (Monica Sandor) was appointed to this position.

error nevertheless. For, rather than being a marginal aspect of medieval studies, feminist scholarship embodies some of the very best traditions of our field.

Best traditions? Who defines what is a "tradition" and what is "best" from it? Let us turn to *Speculum* itself as our arbitrator. In the sixty-seven years of its publishing history, *Speculum* has offered its readers a handful of special articles reflecting upon the nature, objectives, and challenges of medieval studies. In 1941, as war threatened much of the world, C. H. McIlwain spoke at the annual meeting of the Medieval Academy on the importance of "Mediaeval Institutions in the Modern World." His comments were published in *Speculum* later that year. McIlwain, who was then nearing retirement after a distinguished career as a constitutional historian at Harvard, spoke movingly about the "cruelty and inhuman savagery" of events in Europe and tried to draw from them new insights about the "limitation of governmental authority by private right" in medieval Europe.[27]

Under the shadow of McCarthyism a decade later, *Speculum* published two more essays on the state of medieval studies. In 1952 E. N. Johnson addressed a joint dinner session of the American Historical Association and the Medieval Academy on the subject "American Mediaevalists and Today." Johnson, a professor at the University of Nebraska who was particularly noted for his textbooks on medieval Europe and Western civilization, spoke of his "heart-sickening despair" at attacks on academic freedom and his unhappy finding that *Speculum* in particular and medievalists in general were failing "to relate the mediaeval to the contemporary scene" (or as he sarcastically put it later, were largely "unstained by the sin of contemporaneity").[28] In 1955 Barnaby C. Keeney, who would shortly thereafter be elected president of Brown University, spoke at another Medieval Academy dinner on the subject "A Dead Horse Flogged Again." Keeney, who went on to chair the National Council of the Humanities in the late 1960s, castigated humanists in general and medievalists in particular for the aridity of our research and teaching: "Not content with boring our students, we likewise bore ourselves."[29]

Perhaps significantly, no similar reflections were published by *Speculum* during the turmoil of the 1960s or during the more complacent 1970s and 1980s. Then, after a thirty-five–year silence of criticism, Lee Patterson's "On the Margin" in 1990 again challenged us to think hard about the intellectual structures and values of medieval scholarship. Patterson's essay (the only essay in our group that did not originate in a dinner speech) pointedly questioned the interdisciplinary paradigm at the heart of medieval studies. In Patterson's view, we have retreated into an isolated and marginalized enclave of medieval studies, a field now viewed by other scholars as "a site of pedantry and antiquarianism."[30]

Clearly, these essays fall within a single genre: exhortatory critiques of me-

---

[27] C. H. McIlwain, "Mediaeval Institutions in the Modern World," *Speculum* 16 (1941), 275–83.
[28] E. N. Johnson, "American Mediaevalists and Today," *Speculum* 28 (1953), 844–54.
[29] Barnaby C. Keeney, "A Dead Horse Flogged Again," *Speculum* 30 (1955), 606–11.
[30] Lee Patterson, "On the Margin: Postmodernism, Ironic History, and Medieval Studies," *Speculum* 65 (1990), 87–108.

dieval studies. Bewailing the state of our field, McIlwain, Johnson, Keeney, and Patterson have urged us to revise our practices in quite specific ways. What they say cannot be taken as representative of either actual practices or common values, and indeed, they seem to speak, at the same time, from both the margins and the center of medieval studies. On the one hand, their essays can be construed as the ignored mutterings of malcontents. Certainly, if all medievalists had agreed with McIlwain in 1941 and put his ideas into practice, Johnson, Keeney, and Patterson would not have had much to criticize later on. On the other hand, their essays seem to constitute a long and distinguished tradition of self-criticism within medieval studies. Since McIlwain, Johnson, Keeney, and Patterson are, after all, the only critics who have merited space in the pages of *Speculum*, the editors of our flagship journal must have determined that their ideas were particularly significant and laudable.[31] On balance, although these essays might not represent the practices or ideals of most medievalists (past or present), they do represent a distinguished tradition within our field, a tradition expressed by eminent scholars and sanctioned by repeated publication in *Speculum*.

What, then, do these scholars have to say about feminist scholarship? In direct terms, very little. To my knowledge, none of the authors of these essays have been enthusiastic feminists, and since McIlwain, Johnson, and Keeney wrote before the 1960s, only Patterson was able to address directly the current work of feminist scholars. Yet, as I read all of these essays, they indirectly but substantively support feminist scholarship. Indeed, the qualities that McIlwain, Johnson, Keeney, and Patterson set out as the ideals of our profession are the very characteristics of feminist scholarship that offend so many medievalists today. Let me elaborate.

One of the most threatening aspects of feminist scholarship has been its assault on positivism, on the idea that any scholar can uncover the "truth" about the past. Revealing the male-centeredness of much so-called "objective" and "value-free" research, feminists have questioned the objectivity not only of past scholars but also of ourselves. We have argued that every scholar works within an inescapable framework of experience, attitudes, training, and politics, a framework that inevitably affects any final product. Given this inescapable context, "truth" is quite simply unattainable—a false god who has too often shielded prejudice and poor judgment. This rejection of the positivist ideal is not peculiar to feminism; it has a long and distinguished intellectual pedigree and a very wide-

[31] I have excluded presidential addresses from my pool for two reasons. First, these addresses are, in a sense, "command publications." Since the editor of *Speculum* has no choice but to publish them, the views expressed therein do not carry the same imprimatur of essays *chosen* for publication. Second, very few presidential addresses have reflected on the state of medieval studies (and none has provided the sort of sustained critique offered by McIlwain et al.). Nevertheless, insofar as past presidents have considered the subjects treated below in their addresses before the Medieval Academy, I have attempted to note their views in footnotes. Milton McC. Gatch's recent ruminations of "The Medievalist and Cultural Literacy" (*Speculum* 66 [1991], 591-604) appeared after this essay was completed, and its focus on education per se makes it, in any case, a poor match with the broader issues considered by McIlwain, Johnson, Keeney, and Patterson. I would, however, like to call attention to Gatch's attempt to defend women's history (pp. 598–600).

spread contemporary presence in the postmodernist movement.[32] Although perhaps more clearly apparent in works of interpretive history than in philological or antiquarian studies, the situatedness of the author is, feminists and many others argue, always present. We might aim for truth, but we must also recognize that we will inevitably fall short of our goal. Among feminist medievalists, both the questioning of previous orthodoxy and the asserting of the inevitable judgments entailed in scholarship have been relatively mild; it is perhaps most visible in studies suggesting that many of the "progressive" movements of the Middle Ages—the Carolingian renaissance and Gregorian reform are good examples—might have been much less progressive for women than for men.[33]

What do our referees—the authors of *Speculum*'s select critiques of medieval scholarship—have to say about the ability of scholars to cast an "innocent eye" upon the past? McIlwain conceded the point entirely, noting that our understanding of the Middle Ages "will be affected by our temperament, our traditions, and our peculiar studies."[34] Johnson agreed, stating quite clearly that "there is no final historical truth to be distilled from our documents."[35] Keeney also had little hesitation on this point, arguing against the ideal of value-free scholarship in the humanities, bewailing the "wistful imitation of the scientists by humanists," and condemning scholarship in which "the past has sometimes been presented with a certainty which is in itself inaccurate by its very nature."[36] Patterson similarly dismissed what he called the "outmoded positivism" of medieval studies, noting that "those who write history, make history."[37] In short, in questioning the search for truth and asserting the situatedness of all scholars, feminists are not introducing a new heresy into the pure orthodoxy of medievalism; instead, feminists are simply putting into practice a principle that some medievalists have long accepted and other medievalists have long been urged to adopt.[38]

---

[32] Among historians, this matter has received much recent attention in the wake of Peter Novick's *That Noble Dream: The "Objectivity Question" and the American Historical Profession* (New York, 1988). See also a recent forum on this book published in the *American Historical Review* 96 (1991), 675–708. For literary scholars, the best recent discussions can be found in Lee Patterson, *Negotiating the Past: The Historical Understanding of Medieval Literature* (Madison, Wis., 1987), esp. chapters 2 and 3.

[33] See, for example, Suzanne Fonay Wemple, *Women in Frankish Society* (Philadelphia, 1981), and Brenda Bolton, "Mulieres Sanctae," in *Women in Medieval Society*, ed. Susan Mosher Stuard (Philadelphia, 1976), pp. 141–58. The classic study of this genre is from the Renaissance; see Joan Kelly, "Did Women Have a Renaissance?" (1977), reprinted in *Women, History and Theory* (Chicago, 1984), pp. 19–50.

[34] McIlwain, p. 276.

[35] Johnson, p. 846.

[36] Keeney, p. 611.

[37] Patterson, pp. 103 and 106–7.

[38] I have found one possibly dissenting voice among past presidents of the Medieval Academy. In his presidential address in 1977, Paul Oskar Kristeller urged medievalists to be prepared to make sacrifices for the "search for truth" ("Medieval and Renaissance Studies: Reflections of a Scholar," *Speculum* 52 [1977], 1–4). About a decade later, however, another president of the Medieval Academy, Eleanor Searle, noted that scholars can only approximate the truth and that "any individual scholar's sense of configuration and of significance will depend strongly on his/her own world view" ("Possible History," *Speculum* 61 [1986], 779–86). It is perhaps worth noting that even E. K. Rand,

Many medievalists also nurture a haughty aversion to politically inspired scholarship on the Middle Ages. Feminism is a very wide-ranging political movement, but certainly all feminist scholars bring to our work a basic political aspiration: the hope that women and men might do a better job in the future of sharing human resources and responsibilities. This is, I think, a very common aspiration. Few of my students will call themselves feminists, but almost all of them expect that female graduates will have the same opportunities as male graduates to live healthy, safe, prosperous, and satisfying lives. Most parents hope the same for our daughters as for our sons.[39] In any case, what medievalists most fear from politically inspired scholarship is, I think, that it will dictate a rigid interpretive scheme, what McIlwain has called a "pattern ready-made."[40] This has certainly *not* happened. Some feminist medievalists argue that the Middle Ages were a high point for women, a time when women enjoyed more opportunities and higher status than would be the case in the modern era; others argue that little changed in women's status from the medieval to the modern era.[41] Some feminist scholars depict medieval women as active agents who, despite some obstacles, asserted considerable control over their lives and destinies; others tend to see medieval women as victims whose lives were ever circumscribed by patriarchal constraints.[42] Some feminists blame the church for promoting misogynistic ideas about women; others praise the church for offering to nuns some measure of education, respect, and autonomy.[43] And some feminist scholars call Christine de Pisan a feminist; others argue that this term is anachronistic.[44] These examples

in his introductory preface to the first issue of *Speculum*, acknowledged that medieval scholarship was shaped by "shades of belief or point of view" ("Editor's Preface," *Speculum* 1 [1926], 4). I would like to emphasize that the rejection of positivism does not necessitate any extreme sort of relativism. At the same time that feminist scholars and others argue that there are many "possible histories" (to use Searle's phrase), they also recognize that there are other "impossible histories."

[39] I think that the difference between many feminists and nonfeminists might be less a difference of aspiration and more a difference of assessment. Feminists tend to assess the current position of women—e.g., the possibility that our daughters will have the same chances as our sons—very pessimistically. Nonfeminists tend to assess the current relation between the sexes much more positively. For example, Geoffrey Elton, a scholar who seems to be building his latter-day career by attacking feminist scholarship, has even gone so far as to claim that "Most people are prejudiced in favor of women" (see the interview published in the *National Humanities Center Newsletter* 10/3–4 [1989], 3). I would like to direct those inclined to agree with Elton to the recent United Nations report on *The World's Women, 1970–1990: Trends and Statistics* (New York, 1991).

[40] McIlwain, p. 277.

[41] For example, see discussions of this historiographical debate in terms of women's work in my "History That Stands Still: Women's Work in the European Past," *Feminist Studies* 14 (1988), 269–83, and "Medieval Women, Modern Women: Across the Great Divide," in *Culture and History, 1350–1600: Essays on English Communities, Identities and Writing*, ed. David Aers (London, 1992), pp. 147–75.

[42] Compare, for example, the different interpretations of women religious found in Jane Schulenburg, "Heroics of Virginity: Brides of Christ and Sacrificial Mutilation," in *Women in the Middle Ages and the Renaissance*, ed. Mary Beth Rose (Syracuse, N.Y., 1986), pp. 29–72, and Caroline Walker Bynum, *Holy Feast and Holy Fast: The Religious Significance of Food to Medieval Women* (Berkeley, 1987).

[43] The different interpretations of Schulenburg and Bynum again illustrate this point.

[44] Joan Kelly, "Early Feminist Theory and the *Querelle des Femmes*," *Signs* 8 (1982), 4–28. Susan Schibanoff, "Comment on Kelly's 'Early Feminist Theory and the *Querelle des Femmes*,'" *Signs* 9

could be almost endlessly multiplied, but the point is a simple one: feminism has prompted scholars to look at the Middle Ages in new ways, but it has not dictated either what we have found or how we have described our findings.[45]

Feminist politics have also not undermined the fundamental disinterestedness of medieval research. As a feminist medievalist, I respect the possibilities and limitations of my sources; I approach the dead and different people of the Middle Ages with what Ruth Roach Pierson has recently called an essential "epistemic humility"; and I would never manipulate my research findings to suit present-minded concerns.[46] Yet I am more than an antiquarian, more than a reporter of facts newly uncovered; I am also a historian, an interpreter of the facts as I find them. In its interpretive aspects, my work necessarily reflects my feminist politics, just as the interpretations of *all* historians reflect their political views. Tacitus taught that the first duty of historians was to help people remember "virtuous actions" and abhor "evil words and deeds."[47] To accomplish this, historians must exercise judgment (what *is* virtuous? what *is* evil?), and judgments differ with, among other things, the political beliefs of judges. Perhaps Adrienne Rich has best stated the inevitability of political and moral judgments in the writing of history:

> Feminist history . . . is, indeed, as the department chairmen and the deans of liberal arts suspect, political. So, of course, is the history of white men, as told by themselves, political, having to do with the retention of power.[48]

(1983), 320–26. Beatrice Gottlieb, "The Problem of Feminism in the Fifteenth Century," in *Women of the Medieval World*, ed. Julius Kirshner and Suzanne F. Wemple (Oxford, 1985), pp. 337–64. Sheila Delany, " 'Mothers to Think Back Through': Who Are They? The Ambiguous Example of Christine de Pizan," in *Medieval Texts & Contemporary Readers*, ed. Laurie A. Finke and Martin B. Shichtman (Ithaca, N.Y., 1987), pp. 177–200.

[45] For an introduction to some of the many varieties of feminist theory, see Rosemarie Tong, *Feminist Thought: A Comprehensive Introduction* (Boulder, Colo., 1989).

[46] Ruth Roach Pierson, "Experience, Difference, Dominance and Voice in the Writing of Canadian Women's History," in *Writing Women's History*, ed. Karen Offen, Ruth Roach Pierson, and Jane Rendall (Bloomington, Ind., 1991), pp. 79–106.

[47] Tacitus, *Annals* 3.65.

[48] Rich, "Resisting Amnesia" (above, n. 18), p. 149. Rich agreed with Tacitus about the importance of recording the bad as well as the good, saying "And if we are serious about empowerment for women and about changing the very definitions of power, we need to know both the worst and the best." I would like to emphasize that what distinguishes Marxist, progressive, and feminist scholars from other seemingly apolitical medievalists is merely that we are more explicit about our politics. If we agree with Eleanor Searle (as quoted in n. 38) that "any individual scholar's sense of configuration and of significance will depend strongly on his/her own world view," we must accept that *all of us* bring viewpoints with political import to our work. As Allan Pred recently put it, "Through their selection of categories and emphases even the most vehement opponents of theory-informed historical inquiry cannot avoid building their scholarship upon an implicit theory of how the world works in a given setting" (*Place, Practice and Structure: Social and Spatial Transformation in Southern Sweden: 1750–1850* [Totowa, N.J., 1986], p. 2; my thanks to Kären Wigen for bringing this book to my attention). The inevitability of the presence of both theory and politics in historical work has been underlined recently in a controversy about the English Civil War that pits John Adamson (a scholar trained by Geoffrey Elton, perhaps the most vocal advocate of the possibility of finding "truth" in the archives) against Mark Kishlansky. As Lawrence Stone has recently summarized the debate, what it "makes very clear is that Sir Geoffrey's belief in pure and open minds, unsullied by ambition or ideology, going into the archives and emerging with the 'truth', bears no relation to

The politics of feminism, in short, have brought to medieval studies a present-day concern that has inspired new research and diverse interpretations; it has promoted neither doctrinaire nor biased scholarship. Of course, many medievalists would also object even to the relevance of feminist scholarship, to the "sin of contemporaneity."[49] Yet *Speculum*'s commentators on the state of medieval studies would not concur. In 1941 McIlwain sought as the main purpose of his speech to establish some sort of link between the present and the past. Speaking rather tentatively and garnering support from both Aristotle and Maitland, McIlwain suggested "the possibility that events, even of today, may or should affect our interpretation of an epoch as far behind us as the Middle Ages."[50] He applied this principle to constitutional history; feminist medievalists today are doing just the same in our studies of women and men in the Middle Ages. During the McCarthy era, Johnson and Keeney spoke even more directly to the importance of present-day concerns in medieval studies. Johnson stated as a premise of his argument (a premise that, I assume, he expected most of his readers to accept readily) that "history is the interpretation of the past which a given generation needs to help meet contemporary crises."[51] Keeney asserted the importance of medieval studies by arguing that "there is perhaps no other age that can be of more direct application to the problems of the present."[52] And Patterson, our only commentator to write explicitly about feminist medievalists, praised "the sense of connectedness [between the past and the present] that lends urgency to their work."[53] Hence, in drawing inspiration from a critical engagement between present concerns and the past remains, feminist medievalists are working within an intellectual tradition of medieval studies that is both long and distinguished.

Because feminist scholars have sought part of our inspiration from a mass movement quite separate from the academy, our work is also sometimes dismissed as trendy and popular. Yet surely, feminist scholarship on the Middle Ages, reaching perhaps its one-hundredth anniversary this year, is scarcely trendy. As for the accusation of popularizing, listen especially to our arbitrators from the 1950s. Johnson suggested in 1953 that "some of us at least abandon for the moment our programs of esoteric research, and devote ourselves to a re-writing of mediaeval history that will help solve the major problems of today."[54] And he advised quite straightforwardly that "we shall have to write for a wide, popular, even newstand audience, and with all the adaptations however difficult or uncomfortable, such an audience will require."[55] Keeney in 1955 was even more explicit about the failings of scholars in the humanities to communicate with the general public in a meaningful way:

---

reality." For Stone's remarks, see the *Times Literary Supplement* (31 January 1992), p. 3 (see also subsequent issues of the *TLS* for responses to Stone's comments).

[49] Johnson, p. 844. Johnson, of course, was being sarcastic.

[50] McIlwain, p. 278.

[51] Johnson, p. 846.

[52] Keeney, p. 609.

[53] Patterson, p. 107.

[54] Johnson, p. 847.

[55] Johnson, p. 854.

I shall bewail their preoccupation with the obscure and curse their avoidance of things that are important and therefore interesting. I shall point with scorn to their contempt for intelligibility, for communication to lay audiences, and for their lack of interest in synthesis, and pity them for their general desiccation. I shall deplore their scholarly avoidance of judgments of value and ethics. (P. 606)

Insofar as feminist medievalists have responded to a wider audience, we have been doing just what Johnson and Keeney advised to an earlier generation; we have been making the Middle Ages more pertinent and more accessible to more people.[56]

As a feminist scholar myself, it is hard for me to reconstruct fully what might offend some medievalists about feminist scholarship. Yet I hope that I have presented the major objections fairly, and I hope that I have shown that much that prima facie troubles many medievalists about feminist scholarship is, in fact, innocuous, beneficial, and even downright desirable. I do not mean to suggest that the authors of *Speculum*'s few essays on the state of medieval studies were feminists themselves, and I do not mean to suggest that these men have spoken for all medievalists, past or present. If nothing else, the repetition of themes from the 1940s and 1950s in Patterson's essay of 1990 indicates that however much medievalists might be stimulated and provoked by these critiques, many of us have changed very little. Many medievalists still aspire to the "noble dream" of objective research; many still believe it most proper to eschew all engagement between present-day concerns and our scholarly work; many still write solely for our fellow scholars. Yet these are not the only traditions of medieval studies, not even the most eminent traditions of medieval studies. For decades, distinguished scholars have embraced other ideals, ideals that seek to engage actively with the ways in which the present impinges on our views of the past. I have traced this tradition in the critiques of McIlwain and his fellows, but it has existed in practice as well as theory—in the work, for example, of such distinguished medievalists as Eileen Power, Marc Bloch, and Rodney Hilton.[57] When we remember the arguments of McIlwain et al. and the work of

[56] In their presidential addresses, both Kristeller and Searle have spoken against this point. Kristeller argued that "the acquisition and increase of knowledge is intrinsically valuable, and it is the heart of our enterprise" (p. 3). Because Kristeller's presidential address seems to have disagreed with our commentators on two crucial issues (truth and relevance), it might be worth noting that he also urged medievalists to welcome new scholarship (among which, I hope, he would include feminist scholarship). He advised that established medievalists "should not be dogmatic about their fields and theories, but tolerant of other subjects and approaches" (p. 3). In her presidential address, Searle spoke quite explicitly against the notion that medievalists should seek wider audiences: "For myself I feel no responsibility to please the living or to entertain or to improve them. . . . I do not intend to be speaking to my contemporaries, save to my colleagues" (pp. 779 and 786).

[57] As Patterson has noted in his article, medieval literary studies also boasts a long tradition of scholars whose political commitments have enhanced their scholarship. Patterson's examples are of politically motivated "old philologists" (p. 107). Of course, the politics of some medievalists now strike us as repugnant, particularly those who supported the Nazi regime. I would argue, however, that such scholars were not wrong to engage the past and the present—they were simply (and terribly) wrong in their politics. With these exceptions aside, the politics of many past medievalists might seem, from a distance, much more tame and acceptable than the politics of feminist medievalists in the 1990s. Yet the difference is one of perspective rather than kind. I hope that someday the

Power et al., we remember a long and proud history of medievalists who have sought engagement between the past and the present. Feminist medievalists are part of this tradition.

Building upon this tradition, feminist medievalists have already substantially changed medieval studies and will change it even more in the future. Where will feminist scholarship lead medieval studies in the twenty-first century? Certainly, feminist scholarship on the Middle Ages will continue to transform medieval studies itself, helping to create a fuller and more nuanced understanding of medieval life and culture. Yet it is also my hope that we will help to direct medieval studies back to the present, back to critical engagement not only with contemporary issues and audiences but also with our nonmedievalist colleagues. Feminist medievalists have already breached the walls of the "medieval enclave" to reach out to other scholars; let us hope that those walls will entirely crumble away in coming years. In any case, feminist medievalism has two fields of play at the present and for the future: medieval studies (where feminist medievalists are enriching our empirical and interpretive possibilities) and scholarship at large (where feminist medievalists are reawakening a general interest in the Middle Ages).

Within medieval studies itself, there can be no question that research undertaken by feminist scholars has added in substantial ways to our corpus of information about the Middle Ages. Consider, for just one example, the history of medieval monasticism in England. In the 1940s and 1950s David Knowles almost entirely ignored nuns in his three-volume study of English monasticism, claiming in his defense that he could not study women because there was simply no information extant on female monasticism:

> In truth, intimate or detailed records of the nunneries are almost entirely wanting over the whole period between *c.* 1200 and the Dissolution. . . . The religious historian of medieval England cannot help remarking, in every century after the eleventh, upon the absence from the scene of any saintly or commanding figure of a woman.[58]

Knowles was wrong, and he should have known he was wrong. More than twenty years before he offered his excuse, Eileen Power had already proven it quite fallacious, using extensive documentation to produce her *Medieval English Nunneries*. And in more recent years, scholars such as Janet Burton, Sharon Elkins,

---

advocacy of equal opportunity for women will seem as ordinary and admirable as today seem to be the views of those who opposed Nazism or objected to McCarthyism or supported civil rights. Feminist scholars practice an inclusive politics addressed to the common interests of both women and men.

[58] David Knowles, *The Religious Orders in England,* 2: *The End of the Middle Ages* (Cambridge, Eng., 1955), p. viii. Let me add two caveats. First, Knowles did concede that it might be possible "after a long course of research" to reconstruct the economic and social histories of nunneries, but not their spiritual circumstances. We must note, however, not only the effort Knowles expended on the economic and social histories of *male* religious houses but also the spiritual information about female religious that the authors cited below have uncovered. Second, Eileen Power would probably have agreed with Knowles about the absence of saintly women in late-medieval England. Still, it is very telling that Knowles never listed Power's *Medieval English Nunneries* in any of the extensive bibliographies that accompanied his three-volume study.

Marilyn Oliva, and Sally Thompson have also found in the archives what Knowles dismissed as unfindable—extensive evidence about the institutions, lives, and religious experiences of medieval English nuns.[59]

What happened in this specific instance has been duplicated in dozens of different areas of medieval studies; information about women that scholars once proclaimed simply irretrievable has been sought out, recovered, and reported by feminist scholars. In the discipline of history, this process has produced what is often now called "herstory," a collection of new information about women that has validated the claim that women are legitimate subjects of historical inquiry. In literary and artistic studies this process has expanded the canon, by editing, anthologizing, translating, and bringing to critical notice the creative works of medieval women.[60] And throughout medieval studies this process has revitalized research, as feminist medievalists have developed new methods of archival investigation, extracted new sorts of information from old sources, and searched out new documents and texts.

Of course, feminist medievalists are doing much more than simply adding to the amount of material that constitutes the empirical corpus of medieval studies; we are also challenging old interpretations and providing new ways of seeing familiar things. In history, for example, some feminist historians are questioning the very periodization of the Middle Ages (suggesting that the so-called high Middle Ages were not, in fact, a high point for women at all), and others (most notably, Caroline Bynum) are reinterpreting well-known texts about and by medieval mystics in startlingly new ways.[61] In literary studies, for example, Kathryn Gravdal is rereading encounters between knights and shepherdesses in French pastoral poetry (emphasizing rape where other critics have emphasized playful sex), and Helen Solterer and Sarah Westphal-Wihl are looking anew at tales about ladies' tournaments (found in both the French and German tradi-

[59] Janet Burton, *The Yorkshire Nunneries in the Twelfth and Thirteenth Centuries*, Borthwick Paper no. 56 (York, 1979); Sharon K. Elkins, *Holy Women of Twelfth-Century England* (Chapel Hill, 1988); Marilyn Oliva, "The Convent and the Community in the Diocese of Norwich from 1350 to 1540," Ph.D. dissertation, Fordham University, 1991; and Sally Thompson, *Women Religious: The Founding of English Nunneries after the Norman Conquest* (Oxford, 1991).

[60] Although there is some risk of winnowing an extensive effort into just a few texts, I would like to call readers' attention particularly to the following studies of medieval women writers: Peter Dronke, *Women Writers of the Middle Ages* (Cambridge, Eng., 1984), and Katharina M. Wilson, ed., *Medieval Women Writers* (Athens, Ga., 1984). One of the most interesting recent developments in the study of medieval literature is the attempt to claim female authorship for some anonymous texts; see Janet Nelson, "Gender and Genre in Women Historians of the Early Middle Ages," in *L'historiographie médiévale en Europe*, ed. Jean-Philippe Genet (Paris, 1991), pp. 149–63. For the study of women in medieval art, see Lila Yawn-Bonghi, "Medieval Women Artists and Modern Historians," *Medieval Feminist Newsletter* 12 (1991), 10–19.

[61] An early reassessment of the periodization of the Middle Ages can be found in Jo Ann McNamara and Suzanne Wemple, "The Power of Women through the Family in Medieval Europe, 500–1100," *Feminist Studies* 1 (1973), 126–41. For more recent statements, see Susan Stuard, "The Dominion of Gender: Women's Fortunes in the High Middle Ages," in *Becoming Visible: Women in European History*, ed. Renate Bridenthal, Claudia Koonz, and Susan Stuard, 2nd ed. (New York, 1987), pp. 153–74; and David Herlihy, *Opera Muliebria: Women and Work in Medieval Europe* (New York, 1990). For Bynum's work on female mysticism, see especially her *Holy Feast and Holy Fast*.

tions), showing how these tales betray a delicate gender balancing of conformity and nonconformity, restriction and possibility.[62]

In some respects this feminist reinterpretation of medieval studies is quite properly reactive, seeking to revise or reinterpret traditional questions and texts. Yet in other respects this process is also creating new interpretive agendas, independent of the traditional problems and discussions of medieval studies. Hence, Bynum has not just reread well-known mystical texts in new ways; she has also created a new series of questions—about female and feminine religiosity—that demand scholarly examination. Many of these new subjects derive not from the traditional research programs of medievalism, but instead from the research programs of feminism. E. Jane Burns in her new study *Bodytalk* has tackled the critical feminist problem of women's speech by using medieval literature; Susan Mosher Stuard has taken new feminist ideas about gender into medieval scholarship, arguing that the twelfth and thirteenth centuries brought a new notion of difference between men and women to Europeans; in my own work on alewives, I have tried to give feminist concerns about misogyny a historical base, by tracing how misogynistic ideas might have had very real effects on women's work.[63] In dealing with issues such as these, feminist medievalists are still working within medieval studies, to be sure, but we are working to create an entirely new set of scholarly questions, methods, and discussions. We are also enriching medieval studies with theories, insights, and questions drawn from feminist studies.

Feminists, then, are revising the field of medieval studies from three directions: adding new information, answering old questions in new ways, and creating entirely new research agendas. We have helped to introduce the "linguistic turn" to medieval studies, and we are taking *all* of the Middle Ages (men as well as women, masculinity as well as femininity) under our view.[64] Medieval studies will never be the same. At the same time that all of these revisions of medieval studies have been going on, feminist medievalists have also enjoyed some modest success on our second field of play—in our attempts to awaken an interest among feminist scholars generally in the Middle Ages. As every medievalist knows, this playing field has not been level and never will be; in a modern world, scholarship on the Middle Ages will always be somewhat pe-

---

[62] Kathryn Gravdal, *Ravishing Maidens: Writing Rape in Medieval French Literature and Law* (Philadelphia, 1991), and "Chrétien de Troyes, Gratian, and the Medieval Romance of Sexual Violence," *Signs* 17 (1992), 558–85. Sarah Westphal-Wihl, "The Ladies' Tournament: Marriage, Sex and Honor in Thirteenth-Century Germany," *Signs* 14 (1989), 371–98. Helen Solterer, "Figures of Female Militancy in Medieval France," *Signs* 16 (1991), 522–49.

[63] E. Jane Burns, *Bodytalk: When Women Speak in Old French Literature* (Philadelphia, 1993); Susan Stuard, "The Dominion of Gender"; Judith M. Bennett, "Misogyny, Popular Culture, and Women's Work," *History Workshop Journal* 31 (1991), 166–88.

[64] For examples of the linguistic turn, see Nancy F. Partner, "Making Up Lost Time: Writing on the Writing of History," *Speculum* 61 (1986), 90–117, and Gabrielle M. Spiegel, "History, Historicism, and the Social Logic of the Text in the Middle Ages," *Speculum* 65 (1990), 59–86. Both of these articles also illustrate my second point about the breadth of feminist scholarship on the Middle Ages, for they are *by* feminist medievalists but not *about* medieval women. Another example is the conference held at Fordham University in March 1990 on "Gender and Society II: Men in the Middle Ages."

ripheral. Yet for feminist medievalists the challenge presented by the marginality of medieval studies is even more acute. Women's studies faculties are especially dominated by scholars working on contemporary concerns, and although historical perspectives have a distinguished place in women's studies, it is a place that has focused mostly on the modern era and especially on the United States. Given both the political impetus of feminist scholarship and its American locus, this modern tilt is scarcely surprising, but it does pose a challenge for feminist medievalists. We have had to find a larger scholarly audience for our work among feminist scholars mostly interested in investigating the present (or the quite recent past) and mostly inclined to consider research on the Middle Ages to be a frivolous and irrelevant indulgence.

Despite these obstacles, feminist medievalists have made strong preliminary steps towards creating a wider audience for medieval research. Four years before *Speculum* became, with this issue, the first major medieval journal to publish a special issue on women, *Signs: Journal of Women in Culture and Society* devoted an entire issue to medieval women.[65] And long before the Medieval Academy was offering any (or many) papers on women at its annual meetings, the Berkshire Conferences on the History of Women were regularly scheduling numerous papers on medieval women.[66] The battle is not entirely won, to be sure. After publishing three articles on medieval women in its first three volumes in the early 1970s, *Feminist Studies* has yet to publish another. And some of the the newest feminist journals have yet to publish many articles on medieval women.[67] Still, although feminist medievalists have a way to go, we are at least on the right track. More than most medievalists, we have broken out of the medieval enclave and found new audiences for our work.

I hope that feminist medievalists (as well as all medievalists in general) will learn from these early successes and build upon them. Some successes have been based on networking and personality; the right feminist medievalists have been at the right places at the right times.[68] But the most crucial factor seems

[65] This was an issue on "Working Together in the Middle Ages: Perspectives on Women's Communities," *Signs: Journal of Women in Culture and Society* 14 (1989).

[66] At most recent Berkshire Conferences (with the exception of the 1990 conference), each time slot has offered at least one session (with multiple papers) on medieval women. At most Medieval Academy meetings, medievalists have been able to hear either no papers on women (as in 1970, 1971, 1973, 1975, 1977, 1980, 1985, and 1986) or only a handful. The only exceptions have been the 1989 and 1992 meetings, at which about a dozen papers on women were presented. One of the organizers of the 1989 meeting has reported to me that there were many complaints from members of the Academy about the "excessive" attention given to medieval women at this meeting. The first session devoted entirely to women at a Medieval Academy meeting was tellingly titled "Troublemakers: Women in Medieval Society" (1981 meeting).

[67] When I surveyed *Gender and History, Journal of Women's History, NWSA Journal,* and *differences* in December 1991, I found only one article on medieval women: Megan McLaughlin, "Gender Paradox and the Otherness of God," *Gender and History* 3 (1991), 147–59. To my knowledge, only one article on a medieval topic has appeared since my survey: Susan Mosher Stuard, "The Chase after Theory: Considering Medieval Women," *Gender and History* 4 (1992), 135–46.

[68] For example, Jo Ann McNamara played a critical role in promoting sessions on medieval women at early Berkshire Conferences, and the presence of three premodern specialists among the associate editors of *Signs* in the late 1980s (Elizabeth Clark, Sarah Westphal-Wihl, and me) was the main impetus behind the special issue on medieval women.

to be the willingness of feminist medievalists to read outside of medieval studies. Hence, Gravdal focused primarily on medieval texts and medievalist interpretations for her study *Ravishing Maidens*, but she also read Susan Brownmiller, Catharine MacKinnon, Sylvana Tomaselli, and Susan Estrich, not to mention Michel Foucault, Sigmund Freud, and Jacques Derrida. By reading widely in this fashion, feminist medievalists gain two advantages. First, we are able to do a better job of making our work accessible, relevant, and interesting to other scholars. Of course, it is not always possible or even desirable to write for an audience of modernists; sometimes our findings are highly technical, and sometimes our discussions are directed solely at other medievalists. But wide-ranging reading ensures that we know, whenever we want to bridge the medieval-modern gap, how simply to build the bridge—what language to use, what issues to pinpoint, what contexts within which to place our work. Second, reading of this sort also provides us with theories, materials, and practices that directly enrich our work. Judith Walkowitz has things to say about nineteenth-century prostitution that are pertinent to our understanding of medieval prostitution; Alice Kessler-Harris has ideas about modern wage rates that can enhance our understandings of wage differentials in medieval Europe; Luce Irigaray has theorized about female speech in ways that enrich our readings of medieval literature. In short, as feminist medievalists read feminist scholarship outside of medieval studies, we are able not only to communicate more effectively with nonmedievalists but also to develop new ways of interpreting medieval sources.[69]

Most of us would like to have wider audiences, reason enough for feminist medievalists to cast our voices a bit farther afield. Yet there is a more compelling reason: feminist scholarship quite simply needs medieval scholarship. Feminist medievalists contribute two critical perspectives to the larger community of feminist scholars: chronological and theoretical. Feminist medievalists, working on the premodern side of the most profound divide in Western history, provide a critical counterweight to the present-mindedness of much feminist scholarship. As the editors of the *Signs* special issue on medieval women put it in 1989, "A fully multicultural feminism that lacks a history before 1750 is as impoverished as a feminism that attends to historical differences but lacks a multicultural appreciation."[70] This chronological perspective on Western women and Western feminism—a perspective that *only* feminist medievalists can provide—is already altering feminist scholarship and theory. For example, medievalists are playing

[69] Of course, medievalists need to build bridges with classicists as well as with modernists. Indeed, we have much to learn from classicists who, in the last few years, have produced work in the history of sexuality that has generated intense and wide-ranging interest. These classicists, whose problems of documentary survival and interpretation certainly rival our own, have enriched their study of ancient sexualities by building, often brilliantly, on inspirations found in psychology, postmodernism, feminism, and cultural anthropology. See Peter Brown, *The Body and Society: Men, Women, and Sexual Renunciation in Early Christianity* (New York, 1989); David Halperin, *One Hundred Years of Homosexuality and Other Essays on Greek Love* (London, 1990); John Winkler, *The Constraints of Desire: The Anthropology of Sex and Gender in Ancient Greece* (London, 1990); and Halperin, Winkler, and Froma Zeitlin, eds., *Before Sexuality: The Construction of Erotic Experience in the Ancient Greek World* (Princeton, N.J., 1990).

[70] *Signs* 14 (1989), 260.

a critical role in debates about the low working status of women *in our own times*. By documenting remarkable similarities between the working lives of medieval women and modern women, we have been able to raise a critical perspective, a perspective suggesting that neither capitalism nor industrialism can be held responsible for the low status of working women in the 1990s.[71] The medieval West is not, to be sure, the *only* chronological perspective important in feminist scholarship, but it is currently a *critical* perspective (for the past of the West is exceptionally influential and exceptionally well documented). In developing chronological perspectives within feminist scholarship, therefore, feminist medievalists play an essential role within feminist studies.

The study of the Middle Ages also offers unusual possibilities for the further development of feminist theory. To date, feminist medievalists have mostly been *consumers* of feminist theory; informed by the ideas of others, we have used them to see the Middle Ages in new and different ways. I hope that in the future we will also be *producers* of feminist theory, taking from our medieval scholarship insights that can inform the research of our nonmedievalist colleagues.[72] We might be particularly effective in further elaborating feminist theories of "difference." In the social sciences these theories have mostly explored the very modern intersections of race, class, and gender. What better context to develop fuller theories about such differences than in a medieval society that did not replicate such modern categories as race and class but was nevertheless rife with divisions between Christian and Jew and Muslim, between peasants and townspeople and warriors, between women and men? In cultural studies, feminist theories of difference have often emphasized the instability of texts and their readers. What better context in which to explore further the theoretical implications of textual instability than by reading medieval texts that so often embody—in their anonymous authorship and audiences, in their shifting content, and in their uncertain transmission—instability?[73] The medieval West, in its likeness and unlikeness to the modern West, provides many singular possibilities for feminist study, possibilities that should allow feminist medievalists to contribute substantially to the further development of feminist thought.

Feminist medievalists, then, are changing medieval studies in two fundamental ways: we are enriching medieval scholarship per se, and we are expanding the audience for that newly enriched scholarship. In the process we have also revitalized medieval studies in general—attracting new students, stimulating new archival work, provoking new discussions. Medieval studies will never become feminist studies, and *Speculum* will probably never develop into a journal of feminist medieval scholarship, but medieval studies, as a whole, owes a large

[71] Bennett, "History That Stands Still" (above, n. 41).

[72] In "The Chase after Theory" Susan Mosher Stuard presents a more optimistic view of the theoretical work done by feminist medievalists. In her view, feminist medievalists have long generated theory through practice, because they have "invented or tried new approaches out of need" (p. 135).

[73] In this regard, see particularly E. Jane Burns, Sarah Kay, Roberta L. Krueger, and Helen Solterer, "Feminism and the Discipline of Old French Studies: Une Bele Disjointure," in *The Discipline of the Discipline*, ed. R. Howard Bloch and Stephen G. Nichols, Jr. (forthcoming from Johns Hopkins University Press).

debt to female medievalists and feminist scholarship. That debt can best be repaid not in reparations but in appreciation and emulation. We have been part of medieval studies from its nineteenth-century beginnings; we work within some of the best traditions of medieval scholarship as it has been practiced in the twentieth century; and we are pointing the way towards a medieval studies that will survive and flourish in the twenty-first century. What Nellie Neilson told the American Historical Association in her presidential address in 1943 still speaks for us today: "The roots of the present lie deep in the past, a truism we cannot today despise if we seek a solution of our own difficult problems."[74]

[74] *American Historical Review* 49 (1944), 200.

I would like to thank many people who have read and commented on drafts of this essay. My colleagues in the North Carolina Research Group on Medieval and Early Modern Women offered trenchant criticism of an early draft. Stanley Chojnacki, Jan Ewald, Monica Green, Barbara Harris, Nancy Hewitt, Ruth Mazo Karras, Mavis Mate, Janet Nelson, Lee Patterson, Helen Solterer, and Susan Stuard provided me with valuable written critiques. Cynthia Herrup, Maryanne Kowaleski, Nancy Partner, and Lyndal Roper generously took the time to read and comment upon multiple drafts. I would also like to state emphatically that I cannot and do not speak for all feminist medievalists. We are a very diverse group with very diverse ideas about the present and future of feminist scholarship in medieval studies. Although I have sought ideas, suggestions, and criticisms from some of my feminist colleagues, this essay necessarily reflects *only* my thoughts and my opinions.

Judith M. Bennett is Professor of History at the University of North Carolina, Chapel Hill, NC 27599.

Patron or Matron?
A Capetian Bride and a
Vade Mecum for Her Marriage Bed

By Madeline H. Caviness

> Since marriage is so often the context within which a woman works out
> her destiny, it has always been the object of feminist scrutiny.
> —Phyllis Rose[1]

This contribution to feminist studies provides a new decoding of the imagery
in the Hours of Jeanne d'Evreux. I propose layered readings, registering a
modern woman's critical perceptions, informed by knowledge of the historical
context, to reconstruct the impression these images might have made on the
original female owner.

Jeanne d'Evreux's tiny prayer book, now in the Cloisters, New York, is almost
universally accepted to be the one documented in her will as having been illuminated by Jean Pucelle at the behest of Charles IV le Bel, king of France;
it was probably a wedding present for her in 1324, when, at about fourteen
years old, she became his third wife.[2] The prayers are arranged according to
Dominican use (Figs. 2 and 21).[3] They comprise the usual hours of the Virgin,
with illustrations of the Infancy and the Passion of Christ in facing pairs, and—
unusually—the hours of St. Louis of France, with scenes of his life. The queen

---

[1] Phyllis Rose, *Parallel Lives—Five Victorian Marriages* (New York, 1983), p. 5.

[2] New York, The Metropolitan Museum of Art, The Cloisters 54.1.2; the book measures 3⅝ x
2⅜ inches. The correct date for the marriage is given by Joan A. Holladay, "The Education of
Jeanne d'Evreux: Role Models and Behavioral Prescriptions in Her Book of Hours at the Cloisters"
(in press), n. 3, citing the *Grandes chroniques de France*, ed. J. Viard, 9 (Paris, 1937), p. 31; July 5,
1324, is given in the *Recueil des historiens des Gaules et de la France . . . depuis MCCXXVI jusqu'en
MCCCXXVIII*, 21 (Paris, 1855), p. 682. Two issues of *The Metropolitan Museum of Art Bulletin*, 16/
10 (June 1958) and 19 (1971), have been dedicated to studies of the manuscript. A partial enlarged
facsimile with an introduction by James J. Rorimer, *The Hours of Jeanne d'Evreux Queen of France,
at the Cloisters* (New York, 1957), is now out of print, but several color reproductions are in François
Avril, *Manuscript Painting at the Court of France: The Fourteenth Century (1310–1380)* (New York,
1978), pp. 44–59, pls. 3–10. See also François Avril, *Les fastes du gothique: Le siècle de Charles V*
(Paris, 1981), no. 239, pp. 292–93, 434; Michaela Krieger, "Die 'Heures de Jeanne d'Evreux' und
das Pucelle-Problem," *Wiener Jahrbuch für Kunstgeschichte* 42 (1989), 101–32; and Karen Gould,
"Jean Pucelle and Northern Gothic Art: New Evidence from Strasbourg Cathedral," *Art Bulletin*
74 (1992), 51–74. Krieger is the only art historian to argue recently against the date and attribution
of the Cloisters Hours; I cannot deal with her argument in this context.

[3] In the rubrics for matins, fol. 15v: "Incipiunt hore beate marie virginis secundum usum pre-
dicatorum," and for the hours of St. Louis, fol. 102v.

is shown on the page openings that have the first prayer of each cycle, kneeling in devotion before the Virgin and St. Louis (Figs. 2 and 21).[4]

Four levels of imagery are clearly distinguished in the Hours. First: scenes from sacred history, either Gospel or hagiographic events, are elaborately framed and partially colored to set them apart from the other images and the Latin text pages. The effect is that of a series of icons or holy pictures removed from other orders of existence; the Betrayal and Crucifixion of Christ alone are unframed, and the latter is unique in occupying a whole page (Figs. 1, 2, 26, 32).[5] Second: the queen, twice represented as suppliant, is depicted in another (time-)frame either outside and below the Gospel event or in an antechapel at the shrine of the royal saint who was her paternal great-grandfather (see the Genealogical Table and Figs. 2 and 21). Third: uncolored and unframed figures involved in secular activities occupy the bas-de-pages and margins adjacent to images of sacred history (Figs. 1, 2, 21, 22, 26, 32, 40, 42). Fourth: uncolored and unframed "decoration," using human figures, chimeras, and beasts, forms line endings or fillers in the margins and around the initials. On colored grounds, these motifs invade the initials themselves (Figs. 1, 2, 5, 8, 10–12, 16, 18–21, 23–27, 32, 33, 37–39). The hybrids or chimeras are now often referred to as drôleries or grotesques, blurring the distinction between the comical and the strange.

In the book as a whole, the accumulative impact of the grotesques is the most telling element. The marginalia are so invasive and aggressive that the only safe havens from the nightmarishness of the pages' shivaree are the tiny places assigned to Jeanne d'Evreux for prayer (Figs. 2, 21). As a reader, she would also find a safe place in the written word.

DYNASTIC ANXIETIES

The historical moment when fourteen- or fifteen-year-old Jeanne received the Hours from her newly wedded husband was fraught with tension. Charles was the third and last son of Philippe le Bel to ascend the throne of France, and without a male heir he was to be the last of the Capetians (Genealogical Table). The end of Philippe's reign had been disastrous. In 1314 Jacques de Molay, master of the Templars, was burned in Paris, following the fate of many other members of the order, condemned for homosexual acts among other more serious charges; he died calling for vengeance against those who had wrongly condemned him.[6] That same year Philippe's three sons' wives, Marguerite de

---

[4] The makeup of the book is very clearly described by John Harthen, *Books of Hours and Their Owners* (London, 1977), pp. 14–19, 40–44.

[5] The Crucifixion (fol. 68v) is reproduced in Rorimer, *Hours*, and in Avril, *Manuscript Painting*, pl. 6.

[6] H. Géraud, ed., *Chronique latine de Guillaume de Nangis [= Jean Fillons de Venette] de 1113 à 1300, avec la continuation de cette chronique de 1300 à 1368*, 1 (Paris, 1843), pp. 403–4, and records of the inquisition analyzed by Edward J. Martin, *The Trial of the Templars* (London, 1928), pp. 65–77; and Malcolm Barber, *The Trial of the Templars* (Cambridge, Eng., 1978), pp. 165, 178–92. The main charges were that they denied Christ, spat on the Cross, adored an idol, and received absolution from the grand master.

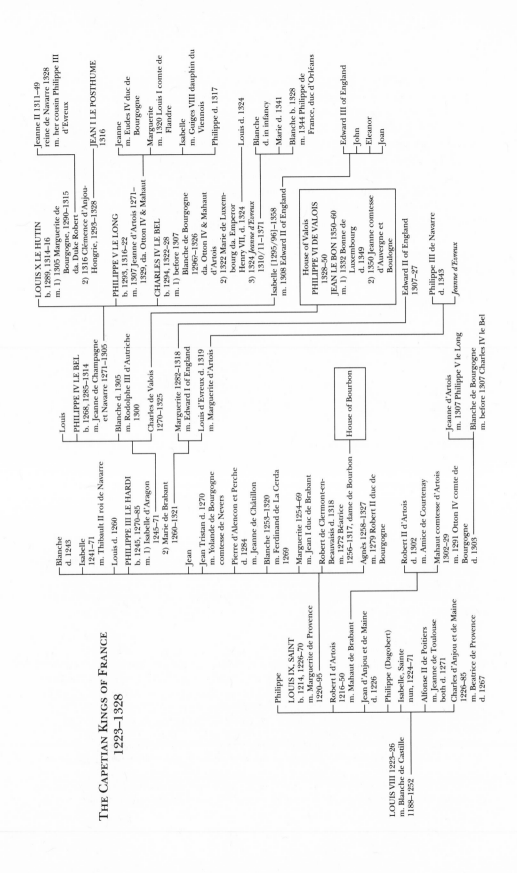

THE CAPETIAN KINGS OF FRANCE 1223–1328

Bourgogne and her cousins, the sisters Jeanne d'Artois and Blanche de Bourgogne, were accused of adulterous affairs of such catastrophic import that, according to one poet, they were marked by a double eclipse of the sun and moon.[7] Their sins were doubly offensive because they had made love on high feast days ("temporibus sacrosanctis"). Their lovers were instantly castrated and executed. Marguerite and Blanche had their heads shaved and were imprisoned in Château Gaillard. Jeanne was sent to Dourdan and released in 1314 after her trial, but her mother, Mahaut, was accused of using sorcery to enable her to retain Philippe's love and even of poisoning Louis because he would not pardon Marguerite.[8] The Templars were not the only ones accused of homosexuality in this bleak decade. Philippe le Bel's fourth child, his daughter Isabelle, had married Edward II of England in 1308 only to find that Piers Gaveston was more often in his bed than she. Her father protested until Gaveston was removed from court and exiled.[9] Gaveston was executed for treason in 1312, against Edward's wishes.[10]

At Philippe le Bel's death his oldest son, Louis X le Hutin (the Quarrelsome), had a wife in prison and no way to dissolve the marriage because the cardinals had been unable to elect a new pope.[11] According to the chronicle of Jean de Saint-Victor, Louis "loosed the reins of passion" and sired an illegitimate daughter.[12] He also openly courted his future second wife and married her as soon as Marguerite mysteriously died in prison. These events placed the whole realm in jeopardy.

The collection of texts and images in MS français 146 in the Bibliothèque Nationale, which seems to have been put together in the royal chancery no earlier than 1317, allegorizes Louis's short reign (1314–16).[13] It is probable, as

[7] Armel Diverrès, ed., *La chronique métrique attribuée à Geoffroy de Paris* (Strasbourg, 1956), pp. 202–5, ll. 5868–6070; cf. *Chronique de Guillaume de Nangis*, 1:404–6, and other sources that are culled by Paul Lehugeur, *Histoire de Philippe le Long, roi de France (1316–1322)* (Paris, 1897), pp. 16–18, 41, 168–69, and discussed by Elizabeth A. R. Brown, "Political Allegory and Political Dissent at the Court of Philip V of France: *Les livres de Fauvel*," an unpublished paper given in the symposium "Christendom and Its Discontents: Exclusion, Persecution, and Rebellion, 1000–1450" at the University of California, Los Angeles, January 1991; and E. A. R. Brown, chap. 9, "The Adultery Scandal and the New *Fauvel*," in her forthcoming book on the manuscript. See also Jean Favier, *Philippe le Bel* (Paris, 1978), pp. 456–531; Joseph R. Strayer, *The Reign of Philip the Fair* (Princeton, 1980), pp. 19, 417.

[8] Lehugeur, *Philippe le Long*, pp. 168–70.

[9] Elizabeth A. R. Brown, "The Political Repercussions of Family Ties in the Early Fourteenth Century: The Marriage of Edward II of England and Isabelle of France," *Speculum* 63 (1988), 582–84, who notes that the affair of the Templars occupied Philippe le Bel at the same time as Gaveston's infractions. Executions of homosexuals continued: Louis Crompton, "The Myth of Lesbian Impunity: Capital Laws from 1270 to 1791," *Journal of Homosexuality* 6 (1980/81), 17.

[10] May McKisack, *The Oxford History of England: The Fourteenth Century* (Oxford, 1959), pp. 22–28.

[11] For this and the following information I depend on Brown, "Political Allegory."

[12] ". . . juvenili ardore accensus fraena incontinentiae laxavit," cited by Brown, "Political Allegory," p. 20.

[13] Brown, "Political Allegory." An older facsimile by Pierre Aubry, *Le roman de Fauvel: Reproduction phototypique du manuscrit français 146* (Paris, 1907), has been surpassed by a new reproduction: *Paris,*

Elizabeth Brown argues, that no one in Paris on the eve of the royal wedding would have dared to take part in a shivaree, so one is represented in the manuscript instead—including a man with cuckold's horns (Fig. 4).[14] Among the texts in this collection is the allegory of a horse called Fauvel ("Unbridled Passion") that takes over the kingdom of France and marries Vainglory in the Sainte-Chapelle.[15] Carnality, Fornication, Adultery, Cupid, and Venus attend the wedding but are afterwards defeated in a tournament by the virtues, led by Virginity and Chastity.

To return to the historical narrative, Louis's posthumous son, Jean, died in infancy, and he otherwise had only a daughter, Jeanne (later of Navarre). Thus his brothers succeeded: First, Philippe le Long (1316–22), whose wife, Jeanne d'Artois, had been reinstated, but he was survived only by daughters (Genealogical Table). His reign was marked by famine and persecutions of Jews, lepers, and heretics. Next to rule was Charles IV (1322–28), who repudiated Blanche de Bourgogne when he ascended the throne. His second wife, Marie de Luxembourg, daughter of Emperor Henry VII, is said to have worn the Dominican habit before her marriage.[16] She died in childbirth during Lent 1324, at the age of eighteen, seven days after the premature birth of their baby boy, Louis.[17] By then it had been proclaimed that women could not inherit, nor could they succeed to *dignitas*, which made it impossible for a princess to succeed to the throne.[18] When Marie died, Charles was nearly thirty years old. His marriage to Jeanne d'Evreux, who was his cousin, required papal dispensation, and Jeanne became the last hope of the Capetian line. Although the marriage was hastily concluded within four months of Marie's death, Jeanne was not crowned until

---

Bibliothèque Nationale, MS fonds français 146: A Facsimile of the Manuscript, ed. E. H. Roesner with an introduction by F. Avril and N. F. Regalado (New York, 1990). A political satire on the Gaveston affair, a "Song of the Times," was written in England ca. 1310: Francis Klingender, *Animals in Art and Thought to the End of the Middle Ages* (London, 1971), p. 368.

[14] Brown, "Political Allegory." On shivarees, see P. Fortier-Beaulieu, "Le charivari dans le Roman de Fauvel, MS du XIVe s: B.N. fr., 146," *Revue de folklore français* 11 (1940), 1–16; and Nancy Freeman Regalado, "Masques réels dans le monde de l'imaginaire: Le rite et l'écrit dans le charivari du *Roman de Fauvel*, MS. B.N. Fr. 146," in *Masques et déguisements dans la littérature médiévale,* ed. Marie-Louise Ollier (Montreal, 1988), pp. 149–64. An invaluable broad survey of the phenomenon is that of Henri Rey-Flaud, *Charivari: Les rituels fondamentaux de la sexualité* (Paris, 1985).

[15] Paris, Bibliothéque Nationale, MS fr. 146, fol. 36v. The text was edited by Emilie Dahnk, *L'hérésie de Fauvel* (Leipzig and Paris, 1935). For phallic connotations of the horse: R. Howard Bloch, *The Scandal of the Fabliaux* (Chicago, 1986), pp. 88–89. For its association with the flesh, and therefore sometimes with women: D. W. Robertson, Jr., *A Preface to Chaucer* (Princeton, 1963), p. 254. Above all, horses were associated with rape and adultery: Rey-Flaud, *Charivari,* pp. 33, 38–40 (as was the centaur, a guise in which Fauvel also appears in the manuscript: Rey-Flaud, pp. 22–23), and in Dürer's print *The Ill-Assorted Couple* of 1495/96 (H. Diane Russell, *Eva/Ave: Woman in Renaissance and Baroque Prints,* exhibition catalogue, Washington, D.C., The National Gallery of Art [New York, 1990], p. 192, no. 122).

[16] Jean François Dreux de Radier, *Mémoires historiques, critiques et anecdotiques des reines et régentes de France,* 3 (Paris, 1808), pp. 84–85, citing several chronicle sources.

[17] *Recueil des historiens,* 21:682.

[18] Andrew W. Lewis, *Royal Succession in Capetian France: Studies on Familial Order and the State* (Cambridge, Eng., 1981), pp. 153–54, mentions proclamations and decisions of 1317 and 1322.

May 1326.[19] Before the king died in 1328 she had two daughters, Blanche, who died very young, and Marie, who never married.[20] A third daughter, also named Blanche, was born a few months after the king's death.[21] Jeanne held the future Charles VI at his baptism in 1368 but eventually retired from public life to follow Blanche de Bourgogne to the Cistercian nunnery at Maubuisson, near Vincennes.[22] Jeanne died at Maubuisson in 1371, bequeathing Pucelle's Hours to the Valois king Charles V and three other books of hours to her only surviving child, her daughter Blanche.[23]

DIDACTIC IMAGES

In the fraught atmosphere of a failing dynasty, betrayed by female lasciviousness and punished by a lack of male heirs, more than lessons of conventional piety had to be directed at the girl-bride who was supposed to become the chaste mother of indubitably legitimate male children. The Annunciation-Betrayal page opening (Fig. 2) suggests ways in which the imagery of her book could instruct Jeanne. The images can be examined in light of the sociological and psychosexual conditions and systems of belief in which the work was created and first read. I will begin to draw at this point on the sources used by Danielle Jacquart and Claude Thomasset, especially the *De secretis mulierum libellus*, a popular work that would have been known to Jeanne's Dominican confessor and was at one time attributed to Albertus Magnus, the great Dominican who died in 1280.[24]

[19] A contemporary illustrated account of the coronation, however, shows it as an immediate sequel to Charles IV's coronation: Anne D. Hedeman, "The Commemoration of Jeanne d'Evreux's Coronation in the *Ordo ad Consecrandum* at the University of Illinois," *Essays in Medieval Studies: Proceedings of the Illinois Medieval Association* 7 (1990), 13–26.

[20] *Recueil des historiens*, 21:64, 69, 684, 687, 688.

[21] *Recueil des historiens*, 21:70, 145, 733.

[22] The baptismal procession is illustrated in the *Grandes chroniques de France*, Bibliothèque Nationale, MS fr. 2813, fol. 446v: Anne D. Hedeman, *The Royal Image: Illustrations of the Grandes chroniques de France, 1274–1422*, California Studies in the History of Art 28 (Berkeley, 1991), pp. 114–15. A brief entry for Blanche de Bourgogne is in Alain Décaux and André Castelet, *Dictionnaire d'histoire de France* (Paris, 1981), p. 101. For the foundation at Maubuisson, which had earlier served as a refuge for Blanche de Castille, widow of Louis VIII: Elizabeth M. Hallam, *Capetian France, 987–1328* (London, 1980), pp. 232–33, 282.

[23] For the books mentioned in Blanche's will that had belonged to her mother, see Harthen, *Books of Hours*, pp. 33, 44.

[24] Danielle Jacquart and Claude Thomasset, *Sexuality and Medicine in the Middle Ages*, trans. Matthew Adamson (Princeton, 1988; orig. *Sexualité et savoir médical au moyen âge* [Paris, 1985]), pp. 128–29; they used an anonymous, undated French translation, *Les secrets des hommes et des femmes composés par Grand Albert traduits du latin en français*. For the misattribution: B. Kusche, "Zur *Secreta Mulierum*—Forschung," *Janus* 62 (1975), 103–23; the text is not included in the authoritative edition of Albertus's writings: Albertus Magnus, *Opera omnia*, ed. Augustine Borgnet, 38 vols. (Paris, 1890–99), and there is no recent Latin edition. Nor is the work included in Michael R. Best and Frank H. Brightman, eds., *The Book of Secrets of Albertus Magnus; of the Virtues of Herbs, Stones and Certain Beasts; also A Book of the Marvels of the World* (London, 1974). I have not yet seen the translation by Helen Rodnite Lemay in the SUNY Series in Medieval Studies (Albany, 1992). For French and Latin editions available to me, see below, n. 31. A critical review of related literature is given by Monica H. Green, "Female Sexuality in the Medieval West," *Trends in History* 4 (1990), 127–58.

The young queen kneels, intent upon reading her (= this) book, no doubt praying to the Virgin for a male child, as Laura Good has emphasized.[25] Locked in the initial of the Lord and guarded by a seneschal with a candle—also a fertility symbol—to light her midnight vigils, she begins the prayer "Domine labia mea aperies."[26] The word *labia* stands out, center page. The bas-de-page below her shows a flirtatious party game (a kind of froggy in the middle or blindman's buff) that alludes to the life she must avoid.[27] This combination of subjects appears later on a marriage casket, where games and grotesques are on the outside and the Annunciation on the interior, symbolic of entering a new life.[28]

An ape clambers toward Jeanne (and her cat or squirrel, perched at the top of the bush), but for the queen there is to be no monkeying around, no plea-surable foreplay; the Lord (= her lord) will open her lips.[29] The ape often represented uncleanliness and sensuality, whether lasciviousness or gluttony; in the initial under the Flight into Egypt it mimics the crouched position and nudity of the falling pagan idol below it, while holding the flame of its lust to be fanned by the bellows of a grotesque fallen angel (Fig. 1).[30] According to *De secretis mulierum*, following Gratian and William of Auxerre, food and sex were alike in that each is necessary to the continuation of the race, but neither should be

[25] Laura Good, "A Lesson in Queenly Behavior: Reinterpreting the Hours of Jeanne d'Evreux," lecture given at the Boston University Symposium on the History of Art at the Isabella Stewart Gardner Museum, March 23, 1991. The paper was first presented in my class on fourteenth-century art in 1990.

[26] For the use of a single lighted candle at weddings, see Erwin Panofsky, "Jan van Eyck's 'Arnolfini' Portrait," *Burlington Magazine* 64 (1934), 117–27, repr. in W. Eugene Kleinbauer, *Modern Perspectives in Western Art History* (New York, 1971), at p. 200.

[27] Richard H. Randall, Jr., "Frog in the Middle," *The Metropolitan Museum of Art Bulletin* 16 (1958), 269–75. My reading does not, of course, exclude the allegorical relationship between the buffeting and the mocking of Christ, as elucidated by Lilian M. C. Randall, "Games and the Passion in Pucelle's Hours of Jeanne d'Evreux," *Speculum* 47 (1972), 248–53; she suggested that the tilting scene under the Betrayal refers to the "God buffeter" or the Wandering Jew (pp. 253–57), a resonance that is quite compatible with the one I am suggesting.

[28] J. Cherry, "The Talbot Casket and Related Late Medieval Leather Caskets," *Archaeologia* 107 (1982), 131–40, who assigns it to north France or Flanders toward the end of the century.

[29] *Labia* was used to denote female genitals, though rarely, in antiquity: J. N. Adams, *The Latin Sexual Vocabulary* (Baltimore, 1982), pp. 99–100, citing Celsus. Medieval use seems to have preferred *labra*: Frederick Charles Forberg, *Manual of Classical Erotology (De figuris Veneris)*, 1 (Manchester, Eng., 1884), pp. 39, 83. The first passage, attributed to Aloysia Sigaea, resembles *Carmina Burana* 185 but is actually postmedieval (cf. *Carmina Burana mit Benutzung der Vorarbeiten Wilhelm Meyers*, ed. Alfons Hilka and Otto Schumann, 2 [Heidelberg, 1961], p. 310). In the late-fifteenth-century Playfair Hours the opening phrase is inscribed on a plinth directly below Joachim and Anne at the Golden Gate and the Birth of the Virgin: London, Victoria and Albert Museum, MS L.475-1918, fol. 36r, reproduced in Kathleen Ashley and Pamela Sheingorn, *Interpreting Cultural Symbols: Saint Anne in Late Medieval Society* (Athens, Ga., 1990), p. 24, fig. 7.

[30] In some cases the ape symbolized the sense of taste; its greed for apples signified the Fall, its thirst for wine, drunkenness: Horst W. Janson, *Apes and Ape Lore in the Middle Ages and Renaissance* (London, 1952), pp. 239–46; also Klingender, *Animals in Art*, pp. 428–29, fig. 262. The view of apes as morally depraved is emphasized by Janson, pp. 16–20, 29–34, 54–55. For Albertus Magnus's view of the ape as a superior beast/bestial humanoid see Janson, pp. 80–90.

enjoyed.[31] This represents a fundamental revision of the medical view prevalent before the mid-thirteenth century, that a woman's pleasure contributed to the likelihood of conception.[32] The bas-de-page shows young women as the instigators of sexual arousal, as in the nursery rhyme "she can hop, she can skip, she can turn the candlestick"; below the youth whom they are buffeting a mouse begins to peek out of its hole.[33] In a bas-de-page in the Ormesby Psalter (an earlier East Anglian book), decoded by Lucy Freeman Sandler as a "bawdy betrothal," a phallus-dagger, vulva-ring, and a cat and mouse are very noticeable (Fig. 3).[34] With the help of the fabliaux, she demonstrated that the preying, hungry female is a "pussy," stalking the male mouse that emerges cautiously from cover, only to retreat back into it. Pliny even referred to a lecherous woman as "an absolute mousehole" because of the comings and goings of "mice."[35] The pussy in Jeanne's case crouches in the foliage behind her feet, while her faithful dog remains in view.

The female was regarded as the sexual aggressor in Christian theology—whether as Eve, who handed the fruit to Adam; Salome, whose wiles and erotic dance destroyed John the Baptist (as imaged on the eleventh-century Hildesheim column); or in the form of female personifications of Luxuria (Figs. 6 and 7).[36] One of the few female grotesques in the Hours blows her own horn; bare-breasted with flowing hair, she is like the personification of Lust in the early-twelfth-century porch sculpture at Moissac (Figs. 5 and 7).[37] Yet the hairy lower

---

[31] *De secretis mulierum et virorum* (Amsterdam, 1625), p. 23; *Les admirables secrets d'Albert le grand, contenant plusieurs traités sur la conception des femmes, sur les vertus des herbes, des pierres précieuses et les animaux* (Lyons, 1777), pp. 22–23; Jacquart and Thomasset, *Sexuality and Medicine*, pp. 87–90 (contraception was banned, as a logical corollary). Another survey of theological positions is less historically focused than it promises to be: Jean-Louis Flandrin, "Sex in Married Life in the Early Middle Ages: The Church's Teaching and Behavioral Reality," in Philippe Ariès and André Béjin, eds., *Western Sexuality: Practice and Precept in Past and Present Times*, trans. Anthony Forster (Oxford, 1985), pp. 114–29.

[32] Jacquart and Thomasset, *Sexuality and Medicine*, pp. 130–38; in the thirteenth century Averroes had many followers in supposing pleasure was not necessary, including Albertus Magnus in his *Questions on Animals* (Jacquart and Thomasset, *Sexuality and Medicine*, pp. 66–69).

[33] Beryl Rowland, *Animals with Human Faces: A Guide to Animal Symbolism* (Knoxville, 1973), p. 127.

[34] Lucy Freeman Sandler, "A Bawdy Betrothal in the Ormesby Psalter," in *A Tribute to Lotte Brand Philip, Art Historian and Detective*, ed. W. Clark et al. (New York, 1985), pp. 154–59.

[35] Rowland, *Animals*, p. 127; she mistakes the gender of the mouse metaphor, however, applying it to the female sex, which is clearly the hole.

[36] John A. Phillips, *Eve: The History of an Idea* (San Francisco, 1984), pp. 38–51, gives a general overview of the various "blaming" mythologies; see also Elaine Pagels, *Adam, Eve, and the Serpent* (New York, 1988), esp. chap. 6. An analysis of Dante's views of women is given by Marianne Shapiro, *Women Earthly and Divine in the "Comedy" of Dante* (Lexington, Ky., 1975), pp. 18–79. For the bronze paschal column in St. Michael's, Hildesheim, see Francis J. Tschan, *Saint Bernward of Hildesheim*, 3: *Album* (Notre Dame, 1952), figs. 147–91, esp. 165–66. Lust dancing to a piper in an Anglo-Saxon *Psychomachia* manuscript of the late tenth century (London, British Library, Add. MS 24199, fol. 18r) is briefly discussed by Francis Wormald, *English Drawings of the Eleventh and Twelfth Centuries* (London, 1952), pp. 28–29, 66, fig. 6a; the sequel, Luxuria reviled by Sobrietas, is illustrated from another recension, fig. 6b.

[37] There are fewer than 20 female grotesques, a ratio of less than 1 female to 26 males; I am

parts, with a bearded face, suggest a hermaphrodite. In another initial a matron plays the cymbals and a monster with phallic tail and bat's wings emerges from her skirts; the squirrel perched behind her shoulder is another form of "pussy" (Fig. 8). Not much later, witches were thought to ride cockhorses (referred to as palfreys) made of broomsticks, and this "cross-dressing" incited anxiety and rage.[38] A third aggressive female with flowing hair plunges a sword into the jaws of the man-headed grotesque she rides (Fig. 10). Such terrifying figures could be contained by the name of the Lord God when invoked in prayer; each is inscribed in the *D* of *Domine* or *Deus*, which becomes a magical or apotropaic sign (as elsewhere, when it contains the lecherous ape, who is under the sway of the devil; see Fig. 1). The angel of the Annunciation crushes a woman-headed beast under his foot against the letter *D* that holds Jeanne; no doubt it refers to the serpent that tempted Eve (Fig. 2).[39]

The most charged of the sacred images on these facing pages, the Betrayal and Arrest of Christ, is remarkable for its concentration of male aggression (Fig. 2). A contemporary sensibility can help my reading. The assortment of arms that jut out into the margins, unrestrained by a frame, and an assault scene below bring to mind a series of paintings by Jonathan Borofsky, entitled *Male Aggression Now Playing Everywhere* (Fig. 13).[40] Elsewhere in the margins a boy with a crossbow also resembles the Borofsky, a large belt buckle with pro-

---

grateful to Sharon Salvadori, for checking my charting of all the marginal motifs in the Hours from the Metropolitan Museum microfilm, and to Nancy Chute, for helping to tabulate the results; see M. H. Caviness, "(En)gendering Marginalia in Books Made for Men and Women," *Medieval Europe, 1992: Art and Symbolism,* Pre-printed Papers 7 (York, 1992), p. 101. For Moissac: Meyer Schapiro, *Romanesque Art* (New York, 1977), pp. 235–36, fig. 114.

[38] Lewis Spence, *Myth and Ritual in Dance, Game, and Rhyme* (London, 1947), p. 71, refers to the witch's broom as "nothing but a magical makeshift for the horse," yet immediately describes fertility rites. The hobbyhorse has similar associations in some nursery rhymes: Iona and Peter Opie, eds., *The Oxford Dictionary of Nursery Rhymes* (Oxford, 1977), pp. 209–10. Dürer's and Baldung Grün's witches ride backwards (another reversal) on long-haired billy goats, but they hold a spindle or a pitchfork at their pubis: Russell, *Eva/Ave,* p. 166, no. 103 and fig. 103a. Josephine Donovan, *Feminist Theory: The Intellectual Traditions of American Feminism* (New York, 1990), p. 29, encapsulates "the post-medieval world view, of a division between the rational and the non-rational [according to which] rational calculation governs the public world amorally; it is a masculine sphere. On the other hand is the nonrational sphere, the world of women, which must be kept in its place, or if it strays into the public realm, must be brutally subdued." Jeffrey Burton Russell, *Witchcraft in the Middle Ages* (Ithaca, N.Y., 1972), views heresy and the inquisitions as witchcraft and persecution. Men in drag enraged at least one twelfth-century writer, quoted by Roger de Hoveden: Christie Davies, "Sexual Taboos and Social Boundaries," *American Journal of Sociology* 87 (1982), 1049–51.

[39] As twined around the tree and balancing an apple on one cloven hoof in the Temptation scene in a late-thirteenth-century north French Bible, London, British Library, Add. MS 11639, fol. 520v, illustrated in Florens Deuchler, *Gothic Art* (New York, 1973), fig. 155. Guido delle Colonne, citing Bede, refers to a serpent with a girl's face chosen by the devil to speak for it: Michael Camille, *The Gothic Idol: Ideology and Image-making in Medieval Art* (Cambridge, Eng., 1989), p. 59.

[40] Rosie Erph secured the loan of a photograph from the Paula Cooper Gallery. For two earlier versions: Mark Rosenthal and Richard Marshall, *Jonathan Borofsky,* exhibition catalogue, Philadelphia Museum of Art (Philadelphia, 1984), pp. 27, 80–81. For the series: Hood Museum of Art, Dartmouth College, *Subject(s): The Prints and Multiples of Jonathan Borofsky, 1982–1991,* exhibition catalogue by James Cuno (Hanover, N.H., 1992), pp. 74–75.

truding tongue acting as referents for his genitals (Fig. 12). Male aggressiveness
provides an essential clue for a historicized reading of the Hours.

The Betrayal scene forms a remarkable pendant to the Annunciation that
opens the matins prayer, in that the curve of the now-pregnant Virgin's body
is mirrored in that of Christ, who thus takes on an effeminate or (given his slight
beard) androgynous appearance (Fig. 2).[41] The thrust of Christ's pelvis and the
way he is hemmed in by sexually charged symbols bring to mind a contemporary
ivory mirror back (Fig. 9); chess is not the only game in town as the lady opens
to her lover's advances, the folds of her skirt taking on the form of labia, and
her attendant holding the "crown" that she will bestow on him.[42]

The kiss of Judas finds a resonance in the central word of the opening prayer,
labia, as well as with kissing grotesques elsewhere in the book (Figs. 2, 11).[43]
The kiss signified the vice of lewdness, as in Amiens sculpture.[44] The various
recensions of the *Bible moralisée* show devils joining together kissing, and even
copulating, couples, sometimes homosexual, below the Fall of Adam and Eve
(Fig. 15).[45]

The beginning of Christ's Passion is marked by a homosexual kiss. The dark-
ness of the moment is recalled by the lamp held above Christ (the hour of prayer
is midnight). Below, a barrel is held aloft on a pole while two oddly dressed
men riding rams tilt at it with spears (Fig. 2). Rams were considered lascivious
and hermaphrodite, and the barrel that the riders fail to penetrate has the
appearance of a uterus as diagramed in a contemporary anatomical manuscript
(Fig. 14).[46] *Aforer le tonel* is a euphemism for *foutre* in the fabliaux.[47] These

[41] This stance has always been dismissed as inherent in courtly style.

[42] Raymond Koechlin, *Les ivoires gothiques français* (Paris, 1968), 3:384, pl. CLXXX, no. 1053;
nos. 1046, 1049, 1056 (also illustrated) have the same drapery configuration.

[43] Figures playing the cymbals, e.g., Fig. 8, also connote kissing (or coitus): Rabanus Maurus
likened them to human lips, though without sexual innuendo (quoted by Théodore Gérold, *Les pères
de l'église et la musique* [Paris, 1931], pp. 178–79), but a later vernacular proverb indicates otherwise:
"Sa femme avec le chevalier jouoit des cimbales," cited in James Woodrow Hassell, Jr., *Middle
French Proverbs, Sentences, and Proverbial Phrases*, Subsidia Mediaevalia 12 (Toronto, 1982), p. 141,
J27.

[44] For the Amiens sculpture and attitudes to kissing in relation to procreation, see Madeline H.
Caviness, " 'The Simple Perception of Matter' and the Representation of Narrative, ca. 1180–1280,"
Gesta 30 (1991), 60; 64, n. 78; fig. 22.

[45] Camille, *Gothic Idol*, pp. 59–60, 90, figs. 30, 48.

[46] For the manuscript, Oxford, Bodleian Library, MS Ashmole 399, and its relatives see Ynez
Violé O'Neill, "The Fünfbilderserie—A Bridge to the Unknown," *Bulletin of the History of Medicine*
51 (1977), 538–49. For the evil connotations of riding a horned ram, see Robertson, *Chaucer*, p.
255; Beryl Rowland, "Animal Imagery and the Pardoner's Abnormality," *Neophilologus* 48 (1964),
56–60; and Russell, *Eva/Ave*, p. 167. Lust rides a ram in a late-fifteenth-century illumination (London, British Library, MS Yates Thompson 3, fol. 172v): Margaret Wade Labarge, *A Small Sound of
the Trumpet: Women in Medieval Life* (Boston, 1986), fig. 47. For the whole cycle, which illustrates
the penitential Psalms in a book of hours made for Jean Dunois about 1450, see William M. Voelkle,
"Morgan Manuscript M.1001: The Seven Deadly Sins and the Seven Evil Ones," in *Monsters and
Demons in the Ancient and Medieval World*, ed. Ann E. Farkas, Prudence O. Harper, and Evelyn B.
Harrison (Mainz, 1987), p. 108, figs. 14–16.

[47] Roy J. Pearcy, "Modes of Signification and the Humor of Obscene Diction in the Fabliaux,"
in *The Humor of the Fabliaux: A Collection of Critical Essays*, ed. Thomas D. Cooke and Benjamin L.
Honeycutt (Columbia, Mo., 1974), pp. 167, 183.

hermaphodite men threaten to violate Christ. Such diffuse and unexpected threats, premonitions of sex and sin in strange costumes and disguises, fill Jeanne's exquisite prayer book.

MORE LESSONS FOR A ROYAL BRIDE

The reading response that I am establishing for the Cloisters Hours is that of the very young bride; in later life she would have been less susceptible. The imagery can be seen in the context of instructional manuals on good behavior prepared by men for married women; in fact the secular tradition goes back to letters that St. Louis wrote to his married daughters stressing the need for modesty, obedience, and piety, for the avoidance of pride, lechery, laziness, and gluttony and of any behavior that might be thought flirtatious.[48] Following the *Miroir des bonnes femmes* of about 1300, the courtesy books of the later fourteenth century include a guide for daughters by Geoffrey de la Tour-Landry, which circulated widely, and an anonymous tract for a young wife written in Paris by a household manager (the *Ménagier de Paris*) at the court of Charles V. The *Ménagier* advocates religious devotion and offers biblical role models for continence, devotion, and obedience.[49] The *Ménagier* also exhorts a wife and mother to preserve "the honor of her husband's line" and notes the precautions taken by the queens of France to avoid suspicion by never kissing any man but their husbands and never opening a sealed letter in private unless it is from him.[50] Furthermore, a cycle of bas-de-page scenes in a noble woman's prayer book, the Taymouth Hours, has been recently understood in light of a didactic purpose: her duty to respect the knight's honor is emphasized at the opening to the hours of the Virgin and at the beginning of the vernacular prayers for mass.[51] Embedding didactic images in the devotional text that was in constant use would keep the lessons in mind, and prayer and visual exempla worked together toward the same end, the construction of gender.

Several images instructed Jeanne about sexuality and procreation. One animal that figures largely in the margins is the rabbit or hare, sometimes pursued by

[48] Diane Bornstein, *The Lady in the Tower: Medieval Courtesy Literature for Women* (Hamden, Conn., 1983), pp. 48–49, 126. An illustrated *Manuel des péchés* in Princeton, made for a noblewoman, emphasizes marital fidelity: Princeton University Library, MS Taylor Medieval 1; see Adelaide Bennett, "A Book Designed for a Noblewoman: An Illustrated *Manuel des péchés* of the Thirteenth Century," in *Medieval Book Production: Assessing the Evidence*, ed. Linda L. Brownrigg (Los Altos Hills, Calif., 1990), pp. 163–81.

[49] J. L. Grigsby, "Miroir des bonnes femmes," *Romania* 82 (1961), 458–81, and 83 (1962), 30–51; Bornstein, *Lady in the Tower*, pp. 53–59; M. Y. Offord, ed., *The Book of the Knight of the Tour, Translated by William Caxton* (London, 1971).

[50] Bornstein, *Lady in the Tower*, p. 55; Eileen Power, trans., *The Goodman of Paris (Le Ménagier de Paris), a Treatise on Moral and Domestic Economy by a Citizen of Paris (c. 1393)* (London, 1928), pp. 105–6.

[51] Linda Brownrigg, "The Taymouth Hours and the Romance of *Beves of Hampton*," *English Manuscript Studies* 1 (1991), 222–41; I am grateful to Jonathan Alexander for this timely reference. For this book, perhaps made for Edward III's sister Joan, see Lucy Freeman Sandler, *Gothic Manuscripts, 1285–1385* (London, 1986), 2:107–9.

a tongue-lolling hound.[52] The female was not always imaged as the sexual aggressor, and a woman viewing a hunt is more likely to identify with the quarry than with the hunter.[53] The rabbit hunt is a reversal of the cat-and-mouse construction, punning on the pursuit of *con* and *coni* (*cunnus* and *cuniculus*); "faire la chasse aux conins" still carries a sexual meaning.[54] In one case a hare is lodged between the sacred script and the spearing of the unicorn (Fig. 16). The mythic unicorn (illustrated more lustily in color in a bas-de-page of the Ormesby Psalter) was captured when it laid its horned head in a virgin's lap (*con*). Only then could it be penetrated by the spear (sexually initiated in metaphor), which makes the unicorn a surrogate or sacrificial scapegoat for the virgin. The unicorn legend was illustrated in bestiaries such as a book of about 1230 from Rochester abbey; there the virgin is nude and covers her pubis with one hand and the unicorn's back with the other, while the spear works as a visual pun on deflowering by passing through the rosette in the center of the round shield (Fig. 17).[55] The hare or rabbit (*con-i*) in Jeanne's book is also about to be taken. The anxiety is palpable.

The abundant rabbits in the margins, connoting fertility, would remind Jeanne of her duty to produce an heir, and might enhance her desire for offspring. In the bestiaries hares and rabbits were lascivious, no doubt because of their frequency of copulation and conception; less often they were credited with virginal fecundity.[56] One large beast hovers below the Visitation, the moment when the pregnant Elizabeth and Mary greet each other (Fig. 18). The bas-de-page players welcome a piper, while a conjurer looks intently at a vessel. The *De secretis mulierum* tells us that if a woman wished to conceive a male child, she might take the intestines or testicles of a hare or rabbit, dry them, and drink them powdered in wine before going to bed with her husband. The testicles of a pig could serve the same function, drunk by either man or wife, which may account for the number of wild boars in the Hours.[57] Wish fulfilment is imaged not only in the Christ child but also in infants being carried by their nurses in the margins (Fig. 19) and in occasional playful boys (e.g., Figs. 8 and 12); there are no girls.[58]

The inclusion of the hours of Jeanne's great-grandfather, St. Louis, provided her with a gender-exchanged role model for a woman's acts of charity and

[52] There are 34–35 coneys, and another 18–21 being chased by dogs, or 52–56 in all.

[53] Male response to my lectures has often urged a naturalized reading of the hunt scenes as merely a normal medieval activity. Any woman who has been followed in the street experiences the sport differently.

[54] Rowland, *Animals*, pp. 133–35; Robertson, *Chaucer*, pp. 113, 255, fig. 6, refers to the hare and hounds as the hunt of Venus. The hunted stag, which appears in some women's books, also signified a sexual quarry: Marcelle Thiebaux, *The Stag of Love: The Chase in Medieval Literature* (Ithaca, N.Y., 1974).

[55] London, British Library, MS Royal 12 F.XIII, fol. 10v: Klingender, *Animals*, pp. 93–94, 396–97.

[56] Of the two, the fecundity and frenzied mating of the hare were better known (Rowland, *Animals*, pp. 89–93). The idea lives on in the locker room: "She screws like a rabbit."

[57] *De secretis*, pp. 116–17; *Les admirables secrets*, p. 66. Boars, with tusks, number 8 or 9. A tusked boar, however, is trodden down by Chastity in the *Somme le Roy*.

[58] There are 3 infants and 19–25 boys (depending on the age cutoff).

humility and for a chaste progenitor (see the Genealogical Table—he had eleven children).[59] His hours are also included in Jeanne's breviary and in the Hours of her niece Jeanne II de Navarre.[60] St. Louis is shown as a young man being disciplined in his antechamber by his confessor, as described in the life of the saint by Guillaume de Saint-Pathus (Fig. 21); he later sent his daughter Isabelle ivory boxes containing chains to discipline herself with, as Joan Holladay has recently shown.[61] On the same page, in parallel with this beating, a knight clubs a youthful male grotesque with genital mask/cockhorse and confines it to the *D* of *Domine*; others beat the foliage in which a cat chases what appears to be a mouse, and a peasant grasps a female grotesque by her long hair to club her, pulling her away from a young man with a cowl. On the left, in the equivalent position to Jeanne on the facing page, a young nobleman sheathes his sword to enter a porch. Sexuality is to be curbed.

Under the guidance of his mendicant confessors St. Louis is seen in the pictures that follow, ministering to the sick and washing the feet of the poor. In one scene, where he feeds a leper, a lion sits obediently at his foot (Fig. 22). On another page a young man is watched by a lion as he sheathes or unsheathes his sword (Fig. 20). The lion, according to the *De secretis*, symbolized the testicles.[62] Albericus of London likened the carnal love that "invades us fiercely at adolescence" to a lion.[63] In the "bawdy betrothal" of the Ormesby Psalter a half-man figure with a lion's mask at the genitals watches the cat and mouse (Fig. 3). For Jeanne's Hours, the climate of the moment favored the sheathing of the sword. The church had put limits on coitus between married couples: there was to be no intercourse during the forty days of Lent, the forty days after Pentecost, and the forty days before Christmas; on sixteen other feast days; on Wednesdays, Fridays, Saturdays, or Sundays; and while the woman was menstruating or nursing.[64] This amounts to about three days of taboo for every day

---

[59] Holladay, *The Education of Jeanne d'Evreux* (above, n. 2).

[60] For a text-image analysis: Emile Mâle, *Art et artistes du moyen âge* (Paris, 1927), pp. 247–60; he compares the cycle to one recorded in the stained glass of Saint-Denis by Montfaucon. For the breviary: Léopold Delisle, *Notice de douze livres royaux du XIIIe et du XIVe siècle* (Paris, 1902), pp. 65–66, pls. XIX–XX.

[61] Joan Holladay, "Men's Intervention in the Structuring of Female Devotion: Artistic and Textual Evidence," paper read in a session entitled "Late Medieval Lay Piety: Gender Issues" at the Twenty-Sixth International Congress on Medieval Studies, Kalamazoo, 1991.

[62] *De secretis*, p. 4; *Les admirables secrets*, p. 17. This is oddly at variance with the astrological diagrams of the male body illustrated in Fritz Saxl and Hans Meier, *Catalogue of Astrological and Mythological Illuminated Manuscripts of the Latin Middle Ages*, 3/2: *Manuscripts in English Libraries* (London, 1953), pl. XCII, where the genitals are between Scorpio and Sagittarius.

[63] Robertson, *Chaucer*, p. 155 (and p. 91, n. 65, for the text).

[64] For the early proscriptions: Jean-Louis Flandrin, *Un temps pour embrasser: Aux origines de la morale sexuelle occidentale (VIe–XIe siècle)* (Paris, 1983), pp. 42–55; Pierre J. Payer, *Sex and the Penitentials: The Formation and Transmission of a Sexual Code, 550–1150* (Toronto, 1984), appendix B and pp. 19–30. John T. McNeill and Helena M. Gamer, *Medieval Hand-Books of Penance: A Translation of the Principal Libri Poenitentiales and Selections from Related Documents* (New York, 1965), p. 413, among later texts cites the Council of Westminster, ca. 1200, which especially emphasized the importance of penance to wives so that they may not be suspected of "secret and heinous sin" by their husbands.

of license in a year without a birth. Apparently such proscriptions were increas-ingly enforced by the mendicants in the face of the illicit love sung by the troubadours and the supposed orgiastic behavior of heretics.[65]

The tensions between sexual taboo and the need to procreate are also ap-parent in the calendar illustrations. Although they ostensibly present a normal cycle of labors and zodiac signs, the imagery is adapted to exploit sexual in-nuendo in relation to taboo and procreation. In April, the first stirrings of spring are marked by a young man who with one hand pulls his mantle aside to reveal the center opening of his surcoat while in the other he holds a budding sapling (Fig. 27); the *verge* puns on phallus. At least part of the month would fall outside the Lenten proscription. The entire month of May, on the other hand, was forbidden for weddings, because of the danger of sexual license, even though Pentecost might fall at the end or in June (Fauvel wed in May on Pentecost, a double infringement). The calendar pages show a young man on a spirited horse in the chase with hounds and falcon; he has loosed the reins to place his hand on his thigh close to the hilt of his sword; the suggestion is completed by his round shield, partly hiding the blade, and by a young peasant who bends with the weight of not one but two huge *verges* (Fig. 24). The sexual potency of the horse and the leafy tree are reinforced later in the book, in the initial placed between the Adoration of the Magi and Herod inspired by a hairy demon to order the massacre of the innocents (Fig. 26). The wise kings have left passion behind to humble themselves before the infant Christ, but the horses paw at the ground and their stableboy places one hand on his genitals while raising the other to beat the horses into submission. On a contemporary mirror back a stableboy beats a pawing horse while its young owner makes advances to a girl (Fig. 29).[66] An image of masturbation that reinforces the reading of the stableboy in the Hours of Jeanne d'Evreux is in the *Roman de la Rose* of ca. 1400; Oiseuse arouses a young man by combing her hair (Fig. 28).[67]

In the facing bas-de-page for May the sign of Gemini is represented by the incestuous union of a young nude male and female, their sex hidden behind their common shield (Fig. 24).[68] In March, a Lenten month, the sexually mature ram nibbles at foliage, but the vines on the facing bas-de-page are still bare,

---

[65] Julien Cheverny, *Sexologie de l'Occident* (Paris, 1976), esp. pp. 97–100, 124–29, 161–63.

[66] The motif of beating the horses is simplified in the Hours of Jeanne de Navarre, daughter of Louis le Hutin, a manuscript illuminated by Pucelle's follower Jean le Noir; the owner turns her back on them to pray, and a grotesque with phallic tail flees from her: Avril, *Manuscript Painting*, pp. 68–71, pl. 16. For the ivory mirror back: Koechlin, *Ivoires gothiques*, p. 367, no. CLXXVI.

[67] Oxford, Bodleian Library, MS Selden Supra 57, fol. 10r: John B. Friedman, "L'iconographie de Vénus et de son miroir à la fin du moyen âge," in Bruno Roy, ed., *L'erotisme au moyen âge: Etudes présentées au Troisième Colloque de l'Institut d'études médiévales* (Montreal, 1977), pp. 77–81, fig. 18, who, however, concentrates on the female figure of Luxuria.

[68] A few other books of the period show couples embracing or caressing each other, even in a bathtub: Robertson, *Chaucer*, p. 257, figs. 105, 106 (esp. the Flemish Hours, London, British Library, MS Stowe 17, fol. 7r). The zodiac sign was traditionally represented by ungendered nudes; see, for instance, the cycle in the north rose of Braine: Madeline H. Caviness, *The Sumptuous Arts at the Royal Abbeys of Reims and Braine* (Princeton, 1990), appendix A, no. 25.

and one old peasant directs another to empty the basket of manure, which he does with his crook lowered (Fig. 23).

Late summer, on the other hand, was a better time to procreate, so appetites could be indulged. At the September vine harvest a women stuffs herself and her basket, denoting fecundity; there is a play between *uva* ("grape") and *ova* ("eggs," hence womb) (Fig. 25).[69] Facing her, the woman holding the sign of Libra appears pregnant. But in November and December, the signs of Sagittarius, as a centaur (resembling Fauvel), and Capricorn, the goat, provide a cautionary note; the lascivious goat is a chimera with dragon's wings and tail, and both are reminders of the taboo before Christmas (Fig. 39).[70] The signs of the zodiac were not traditionally treated in this way, but an earlier example is in another Capetian queen's book, the Psalter of Ingeborg.[71] These images resonate with the grotesques and chimeras on the text pages.

Jeanne's Dominican confessor surely pointed out to her that her holy progenitor controlled his bestiality by mortifying the flesh, as illustrated in the emblems surrounding this scene (Fig. 21, right). St. Louis also, however, cured some of the evils that accrued from too much sexual activity, such as blindness; this is probably the miracle at St. Louis's tomb on the facing page that opens the cycle of the Hours (Fig. 21, left).[72] Leprosy was similarly regarded as a venereal disease or, in the newborn, as the result of conception during menstruation.[73] In fact, the lion that I noted before cowers below the saintly king as he feeds a leprous monk (Fig. 22). The queen must learn to help her husband tame *leo*, as St. Louis had done, and to escape his advances when she was menstruating, like the *con-coni* that defies natural law by taking refuge in a tree behind his back! At such a time the "natural" law that allowed men to beat their wives but not otherwise might also be overturned, as in the bas-de-page: a woman who uses a stick to defend her basket (i.e., the womb) is aided by an older man who holds back her husband's instrument to prevent him from knocking her up.[74]

[69] Baskets, bowls, barrels, buckets, and pots are common in the margins of the Hours: there are 47 in all. Laura Kendrick, *The Game of Love: Troubadour Wordplay* (Berkeley, 1988), p. 146, quotes the tenth-century St.-Martial songbook, Paris, Bibliothèque Nationale, MS lat. 1338, fol. 24r–v: "Maria est intacta sportula" ("Mary is a spotless little basket"). In the Taymouth Hours, MS Yates Thompson 13, fol. 59v, the bas-de-page facing the Annunciation shows a woman at a well receiving a large pot from an angel.

[70] Rowland, *Animals*, pp. 80–85.

[71] Florens Deuchler, *Der Ingeborgpsalter* (Berlin, 1967), figs. 11–12.

[72] Many scientific texts, from Aristotle on, linked semen to the fluid that was supposedly in the brain and that also provided moisture for the eyes; its depletion would damage both. See Jacquart and Thomasset, *Sexuality and Medicine*, pp. 56, 181–82. Avril, *Manuscript Painting*, p. 53, prefers to identify the men with closed eyes as the guards who protected the tomb.

[73] *De secretis*, pp. 50–51; *Les admirables secrets*, p. 33. Jacquart and Thomasset, *Sexuality and Medicine*, pp. 185–86, quote O. Pontal, *Les statuts de Paris et le synodal de l'ouest, XIIIe siècle*, vol. 1 of *Les statuts synodaux français du XIIIe siècle*, Collection de Documents Inédits sur l'Histoire de France, ser. in 8vo, 9 (Paris, 1971), pp. 205–7, for the infection of the fetus. On the recurrent association of menstruation with pollution and danger: Mary Douglas, *Purity and Danger: An Analysis of the Concept of Pollution and Taboo* (London, 1966), pp. 121, 147, 151, 176–77.

[74] The norm, a (choleric) man beating a woman with a club, is illustrated from London, British

VISUAL PUNS AND ANAGRAMS

Many of the other images throughout the book communicate at a more intuitive, subliminal level. This marginal "decoration" has never been seriously analyzed as a whole.[75] The traditional view is that these grisaille figures are playful and whimsical, perhaps a bit raunchy, as if to offer comic relief in the face of gruesome scenes such as St. Louis piously collecting the decaying remains of crusaders for burial (Fig. 10). Just a few of the vignettes seem to bear this out—such as the uncouth comedians who grimace at each other across the top of a page, facing the deathbed scene of the saintly king (fols. 165v–166r). Yet it could scarcely have escaped the young bride's notice that most of these motifs are far more grotesque than funny (e.g., Figs. 1, 5, 18, and 21).

The sexual innuendo and cumulative impact on the viewer of the grotesques have been underestimated, since the color, size, and centrality of the sacred subjects demand attention; these others are marginal, yet I find them as insistent as a hoard of small children tugging at my skirts and sleeves. They seem to struggle against the ordered lines of the written word (which constitute the prayers), powerful distractions to be resisted by the reader intent upon her devotions. Indeed, most were sufficiently repellent as to direct the eye back into the words, and thus they control the reader. The use of such line endings had been developed by previous generations, beginning from obvious signs such as pointing hands.[76] No such specific lexical functions are found in the line endings of the Hours, but their repetitious punctuation of the text may have aided the line-to-line process of reading.

Before describing the prevalent types and themes of these grotesques, it

---

Library, Add. MS 17987, fol. 88v, in Saxl and Meier, *Catalogue of Astrological and Mythological Illuminated Manuscripts*, 3/2, pl. 88, fig. 228. As noted by Veronica Sekules, "Women and Art in England in the Thirteenth and Fourteenth Centuries," in Jonathan Alexander and Paul Binski, eds., *Age of Chivalry: Art in Plantagenet England, 1200–1400*, exhibition catalogue, Royal Academy (London, 1987), p. 41, women who are depicted reversing this order usually belong to the lower class. An aristocratic woman, however, beats a man with her spindle (a symbol of her sexuality) in the margins of the Luttrell Psalter, London, British Library, Add. MS 42130, fol. 60r (I owe this example to Vera Beattie of the Institute of Fine Arts). For a later example of this *monde renversé*, with satirical rather than moral overtones, see Diane G. Scillia, "Israhel Van Meckenem's Marriage à la Mode: The *Alltagsleben*," in *New Images of Medieval Women*, ed. Edelgard E. DuBruck (Lampeter, Wales, 1989), pp. 211–13; 226, n. 27; fig. 6; she refers to Frances and Joseph Gies, *Women in the Middle Ages* (New York, 1978), pp. 46–48, and other literature on the right of men to beat their wives.

[75] Lilian M. C. Randall, *Images in the Margins of Gothic Manuscripts* (Berkeley, 1966), the basis for all serious study of marginalia, lays good groundwork, but its comparative apparatus is organized according to representational images, which makes it more a work of reference than an analytic tool.

[76] In the East Anglian Ramsey Psalter of ca. 1303–16 a line ending with a hand pouring the contents of a flask into a bowl held by a grotesque at the foot of the page wittily brings the reader's attention to two lines that had been omitted halfway up and inserted at the bottom; in the left margin three mice climb up a leash attached to a cat waiting for them on a branch that leads back to the next line to be read: St. Paul im Lavanttal, Stiftsbibliothek, Cod. XXV/2, 19, fol. 108v; see Lucy F. Sandler, *The Peterborough Psalter in Brussels and Other Fenland Manuscripts* (London, 1974), pp. 116, 148, fig. 345.

should be emphasized that they contrast with the mode of depiction in the devotional frames in ways that enhance the reading of both genres. For instance, fully draped figures represent the highest social and spiritual ranks (Jeanne, the Virgin, angels visiting earth), their feet peeking demurely from overly long skirts to confirm a human termination (Figs. 1, 2, 18, 32). On the other hand, the purest angels in heaven are half-length (Figs. 2 and 32, angels in heaven). One very unusual standing figure is a nude Christ child, his sex delicately—but scarcely—masked, reminding the viewer of the humanity of Christ (Fig. 26).[77] All of these figures contrast with the fantastic semihuman grotesques in the margins, which have bestial lower halves (Figs. 1, 10, 21, 33).

The margins and line endings, then, constitute a discrete zone, one that is negatively defined as outside the sacred spaces of picture frames and written words. When a modern woman reader (and perhaps *any* reader) free-associates in scanning these unhallowed areas of the page, a surprising amount of phallic imagery surfaces. Several "shaggy" and "horny" beasts, metaphors for *mots poilus*, have already been noted. Extremely prevalent in the initials, line endings, and margins are swords, often held erect, sticks, clubs, crooks, horns, and horned animals, recalling the weapons with which the Passion cycle opened (Figs. 2, 5, 16, 20, 22, 23).[78] Many are wielded so as to project into the margins of the page (e.g., Figs. 12, 16, 33). Battering rams and arrows are also metaphors for penetration in medieval love poetry. The *Carmina Burana* often expresses especially violent male fantasy:

> *Er warf mir uf daz hemdelin.* / corpore detecta,
> *er rante mir in daz purgelein* / cuspide erecta
>
> Hoy et oe! / maledicantur tilie / iuxta viam posite!
>
> *Er nam den chocher unde den bogen,* / bene venebatur!
> *der selbe hete mich betrogen.* / "ludus compleatur!"[79]

Lower-class instruments are clubs and cudgels, sometimes with shoots lopped

---

[77] Stylistic analyses used to claim this as an Italianate feature. The same is usually said of the origin of the fainting Virgin at the Crucifixion, but Judith H. Oliver, *Gothic Manuscript Illumination in the Diocese of Liège*, Corpus of Illuminated Manuscripts from the Low Countries (Louvain, 1988), fig. 169, has demonstrated use of this motif in a mid-thirteenth-century Psalter from the Low Countries, the former Donaueschingen MS 316, fol. 13v (the manuscript was sold at Sotheby's in 1982).

[78] The tables compiled from the microfilm in the Metropolitan Museum library revealed: 37/38 clubs, crooks, axes, and billhooks; 18 spears/bows and arrows/lances; 41 swords, daggers, and cutlasses.

[79] Hilka and Schumann, eds., *Carmina Burana* (above, n. 29), 1/2 (Heidelberg, 1941), p. 310: CB 185.9–10, rather freely translated by David Parlett, *Selections from the Carmina Burana: A Verse Translation* (Harmondsworth, 1986), pp. 147–49, "Under the Linden Tree":

> *Then tearing off my little gown* / he bared me pink as ham
> *and battered down my last defence* / with a rampant battering ram!
> [lit. he rammed my little keep with his erect spear-head]
>
> Alas and lack-a-day! / Thrice cursed be the linden tree that grows along the way!
> *Up with his bow and arrows then—* / how well his hunt did go!
> *For he had played me false, and won.* / "Thanks, darling, Cheerio!"
> [lit. the game is over].

off, like live wood (e.g., Figs. 22, 23).[80] Resonating with the *verge* as fertility symbols, they are its secular equivalent (Figs. 24, 27, 36).[81] Peasants seldom appear in the holy pictures, but in the Angel's Announcement to the Shepherds they invade sacred space with their clublike crooks and spill out of it into the margins and bas-de-page (Fig. 32). Some crooks assume the position of cock-horses, and a splay-legged boy observing from the shrubbery in the margin has an ambiguously placed dog's head projecting at his thigh. Aggressive and insistent, these simple phallic signs transfer meanings to slumped phrygian caps and even a tonsured monk's head (Fig. 33).[82]

A modern photograph, Robert Mapplethorpe's *James Ford* (1979), provides a formal analogue of a comparably charged image (Fig. 34).[83] The phallic resonance is supplied by visual metaphor rather than representation. *James Ford* is a visual pun, a Jesse without issue, whereas in a twelfth-century manuscript the pun is verbal as well: the *virga/verge* of Isaiah's prophecy is a phallus, and the English rendering as rod has the same modern connotation (Fig. 35).[84] A very early Jesse Tree, in the Shaftesbury Psalter, was notably painted in a women's book, probably for an abbess at Shaftsbury, and it is much more explicit in its anatomical rendering of the rod than are later versions of the Jesse Tree.[85] Virtually within sight of Shaftesbury, across the downs, is the phallic chalk carving known locally as the Long Man or Giant of Cerne (Fig. 36).[86] Such a figure is a dramatic reminder that pre-Christian fertility symbols were still visible

[80] For the association with a grotesque herdsman in Chrétien de Troyes, and other examples: Alice M. Colby, *The Portrait in Twelfth-Century French Literature: An Examination of the Stylistic Originality of Chrétien de Troyes* (Geneva, 1965), pp. 171–72.

[81] The cross of Christ is also often shown cut from the *lignum vitae* of green wood: e.g., in the Psalter of Robert de Lindseye, abbot of Peterborough (d. 1222), London, Society of Antiquaries, MS 59, fol. 35v: Nigel Morgan, *Early Gothic Manuscripts*, 1: *1190–1250* (London, 1982), no. 47, pp. 94–95, fig. 157.

[82] For a similar reading of the phrygian caps worn at the time of the French Revolution, see Neil Hertz, "Medusa's Head: Male Hysteria under Political Pressure—A Vermiform Appendix: The Phrygian Cap," *Representations* 4 (1983), 40–54.

[83] Janet Kardon et al., *Robert Mapplethorpe: The Perfect Moment* (Philadelphia, 1988), pp. 53, 120.

[84] Isaiah 11.1, "Et egrediatur virga de radice Iesse, et flos de radice eius ascendet." Cf. the expression "having a rod on" for having an erection.

[85] London, British Library, MS Lansdowne 383, fol. 15r; an abbess kneels at the feet of Christ in Majesty on fol. 14v; see C. M. Kauffmann, *Romanesque Manuscripts, 1066–1190*, A Survey of Manuscripts Illuminated in the British Isles (London, 1975), no. 48, figs. 131–34, pp. 82–84, with a date ca. 1130–40 and earlier bibliography; and George Henderson, " 'Abraham genuit Isaac,' " *Gesta* 26 (1987), 128 and 138, nn. 7–8. The latter also notes that the abbreviation of the kings to one, thus privileging the role of the Virgin, is shared with Herrad of Landsberg's *Hortus deliciarum*, another book made for women.

[86] The outline of this 180-foot figure is cut 2 feet into the chalk; it may be a Romano-British Hercules: Royal Commission on Historical Monuments, England, *An Inventory of the Historical Monuments of Dorset*, 1: *West* (London, 1952), p. 82, pl. 107. Ronald Sheridan and Anne Ross, *Gargoyles and Grotesques: Paganism in the Medieval Church* (Boston, 1975), pp. 24–27, prefer to relate it to Celtic deities, and notice giants with clubs carved on the local fifteenth-century church of Cerne Abbas.

in the Middle Ages, and some cults even survived.[87] Hollow male statues were fabricated as fire blowers, and a crouching male exposes himself in the four-teenth-century choir stall paintings of Cologne cathedral.[88] Such blatant images overlap their strong meanings onto nonrepresentational objects in the same culture.

Phallic resonances in the Hours are corroborated by other clues. In the case of a beggar whose deflated bagpipes (or cane and purse?) hang down over his belt, the foliage in the initial behind him signals fertility (Fig. 38). Elsewhere, bagpipes and caps perk up in unison (Fig. 39). The inflated bladder of the drone and the erect horn of the chanter when it is ready to perform made the bagpipe an ideal purveyor of sexual meaning (as in the Visitation page, Figs. 18, 32), though they were also associated with gluttony. Hence the beggar holds out his empty bowl, the bagpipe also signifying his empty belly. Such base appetites were probably seen to fit the lower classes, who celebrated to the raucous sound of bagpipes (Figs. 31 and 32).[89] Inflated bladders, often carried in a shivaree, signified fecundity.[90]

There is also a burlesque element to some wind instruments. In several cases a bellows serves as a bagpipe; it preserves the form but not the function, es-pecially when it is used to puff up the "player" instead of the other way around, connotating a blow job (Figs. 37, 38).[91] In one bas-de-page a small dog serves as a kind of bagpipe, its tail used as a mouthpiece and its hind legs as stops (Fig. 40). It puns in the vein of "playing the skin flute" (fellatio).

Other musical instruments that have sexual allusions are horns and flutes

[87] For phallic cults in medieval France: Raphael Blanchard, "Persistance du culte phallique en France," *Bulletin de la Société Française d'Histoire de la Médecine* 3 (1904), 106–21, and Germain Bapst, "L'orfèvrerie d'étain dans l'antiquité," *Revue archéologique*, 3rd ser., 2 (1984), 99–100; for Scandinavia and the British Isles: Thorkil Vanggaard, *Phallòs: A Symbol and Its History in the Male World* (New York, 1972), chaps. 14–16, esp. pp. 160–63, and Joseph Stevenson, ed., *Chronicon de Lanercost, M.CC.I–M.CCC.XLVI* (Edinburgh, 1839), p. 85; for Pavia ca. 1350: Defendente Sacchi, *Delle condizione economica, morale e politica degli Italiani ne'tempi municipali* (Milan, 1829), pp. 31–33 (I am extremely grateful to Catarina Pirina for a Xerox copy from this work, which was otherwise unavailable to me).

[88] R. Plot, *The Natural History of Staffordshire* (Oxford, 1686), p. 433, pl. XXXII (the engraver has wrapped the erect penis of the aeolipile in a grape leaf!); W. L. Hildburgh, "Aeolipiles as Fire-Blowers," *Archaeologia* 94 (1951), 25–55; Gerhard Schmidt, "Die Chorschrankenmalereien des Köl-ner Domes und die europäische Malerei," *Kölner Domblatt* 44/45 (1979), 308, fig. 16. For a group of later pilgrims' badges: Brian Spencer, *Salisbury Museum Medieval Catalogue*, 2: *Pilgrim Souvenirs and Secular Badges* (Salisbury, 1990), pp. 115–16, figs. 304–6.

[89] For both appetites see Edward A. Block, "Chaucer's Millers and Their Bagpipes," *Speculum* 29 (1954), 241–43. Also Jean Gagné, "L'erotisme dans la musique médiévale," in Roy, ed., *L'erotisme* (above, n. 67), p. 91; Folke Nordström, *Virtues and Vices on the 14th Century Corbels in the Choir of Uppsala Cathedral* (Stockholm, 1956), pp. 95–99 and 108, where bagpipes are associated with Luxury/Venus and with a monster. Emanuel Winternitz, "Bagpipes for the Lord," *Metropolitan Museum of Art Bulletin* 16 (1958), 276–86, is more circumspect, though he introduces the theme with a general comment on "wild and fantastic creatures, pipes and drums, satyrs and nymphs, jugglers and beggars, foaming with sin and sex."

[90] Rey-Flaud, *Charivari* (above, n. 14), pp. 28, 53–54, 138.

[91] There are 5 bellows and 8 or 9 bagpipes in all.

(Figs. 1, 5, 6, 32, 33).[92] *Instrument* in French and *istrumento* in Italian refer to male sex.[93] Jean Gagné cites the lines from a fifteenth-century poem:

> Je ne puis plus jouer de l'instrument
> Duquel les femmes ont grant joie

and points out that the pun *jouer (avec) son instrument* is illustrated in a fifteenth-century woodblock print in the Shepherds' Calendar of 1491, which shows erotic love play between a couple accompanied by a flute (Fig. 41).[94]

Such multilayered and apparently conflicting readings of an illuminated prayer book would be natural for an audience of the time. In texts one can also find examples of the vivid overlay of sacred and profane that coexist here—the *Carmina Burana* owes most of its erotic phrases to the *Song of Songs*, and in a thirteenth-century motet one voice chanted a Latin hymn in praise of the Virgin while the other simultaneously sang a love song in French.[95] And from the end of the Middle Ages comes a riddle: What is the filthiest word in the Psalms? The answer is *conculcavit* ("he has trampled underfoot"), because broken into syllables and read in French it gives *con* ("cunt"), *cul* ("ass"), *ca* ("shit"), and *vit* ('cock').[96] The habit of breaking down signifiers to find other signs, frequently punning by moving from Latin to vernacular and from sacred to scatological, is extensively commented on by Laura Kendrick, who finds it an oral mechanism that destabilizes the text in troubadour poetry.[97] Scatological references were much closer to the surface in a culture that daily dealt with sobriquets such as Letcher, Cunteles, Pryketayle, Shakespeare, and Grosseteste (not "Big Head" as I once thought—but whoever could imagine a Bishop Big Balls of Lincoln now?), or Rabelaisian French names such as Conillaud, Vitu, Chiart, and Poile au Cul.[98]

[92] These occur 23/24 times in the Hours. Robertson, *Chaucer*, p. 129, fig. 34, has made the same observation.

[93] I owe knowledge of the sixteenth-century Italian usage to Elizabeth S. Cohen, "Between Oral and Literate Culture: The Social Meaning of an Illustrated Love Letter," unpublished paper given at "Dialogues with the Past: A Cultural History Symposium in Honor of Natalie Zemon Davis," November 15–17, 1990, Boston University.

[94] "I am no longer able to play the organ that so delights the women": Gagné in Roy, *L'erotisme*, pp. 89, 92, and fig. 24.

[95] John Brückmann and Jane Couchman, "Du 'Cantique des cantiques' aux 'Carmina Burana': Amour sacré et amour érotique," in Roy, *L'erotisme*, pp. 35–50; Bruce R. Smith, "The Contest of Apollo and Marsyas: Ideas about Music in the Middle Ages," in David L. Jeffrey, ed., *By Things Seen: Reference and Recognition in Medieval Thought* (Ottawa, 1979), pp. 98–99. Russell A. Peck, "Public Dreams and Private Myths: Perspective in Middle English Literature," *PMLA* 90 (1975), 465–67, has also pointed out the multiple meanings, from scatological to sacred, of the poem "Erthe took of erthe."

[96] "Quel est le mot le plus poilu du psautier?" quoted by Bruno Roy, "L'humeur érotique au XVe siècle," in Roy, *L'erotisme*, p. 157, from a Flemish source.

[97] Kendrick, *The Game of Love* (above, n. 69), pp. 10, 53–73; she also notes that Saint Cunegonde ("San Con") was called upon by women in childbirth, p. 69.

[98] David L. Jeffrey, "Introduction," in Jeffrey, ed., *By Things Seen*, p. 13; Albert Dauzat, *Dictionnaire étymologigue des noms de famille et des prénoms de France*, 3rd ed. (Paris, 1967), pp. xvi, 598, and *Les noms de famille de France* (Paris, 1945), pp. 180, 187–88; Henri Carrez, "Anthroponymie: Surnoms évoquant des infirmités portés dans la région dijonnaise du XIIe au XVe siècle," *Onomastica* 1 (1947), 43, 49–50.

If the manuscript pages seem to pulsate with male sexual energy deriving from so many large bows and arrows, swords, spears, instruments, cockhorses, and phallic tails, how can this reading be reconciled with a devotional book destined for the virginal bride of a king? Is this a Book of Hours or a cocktail hour?[99] One might be tempted to offer the historical hypothesis that so much phallicity (to coin a term) in the marginalia constituted an erotic aid to Charles IV's bride, deconstructing the proscriptive exempla. To the contrary, eroticism is precisely what is lacking.

By far the most common allusion to male sexuality is the part-man, part-beast grotesque with hairy hind parts and a huge phallic tail emerging from his cape like a cockhorse (Figs. 10, 39, 40).[100] A modern male viewer might recall Maria Schell (eyeing her audience and running her tongue over her upper lip) in the delicious bedroom-comedy film *Diable par la Queue*: "Et parfois je me demande ce que ça veut dire, *tenir* le diable par la *queue*?"[101] A feminist reading of the images, on the other hand, notes that the more than 530 such creatures in the margins insistently image sexuality as repulsive and bestial; and penetration (suggested by the spears and arrows) is aggressive and wounding (Fig. 16).

Furthermore, men with tails had extremely degraded meanings for the fourteenth century: "disloyalty, falsity, and treacherous behavior" were to be expected from such creatures, as from vipers and scorpions.[102] Albericus of London wrote in the thirteenth century of a monster with the "head of a lion, the belly of a goat, and the tail of a serpent," the three parts signifying the stages of carnal love: desire and lechery (the lion and horned goat, as noted before) and "the prick of penance that goads the mind" after the act (the dragon's tail).[103] Grotesques with genital masks were explicitly demonic to a fourteenth-century audience.[104] The Taymouth Hours, a contemporary English manuscript with links to the Pucelle shop, has several bas-de-page scenes of damnation presided over by such demons (Fig. 43).[105] In the bas-de-page of Jeanne's Hours,

[99] A similar scatological conjunction with the Hours is made in the fabliaux: "Une fois la fout, en mains d'eure / Que l'en éust chanté une Eure (He fucked her once in less time than it would have taken to say a prayer)," quoted by Pearcy in *Humor of the Fabliaux*, p. 172.

[100] The tail (*cauda*) is cited, along with the stem, pike, javelin, tree, shaft, dart, and verge, as synonyms for the penis: Forberg, *Manual of Erotology* (above, n. 29), pp. 82–83.

[101] "Every now and then I wonder what exactly it means to *hold* the Devil by his *tail*?" Schell's role as the impecunious heiress of a decaying château that her mother runs as a hotel is to lure male patrons to it and entice them to stay with ever-unfulfilled promises of sexual favors.

[102] Lilian M. C. Randall, "A Medieval Slander," *Art Bulletin* 42 (1960), 33–35. A composite creature with a man's head, serpent's body, and scorpion's tail is held by the Duke of Athens as he is expelled from Florence as a traitor in a fresco of 1343: Roger J. Crum and David C. Wilkins, "In the Defense of Florentine Republicanism," in Ashley and Sheingorn, eds., *Interpreting Cultural Symbols* (above, n. 29), pp. 138–39, fig. 3; they identify the chimera with the Gerione, "that foul image of fraud," described by Dante in the *Inferno*.

[103] Quoted by Robertson, *Chaucer*, p. 155.

[104] Jurgis Baltrušaitis, *Le moyen âge fantastique: Antiquités et exotismes dans l'art gothique* (Paris, 1955), pp. 30–31, cites many examples in English and French art and chronicles of the period, and traces their derivation from ancient grilles (pp. 18–29). Later examples are in Voekle, "Morgan Manuscript M.1001" (above, n. 46), fig. 9.

[105] Also fols. 138r, 139v, 149r. For this book, see above, n. 51.

an unclean ape cavorts to the beat of a demonic-grotesque street player's drum (Fig. 42). In a unique case where these hybrids invade sacred history, the fleeing Holy Family are urged on by grotesques and chimeras, evidently portents of evil, entwined in the foliage behind them (Fig. 1).

A contextual reading reveals a remarkable coherence in the illuminated motifs of the Hours. The density of imagery on the tiny pages of the book makes its scrutiny intensely private; open, it barely fills the palm of one hand and has to be held close. The feelings aroused by the cumulative imagery, far from being erotic, might range from surprise and fear to repulsion and disgust. If ribald humor is also involved, perhaps it alleviates sexual tensions, as in the ritual joking described by anthropologists in situations where incest or other taboo breaking could occur.[106] Hildegard of Bingen uses a genital mask apotropaically in her *Scivias*, donned by the Giving of Life to ward off a rapist.[107] The medieval theological discourse of sexuality dictated that the passions are bestial and must be controlled, even in propagation. The social function of the shivaree in a Christian context was to dissuade both sexes from second marriages.[108] The combination of grotesque images and grisaille execution resonates with the convergence of Carnival and Lent: on "Fat Tuesday" (Mardi Gras) masking, rough music, and *monde renversé* mime were the norm, followed by "Ash Wednesday," when colored altar cloths were replaced by penitential gray. The magnificent painted silk altar hanging known as the Parement de Narbonne, made for Charles V (now in the Louvre), is a Lenten altar covering.[109] Pucelle's use of grisaille has often been discussed in terms of its reliance on tonal modeling to elucidate forms, but the primary resonance for an audience of the time would have been the sensual deprivations of Lent. By a similar deprivation, the grotesques belong to a discourse of sexuality that is devoid of pleasurable eroticism, a distinction that is clarified by comparing an earlier and later image.

The famous image of shivaree in the fourteenth-century Fauvel manuscript illustrates the mocking rites that may have been believed to put to rest a departed spouse on the remarriage of his/her surviving widow/er (Fig. 4).[110] Here are the familiar ingredients of hairy men, horned masks, lions, and drums, which emulate the sexual act.[111] The male grotesque with hairy hind parts and a wind

---

[106] Edward Evans-Pritchard, "Some Collective Expressions of Obscenity in Africa," *The Position of Women in Primitive Societies and Other Essays in Social Anthropology* (New York, 1965), pp. 86–94 (concerning in-law relationships); Alice Schlegel, "Gender Meanings: General and Specific," *Beyond the Second Sex: New Directions in the Anthropology of Gender*, ed. Peggy Reeves Sanday and Ruth Gallagher Goodenough (Philadelphia, 1990), pp. 33–37 (Hopi sibling relationships).

[107] Hildegard of Bingen, *Wisse die Wege: Scivias*, ed. Maura Böckler (Berlin, 1928), pl. IV. This is a photograph of the original twelfth-century illumination, destroyed in the war. Unfortunately the 1954 edition and all subsequent publications have relied on copies, or even copies of copies, of this cycle.

[108] Kathleen Ashley, "Image and Ideology," in Ashley and Sheingorn, eds., *Saint Anne*, p. 127, n. 19.

[109] Molly Teasdale Smith, "The Use of Grisaille as Lenten Observance," *Marsyas* 10 (1957–59), 43–54, with other examples.

[110] See above, nn. 7 and 14.

[111] For Leo, see n. 62 above. For the lewd action of drums, Gagné in Roy, *L'erotisme*, pp. 93–94.

instrument, frequently seen in the margins of the Hours, reappears in Dürer's engraving two hundred years later as a classical satyr, complete with horns *and* genitals, fertility tree *and* fecund nymph (Figs. 38–40, 44). The medieval grotesque has been historicized and eroticized, the carnivalesque element thus eliminated, replaced by the literary reference to classical mythology.[112] The mood in the *Musical Satyr* is one of bucolic celebration of life. The shivaree and grisaille of the Hours fit a time of penitence prior to marriage, rather than nuptial celebration.[113]

A WOMAN'S READING: FLUSHING MALE HUMOR OUT OF THE LOCKER ROOM

It is important to distinguish between medieval and modern discourses of sexuality. I have stressed a lack of sensuality or eroticism in most of the motifs in the margins of the Hours of Jeanne d'Evreux. Indeed, in medieval art in general there are virtually no erotic images in the sense of female (or male) sex objects—a reason I suspect that so many women have chosen that field of study, as opposed to baroque art for instance.[114] Yet what I found was a discourse of veiled sexuality that is equally detrimental to the feminine, and equally controlling.[115] An encoding of aggressive phallic forms in visual puns and metaphors, and in the blatantly absurd hybrid grotesques, destabilizes representational codes, eliciting negative responses in the female viewer.

Given the historical context, I believe the many images that repel female readers rather than amuse us may well have frightened the adolescent Jeanne; everything warned her to keep her mind on her prayers and to avoid adultery. Not only the aggressive phallic symbols that I have dwelt on, but also the negative images of women would act as warnings. The resonances of these images derived both from popular notions that were embedded in vernacular and oral culture and from learned discourse of the kind that was textualized in Latin. I have made the assumption that as a child Jeanne was not cut off from vulgar culture, in which bawdy language was less repressed than now. She had access to learned discourse through her Dominican confessor; just as she would need instruction

[112] In a later manifestation, Rembrandt's etching *The Flute Player*, the lecherous shepherd directs his gaze and his instrument at a shepherdess who prepares a floral coronet; the animal elements are reduced to an ignoble owl and rutting sheep: Alison McNeil Kettering, "Rembrandt's *Flute Player*: A Unique Treatment of Pastoral," *Simiolus* 9 (1977), 19–21, 33–40; I am grateful to T. Kaori Kitao for the reference.

[113] Confession and penitence before marriage are advocated in an early-thirteenth-century sermon attributed to Jacques de Vitry: Jean-Claude Schmitt, *Prêcheur d'exemples: Récits de prédicateurs du moyen âge* (Paris, 1985), p. 55.

[114] The issue of eroticism has been debated by Caroline W. Bynum, "The Body of Christ in the Later Middle Ages: A Reply to Leo Steinberg," *Renaissance Quarterly* 39 (1986), 399–439, in response to Leo Steinberg, *The Sexuality of Christ in Renaissance Art and in Modern Oblivion* (New York, 1983).

[115] For a reflection on the coercive aspects of public images of female sex objects, and the liberating effect of being in a culture, such as the former USSR (or in my own experience, the former German Democratic Republic), where they were not tolerated, see Jo Anna Isaak, "Representation and Its (Dis)contents," *Art History* 12 (1989), 362–66.

in reading her Latin prayer book, she would need the mediation of her confessor to verbalize the exempla that are suggested by some of the pictures.[116] How else was she to learn the church's teaching on sexuality? Once made known, the lessons of the images would be recalled, and accumulatively enriched, in the constant round of daily and yearly prayer. The Book of Hours was thus a far more effective schoolbook than a separate treatise on the virtues and vices, which like any schoolbook might be laid aside.[117] Page after page, the imagery in the Hours never relinquishes its controlling ideology, using grotesques and exempla to incite fear or to inspire imitation, thus constructing the young queen's gendered role.

An additional powerful mediating agent was the act of giving. The adolescent virgin bride who received the book from her much older ruling king might be influenced to abhor sex in a way that fit the historical moment. Denial of sexual pleasure to a wife would help allay the fears of a recently cuckolded husband. A psychological clitoridectomy would give him complete control of his wife's sexuality.[118] This case study is additionally important for women's history since it provides a caveat in dealing with "women's books": we should not assume the female owner/reader exercised the control we normally ascribe to a patron; the term "matron," symmetric in gender but asymmetric in meaning, fits the role assigned to Jeanne.

If I were to conclude at this point that my "take" on Jeanne's reading of her book constitutes a historical truth that should silence other readings, this study might be valued or contested in relation to women's history. That phase of the feminist project has indeed been useful in dis/re-covering women artists, "patrons," and subjects, yet it operates within the traditional parameters of argumentation.[119] Proofs, however, are seldom available for a historical reconstruction of the affective impact of a medieval work of art, even when its audience is precisely known. I do not propose to substitute a monolithic personal reading but to allow the work a multiplicity of affective possibilities that might be accounted for by differences of mood, life stage, and gender in the readers of this particular book; it not only may have looked different to Jeanne in her celibate widowhood, but certainly must have done so to Charles V when he inherited it. That it looks different to me now than to male art historians in the

---

[116] Although I am not concerned with the authorship of Jean Pucelle, it is of interest that recent studies have noted the strong Dominican flavor of his work: Lucy Freeman Sandler, "Jean Pucelle and the Lost Miniatures of the Belleville Breviary," *Art Bulletin* 66 (1984), 74, 90, who also attributes the textualization of the pictures to the artist; Karen Gould, "Jean Pucelle," in *Great Lives from History: Ancient and Medieval Series*, ed. Frank N. Magill (Pasadena, 1988), p. 1763; and Gould, "Jean Pucelle" (n. 2 above).

[117] Cf. the courtesy books (n. 49 above) and the summa (*La Somme le Roy*) composed by the Dominican brother Laurent in 1279 for Philippe III le Hardi, and illuminated by Maître Honoré, now in London, British Library, Add. MS 54180: Eric C. Millar, *The Parisian Miniaturist Honoré* (New York, 1959), pp. 20–30, pls. 3–8.

[118] Donovan, *Feminist Theory* (above, n. 38), p. 94, discusses Freud's theory that the clitoris becomes anesthetic in the young wife as a result of socialization.

[119] Thalia Gouma Peterson and Patricia Mathews, "The Feminist Critique of Art History," *Art Bulletin* 69 (1987), 326–57.

1950s is part of the process of historical distancing. The central issue I have struggled with is learning how to read as a woman, and a book made for the private use of a woman was a deliberate choice of arena.[120] At the outset this reading involved trusting instinctual responses that deconstructed the sacred meanings conventional in a book of hours. Others had begun a similar process, isofar as they found the grotesque marginalia humorous and playful, but they regarded the margins as separate from the center; some women shared that predominant view. The disparity between this standard reading and mine was very evident in the course of lecturing and teaching.[121]

In addition to sexuality and marriage, humor is a cultural practice that leads to easily definable masculinist readings and that demands feminist scrutiny. Any analysis of humor requires recognition not only of who laughs but also what or who is laughed at.[122] It helps us to understand patterns of dominance, since humor is itself an agent of domination and of behavior formation. Symptomatic of gender relationships, for instance, the medieval riddles studied by Bruno Roy revealed that *con* was more often referred to directly than *vit*, especially by the questioner; the male part was more often referred to metaphorically.[123] The traditional view of grotesques as comic elements, whether articulated by Horace or Bakhtin, Robertson or Schapiro, is essentially masculinist; yet it was often cited as "normal" in rebuttal of my reading of the Hours of Jeanne. Several attitudes emerge in a closer examination of this normalized reading.

A popular version of this view was expressed in the introduction to the 1957 publication of the Hours of Jeanne:

> The medieval man had time for play and fun. If there were to be outlets for humor, a private prayer book was a place for the whimsy of the imaginative artist. Apart from any meaning these decorative additions may suggest, they constitute a considerable part of the charm of Jeanne d'Evreux's Book of Hours.[124]

So stated, that view of marginalia may be defined in relation to several terms: It privileges the creative genius of the (male) artist, giving him license for "self"-

---

[120] The clearest exposition of this process is that by Jonathan Culler, with the acknowledged help of his female students: "On Reading as a Woman," in *On Deconstruction: Theory and Criticism after Structuralism* (Ithaca, N.Y., 1982), pp. 43–64.

[121] Two masters candidates, Renata Hejduk in 1989 and Laura Good in 1990, noticed the mediating role of Jeanne's husband as the real patron of the work, in relation to the wish for fertility. Yet they accepted the old formulation that the marginalia were amusing.

[122] Armand Strubel, "Le rire au moyen âge," in Daniel Poirion, ed., *Précis de littérature française du moyen âge* (Paris, 1983), pp. 186–87.

[123] Roy, "L'humour," in *L'erotisme*, p. 158. In modern usage, an analysis of slang has revealed 220 sexual sobriquets for women as opposed to 22 for men: analysis by Julia Stanley, cited by Barbara W. Eakins and R. Gene Eakins, *Sex Differences in Human Communication* (Boston, 1978), p. 113. Gershon Legman, *Rationale of the Dirty Joke: An Analysis of Sexual Humor* (New York, 1971), pp. 9–14, 221–85, 437–525, emphasizes aggression, even calling jokes "verbal rape," and notes the prevalence of male anxieties that are expressed in this way, especially concerning marriage and the vagina.

[124] *Hours*, pp. 6–7. The introduction was signed by James Rorimer, but I am told by Lilian Randall that Harry Bober actually wrote it.

expression that allows him to disregard the devotional function of the book and
the program decided on by a theological adviser. It overlooks the reading of
the imagery by the female recipient of the book, or by a modern woman reader,
claiming the margins instead as a zone for the expression of male fantasy, leading
to the private exchange of men's jokes, or a metaphorical locker room.

License to create and laugh at female grotesques was given to his fellow men
by Horace at the opening of his poem *On the Art of Poetry*:

> If a painter chose to join a human head to the neck of a horse, and to spread feathers
> of many a hue over limbs picked up now here now there, so that what at the top is a
> lovely woman ends below in a black and ugly fish, could you, my friends, if favored
> with a private view, refrain from laughing? Believe me, dear Pisos, quite like such
> pictures would be a book, whose idle fancies shall be shaped like a sick man's dreams,
> so that neither head nor foot can be assigned to a single shape. "Painters and poets,"
> you say, "have always had an equal right in hazarding anything." We know it: this
> license we poets claim and in our turn we grant the like; but not so far that savage
> should mate with tame, or serpents couple with birds, lambs with tigers.[125]

This passage alone contains most of the ideas expressed in James Rorimer's
introduction to the facsimile edition. Like the treatise *De secretis mulierum*, it is
male-to-male discourse.[126]

Robertson's richly nuanced study of pre-Chaucerian imagery occasionally re-
iterated this masculinist formula, as when he found the incongruities of Chaucer's Prioress's behavior grotesque and humorous, or when he suggested a
contrast between the Chaucerian and Rabelaisian use of allegory "as a human-
istic device" and the use of allegory by Christine de Pisan.[127] Most blatant, he
viewed the grotesques that enact a byplay to the events of Amnon's seduction
and rejection of Thamar as humorous; the narrative is scarcely funny from a
woman's point of view, and Robertson had elsewhere carefully documented
from theological sources the prevalent medieval view of the chimera as an emblem of evil.[128]

Another common claim made for the margins is that they set the artist's
creativity free. In 1952 H. W. Janson characterized drôleries as "flights of
fancy."[129] Meyer Schapiro, referring to the Hours of Jeanne d'Evreux as an
example, also used the concept of freedom of expression, which fit his thesis
that medieval art was not uniformly ordered by theological intellection:

> The margins of books committed to a most disciplined spirituality were open to prim-

---

[125] Horace, *Satires, Epistles and Ars Poetica*, ed. and trans. H. Rushton Fairchough (Cambridge,
Mass., 1978), pp. 450–51. I am grateful to John Czaplicka for this reference.

[126] *De secretis mulierum*, pp. 50–51; *Secrets des femmes*, p. 33. This aspect of the work is discussed
by Margaret Schleissner, "A Fifteenth-Century Physician's Attitude toward Sexuality: Dr. Johann
Hartlieb's *Secreta Mulierum* Translation," in Joyce E. Salisbury, ed., *Sex in the Middle Ages: A Book
of Essays* (New York, 1991), p. 110.

[127] Robertson, *Chaucer*, pp. 247, 253, 361, 389.

[128] Robertson, *Chaucer*, p. 223; cf. his use of the text attributed to Alanus the Englishman concerning the chimera with a lion's head, goat's body, and serpent's tail (p. 155).

[129] *Apes and Ape Lore* (above, n. 30), p. 164.

1. The Flight into Egypt; fallen idols.
   Hours of Jeanne d'Evreux (New York, The Cloisters, 54.1.2),
   fol. 83r (enlarged).
   (See n. 146 for illustration credits.)

Inapiunt hore le marie uir
gis scdm usum pdicatox.

2. The Betrayal; tilting at a barrel.
   With *titulus* of the hours of the Virgin.
   Facing page: The Annunciation; Queen Jeanne; blindman's buff.
   With beginning of matins, hours of the Virgin.
   Hours of Jeanne d'Evreux, fols. 15v–16r (enlarged).

3. Betrothal. Ormesby Psalter. Oxford, Bodleian Library,
MS Douce 366, fol. 131r (detail; bas-de-page).

4. Shivaree. *Roman de Fauvel.*
Paris, BN, MS fr. 146,
fol. 36v (detail).

5. Hours of St. Louis,
beginning of prime.
Hours of Jeanne d'Evreux,
fol. 143r.

6. Salome dancing before
   Herod.
   Bronze Paschal Column,
   ca. 1015, Hildesheim
   Cathedral.

7. Lust.
   South Porch, ca. 1115,
   St.-Pierre, Moissac.

8. Beginning of Seven
   Penitential Psalms.
   Hours of Jeanne d'Evreux,
   fol. 183r.

9. Game of Chess.
   Ivory mirror back.
   Paris, Musée du Louvre.

11. Young man embracing
    a female grotesque.
    Hours of Jeanne d'Evreux,
    fol. 52r (detail).

10. Hours of St. Louis,
    beginning of nones.
    Hours of Jeanne d'Evreux,
    fol. 160r.

12. Archer and grotesque
    (line endings).
    Hours of Jeanne d'Evreux,
    fol. 53r (detail).

13. Jonathan Borofsky,
    Male Aggression Now Playing Everywhere.
    Acrylic on canvas, 1985,
    129.5 × 145.5 in.

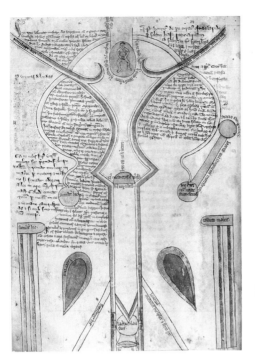

14. Anatomy of the uterus and adnexa.
    Early-fourteenth-century
        medical treatise.
    Oxford, Bodleian Library,
        MS Ashmole 399, fol. 13v.

15. Adam and Eve; devils urging
        homosexual couples to embrace.
    Bible Moralisée.
    Vienna, Österreichische
        Nationalbibliothek, MS
        2554, fol. 48r (detail).

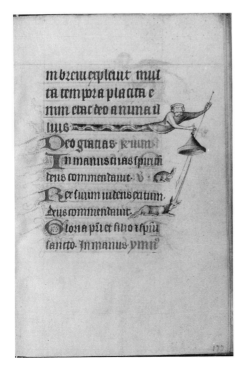

17. Capturing the unicorn in a
        virgin's lap. Rochester Bestiary.
    London, BL, MS Royal 12.F.XIII,
        fol. 10v (detail).

16. (*Left*) Capturing a rabbit and
        unicorn (line endings).
    Hours of Jeanne d'Evreux,
        fol. 177r.

19. Grotesque carrying two infants (line ending). Hours of Jeanne d'Evreux, fol. 33r (detail).

18. Visitation page, hours of the Virgin, beginning of lauds. Hours of Jeanne d'Evreux, fol. 35r (reduced).

20. "Gladiator" initial. Hours of Jeanne d'Evreux, fol. 82r.

21. Queen Jeanne at St. Louis's tomb; chastisement of the saint. Beginning of hours of St. Louis. Hours of Jeanne d'Evreux, fols. 102v–103r (reduced).

22. St. Louis feeds a leprous monk; a man is restrained from knocking up his wife.
Hours of Jeanne d'Evreux, fol. 123v (enlarged).

23. Manure spreading; Zodiac sign for Aries. Calendar for March.
Hours of Jeanne d'Evreux, fols. 3v–4r (detail; bas-de-pages).

24. Falconer; Zodiac sign for Gemini. Calendar for May.
Hours of Jeanne d'Evreux, fols. 5v–6r (detail; bas-de-pages).

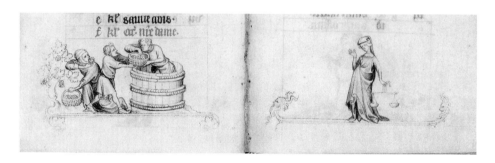

25. Grape harvest; Zodiac sign for Libra. Calendar for September.
Hours of Jeanne d'Evreux, fols. 9v–10r (detail; bas-de-pages).

27. Young man with budding trees.
    Calendar for April.
    Hours of Jeanne d'Evreux,
        fol. 4v (detail; bas-de-page).

26. Adoration of the Magi;
    Massacre of the Innocents.
    Hours of Jeanne d'Evreux, fol. 69r.

28. "Oiseuse," *Roman de la Rose*, ca. 1400.
    Oxford, Bodleian Library, MS Selden
        Supra 57, fol. 10r (detail).

29. Courtship, with restless horses.
    Ivory mirror back.
    Florence, Museo Nazionale,
        ex-Carrand Collection.

30. Zodiac sign for Capricorn.
    Calendar for December.
    Hours of Jeanne d'Evreux,
        fol. 13r (detail; bas-de-page).

31. The Angel's Announcement to
    the Shepherds.
    Translucent enamel plaque, base
        of statue of Virgin and Child
        given to the Abbey of St.-Denis
        by Jeanne d'Evreux.
    Trésor de Saint-Denis.

32. The Angel's Announcement
    to the Shepherds.
    Hours of Jeanne d'Evreux,
        fol. 62r.

33. Text pages. Hours of Jeanne d'Evreux, fols. 158v–159r.

34. Robert Mapplethorpe, *James Ford*.
Photograph (1979).

35. Jesse Tree. Shaftesbury Psalter
(ca. 1130–40). London, BL,
MS Lansdowne 383, fol. 15r.

36. Long Man of Cerne.
Hillside chalk carving
(Romano-British?).

37. Grotesque with bellows.
Hours of Jeanne d'Evreux,
fol. 203r (detail).

38. Hours of St. Louis,
beginning of terce.
Hours of Jeanne d'Evreux,
fol. 149r.

39. Hours of St. Louis,
beginning of sext.
Hours of Jeanne d'Evreux,
fol. 155r.

40. Grotesques, below Christ before Pilate.
Hours of Jeanne d'Evreux, fol. 34v
(detail; bas-de-page).

41. Venus and lovers bathing.
Kalendrier des Bergiers (Paris, 1493).

42. Grotesque drummer with genital mask and performing
ape, below the Presentation in the Temple.
Hours of Jeanne d'Evreux, fol. 76r (bas-de-page).

43. Demons. Taymouth Hours (ca. 1325).
London, BL, MS Yates Thompson 13, fol. 139v (bas-de-page).

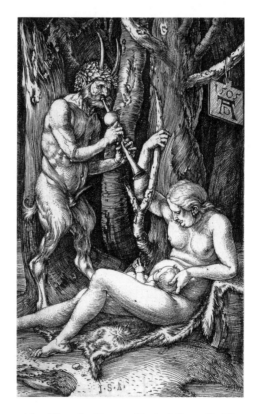

44. Albrecht Dürer, *Musical Satyr*, B. 69.
Engraving (1505), 4.5 × 2.75 in.
Boston, Museum of Fine Arts, P333.

itive impulses and feelings, and in a context of exquisite writing these miniatures, which are whimsical and often gross in idea, compete for the reader's attention. Though scattered capriciously on the margins, they are done with the same precision of detail and calligraphic finesse as the richly framed religious imagery on the same page. They are a convincing evidence of the artist's liberty, his unconstrained possession of the space, which confounds the view of medieval art as a model of systematic order and piety. There is also in these images a sweetness and charm. . . .[130]

He deemphasized the hybrids, noting instead that humans are reduced to the same size as animals and birds, a process that used "irreverent playfulness" to arrive at "desublimation through which the distance between the natural and the civilized is abolished." It takes a while to realize that desublimation may be debasement, and that the human-become-equal-with-animals may be bestial.

The most influential writer of this century on the topics of "carnival liberties and carnival truth," shivaree, and the grotesque is the Russian structuralist Mikhail Bakhtin, whose *Rabelais and His World* was written in 1940, though not published until twenty-five years later.[131] He formulated a binary polarity between the serious and the laughing aspects of medieval life, one that likely fit his personal experience of Stalinism:

> The men of the Middle Ages participated in two lives: the official and the carnival life. Two aspects of the world, the serious and the laughing aspect, coexisted with their consciousness. This coexistence was strikingly reflected in thirteenth- and fourteenth-century illuminated manuscripts, for instance in the legendaries, that is, the hand-written collections of the lives of saints. Here we find on the same page strictly pious illustrations of the hagiographical text as well as free designs not connected with the story. The free designs represent chimeras (fantastic forms combining human, animal, and vegetable elements), comic devils, jugglers performing acrobatic tricks, masquerade figures, and parodical scenes—that is, purely grotesque, carnivalesque themes. All these pictures are shown on the same page, which like medieval man's consciousness contains both aspects of life and the world. . . . However, in medieval art a strict dividing line is drawn between the pious and the grotesque; they exist side by side but never merge.[132]

The essential aspect of Bakhtin's analysis is that he used Rabelais as a literal reflection of a monolithic Middle Ages, taking cues from him on when to laugh. It was already a postmedieval view. Devils are only comical to those who do not believe in them. From Bakhtin's view that medieval laughter "remained outside all official spheres of ideology and outside all official strict forms of social relations," it followed that what was relegated to the margins was funny.[133] And the laughter dispelled fear, though not in the sense used by later anthropologists:

---

[130] Meyer Schapiro, "Marginal Images and Drôlerie" (review of Randall, *Images in the Margins*, originally published in 1970), in *Late Antique, Early Christian and Medieval Art: Selected Papers* (New York, 1979), p. 197.

[131] Mikhail Bakhtin, *Rabelais and His World*, trans. Helene Iswolsky (Cambridge, Mass., 1968), p. x; it was first published as *Tvorchestvo Fransua Rable* in 1965.

[132] Bakhtin, *Rabelais*, p. 96; cf. also p. 121: "folk humor . . . was opposed to the intolerant, dogmatic seriousness of the Middle Ages."

[133] Bakhtin, *Rabelais*, p. 73.

The acute awareness of victory over fear is an essential element of medieval laughter. This feeling is expressed in a number of characteristic medieval comic images. We always find in them the defeat of fear presented in a droll and monstrous form, the symbols of power and violence turned inside out, the comic images of death and bodies gaily rent asunder.[134]

The comic becomes a subversive political tool, as in modern newspaper cartoons. Among the writers reviewed so far, Robertson is the only one who cites a range of texts from the high Middle Ages that define responses to grotesques. Another authority who has been cited for an unsmiling view of chimeras is Dürer—who also avoided the representation of traditional phallic grotesques in his rendering of sensuality (Fig. 44). He is quoted out of context by both Wolfgang Kayser and Margaret Miles.[135] In the context of his theories about the variety and regularity of natural forms, Dürer cautioned artists against "exceeding the limits of the species": "Let every man beware lest he make something impossible, which Nature cannot permit; unless he wish to create a vision, in which he may mingle all kinds of creatures (mingle the species)."[136] This visionary world is clearly not the heaven of the Christian mystic but the hell of Hieronymous Bosch. Dürer had a postmedieval distance from these grotesque chimeras, yet he fully understood their true meaning.

Several other modern analysts of medieval grotesques have seen some of their evil connotations. Kayser's study of the grotesque, first published in 1957, emphasized the dehumanizing, alienating aspects of the genre.[137] So, too, have a number of recent women writers. In 1965 Alice Colby, in a close reading of two descriptions of monstrously ugly human beings by Chrétien de Troyes, already seemed to question the predominent view about comic relief by evoking alterity: it "is very difficult to know exactly what was thought amusing eight hundred years ago." In fact, her analysis of the verse indicated that these creatures are disruptive enough to break the harmony and order of the text itself, an impact that might be thought of as sinister rather than funny.[138]

Another reading that is argued from a specific con-text is Kendrick's, for the chimeras (her term) in the troubadour songbooks.[139] She sees the hybrids as figures for the dual meanings of the verses, the sacred and the profane, the

---

[134] Bakhtin, *Rabelais*, p. 91. That Bakhtin "underplayed the role of anxiety" in the carnivalesque and his relationship to Stalinism are pointed out by Dominick LaCapra, *Rethinking Intellectual History: Texts, Contexts, Language* (Ithaca, N.Y., 1983), pp. 298, 292–93, 321.

[135] "If a person wants to create the stuff that dreams are made of, let him freely mix all sorts of creatures": Wolfgang Kayser, *The Grotesque in Art and Literature*, trans. Ulrich Weisstein (New York, 1963; orig. *Das Groteske: Seine Gestaltung in Malerei und Dichtung* [Oldenbourg, 1957]), p. 22; Margaret R. Miles, *Carnal Knowing: Female Nakedness and Religious Meaning in the Christian West* (Boston, 1989), p. 161.

[136] Paraphrased and quoted from Dürer's *Treatise on Proportion* by Wilhelm Waetzolt, *Dürer and His Times*, enlarged edition (London, 1955), p. 219.

[137] Kayser, *The Grotesque*, pp. 30–31, 188–89. Iswolsky, in the introduction to Bakhtin, *Rabelais*, pp. 46–52, offers a critique of Kayser's modernist bias.

[138] Colby, *The Portrait* (above, n. 80), pp. 170–77.

[139] Kendrick, *Game of Love*, pp. 107–10.

pure and the bawdy, suggesting "the difficulty of controlling the significations of the letter" and allowing for personal interpretation. Along with the verbal punning that is her main theme, these chimeras contribute to the destabilization of the textualized verses. Reading as a woman, she notes their phallic tails (and even the phallic noses of the poets).[140]

In 1980 Gigetta Regoli offered the term "monster" as more appropriate than grotesque or drôlerie, noting its double meaning as a sign or portent (*monstrum*, from *monstrare*) and quoting Augustine to the effect that a portent does not act contrary to nature but only against what is codified as natural.[141] Examining chiefly monastic manuscripts, she sees these marginal images sustaining the seriousness of the text, whether consciously or not; many represent the struggles of the spirit against evil, and monsters are commonly restrained by the initial letters, as I have noted in the Hours of Jeanne d'Evreux.

More recently, Miles has insisted on the alienating aspects of grotesques, whose dismemberment and weird recombinations are essentially threatening and dehumanizing. She quotes Bakhtin's example of ancient terra-cottas that depicted women as "laughing, senile, pregnant hags" and points to a passage in Aquinas where he debates whether women are "monsters of nature."[142] Women have repeatedly been the subject of male definitions of the grotesque and monstrous.

Further insight is provided by a Lacanian analysis of the legends concerning monsters formed in the womb as a result of their mother's gaze on some undesirable (yet desired) image; such legends were commonplace in the fourteenth century. As Marie-Hélène Huët has remarked, in such cases the mother's "normal" role as passive incubator for an offspring conceived in the likeness of its father turned into an "active role . . . that . . . repressed the legitimate father," so that "the repression and abolition of the father by his monstrous creation also amounts to a form of castration."[143] In this model it is the male more than the female viewer who would experience "dismay and terror," yet the blame is laid on "the mother's desiring imagination." Such implications may also have been within the emotional grasp of Jeanne and her husband, though unarticulated.

This brief review indicates the remarkable extent to which modern interpretations of grotesques as comic or not comic are divided along gender lines. Though not exclusively, for the most part it is women who, recognizing the license given (male) artists to deform them, refuse to ridicule themselves and view the laughter of others as an instrument of control over them. In our academic discourses feminist readings must assume pre- and co-existent mas-

---

[140] I came across her analysis after my own was formulated and was immediately struck by how close we are in our responses.

[141] Gigetta Dalli Regoli, *Monstri, maschere e grilli nella miniatura medievale pisana* (Pisa, 1980), pp. xi–xviii.

[142] Miles, *Carnal Knowing*, pp. 160–62.

[143] Marie-Hélène Huët, "Living Images: Monstrosity and Representation," *Representations* 4 (1973), 73–77, 83.

culinist readings, and it is frequently through feminist readings that unspoken ideologies are revealed, operating through naturalized attitudes; indeed the extent to which masculinist ideology has been naturalized is a measure of its success. Even though subversive, and one hopes successful in transforming older hierarchies, feminist readings cannot claim universality.[144] The real struggle for the feminist critic is not to validate her/his own reading by displacing others, but to force other readings that have been naturalized into a position of coexistence; I would claim that the struggle is oppositional, but not the gendered readings per se.[145] The situation will improve when "normal" readings are redefined as masculinist and pull over into their own lane in a multilane highway.[146]

[144] For many of us it is essential to avoid that kind of mastery of the material of history that involves a silencing of others. Even an "oppositional" stance, such as that of Cixous, can be objected to in that it seems to work within "the very ideological system [of 'oppositional' thinking] feminists want to destroy": Robert Con Davis, "Woman as Oppositional Reader: Cixous on Discourse," in *Gender in the Classroom: Power and Pedagogy*, ed. Susan L. Gabriel and Isaiah Smithson (Urbana and Chicago, 1990), p. 97.

[145] For instance, in a recent faculty meeting at Tufts University it took fifteen minutes of debate to strike from a course description for nineteenth-century art a long list of white male (French) artists and to add that special attention would be given to women artists; Prof. Howard Malchow (Department of History) asked if the other were not the "normal" way to teach the art of the period. The matter was settled in favor of change only after mention of a lawsuit.

[146] This article grew out of seminars on women in medieval art and literature that I taught at Tufts University in 1989 and 1990 with Charles Nelson; I am especially indebted to him for helping me shape the theoretical framework. A short version, couched as a Freudian reading, is in press: "A Feminist Reading of the Hours of Jeanne d'Evreux," *Japan and Europe in Art History: Papers of the Colloquium of the Comité International d'Histoire de l'Art, 1991* (Tokyo). Parts of this material were given in 1991 to the women's studies faculty at Tufts University; at a research colloquium in the Fine Arts Department at Harvard University; in the "Feminist Newsletter" session at the Twenty-Sixth International Congress on Medieval Studies at Kalamzoo; in a seminar at the Courtauld Institute of Art in London; at the University of Arizona in Tucson; at the State University College at Cortland, New York; at Swarthmore College; and at the Medieval Club of New York. Each time questions and debate helped me focus the issues more clearly, and I am grateful to the many participants for their comments. Peggy Brown, Caroline Bynum, Joan Holladay, Karen Gould, and Lilian Randall read an early draft, and their suggestions as well as those of Lucy Sandler have been especially valuable; I am additionally grateful to Peggy Brown and Joan Holladay for letting me read their unpublished papers and for saving me from several errors. Above all, Nancy Partner's criticisms and encouragement have been crucial to the formulation of the argument presented here. Timothy Husband took some new photographs of the Hours of Jeanne d'Evreux.

All photographs of the Hours of Jeanne d'Evreux are reproduced by permission of the Metropolitan Museum of Art. Credits for other figures are as follows: Art Resources: 6, 7; Bibliothèque Nationale, 4; Bodleian Library: 3, 14, 28; Boston Museum of Fine Arts: 44; British Library: 17, 35, 43; Paula Cooper Gallery, New York (photograph by James Dee): 13; after Editions des Quatre Chemins, 1926: 41; after Koechlin, 1968: 9, 29; Robert Mapplethorpe Collection: 34; National Monuments Commission: 36; Österreichische Nationalbibliothek: 15; Réunion des Musées Nationaux: 31.

Madeline H. Caviness is Mary Richardson Professor and Professor of Art History at Tufts University, Medford, MA 02155.

Regardless of Sex:
Men, Women, and Power
in Early Northern Europe

By Carol J. Clover

In chapter 32 of *Gísla saga*, two bounty hunters come to the wife of the outlawed Gísli and offer her sixty ounces of silver to reveal the whereabouts of her husband. At first Auðr resists, but then, eyeing the coins and muttering that "cash is a widow's best comfort," she asks to have the money counted out. The men do so. Auðr pronounces the silver adequate and asks whether she may do with it what she wants. By all means, Eyjólfr replies. Then:

> Auðr tekr nú féit ok lætr koma í einn stóran sjóð, stendr hon síðan upp ok rekr sjóðinn með silfrinu á nasar Eyjólfi, svá at þegar støkkr blóð um hann allan, ok mælti: "Haf nú þetta fyrir auðtryggi þína ok hvert ógagn með. Engi ván var þér þess, at ek mynda selja bónda minn í hendr illmenni þínu. Haf nú þetta ok með bæði skǫmm ok klæki. Skaltu þat muna, vesall maðr, meðan þú lifir, at kona hefir barit þik. En þú munt ekki at heldr fá þat, er þú vildir." þá mælti Eyjólfr: "Hafið hendr á hundinum ok drepi, þó at blauðr sé."[1]

In George Johnston's translation:

> Aud takes the silver and puts it in a big purse; she stands up and swings the purse with the silver in it at Eyjolf's nose, so that the blood spurts out all over him; then she spoke: "Take that for your easy faith, and every harm with it! There was never any likelihood that I would give my husband over to you, scoundrel. Take your money, and shame and disgrace with it! You will remember, as long as you live, you miserable man, that a woman has struck you; and yet you will not get what you want for all that!"
>
>   Then Eyjolf said: "Seize the bitch and kill her, woman or not!" [literally, "Seize the dog (masculine) and kill (it), though (it) be *blauðr*"].[2]

Eyjólfr's men hasten to restrain him, noting that their errand is bad enough as it is without the commission of a *níðingsverk* (rendered by Johnston as "a coward's work").

The adjective *blauðr* poses a translation problem.[3] Cleasby-Vigfusson's entries under it and its antonym *hvatr* read as follows:

---

[1] *Gísla saga Súrssonar*, in *Vestfirðinga sǫgur*, ed. Björn K. Þórólfsson and Guðni Jónsson, Íslenzk fornrit [henceforth cited as ÍF] 6 (Reykjavík, 1958). Translations of Old Norse passages throughout are my own unless otherwise indicated.

[2] *The Saga of Gisli*, trans. George Johnston with notes by Peter Foote (Toronto and Buffalo, 1963), p. 51.

[3] Friedrich Ranke has, "Ergreift den Hund und schlagt ihn tot, wenns auch eine Hündin ist!" (*Die Geschichte von Gisli dem Geächteten* [Munich, 1907], p. 85, and [Düsseldorf, 1978], p. 64); Hjalmar Alving has, "Lägg hand på den djävulen och slå ihäl henne, fast hon är kvinnfolk" (*Isländska sagor*,

BLAUÐR, adj. Properly means *soft, weak,* answering Latin *mollis,* and is opposed to *hvatr,* 'brisk, vigorous'; hence the proverb, *fár er hvatr er hrörask tekr, ef í barnæsku er blauðr* [few are *hvatir* in action who are *blauðir* in childhood]. Metaphorically *blauðr* means 'feminine,' *hvatr* 'masculine,' but only used of animals, dogs, cats, fishes; *hvatr-lax = hæingr = salmo mas*; [the feminine noun] *bleyða* is a 'dam,' and metaphorically 'a coward, a craven.' *Blauðr* is a term of abuse, a 'bitch, coward.' . . .

HVATR, adj. 'Bold, active, vigorous.' II. 'Male,' opposed to *blauðr,* 'female,' of beasts.[4]

Attested in both poetry and prose, *blauðr* occurs most conspicuously in verbal taunts toward or about men, and in such cases it is typically rendered in English as "coward" (earlier "craven"), as in Hallgerðr's remark in chapter 38 of *Njáls saga,* "Jafnkomit mun á með ykkr, er hvárrtveggi er blauðr" (translated in the Penguin edition, "The two of you are just alike; both of you are cowards"), directed to her pacifist husband and his equally pacifist friend Njáll, a man who not only favored Christianity but was unable to grow a beard.[5] When *blauðr* is used in reference to women or female animals, however (as in the *Gísla saga* passage above), it is rendered "woman" or "female"; clearly "coward" will not do in the *Gísla saga* passage. The need in English for two words ("coward" and "female") where Norse uses one (*blauðr*), and Cleasby-Vigfusson's brave, but on the face of it hopelessly bedeviled, effort to distinguish "metaphoric" from presumably "real" or "proper" usages, and human from animal, hint at the aspect of early Scandinavian culture, and perhaps Germanic culture in general, that this essay is about: a sex-gender system rather different from our own, and indeed rather different from that of the Christian Middle Ages.

Certainly the *Gísla saga* passage seems a snarl of gender crossings. If her sex qualifies Auðr as *blauðr,* bloodying the nose of a person qualifies her as *hvatr*; and if being a man qualifies Eyjólfr as *hvatr,* having his nose bloodied qualifies him as *blauðr,* and having his nose bloodied by a creature he himself wishes to designate as *blauðr* by virtue of her sex qualifies him as *blauðr* in the extreme—which is, of course, the point of Auðr's reminder that he has been not only struck in the nose, but struck in the nose by a *woman.* When Eyjólfr calls out his order to have her seized despite the fact that she is *blauðr,* he acknowledges that whatever properties are assumed to attach to her bodily femaleness have

---

2 [Stockholm, 1936], p. 66); Vera Henriksen has, "Ta fatt i den bikkja og drep den, selv om det er en tispe!" (*Gisle Surssons saga* [Oslo, 1985], p. 85); George Webbe Dasent has, "Lay hands on and slay her, though she be but a weak woman" (*The Story of Gisli the Outlaw* [Edinburgh, 1866], p. 98); Preben Meulengracht Sørensen has, "Grib hunden og dræb den, selv om den er af hunkøn" (*Norrønt nid: Forestillingen om den umandige mand i de islandske sagaer* [Odense, 1980], p. 94), which translator Joan Turville-Petre renders, "Lay hands on the hound and kill it, even though it is female" (*The Unmanly Man: Concepts of Sexual Defamation in Early Northern Society* [Odense, 1983], p. 76); and Cleasby-Vigfusson (Richard Cleasby and Gudbrand Vigfusson, *An Icelandic-English Dictionary* [Oxford, 1957]) has, under the entry *blauðr,* "take the dog and kill it, though it be a bitch."

4 I have abbreviated and edited the entries. (The definition of the noun *bleyða* as "a craven" comes from the separate entry under that word.) So too Johan Fritzner, *Ordbog over det gamle norske sprog* (Oslo, etc., 1867; 4th ed. 1973). On *blauðr* (*bleyði,* etc.) see also Margaret Clunies Ross, "Hildr's Ring: A Problem in the *Ragnarsdrápa,* Strophes 8–12," *Mediaeval Scandinavia* 6 (1973), 75–92.

5 *Brennu-Njáls saga,* ed. Einar Ól. Sveinsson, ÍF 12 (Reykjavík, 1954), chap. 38. *Njal's Saga,* trans. Magnus Magnusson and Hermann Pálsson (Harmondsworth, Middlesex, 1960).

been overridden by her aggressive behavior. She wants to be *hvatr*, she gets treated accordingly. And when his men restrain him, saying that they have accumulated enough shame without committing a *níðingsverk*, they in effect redefine her as *blauðr*.[6] It could be argued that the scene, particularly the focus on wifely loyalty, has Christian resonances (like all the Icelandic sagas, this one has roots in the pagan era but was written down during the Christian one), and that some part of its confusion stems from what I shall suggest are different gender paradigms.[7] But the real problem, I think, inheres in the *hvatr/blauðr* term set (presumably ancient) and the inability of the modern languages, and modern scholarship, to apprehend the distinction.

When commentaries on Viking and medieval Scandinavian culture get around (most do not) to the subject of "women" or "sex roles" or "the family," they tend to tell a standard story of separate spheres.[8] Woman's, symbolized by the bunch of keys at her belt, is the world *innan stokks* ("within the household"), where she is in charge of child care, cooking, serving, and tasks having to do with milk and wool. Man's is the world beyond: the world of fishing, agriculture, herding, travel, trade, politics, and law. This inside/outside distinction is formulated in the laws and seems to represent an ideal state of affairs. It is no surprise, given its binary quality, and also given the way it seems to line up with such term sets as *hvatr/blauðr*, that modern speculations on underlying notions of gender in Norse culture should be similarly dichotomous. As labor is divided,

---

[6] "þá er fǫr vár helzti ill, þó at vér vinnim eigi þetta níðingsverk, ok standi menn upp ok láti hann eigi þessu ná" ("Our errand has been bad enough without our committing this *níðingsverk*; up, men, don't let him try it!").

[7] The relation of the thirteenth-century written sources, especially the Icelandic sagas, to preconversion social history is a long-standing point of debate. I am here as elsewhere proceeding on the neotraditionalist assumption that although the written sources may exaggerate or fabricate at some points, there is a large grain of truth in their collective account. For a survey of the relevant literature up to 1964, see Theodore M. Andersson, *The Problem of Icelandic Saga Origins* (New Haven, 1964), and from that date through 1983, my "Icelandic Family Sagas (*Íslendingasögur*)," in *Old Norse–Icelandic Literature: A Critical Guide*, ed. Carol J. Clover and John Lindow (Ithaca, N.Y., and London, 1985), pp. 239–315. On the problem in myth, see John Lindow's "Mythology and Mythography" in the same volume (pp. 21–67).

[8] Two recent full-length studies that go some way in redressing the scant attention paid to women in the literature of the Viking Age are Birgit Sawyer's *Kvinnor och familj i det forn- och medeltida Skandinavien* (Skara, 1992) and Judith Jesch's *Women in the Viking Age* (Woodbridge, Suffolk; and Rochester, N.Y., 1991). Both contain useful bibliographies. See also Roberta Frank, "Marriage in Twelfth- and Thirteenth-Century Iceland," *Viator* 4 (1973), 473–84, and Peter G. Foote and David Wilson, *The Viking Achievement* (London, 1974), esp. pp. 108–16. The fullest modern explorations of the sex-gender system (as opposed to women's status) are Meulengracht Sørensen's *Unmanly Man*, his forthcoming *Fortælling og ære: Studier i islændingesagaerne*, and Clunies Ross's suggestive studies of textual cruces in the mythic tradition ("Hildr's Ring"; "An Interpretation of the Myth of þórr's Encounter with Geirrøðr and His Daughters," in *Speculum Norroenum: Norse Studies in Memory of Gabriel Turville-Petre*, ed. Ursula Dronke, et al. [Odense, 1981], pp. 370–91; and, less directly, "The Myth of Gefjon and Gylfi and Its Function in *Snorra Edda* and *Heimskringla*," *Arkiv för nordisk filologi* 93 [1978], 149–65). Because of the synoptic nature of this essay, I have restricted citations to immediately relevant scholarly sources and those recent books and articles that contain more complete and specific bibliographic information. I owe special thanks to Roberta Frank and William Ian Miller for help in need.

in other words, so must be sexual nature: thus we read, in the handbooks, of the "polarity" of the sexes, of an "antithesis between masculine and feminine," of male-female "complementarity," and so on.[9]

But is it that simple, and, more to the point, is it that modern? Let me begin an interrogation of this sexual binary on the female side. From the outset of the scholarly tradition, readers have been startled and not infrequently appalled by the extraordinary array of "exceptional" or "strong" or "outstanding" or "proud" or "independent" women—women whose behavior exceeds what is presumed to be custom and sometimes the law as well. No summary can do them justice, not least because paraphrase (indeed, translation in general) forfeits the tone of marvelous aplomb, both social and textual, that is such a conspicuous and telling aspect of their stories. But for those unfamiliar with the field, the following list should give a rough idea of the parameters. Heading it is the formidable Unnr in djúpúðga. The overwhelming majority of Iceland's founding fathers (the original land claimants) were fathers indeed, but a handful—thirteen, according to *Landnámabók*[10]—were women, and one of these was Unnr, who, fearing for her life and fortunes in Scotland after the death of her father and son, had a ship built in secret and fled, taking all her kin and retinue with her, to Orkney, then the Faroes, and finally Iceland, where, in about the year 900, she took possession of vast lands and established a dynasty.[11] ("In every respect," Preben Meulengracht Sørensen observes, "she has taken over the conduct and social functions of the male householder and leader.")[12]

In Scandinavia as in the Germanic world in general, men preceded women as heirs, but women did inherit, and a variety of evidence confirms that women could, and a not-insignificant percentage did, become considerable landholders.[13] They could also become traders and business partners. One of the main Scandinavian ventures on the North American continent was significantly bankrolled by a woman—a woman who moreover betook herself on the journey. (During the American winter, she is said to have driven her husband to murder

[9] Writes Meulengracht Sørensen, for example: "Fordi kønnet altid er en del af individet og fra naturens hånd er knyttet til så vigtige dele af menneskelivet, og fordi det seksuelle køn er skabt som en komplementaritet, der så umiddelbart indbyder til fortolkning som både modsætning og helhed, er kønnet måske den mest dynamiske kulturelle kategori. . . . Ikke blot i biologisk og fysisk forstand skal en mand være mand og en kvinde kvinde; han og hun skal også efterleve de idealer, som kulturen sætter for deres køn" (*Fortælling og ære*). See also Sawyer, *Kvinnor och familj*, p. 75.

[10] *Landnámabók*, ed. Jakob Benediktsson, ÍF 1 (Reykjavík, 1968). The calculation is Judith Jesch's (*Women in the Viking Age*, pp. 81–83).

[11] *Laxdæla saga*, ed. Einar Ól. Sveinsson, ÍF 5 (Reykjavík, 1934), chap. 4. The account is borne out in *Landnámabók*, in which she is called Auðr (pp. 136–46 and passim).

[12] In full: "[Unnr] acted as a man because the men who should have acted on her behalf were dead. This was in accordance with the law, which conferred authority on her in this situation, but it became a literary motive too; specifically in *Laxdæla saga* in her role as the revered and authoritative head of the family, when in every respect she has taken over the conduct and social functions of the male householder and leader" (*Unmanly Man*, p. 22). On the "transsexualization" of women for legal purposes, see the discussion of the *Baugatal* passage below.

[13] So suggest place-names and, in eastern Scandinavia, runic inscriptions. See especially Birgit Sawyer's *Property and Inheritance: The Runic Evidence* (Alingsås, 1988) and Barthi Guthmundsson's *Origin of the Icelanders* (Lincoln, Nebr., 1967), pp. 36–40 (translation of *Uppruni Íslendinga* [Reykjavík, 1959]).

several companions while she herself took an axe to their wives.)[14] It may well be that even that most macho of early Scandinavian business activities, organized piracy ("viking" in the proper sense of the term), was practiced by women. *The War of the Gædhil with the Gaill* refers twice to a "red girl" who headed up a viking band in Ireland and invaded Munster in the tenth century, and as any reader of the literature well knows, there are many other such legends of "fierce and imperious women"—legends so numerous and so consistent that, as Peter Foote and David Wilson sum it up, they "must certainly have some basis in reality."[15] More mundane but no less telling, given the "overwhelming maleness" of the enterprise, is the existence of a handful of women skalds.[16] More generally, the sources tell of a number of women who prosecute their lives in general, and their sex lives in particular, with a kind of aggressive authority unexpected in a woman and unparalleled in any other European literature.[17]

Nor was government the exclusive turf of men. It was in principle a male matter, but in practice, if we are to believe the sagas, women could insinuate themselves at almost every level of the process. One source claims that until the year 992, when they were debarred, women in Iceland could bring suit.[18] Normally women were not allowed to serve as witnesses—but exceptions could be made. Likewise service as arbitrators; it was a male business, but we know of at least one woman who "was formally empowered by the disputants to act as an arbitrator in a case."[19] Normally and ideally households were headed by men,

---

[14] *Grœnlendinga saga*, in *Eyrbyggja saga*, ed. Einar Ól. Sveinsson and Matthías Þórðarson, ÍF 4 (Reykjavík, 1935), chap. 8.

[15] Foote and Wilson, *Viking Achievement*, pp. 110–11. For further bibliography, see my "Maiden Warriors and Other Sons," *Journal of English and Germanic Philology* 85 (1986), 35–49.

[16] Jesch, *Women in the Viking Age*, p. 161; the following pages detail the women's poetic production. On women's participation in the production of literature more generally, see Else Mundal, "Kvinner og dikting: Overgangen frå munneleg til skriftleg kultur—ei ulykke for kvinnene?" in *Förändringar i kvinnors villkor under medeltiden: Uppsatser framlagda vid ett kvinnohistoriskt symposium i Skálholt, Island, 22.–25. juni 1981*, ed. Silja Aðalsteinsdóttir and Helgi Þorláksson (Reykjavík, 1983), pp. 11–25; also Helga Kress, "The Apocalypse of a Culture: *Völuspá* and the Myth of the Sources/Sorceress in Old Icelandic Literature," in *Poetry in the Scandinavian Middle Ages*, Proceedings of the Seventh International Saga Conference (Spoleto, 1988), pp. 279–302, and "Staðlausir stafir: Um slúður sem uppsprettu frásagnar í Íslendingasögum," *Skírnir* 165 (1991), 130–56.

[17] The locus classicus is the account of al-Ghazal's embassy to what would appear to be a Scandinavian court and his encounter there with a sexually forward queen who claims, in effect, that her people practice open marriage. The historicity of the text is questioned, but as Jesch's prudent point-by-point analysis concludes, "in spite of the literary tricks, there is nothing that is totally incredible in this account and some of it fits with what we already know of Scandinavian society in the Viking Age. . . . If Arabists reject the story of al-Ghazal's embassy as a fiction, this cannot be because of its inherent improbability as a reflection of royal viking life in the ninth century" (*Women in the Viking Age*, pp. 92–96). The sagas famously present a number of women who arrange their sex lives to their own satisfaction, and the theme of female promiscuity and erotic aggression in the legendary sources confirms the sense that the woman with enough social power was not particularly hindered by the usual sexual constraints. The admiration, grudging or plain, extended to these women conflicts with the scholarly claim, based on the handful of *níð* insults applied to women, that promiscuity in women was the shameful equivalent of effeminacy in men. See nn. 38 and 59 below.

[18] *Eyrbyggja saga*, chap. 38.

[19] William Ian Miller, *Bloodtaking and Peacemaking: Feud, Law, and Society in Saga Iceland* (Chicago

but the laws provide for the female exception, and although the female householder was in principle subject to the authority of male guardians, the sagas
give evidence, as William Ian Miller puts it, that "women were more than mere
title holders with managerial powers lodged solely with men."[20] Women were
in theory exempt from feud violence, but there are cases of their being specifically included together with able-bodied men as targets of vengeance.[21] In
Iceland, not just men but also women were subject to the penalties of outlawry
and execution. Only a man could *be* a *goði*, but it was technically possible for
women to *own* the office.[22] A woman's control over whatever property she might
technically own was less a function of her sex than her marital status: an unmarried and underage girl had none; a married woman, little; a widow, however
(as Foote and Wilson sum it up), "could have charge of her own property, no
matter her age, and administer that of her children; she also had more say in
arrangements that might be made for another marriage."[23] Certainly women's
role, in blood feud, in "choosing the avenger" involved them centrally in the
family politics of honor and inheritance, theoretically male terrain.[24] Normally
women were buried with "female" grave goods (e.g., spinning implements), but
there are enough examples of female graves with "male" objects (weapons,
hunting equipment, carpentry tools) to suggest that even in death some women
remained marked as exceptional.[25]

The examples could be multiplied, but even this summary list should suffice
to prompt the paradoxical question: just how useful is the category "woman"
in apprehending the status of women in early Scandinavia? To put it another
way, was femaleness any more decisive in setting parameters on individual behavior than were wealth, prestige, marital status, or just plain personality and
ambition? If femaleness could be overridden by other factors, as it seems to be
in the cases I have just mentioned, what does that say about the sex-gender
system of early Scandinavia, and what are the implications for maleness? I have

---

and London, 1990), p. 351. The case in question is recounted in *Þórðar saga kakala*, in *Sturlunga
saga*, ed. Jón Jóhannesson, Magnús Finnbogason, and Kristján Eldjárn (Reykjavík, 1946), 1, chap.
8.

[20] Miller, *Bloodtaking and Peacemaking*, p. 27.

[21] Miller, *Bloodtaking and Peacemaking*, pp. 207–8.

[22] *Grágás: Islændernes lovbog i fristatens tid, udgivet efter det Kongelige Bibliotheks haandskrift*, ed.
Vilhjálmur Finsen (Copenhagen, 1852; repr. Odense, 1974), 1a:142. *Grágás* 1a:1–217, trans. Andrew
Dennis, Peter Foote, and Richard Perkins, *Laws of Early Iceland: Grágás* (Winnipeg, 1980). See also
Miller, *Bloodtaking and Peacemaking*, p. 24.

[23] Foote and Wilson, *Viking Achievement*, p. 110. See also Miller, *Bloodtaking and Peacemaking*, esp.
p. 27.

[24] William Ian Miller, "Choosing the Avenger: Some Aspects of the Bloodfeud in Medieval Iceland
and England," *Law and History Review* 1 (1983), 159–204; his *Bloodtaking and Peacemaking*, pp. 211–
14; and my "Hildigunnr's Lament," in *Structure and Meaning in Old Norse Literature*, ed. John Lindow,
Lars Lönnroth, and Gerd Wolfgang Weber (Odense, 1986), pp. 141–83.

[25] The lively discussion of grave goods and sex is nicely summarized in Jesch, *Women in the Viking
Age*, pp. 21–22, 30; see also my "The Politics of Scarcity: Notes on the Sex Ratio in Early Scandinavia," *Scandinavian Studies* 60 (1988), 147–88 (repr. in *New Readings on Women in Old English
Literature*, ed. Helen Damico and Alexandra Hennessy Olsen [Bloomington and Indianapolis, 1990]),
esp. pp. 165–66.

no doubt that the "outstanding" women I enumerated earlier were indeed exceptional; that is presumably why their stories were remembered and recorded. But there is something about the quality and nature of such exceptions, not to say the sheer number of them and the tone of their telling, that suggests a less definitive rule than modern commentators have been inclined to allow. Certainly between women's de jure status and de facto status (as it is represented in literary and even historical texts) there appears to have been a very large playing field, and the woman (especially the divorced or widowed woman) sufficiently ambitious and sufficiently endowed with money and power seems not to have been especially hindered by notions of male and female nature.[26]

The slippage is not only between law and life. It is also between law and law (regional variations pointing to a degree of relativity in the importance of sexual difference), and it is also, on some points, within one and the same law. I turn here to the portion of *Grágás* known as *Baugatal*. A schedule of compensation for slayings, *Baugatal* (literally "ring count") divides the kindred into four tiers depending on their relationship to the slain person. The first tier is composed of near kinsmen of the slain person (father, son, brother, etc.), who are required to pay (if they are defendants) or collect (if they are plaintiffs) the main "ring" or major share of the wergild. Then comes the next tier, made up of less immediately related kinsmen with a lesser share of the wergild, and so on. The extensive list, which explores all possible permutations of payers and receivers, consists exclusively of men, with one exception:

> Sú er ok kona ein er bæði skal baugi bœta ok baug taka ef hon er einberni. En sú kona heitir baugrygr. En hon er dóttir ins dauða, enda sé eigi skapþiggjandi til hǫfuðbaugs en bœtendr lifi, þá skal hon taka þrímerking *sem sonr*, ef hon tók eigi full sætti at vígsbótum til þess er hon er gipt; enda skulu frændr álengr taka. Nú er hon dóttir veganda, en engi er skapbœtendi til bœtendi til hǫfuðbaugs, en viðtakendr sé til, þá skal hon bœta þrímerkingi *sem sonr* til þess er hon kømr í vers hvílu; en þá kastar hon gjǫldum í kné frændum.

> (There is also one woman who is both to pay and to take a wergild ring, given that she is an only child, and that woman is called "ring lady." She who takes is the daughter of the dead man if no proper receiver of the main ring otherwise exists but atonement payers are alive, and she takes the three-mark ring *like a son*, assuming that she has not accepted full settlement in compensation for the killing, and this until she is married, but thereafter kinsmen take it. She who pays is the daughter of the killer if no proper payer of the main ring otherwise exists but receivers do, and then she is to pay the three-mark ring *like a son*, and this until she enters a husband's bed and thereby tosses the outlay into her kinsmen's lap.)[27]

In other words, when the slain man has no male relatives in the first tier (no son, brother, or father) but *does* have a daughter (unmarried), that daughter

---

[26] The discrepancy between women's two "statuses" (in the laws and in the narrative sources) is much discussed. See in particular Rolf Heller, *Die literarische Darstellung der Frau in den Isländersagas* (Halle, 1958); Jenny Jochens, "The Medieval Icelandic Heroine: Fact or Fiction?" *Viator* 17 (1986), 35–50; the same author's "Consent in Marriage: Old Norse Law, Life and Literature," *Scandinavian Studies* 58 (1986), 142–76; and my "Politics of Scarcity," esp. pp. 147–50 and 182.

[27] *Grágás* 1a:200–201. Translation from *Laws of Early Iceland*, p. 181; my italics.

shall function as a son. So compelling is the principle of patrilineage that, in the event of genealogical crisis, even a woman can be conscripted as a kind of pinch hitter. Better a son who is your daughter than no son at all.

That the "surrogate son" provision is of some antiquity in Scandinavia is suggested by the presence of similar statutes on the mainland.[28] It is worth noting that its implications go beyond the matter of wergild, for insofar as a wergild list ranks an individual's kinsmen according to their degree of relatedness to the slain person, it is also assumed to reflect the schedule of inheritance as well. It is moreover assumed to reflect the schedule of actual feud—the order in which the survivors are obliged to take retaliatory action. Thus the law itself contemplates a situation in which, in the genealogical breach, a woman becomes a functional son, not only in the transaction of wergild, but also in the matter of inheritance and also, at least in principle, in the actual prosecution of feud. (That she must revert to female status upon marriage further underscores the expectation that gender will yield, as it were, to the greater good of survival of the line.) Just where and when and how completely the surrogate son clause obtained we have no idea, although the ubiquity of "maiden warrior" legends—legends of unmarried, brotherless daughters who on the death of their fathers become functional sons, even dressing and acting the part—suggests that the idea was very much alive in the public mind.[29] In either case, what concerns us here is not so much historical practice as legal contemplation—the plain fact that even within one and the same law, the principle of sex is not so final or absolute that it could not be overridden by greater interests. *Baugatal* and similar surrogate son provisions not only allow but institutionalize the female exception. Again, to judge from the presence of "male" objects in the occasional female grave, not even death necessarily undid such exceptionality.

I have hesitated over such terms as "femaleness" and "masculinity" in the above paragraphs, for they seem to me inadequate to what they mean to describe. The modern distinction between sex (biological: the reproductive apparatus) and gender (acquired traits: masculinity and femininity) seems oddly inapposite to the Norse material—in much the same way that Cleasby-Vigfusson's distinction between literal and metaphoric seems oddly inapposite to the semantic fields of the words *blauðr* and *hvatr*. What can be the meaning of biological femaleness in a culture that permits women to serve as juridical men? If biological femaleness does not determine one's juridical status, what does it determine—and indeed what does it matter? Is this a culture in which "sex" per se is irrelevant and "gender" is everything? Or is it a culture that simply does

---

[28] See my "Maiden Warriors and Other Sons" for the passages from the *Gulaþing* and the *Frostaþing* laws (p. 46, n. 30) and for an inventory of the relevant literary passages and a bibliography. On the politics of women's becoming "men" in early Christianity, see especially Elizabeth Castelli, " 'I Will Make Mary Male': Pieties of Body and Gender Transformation of Christian Women in Late Antiquity," in *Body Guards: The Cultural Politics of Gender Ambiguity*, ed. Julia Epstein and Kristina Staub (New York, 1991), pp. 29–50.

[29] In nineteenth- and early-twentieth-century Albania (a blood feud society remarkably similar to that of saga Iceland), such surrogate sons did indeed assume the male role (taking up pants, rifles, cigars and moving in the male sphere). For a summary discussion of the theme, with relevant bibliography, see my "Maiden Warriors and Other Sons."

not make a clear distinction but holds what we imagine to be two as one and the same thing? Something of the sort would seem to be the lesson of the *blauðr/hvatr* complex. Cleasby-Vigfusson proposes (in effect) that the word *blauðr* refers to "sex" when applied to a sex-appropriate being (thus to call Auðr *blauðr* is merely to call her female) but to "gender" when applied to a sex-inappropriate being (thus to call a man *blauðr* is to call him cowardly); but the fact that one word does for both (both "sex" and "gender," or in Cleasby-Vigfusson's terms both "proper" and "metaphoric") would seem to suggest that in Old Norse there is no "both" in the modern sense, but a single notion. That this single notion corresponds, at least in the case of the female, more closely to our sense of gender than to our sense of sex (though I shall suggest later that the Scandinavian sense of "gender" wreaks havoc with the concept of gender as we understand it) is clear from the examples of "exceptional" or "outstanding" women I enumerated above. "Woman" is a normative category, but not a binding one. If a woman is normally *blauðr*, she is not inevitably so, and when she is *hvatr*, she is thought unusual, but not unnatural.

Unusual for the better. Although the woman who for whatever reason plays life like a man is occasionally deplored by the medieval author,[30] she is more commonly admired—sometimes grudgingly, but often just flatly. Certainly *Laxdæla saga* is unequivocal about Unnr in djúpúðga: "Hon hafði brott með sér allt frændlið sitt, þat er á lífi var, ok þykkjask menn varla dœmi til finna, at einn kvenmaðr hafi komizk í brott ór þvílíkum ófriði með jafnmiklu fé ok foruneyti; má af því marka, at hon var mikit afbragð annarra kvenna" ("She took with her all her surviving kinsfolk; and it is generally thought that it would be hard to find another example of a woman escaping from such hazards with so much wealth and such a large retinue; from this it can be seen what a paragon amongst women she was").[31] So too Auðr in the same saga, who assumes male

[30] Hallgerðr of *Njáls saga* is perhaps the only "exceptional" female figure who is more or less roundly condemned by her author, whose voice is the most consistently misogynist in Icelandic literature. See Helga Kress, "Ekki hǫfu vér kvennaskap: Nokkrar laustengdar athuganir um karlmennsku og kvenhatur i Njálu," in *Sjötiu ritgerðir helgaðar Jakobi Benediktssyni 20. júlí 1977*, ed. Einar G. Petursson and Jónas Kristjánsson (Reykjavík, 1977), pp. 293–313, and, for a more moderate view, Ursula Dronke, *The Role of Sexual Themes in "Njáls Saga,"* The Dorothea Coke Memorial Lecture in Northern Studies (London, 1980). English-speaking readers of that saga should be aware that Hallgerðr comes off rather worse in translation than she does in the original.

[31] *Laxdæla saga*, chap. 4. Translation from Magnus Magnusson and Herman Pálsson, *Laxdaela Saga* (Harmondsworth, Middlesex, 1969). The word *afbragð*, here rendered as "paragon," means a superior, exceptional, surpassing person. Although *Landnámabók*'s more historical account of Auðr/Unnr does not comment on her character, its length and detail confirm the esteem in which she was held. *Laxdæla saga*'s interest in (and approval of) "strong" women has long been noted, and Helga Kress has argued that it demonstrates "en kvinnlig bevissthet" that may point to female authorship ("Meget samstavet må det tykkes deg," *Historisk Tidskrift* [1980], p. 279). There is no doubt that *Laxdæla*'s representation of women is extraordinary, but I would suggest that the claim of "feminine (or female) consciousness" for that text is compromised by the fact that it is their exceptional (that is, ideally masculine) qualities that qualify its women for history, as it were. What does it mean to speak of "feminine consciousness" in a world in which femininity is for all practical purposes synonymous with effeminacy? The same question may be asked of Foote and Wilson's suggestion that "Outstanding women, real or legendary, must have done something to lift the status of women in general" (*Viking Achievement*, p. 111).

dress and arms and goes off to exact the revenge her brothers refused to take on her behalf; although the saga does not say so in so many words, it is clear that her actions are approved of, legal injunctions against transvestism notwithstanding.[32] Lest we doubt the gender implications of such women's exceptional behavior, it is spelled out for us in the application to them of that most privileged of epithets, *drengr* (*drengiligr, drengskapr,* etc.). Defined by Cleasby-Vigfusson as a "bold, valiant, worthy man," *drengr* is conventionally held up as the very soul of masculine excellence in Norse culture.[33] Yet Njáll's wife Bergþóra is introduced as "kvenskǫrungr mikill ok drengr góðr ok nǫkkut skaphǫrð" ("a women of great bearing and a good *drengr,* but somewhat harsh-natured").[34] Even Hildigunnr, whose goading of Flosi fuels a feud that might otherwise have calmed down, is so designated: "Hon var allra kvenna grimmust ok skaphǫrðust ok drengr mikill, þar sem vel skyldi vera" ("She was the sternest and most hardminded of women but a great *drengr* when need be").[35] This is a world in which "masculinity" always has a plus value, even (or perhaps especially) when it is enacted by a woman.[36]

If the category "woman" is a movable one, what of the category "man"? Is maleness, too, subject to mutation and "exception," or is it alone clear and fixed? Much has been said—though far more *could* be said—about Norse notions of masculinity. On the assumption that readers are generally familar with the ideal, let me proceed directly to that long and broad streak in the literature— a streak that runs through poetry (both mythological and heroic) and prose, Latin and vernacular, legend and history and even law—in which manliness is most garishly contested: the tradition of insulting.

---

[32] *Laxdæla saga,* chap. 35. See Meulengracht Sørensen, *Unmanly Man,* p. 22.

[33] Cleasby-Vigfusson derives the word from *drangr,* "jutting rock," "cliff," or "pillar." See Foote and Wilson's discussion of the term and concept in *Viking Achievement,* pp. 105–8, 425–26, with bibliography.

[34] *Njáls saga,* chap. 20, my translation. Magnússon and Pálsson have, "She was an exceptional and courageous woman, but a little harsh-natured."

[35] *Njáls saga,* chap. 95, my translation. Magnússon and Pálsson have, "She was harsh-natured and ruthless; but when courage was called for, she never flinched."

[36] The "masculine ideal" that underwrites such attitudes is often noted (see, for example, Meulengracht Sørensen, *Unmanly Man,* pp. 20–22, and Sawyer, *Kvinnor och familj,* pp. 74–75). In her "Forholdet mellom born ok foreldre i det norrøne kjeldematerialet" (*Collegium medievale* 1 [1988], 2–28) Else Mundal proposes that it is the belief in bilateral genetic inheritance (that is, the belief that the child, regardless of sex, stands to get as much of its character from the mother as from the father) that accounts for the approval the "strong" woman seems to enjoy: her "masculinity" can be seen as an investment for unborn sons of the future (esp. p. 24). In my "Maiden Warriors and Other Sons," I speculated similarly that "the idea of latent or recessive features, physical or characterological, was undeveloped [in early Scandinavia]; inherited qualities seem to manifest themselves in some degree in every generation. The qualities that Angantýr now bestows [on his daughter Hervör] as the 'legacy of Arngrím's sons,' *afl* and *eljun* [strength and powerful spirit], are emphatically 'male' qualities. They may ultimately be 'intended' for Hervör's future sons and their sons on down the line . . . but in the meantime they must assert themselves in Hervör herself (as indeed they already have)" (p. 39). The very notion that, say, passivity can be inherited from the father and martial propensities from the mother bespeaks a far more tenuous connection between sex and gender than modern ideology would have it.

Although insults are most concentrated in those literary set pieces we call flytings (*senna* and *mannjafnaðr*), they can crop up in just about any venue.[37] In terms more or less formal and more or less humorous, the insulter impugns his antagonist's appearance (poor or beggardly); reminds him of heroic failure (losing a battle, especially against an unworthy opponent); accuses him of cowardice, of trivial or irresponsible behavior (pointless escapades, domestic indulgences, sexual dalliance), or of failings of honor (unwillingness or inability to extract due vengeance, hostile relations with kinsmen); declares him a breaker of alimentary taboos (drinking urine, eating corpses); and/or charges him with sexual irregularity (incest, castration, bestiality, "receptive homosexuality"). (Once again, although most insults are traded between men, there are also women in the role of both insulter and insultee—though a woman in either role usually faces off against a man, not another woman, and although she may score lots of direct hits, in the end she always loses. The most frequent charges against women are incest, promiscuity, and sleeping with the enemy.)[38]

Of these, the most spectacular is the form of sexual defamation known as *níð*. Very likely part of the Germanic legacy, *níð* was prohibited by law. The following passages give a sense of the term.[39] The first is from the Norwegian Gulaþing Code and follows the rubric "If a person makes *níð* against someone":

> Engi maðr scal gera tungu nið um annan. ne trenið. . . . Engi scal gera yki um annan. æða fiolmæle. þat heiter yki ef maðr mælir um annan þat er eigi ma væra. ne verða oc eigi hever verit. kveðr hann væra kono niundu nott hveria. oc hever barn boret. oc kallar gylvin. þa er hann utlagr. ef han verðr at þvi sannr.[40]

---

[37] On the flyting, see Joseph Harris, "The *Senna*: From Description to Literary Theory," *Michigan Germanic Studies* 5 (1979), 64–74; my "The Germanic Context of the Unferþ Episode," *Speculum* 55 (1980), 444–68, and "*Hárbárðsljóð* as Generic Farce," *Scandinavian Studies* 51 (1979), 124–45; and Karen Swensen, *Performing Definitions: Two Genres of Insult in Old Norse Literature* (Columbia, S.C., 1991), which contains an especially useful bibliography.

[38] Applied to a woman, the noun *ergi* (adjective *ǫrg*) "is virtually synonymous with nymphomania, which was a characteristic as much despised in a woman as unmanliness was in a man," according to Folke Ström (*Níð, Ergi and Old Norse Moral Attitudes* [London, 1973], p. 4); for Meulengracht Sørensen, the female use means that she "is generally immodest, perverted or lecherous" (*Unmanly Man*, pp. 18–19). The fact that charges toward women to this effect are so few and far between would seem to suggest that the female use is a secondary formation and a rather unstable one at that. Nor, although space does not permit me to make a full argument here, am I convinced that the *ǫrg* female is as fundamentally different from the *argr* male as these scholars suggest; again I suspect a modern contamination. See n. 17 above.

[39] For a detailed account of these and other legal references, see Bo Almqvist, *Norrön niddiktning: Traditionshistoriska studier i versmagi*, 2 vols. (Uppsala, 1965–74), esp. pp. 38–68. See also Kari Ellen Gade, "Homosexuality and the Rape of Males in Old Norse Law and Literature," *Scandinavian Studies* 58 (1986), 124–41. On *níð* generally, see (in addition to Meulengracht Sørensen and Almqvist) Ström, *Níð, Ergi, and Old Norse Moral Attitudes*; Erik Noreen, "Om niddiktning" in his "Studier i fornvästnordisk diktning II," in *Uppsala Universitets årsskrift: Filosofi, språkvetenskap och historiska vetenskaper* 44 (1922), 37–65; and Joaquín Martínez Pizarro, "Studies on the Function and Context of the *Senna* in Early Germanic Narrative," Ph.D. dissertation, Harvard University, 1976.

[40] *Norges gamle love indtil 1387*, ed. R. Keyser, P. A. Munch, G. Storm, and E. Herzberg (Christiania, 1846), 1:57. Translations from the laws pertaining to *níð* are adapted from Meulengracht Sørensen's *Unmanly Man* (pp. 14–32).

(Nobody is to make *tungu nið* [verbal *nið*] about another person, nor a *tréníð* [wooden *nið*].[41] . . . No one is to make an *ýki* [exaggeration] about another or a libel. It is called *ýki* if someone says something about another man which cannot be, nor come to be, nor have been: declares he is a woman every ninth night or has born a child or calls him *gylfin* [a werewolf or unnatural monster?]. He is outlawed if he is found guilty of that. Let him deny it with a six-man oath. Outlawry is the outcome if the oath fails.)

The second also comes from the Gulaþing Code, in the passage under the rubric *fullréttisorð* (verbal offenses for which full compensation must be paid):

Orð ero þau er fullrettis orð heita. þat er eitt ef maðr kveðr at karlmanne ǫðrum. at hann have barn boret. þat er annat. ef maðr kveðr hann væra sannsorðenn. þat er hit þriðia. ef hann iamnar hanom við meri. æða kallar hann grey. æða portkono. æða iamnar hanom við berende eitthvert.[42]

(There are certain expressions known as *fullréttisorð* [words for which full compensation must be paid]. One is if a man says to another that he has given birth to a child. A second is if a man says of another that he is *sannsorðinn* [demonstrably fucked]. The third is if he compares him to a mare, or calls him a bitch or harlot, or compares him with the female of any kind of animal.)

The corresponding provision in the Icelandic *Grágás* establishes lesser outlawry (three years' exile) for *ýki* and *tréníð*, but full outlawry (exile for life) for the utterance of any of the words *ragr*, *stroðinn*, or *sorðinn*. Indeed, for these three words one has the right to kill.[43]

The legal profile of *nið* is richly attested in the literature. Two examples suffice to give the general picture: Skarpheðinn's taunting suggestion, in *Njáls saga*, that Flosi would do well to accept a gift of pants, "ef þú ert brúðr Svínfellsáss, sem sagt er, hverja ina níunda nótt ok geri hann þik at konu ("if you are the bride of the Svínafell troll, as people say, every ninth night and he uses you as a woman")[44] and Sinfjǫtli's claim to Guðmundr in the eddic *Helgakviða Hundingsbana I*, "Nío átto við / á nesi Ságo / úlfa alna, / ec var einn faðir þeirra" ("Nine wolves you and I begot on the island of Sága; I alone was their father").[45] As the latter example in particular indicates (and there are many more), what is at stake here is not homosexuality per se, for the role of the penetrator is regarded as not only masculine but boastworthy regardless of the sex of the

---

[41] *Tréníð* is the plastic equivalent of *tunguníð* (tongue *nið*). The classic example is the carved effigy in *Gísla saga* of one man sodomized by another (chap. 2), but the term may also refer to a pole of the sort described in *Egils saga Skallagrímssonar*, ed. Sigurður Nordal, ÍF 2 (Reykjavík, 1933), chap. 57. For a fuller discussion, see Meulengracht Sørensen, *Unmanly Man*, esp. pp. 51–61; Ström's *Níð, Ergi, and Old Norse Moral Attitudes*, pp. 10–14; and Almqvist, *Norrön niddiktning*, passim.

[42] *Norges gamle love*, 1:70.

[43] *Grágás* (*Staðarhólsbók*), 2a:392.

[44] *Njáls saga*, chap. 123. Notes Meulengracht Sørensen, "Nobody has suspected Flosi of being homosexual. The charge is symbolic" (*Unmanly Man*, p. 20). Virtually the same insult occurs in two other sources (*Þorsteins saga Síðu-Hallssonar* and *Króka-Refs saga*).

[45] St. 38, in *Edda: Die Lieder des Codex Regius nebst verwandten Denkmälern*, 1: *Text*, ed. Gustav Neckel, 5th rev. ed. by Hans Kuhn (Heidelberg, 1983).

object.[46] The charge of *níð* devolves solely on the penetrated man—the *sorðinn* or *ragr* man. This architecture is a familiar one in the early world and in certain quarters of the modern one as well, but it surely finds one of its most brazen expressions in the Norse tradition of *níð*.

To what extent sodomy, consensual or otherwise, was practiced in early Scandinavia is unknown. What is clear from a survey of *níð* examples is that the charges to that effect are "symbolic" (as Folke Ström would have it) or "moral" (as Meulengracht Sørensen prefers) insofar as they refer not to an act of sex but rather to such "female" characteristics as "a lack of manly courage," "lack of prowess," or " 'unmanliness' in both its physical and its mental sense," or "certain mental qualities, not to mention duties that were considered specifically female."[47] Meulengracht Sørensen distinguishes three meanings of the word *argr/ragr* as it refers to men: "perversity in sexual matters" (being penetrated anally), "versed in witchcraft," and " 'cowardly, unmanly, effeminate' with regard to morals and character." The second and third meanings derive from the first, in his view, by the logic that "a man who subjects himself to another in sexual affairs will do the same in other respects; and fusion between the notions of sexual unmanliness and unmanliness in a moral sense stands at the heart of *níð*."[48]

Symbolic or no, the *níð* taunts figure the insultee as a female and in so doing suggest that the category "man" is, if anything, even more susceptible to mutation than the category "woman." For if a woman's ascent into the masculine took some doing, the man's descent into the feminine was just one real or imagined act away. Nor is the "femaleness" of that act in doubt. Anal penetration constructed the man who experienced it as whore, bride, mare, bitch, and the like—in whatever guise a female creature, and as such subject to pregnancy, childbirth, and lactation. In the world of *níð* (male) anus and vagina are for all imaginary purposes one and the same thing. Men are sodomizable in much the way women are rapable, and with the same consequences. The charge may be "symbolic," but its language could hardly be more corporeal, and although, as I shall suggest below, the separate status of the female body is far from secure, there is no doubt that the body of the *ragr* man looks very much like that of a woman.

But is *níð* really the fundamental truth of early Scandinavian sexual attitudes? It is not surprising that modern scholarship has reified it as such, given its

---

[46] On this pattern in cultures present and past, and on the distinction between person and act, there is an abundant literature. See especially David M. Halperin, "One Hundred Years of Homosexuality," in *One Hundred Years of Homosexuality and Other Essays on Greek Love* (New York, 1989), esp. bibliography on p. 159, n. 21, and p. 162, n. 52; and, for another perspective (and for the most up-to-date bibliography on the discussion), David J. Cohen, *Law, Sexuality, and Society: The Enforcement of Morals in Classical Athens* (Cambridge, Eng., 1991), esp. chap. 7, "Law, Social Control, and Homosexuality in Classical Athens." Mention should be made, on the Norse side, of the passage in chap. 22 of *Bjarnar saga Hítdœlakappa* (ed. Sigurður Nordal and Guðni Jónsson, in *Borgfirðinga saga*, ÍF 3 [Reykjavík, 1938]), which suggests that the position of the aggressor may have been rather more compromised than tradition would have it.

[47] Ström, *Níð, Ergi, and Old Norse Moral Attitudes*, p. 17.

[48] Meulengracht Sørensen, *Unmanly Man*, pp. 19–20.

special status in the laws and also given the way, thanks to its occlusion in the scholarly tradition, it has been handed to modern critics as a kind of blank slate.[49] But it is important to remember that *níð* insults are by no means the only sort of Norse insult; that they are typically found interspersed, as if on roughly equal footing, with insults not immediately sexual; and that in this larger context, *níð* insults seem part and parcel of a shame system in which the claim of femaleness is an especially striking, but by no means the only, element.

Men call each other poor or beggardly—and in quite stinging terms—as often as they call each other women. They call each other slaves and captives. They accuse one another of having fled from danger or having failed to take action to protect themselves and their kin. A great number of insults occur in alternation with boasts and turn on some standard oppositions: action vs. talk, hard life vs. soft life, adventurer vs. stay-at-home, etc. In a particularly grandiose flyting from *Örvar-Odds saga,* the legendary Örvar-Oddr brags of having explored warfare when all the insultee explored was the king's hall; of having fought the Permians while the insultee was safely ensconced at home between linen sheets; of having razed enemy strongholds while the insultee was "chattering with girls"; of having slain eighteen men while the insultee was staggering his way to a bondwoman's bed; of having brought down an earl while the insultee was "at home wavering between the calf and the slave girl." Similar is the claim in the eddic *Helgi Hundingsbana I* that while the "flight-scorning prince" Helgi was off feeding the eagles, Sinfjǫtli was "at the mill kissing slave girls." Insofar as home-staying (especially when it amounts to combat avoidance) is coded as effeminate (even though the accused may be an active "phallic aggressor"[50] within the realm of the household), these insults, too, are haunted by gender, and they indeed on occasion tip over into *níð,* as in the following stanza from *Örvar-Odds saga*: "Sigurðr, vart eigi, / er á Sælundi felldak / bræðr böðharða, / Brand ok Agnar, / Ýsmund, Ingjald, / Álfr var inn fimmti; / en þú heima látt / í höll konungs, / skrökmálasamr, / skauð hernumin" ("Sigurðr, you weren't on Zealand when I felled the battle-hard brothers Brandr and Agnarr, Ásmundr and Ingjaldr, and Álfr was the fifth—while you were lying at home in the king's hall, full of tall stories, a *skauð hernumin*").[51] The participial *hernumin* here means "battle-taken" and suggests the sort of victimization to which a prisoner of war was subject. The feminine noun *skauð* means "sheath" and is a word for a fold or crack in the genital area—used in practice to refer to the female genital and to the fold of skin into which a horse's penis retracts.[52] If *skauð hernumin* defies

[49] The first full-fledged treatment of the subject was an anonymous essay entitled "Spuren von Konträrsexualität bei den alten Skandinaviern," in *Jahrbuch für sexuelle Zwischenstufen unter besonderer Berücksichtigung der Homosexualität* 4 (Leipzig, 1902), pp. 244–63.

[50] Meulengracht Sørensen, following T. Vanggaard (*Phallos* [Copenhagen, 1969], trans. by the author as *Phallos: A Symbol and Its History in the Male World* [London, 1972]), sees in "phallic aggression" the organizing principle of the early Scandinavian sex-gender system (*Unmanly Man,* esp. pp. 27–28).

[51] In *Fornaldar sögur Norðurlanda* 2, ed. Guðni Jónsson (Reykjavík, 1959).

[52] Horse genitalia, both male and female, loom large in the obscene literature of Old Norse, and the pattern is presumably Germanic. See especially Martínez Pizarro, "Studies on the Function and Context of the *Senna* in Early Germanic Narrative." The sense of *skauð* is echoed in the noun *hrukka*

precise translation, its general sense is clear. The insultee is trebly accused: of being a draft dodger, of being a prisoner of war and hence subject to whatever abuse that condition may entail, and of having either no penis or one so soft and hidden—so *blauðr*—that it is useless as such.

Whatever else they may be, these are insults preoccupied with power—or, more to the point, with powerlessness under threat of physical force. That sexual difference is deeply imbricated in this concern is clear. The question is which, if either, is primary. Is power a metaphor for sex (so that the charge of poverty boils down to a charge of femaleness), as Meulengracht Sørensen argues, or is sex a metaphor for power (so that the charge of *níð* boils down to a charge of powerlessness)? Modern scholarship has tended to assume the former. I incline toward the latter, or toward a particular version of the latter. The insult complex seems to me to be driven, not by the opposition male/female per se, but by the opposition *hvatr/blauðr*, which works more as a gender continuum than a sexual binary. That is, although the ideal man is *hvatr* and the typical woman is *blauðr*, neither is necessarily so; and each can, and does, slip into the territory of the other.

If the human body was once taken as the one sure fact of history, the place where culture stopped and biological verities began, it is no longer. Not in the academy, in any case, in which there has arisen a virtual industry of investigating the ways conceptions of bodies, above all sexed bodies, are historically contingent. Of particular interest for students of early Scandinavia are the implications of what Thomas Laqueur calls the "one-sex" or "one-flesh" model of sexual difference that he argues obtained in western Europe from the Greeks through the early modern period.[53] Unlike the "two-sex" or "two-flesh" model, which emerged in the late eighteenth century and which construes male and female as "opposite" or *essentially* different from one another, the "one-sex" model understands the sexes as inside-vs.-outside versions of a single genital/reproductive apparatus, differing in degree of warmth or coolness and hence in degree of value (hot being superior to cool) but essentially the same in form and function and hence ultimately fungible versions of one another. The point here is not that there is no notion of sexual difference but that the difference was conceived less as a set of absolute opposites than as a system of isomorphic analogues, the superior male set working as a visible map to the invisible and inferior female set—for the one sex in question was essentially male, women being viewed as "inverted, and less perfect, men."[54]

("fold" or "wrinkle," referring also to the female genital), related to the verb *hrøkkva* ("fall back, recoil, retreat, cringe"); see Zoe Borovsky, "Male Fears, Female Threats: Giant Women in Old Norse–Icelandic Literature," paper delivered at the annual meeting of the Society for the Advancement of Scandinavian Study, May, 1991. See also Torild W. Arnoldson, *Parts of the Body in Older Germanic and Scandinavian* (Chicago, 1915; repr. New York, 1971), p. 175; and Meulengracht Sørensen, *Unmanly Man*, esp. pp. 58–59.

[53] Thomas Laqueur, *Making Sex: Body and Gender from the Greeks to Freud* (Cambridge, Eng., 1990).

[54] Laqueur, *Making Sex*, p. 26. More particularly, penis and vagina are construed as one and the same organ; if the former happens to extrude and the latter to intrude (in an inside-out and upward-extending fashion), they are physiologically identical, and the same words did for both. Likewise

So the official story, the one told by medical treatises. Popular mythologies were (and to a remarkable degree still are) rather more fluid in their understanding of which parts match which. A millennially popular "set" equates the (male) anus with the vagina—not a correspondence authorized by the medical treatises, but one that proceeds easily from the one-sex body as a general proposition. (The word *vagina* itself, meaning "sword sheath," was also used in Latin sources to refer to the anus.[55] Certainly, Norse words or periphrases for the vagina are typically usable for the anus, and it is indeed with deprecating reference to the male that such terms are conspicuously attested.)[56] What is of particular interest for present purposes is not so much the system of homologues per se, but the fluidity implied by that system. This is a universe in which maleness and femaleness were always negotiable, always up for grabs, always susceptible to "conditions." If "conditions" could go so far as to to activate menstruation in men or a traveling down of the sexual member in women (eventualities attested by medical authorities throughout the early period), then "conditions" could easily enable gender encroachments of a more moderate sort.[57]

A systematic account of the Norse construction of the body, including the sexed body, remains to be written. I presume that the Scandinavians in the early period had some one-sex account of bodily difference—the conflation of anus and vagina and the charges of male pregnancy point clearly in that direction—but no treatise spells out the terms. I also presume that in the same way that the thirteenth-century authors were cognizant of other medical learning (the theory of humors, for example), they were cognizant of the learned hot/cool model of sexual difference—but they did not insinuate that model into the "historical" texts. One can think of several reasons for this: because they preferred to let tradition overrule science, because for narrative purposes strength stood as the objective correlative of heat, because it is the nature of sagas to naturalize learning. But it may also, and above all, be because the medieval authors knew that in the very social stories they had to tell, actual genitals were pretty much beside the point. The first lesson of the foregoing examples is that bodily sex was not that decisive. The "conditions" that mattered in the north—

---

testes (the male ones outside and the female ones inside, again with the same words doing for both), and so too genital fluids (menstrual and seminal emissions being cooler and hotter versions of the same matter).

[55] On the correspondence, see Laqueur, *Making Sex*, pp. 159 and 270, n. 60. According to psychoanalysis, the one-sex model is alive and well in the unconscious—in the form, for example, of penis envy on the part of females and, on the part of males, fantasies of anal intercourse, pregnancy, and birth. In my *Men, Women, and Chain Saws: Gender in the Modern Horror Film* (Princeton, 1992), I have argued that the one-sex model is also alive and well in popular culture; it is in any case an obvious feature of horror movies, which commonly turn explicitly or implicitly on the idea that males and females are essentially the same, genitally and otherwise.

[56] On the conflation of vagina and (male) anus, see Margaret Clunies Ross, "Hildr's Ring," and for a discussion of the equivalence in the modern context, see Leo Bersani, "Is the Rectum a Grave?" *October* 43 (1989), 194–222. For lexical listings, see Arnoldson's *Parts of the Body in Older Germanic and Scandinavian* and William Denny Baskett's *Parts of the Body in the Later Germanic Dialects* (Chicago, 1920). Unavailable to me is the unpublished manuscript "Verba Islandica obscaena," by Ólafur Davíðsson (Reykjavík, Landsbókasafn Íslands, MS 1204, 8vo).

[57] Laqueur, *Making Sex*, pp. 122–34 and passim.

the "conditions" that pushed a person into another status—worked not so much at the level of the body, but at the level of social relations.

The second lesson has to do with the attenuated quality of the category "female." The fact that "femaleness" is so frequently invoked with reference to men (far more often than to women, I suspect), the absence of a language for and lack of concern with features exclusive to women, and the consignment of anything that might qualify as women's sphere to a position virtually outside of history would seem to suggest that what is at stake here is not "femininity" in any modern sense, but simply "effeminacy" or, more to the point, "impotence"—the default category for the person of either sex who for whatever reason fell outside normative masculinity. Scholars who try to distinguish the feminine from the effeminate by suggesting that the female role was ignominious only when it was assigned to a man and that women and female activities as such were not held in contempt are on shaky ground, for the sources point overwhelmingly to a structure in which women no less than men were held in contempt for womanishness and were admired—and mentioned—only to the extent that they showed some "pride" (as their aggressive self-interest is repeatedly characterized in modern commentaries).[58] Again, it seems likely that Norse society operated according to a one-sex model—that there was one sex and it was male. More to the point, there was finally just one "gender," one standard by which persons were judged adequate or inadequate, and it was something like masculine.

What finally excites fear and loathing in the Norse mind is not femaleness per se, but the condition of powerlessness, the lack or loss of volition, with which femaleness is typically, but neither inevitably nor exclusively, associated. By the same token, what prompts admiration is not maleness per se, but sovereignty of the sort enjoyed mostly and typically and ideally, but not solely, by men. This is in any case not a world in which the sexes are opposite or antithetical or polar or complementary (to return again to the modern apparatus). On the contrary, it is a world in which gender, if we can even call it that, is neither coextensive with biological sex, despite its dependence on sexual imagery, nor a closed system, but a system based to an extraordinary extent on winnable and losable attributes. It goes without saying that the one-sex or single-standard system (in the sense I have outlined it here) is one that advantaged men. But it is at the same time a system in which being born female was not so damaging that it could not be offset by other factors. A woman may start with debits and a man with credits, but any number of other considerations—wealth, marital status, birth order, historical accident, popularity, a forceful personality, sheer ambition, and so on—could tip the balance in the other direction. (When Hallgerðr of *Njáls saga*, who acted herself so forcefully into history, says to her father that "Pride is something you and your kinsmen have plenty of, so it's no surprise that I should have some too," she articulates perfectly the economy of the one-sex model, in which, however unequal, men and women are, or can be,

[58] For example: *Níð* "did not require that women or female activities were held in contempt as such, of course, no more than was a woman's sexual role or her maternal capacity. The female role was ignominious when it was assigned to a man" (Meulengracht Sørensen, *Unmanly Man*, p. 24).

players in the same game.)[59] More to the point, because the strong woman was
not inhibited by a theoretical ceiling above which she could not rise and the
weak man not protected by a theoretical floor below which he could not fall,
the potential for sexual overlap in the social hierarchy was always present. The
frantic machismo of Norse males, at least as they are portrayed in the literature,
would seem on the face of it to suggest a society in which being born male
precisely did *not* confer automatic superiority, a society in which distinction had
to be acquired, and constantly reacquired, by wresting it away from others.

Let me take this a step further and propose that to the extent that we can
speak of a social binary, a set of two categories into which all persons were
divided, the fault line runs not between males and females per se, but between
able-bodied men (and the exceptional woman) on one hand and, on the other,
a kind of rainbow coalition of everyone else (most women, children, slaves, and
old, disabled, or otherwise disenfranchised men). Even the most casual reader
of Norse literature knows how firmly drawn is that line, for it suggests itself all
over the lexical and documentary map, including in the laws themselves, which
distinguish clearly and repeatedly between *úmegð* (singular *úmagi*), "depen-
dents" (literally, those who cannot maintain themselves: "children, aged people,
men disabled by sickness, paupers, etc."), on one hand, and "breadwinners"
(*magi/megð*) on the other.[60] What I am suggesting is that this is *the* binary, the
one that cuts most deeply and the one that matters: between strong and weak,
powerful and powerless or disempowered, swordworthy and unswordworthy,
honored and unhonored or dishonored, winners and losers.[61] Insofar as these
categories, though not biological, have a sexual look to them, the one associated
with the male body and the other with something like the female one, and insofar
as the polarity or complementarity or antithesis that modern scholarship has
brought to bear on maleness and femaleness applies far more readily, and with
less need for qualification, to the opposition *hvatr/blauðr* or *magi/úmagi*, they
might as well be called genders. The closest English comes to the distinction
may be "spear side" and "distaff side"—a distinction which, although it is clearly

[59] Cf. Meulengracht Sørensen's claim (in the chapter entitled "Mænds og kvinders ære" in his
forthcoming *Fortælling og ære*) that men's and women's honor systems were essentially different.
His construction proceeds to a considerable extent from the evidence of *níð* insults, which seem to
bespeak a double standard (men are accused of being women, women of being promiscuous). As I
have suggested above, a reading of *níð* in context (both the context of other insults and the context
of praise- and blameworthy deeds in general) leads to a rather different conclusion—a conclusion
buttressed by the paucity and apparent instability of references to female *níð*. See also nn. 17 and
38 above. The "one-sex" argument in this and the preceding sections was presented in short form
in my review of Meulengracht Sørensen's *Norrønt nid*, in the *Journal of English and Germanic Philology*
(1982), 398–400.

[60] Cleasby-Vigfusson, entry under *úmagi*. Related terms (also deriving from *mega* 'to have strength
to do, avail') are *úmeginn* 'impotent', *úmegin* 'unmight, a swoon', *úmætr* 'worthless, invalid', and
úmætta 'to lose strength, faint away'—as opposed, on the positive side, to terms like *megin, megn*
'strong, mighty'.

[61] The equation of women and old men is also evident in the norms governing the appropriateness
of the vengeance target in feud. "The underlying idea," writes Miller, "is that people not socially
privileged to bear arms were excused from having arms brought to bear on them" (p. 207).

(now) welded to sexual difference, is nonetheless one derived from roles (rather than bodies) and hence at least gestures toward gender (insofar as men are in principle able to spin and women to do battle).

To observe that some such binary is a familiar feature of premodern societies (and at the popular level in modern ones as well) should not detract from its decisive importance in Old Norse.[62] Nor is (for example) the Greek distinction between hoplites and *kinaidoi* as it has been outlined in recent scholarship quite apposite to the Scandinavian one between *magi* and *úmagi*, for the gender traffic in Norse involves not only men, but women, and conspicuously so. What Winkler calls the "odd belief in the reversibility of the male person, always in peril of slipping into the servile or the feminine," is matched, in Norse, by the odd belief in the reversibility also of the female person, under the right conditions capable of ascension into the ranks of those who master, and that fact has grave consequences for the male side of the story.[63] Not only losable by men, but achievable by women, masculinity was in a kind of double jeopardy for the Norse man. He who for whatever reason became a social woman stood, to put it crudely, to find himself not just side by side with woman, but under her, and, again, it may be just that ever-present possibility that gives Norse maleness its desperate edge. The literature is in any case rich with scenes, both historical and legendary, that turn on male humiliation or defeat at the hands of women—including, as a relatively gentle example, the encounter between Auðr and Eyjólfr with which this essay began.[64]

Let me turn to a stream in the downward gender traffic that I have not yet mentioned, though it is especially privileged in the documents: men once firmly in category A who have slid into category B by virtue of age. In a literature not given to pathos and little interested in the old, these moments—in which former heroes are shown doddering about, or bedridden, or blind and impotent—stand

---

[62] See esp. John J. Winkler, "Laying down the Law: The Oversight of Men's Sexual Behavior in Classical Athens," in his *Constraints of Desire: The Anthropology of Sex and Gender in Ancient Greece* (New York and London, 1990). "The logic of a zero-sum calculus underlies many of the most characteristic predicates and formulae that were applied to issues of sex and gender," Winkler writes. "Thus, not to display bravery (*andreia*, literally 'manliness') lays a man open to symbolic demotion from the ranks of the brave/manly to the opposite class of women" (p. 47).

[63] Winkler, *The Constraints of Desire*, p. 50.

[64] For example, Egill, mocked and pushed around by women in his old age (*Egils saga*, chap. 85); þorkell, tongue-lashed into submission by his wife Ásgerðr (*Gísla saga Súrssonar*, chap. 9); þorðr Ingunnarson, assaulted in bed by his angry, pants-wearing former wife with a short sword—a gesture loaded with sexual meaning and one that had permanent effect (*Laxdœla saga*, chap. 35); and, of course, any number of heroes' battles with giantesses and warrior women in the *fornaldarsögur* and related traditions. Along different but not unrelated lines, Clunies Ross notes the special ability of women in the mythological sources to humiliate men. The passages she analyzes "reveal the conviction that a dominant woman was more to be feared than a man, for she was able to strengthen herself magically in order to usurp male roles and reduce the men in her power to physical and mental debility, to make them *ragr*. . . . The insult of showing the 'ring' to Hǫgni is a verbal equivalent to Hildr's destructive and debilitating powers, for it accuses him of weakness and effeminacy. It is particularly vicious that, having adopted a maculine role herself, she should accuse her own father of having lost his manhood" ("Hildr's Ring," p. 92).

out in strong relief.[65] We tend to understand the poignancy of such scenes
rather straightforwardly in terms of the past, as a kind of northern sounding
of the *ubi sunt* or *sic transit gloria* themes so richly developed in Old English
verse. Certainly they are that, but with a spin that strikes me as if not uniquely
Norse, then characteristically so. For in the Norse examples it is not just the
ruination of the once-heroic body that is at stake, but the second-class company
such a body is forced to keep.

Consider, for example, just how many of the scenes of Egill Skallagrímsson's
old age are played out in the company of women—who cajole, tease, laugh at,
advise, and humor him, both figuratively and literally pushing him around. His
story could have been told, as others are, with fewer (or indeed none) of these
scenes; certainly the preceding 230-odd pages of that text are as woman-free
as the Icelandic sagas get. The effect of this cluster of women at the end, I
think, is to suggest that Egill has in a sense become one of them—no longer a
man of the public world, but a man *innan stokks*. Viewed in this context, his
composition, on the death of his son(s), of the lament *Sonatorrek* ("Loss of My
Sons")—thought by many the most magnificent poem in the language—takes on
a new dimension. To judge from the extant literature, emotional lamentations
of this woe-is-me sort are very much the business of women in early Scandinavia,
so much so that they seem tantamount to a female industry.[66] Thematically,
metaphorically, and lexically, Egill's poem resembles nothing so much as
Guðrún's lament in the eddic *Hamðismál* and *Guðrúnarhvǫt*,[67] and although his
composition is commonly assumed to be prior, the fact that it is the *only* male-
composed lament of the woe-is-me type in early Scandinavia, and that it is
produced so emphatically *innan stokks* (not only within the house but within the
bedchamber, where he lies mourning) and so specifically in the company of
women (his daughter induces him to compose it, and the audience for its premier
performance consists of "Ásgerðr, Þorgerðr, and the household") leads me to
wonder whether some part of its original pathos did not have to do with the
gendered circumstances of its production.[68] To pose it as a question: is it possible

---

[65] For a new account of emotional expression in Norse literature, see William Ian Miller's forthcoming *Humiliation and Other Essays in Social Discomfort* (Ithaca, N.Y., 1993). On the social place of
aging men, see his *Bloodtaking and Peacemaking*, pp. 207–10.

[66] For a discussion of female lamenting and its role in feud, see my "Hildigunnr's Lament," with
notes.

[67] Common features include (in addition to the characteristic mix of lament and revenge) the
theme of the withering family line and, in that connection, the use of the extremely rare word *þáttr*
(in the meaning "strand," as of a rope); the elegiac conceit of a tree as an image of human growth
and ruin; the "chain-of-woes" construction; the self-pitying woe-is-me tone; the ecstatic "now I die"
conclusion; and the final authorial remarks on the cathartic effects of lamenting. See Ursula Dronke,
The Poetic Edda, 1: *Heroic Poems* (Oxford, 1969), pp. 183–89, and my "Hildigunnr's Lament," pp.
153–62. The "difference" of *Sonatorrek* in the context of Egill's other poetry is often noted. E. O.
G. Turville-Petre, for example, writes that the poem "gives a clear insight into the mind of Egill in
his advancing years, showing him as an affectionate, sensitive, lonely man, and not the ruffianly
bully which he sometimes appears to be in the Saga" (*Scaldic Poetry* [Oxford, 1976], p. 24).

[68] Worth remembering in this connection is the unnamed old man to whom the *Beowulf* poet
compares the old king Hreðel, father of a fratricide (vv. 2441–65). Overcome by grief, and unable
to take revenge, old Hreðel can do no more than the "old man" who "goes to his bed, sings his

that some of *Sonatorrek*'s contemporary force derived from its point of issue on the distaff side and its coding as a "woman's" form?

By way of steadying this suggestion about *Sonatorrek*, let me turn to two proverbs that explicitly link the condition of old men with femaleness. One, which in fact turns on public speech, occurs in a scene in *Hávarðar saga Ísfirðings* in which a woman named Bjargey urges a husband too old for battle to take up the role of whetter. "þat er karlmannligt mál," she moralizes, "at hann, er til engra harðræðanna er forr, at spara þá ekki tunguna at tala þat, er honom mætti verða gagn at" ("It is manly for those unfit for vigorous deeds to be unsparing in their use of the tongue to say those things that may avail").[69] The saying is doubly telling. It acknowledges the equivalence of old men and women, for tongue wielding (whetting, egging) is a conspicuously female activity.[70] But it also acknowledges the commensurability of the tongue and the sword. The homology of physical and verbal dueling is a familiar theme in the literature, cropping up in such phrases as "war of words," "to battle with the voice," "to wound with words," or, to reverse the formulation, "quarrel of swords" (= battle). Saxo's *Gesta Danorum* similarly describes Ericus Disertus (Eiríkr inn mál-spaki or Eric the Eloquent) as an "argument athlete" (*altercationum athleta*) who is as "valorous in tongue as in hand," and Gotwar as a woman for whom "words were weapons," someone who "could not fight" but "found darts in her tongue instead."[71] The tongue may be a lesser weapon, the "sword" of the unsword-worthy, but it is a weapon nonetheless, and one whose effects could be serious indeed (as the legal injunctions against *tunguníð* attest). And like the sword it is less than, the tongue is subject to bold use or cowardly unuse, so that even within the category of unswordworthy persons, conspicuously women and old men, the politics of *hvatr* and *blauðr* play themselves out. "It is *manly*," Bjargey says, for the unswordworthy to use their tongues to make things happen. Better to wield the sword than the tongue, in short, but better to wield the tongue than to wield nothing—in both cases whether one is a man or a woman.

Egill himself states the equation in a pithy half-stanza lamenting the effects of age: "my neck is weak," he says; "I fear falling on my head; my hearing is gone; and *blautr erum bergis fótar borr*."[72] The line in question translates some-

---

cares over (*sorh-leoð*, 'sorrow song'), alone, for the other" and then dies. Again we seem to have a male whose lamentation is precisely the effect of disabled masculinity; the other two funeral-la-menters in *Beowulf* are both women (vv. 1117–18 and 3150–55). Text and translation from Howell D. Chickering, Jr., *Beowulf: A Dual-Language Edition* (Garden City, N.Y., 1977). For an especially useful and bibliographically detailed discussion of elegy and death lament (especially reflexive) in the Germanic tradition, see Joseph Harris, "Elegy in Old English and Old Norse: A Problem in Literary History," in *The Vikings*, ed. R. T. Farrell (London, 1982), pp. 157–64, as well as his "Beowulf's Last Words," *Speculum* 67 (1992), 1–32.

[69] *Hávarðar saga Ísfirðings*, ed. Björn K. Þórólfsson and Guðni Jónsson, ÍF 6 (Reykjavík, 1943), chap. 5.

[70] See Miller, "Choosing the Avenger" and *Bloodtaking and Peacemaking*, pp. 212–14. The syn-onyms *hvetja* and *eggja* mean "whet" in both senses (to sharpen or put an edge on a blade, and to goad or egg on a person).

[71] See my "Germanic Context of the Unferþ Episode," esp. pp. 451–52, for a more complete list and source references.

[72] "Vals hefk vǫfur helsis; / váfallr em ek skalla; / blautr erum bergis fótar / borr, en hlust es þorrin" (*Egils saga*, chap. 85).

thing like: "soft is the bore [= drill bit] of the foot/leg of taste/pleasure," the
bore referring to tongue if one takes *bergis fótar* to mean "head," but to penis
if one takes the kenning to mean "leg or limb of pleasure."[73] If one assumes,
as I do, that the art of the line lies precisely in its duplicity and that *both* meanings
(penis *and* tongue) inhere in it (skaldic verse is nothing if not a poetry of the
double entendre), and if one hears the harmonic "sword" that inevitably sounds
over these two tones (for penises and tongues are repeatedly figured as weapons),[74] and finally if one takes in the sense of effeminacy/femaleness that attaches
to the word *blautr*, "soft" (a word that rhymes both sonically and semantically
with *blauðr*), one has in this five-word verse the full chord: when not only one's
sword and penis go limp but also one's tongue, life is pretty much over. This
is not the first we have heard of Egill's tongue, of course. *Sonatorrek* itself opens
with a complaint about the difficulty of its erection ("Mjǫk erum tregt / tungu
at hrœra / eðr loptvæi / ljóðpundara"—"It is very hard for me to stir my tongue
or the steel-yard of the song-weigher");[75] and although there is no question of
an overt sexual or martial meaning here, the wider system of tongue/sword/
penis correspondences invites us to just such associations, which serve in turn
to confirm our sense that this poem stems from a point very far down the gender
scale—a point at which sword and penis have given way to the tongue, and even
the tongue may not be up to the task. (The one-sex reasoning behind the sword/
penis/tongue construction, and the value of the categories relative to one another, could hardly be clearer. Worth remembering, on the distaff side, is the
figure used to characterize the maiden warrior Hervör's shift from the female
to the male role: she trades the needle for the sword.)[76] Egill's *Sonatorrek* sounds
like a female lament, in short, because in some deep cultural sense it *is* one.

The second proverb is untranslatable, and in its untranslatability is crystallized
the problem on which this essay turns. It occurs in *Hrafnkels saga* and is invoked
by a serving woman in an effort to rouse Hrafnkell from bed as enemies approach
the farm: "Svá ergisk hverr sem eldisk"—"Everyone becomes *argr* who [or: as

---

[73] See Noreen, "Studier i västnordisk diktning" (above, n. 39), pp. 35–36; and *Egils saga*, p. 294,
note on stanza 58. Roberta Frank points out that the duplicitous reading has medieval authority,
in the "Third Grammatical Treatise" of Óláfr hvítaskáld, who observes that Egill's *bergis fótar borr*
works both as a penis kenning and a tongue kenning (*Old Norse Court Poetry: The Dróttkvætt Stanza*
[Ithaca, N.Y., 1978], p. 162). The author of the "head" interpretation of *bergifótr* is, of course,
Finnur Jónsson, who thought it "en af Egils dristige kenningar" (*Lexicon poeticum* [Copenhagen,
1931; repr. 1966]). For other examples of such wordplay, see Kari Ellen Gade, "Penile Puns:
Personal Names and Phallic Symbols in Skaldic Poetry," *Essays in Medieval Studies: Proceedings of
the Illinois Medieval Association* 6 (1989), 57–67.

[74] "Vápn þat er stendr milli fóta manna heitir suerð" ("That weapon which stands between a
man's legs is called a sword"), Snorri declares (*Snorra-Edda*, ed. Rasmus Rask [Stockholm, 1818],
p. 232, line 19). For literary examples and a discussion of the sword/penis figure, see Meulengracht
Sørensen, *Unmanly Man*, pp. 45–78, and Clunies Ross, "Hildr's Ring." As for the tongue: "Tvnga
er opt kavllvð sverþ mals e(ða) mvnz" ("Tongue is often called sword of speech or of mouth," *Edda
Snorra Sturlusonar*, p. 191). Consider, for example, *góma sverð* ("sword of the gums") and *orðvápn*
("word-weapon"); see Rudolf Meissner, *Die Kenningar der Skalden: Ein Beitrag zur skaldischen Poetik*
(Bonn and Leipzig, 1921; repr. Hildesheim, etc., 1984), pp. 133–34.

[75] Text and translation from Turville-Petre, *Scaldic Poetry*, pp. 28–29.

[76] *Saga Heiðreks ins vitra/The Saga of King Heiðrek the Wise*, trans. and ed. Christopher Tolkien
(London, 1960), p. 10.

he/she] gets older."[77] Like the entry under *blauðr*, Cleasby-Vigfusson's entry under *argr* (the banned "a" word of the laws) tries to solve the problem by distinguishing a literal meaning ("emasculate," "effeminate") from a figurative one ("wretch," "craven," "coward"). If we elect the latter, we get something along the lines of "Sooner or later, we all end up cowardly" (E. V. Gordon) or "The older the man, the feebler" (Hermann Pálsson), a choice that occludes the sense of gendered degradation that the term *argr* carries with it.[78] If we elect the former, we get something like "Sooner or later, we all end up effeminate." It is clear why translators would prefer "cowardly" here, for "effeminate" jolts: what can it mean if every man eventually becomes it, and do women become it, too? I would argue that (although neither choice is good) "effeminate" is preferable for two reasons: because it captures so succinctly the default social partnership of old men and typical women, and because it reveals in no uncertain terms that, for all its associations with the female body, the word *argr* (*ergi, ergjask, ragr*, etc.) finally knows no sex. Again, the problem is that Modern English has no language for a system in which the operative social binary *looks* sexual (i.e., is figured in terms of male and female bodies) but is in practice *not* sexual, that is to say, neither exclusively nor decisively based on biological difference (or for that matter *any* inborn characteristic, with the presumable exception of natal defects). What the proverb "Svá eldisk hverr sem eldisk" boils down to is that sooner or later, all of us end up alike in our softness—regardless of our past and regardless of our sex.

It is beyond the scope of this already too synthetic essay to probe the impact on the northern periphery of "medievalization" (the conversion to Christianity and the adoption of European social forms), but by way of ending let me hazard some general propositions. The documentary sources, dating as they do from the Christian period, are notoriously slippery, but no reader of them can escape the impression that the new order entailed a radical remapping of gender in the north. More particularly, one has the impression that femaleness became more sharply defined and contained (the emergence of women-only religious orders is symptomatic of the new sensibility), and it seems indisputably the case that as Norse culture assimilated notions of weeping monks and fainting knights, "masculinity" was rezoned, as it were, into territories previously occupied by "effeminacy" (and other category B traits). (This expansion of the masculine was presumably predicated on the fixing of the female and her relocation at a safe distance.) It may be, as Laqueur argues on the basis of the medical tradition, that the one-sex model of sexual difference did not fully yield to a two-sex one until the late eighteenth century with the invention of a separate femaleness with its own organs and characteristics, but that does not mean that the one-sex era was monolithic or static or that the two-sex model did not have its

---

[77] *Hrafnkels saga*, in *Austfirðinga sǫgur*, ed. Jón Jóhannesson, ÍF 11 (Reykjavík, 1950), chap. 8. The word *ergisk* is the middle-voice verbal form of the adjective *argr* ("to become *argr*"). The word *hverr*, "everyone," is a masculine pronoun usable for a male entity or for the universal person.

[78] E. V. Gordon, *An Introduction to Old Norse* (Oxford, 1927; 2nd ed. rev. by A. R. Taylor, 1957), p. 342 (under *ergjask*); and Hermann Pálsson, trans., *Hrafnkel's Saga and Other Stories* (Harmondsworth, Middlesex), chap. 17.

conceptual harbingers. In the northern world, at least, the social organization of Christian Europe must have been perceived as entailing a profoundly different sex-gender system—one that despite its own stories of real and imagined gender crossings (particularly within religious discourse) drew a line of unprecedented firmness between male and female bodies and natures. The new dispensation would by the same token appear to have blurred the line between able-bodied men and aging men: the portrait of Njáll in that most Christian of sagas seems a conscious attempt to recuperate for Christian patriarchy a man under the old order dismissable by virtue of age, and indeed openly accused of effeminacy by his pagan neighbors. (Egill, on the other hand, born just two decades earlier and hence dead before the conversion, can be construed by his medieval biographer as having missed out.) What I am suggesting is that there are one-sex systems and one-sex systems; that early northern Europe "lived" a one-sex social logic, a one-gender model, to a degree unparalleled elsewhere in the west; and that the medievalization of the north entailed a shift of revolutionary proportions—a shift in the direction of two-sex thinking, and one therefore in kind not unlike the shift Laqueur claims for Europe in general eight hundred years later.[79]

It should by now be clear that the problems of translation with which this essay has been preoccupied are not just unrelated lexical glitches, but cognate symptoms of a larger problem of conceptual translation. Whether the early Scandinavian model is as I have outlined it here—I am aware of having barely scratched the surface—is not clear. What is clear is that their system and ours do not line up and that the mismatch is especially obvious, and especially alien, where women and the feminine are concerned. From the outset, scholars have speculated on what unusual notion of womanhood might account for such startlingly strong female figures in a culture that seems otherwise to hold femaleness in such contempt. (It is a speculation that extends all the way back to Tacitus.) I mean in this essay to turn the question inside out and ask whether the paradox—extraordinary women, contempt for femaleness—may not have more to do with the virtual absence of *any* notion of "womanhood" than it does with the existence of some more spacious or flexible notion than our own. The evidence points, I think, to a one-sex, one-gender model with a vengeance— one that plays out in the rawest and most extreme terms a scheme of sexual

---

[79] That the older system did not die at once, but lived in odd ways well into the Christian era, is suggested by, for example, the anomalous practice of priest marriage in Iceland, a practice that suggests the tenacity not only of the clan system but also of certain pre-Christian notions of masculinity. Writes Miller, "Sexuality and marriage were a part of the world of manly honor and no one thought to mention that divinity and dalliance need be sundered until the episcopate of Thorlak Thorhallson (1178–93). Thorlak zealously attempted to enforce ecclesiastical strictures dealing with sexual practices, but even he did not tackle clerical celibacy, confining himself instead to separating priests and spouses who had married within the prohibited degres . . . or who kept concubines in addition to their wives" (*Bloodtaking and Peacemaking*, pp. 37–38; see also his bibliographic references). Consider, too, such historical details as the one recorded in *Jóns saga helga* to the effect that the cathedral school at Hólar in the year 1110 saw fit not only to admit a girl, one Ingunn, but to permit her to tutor her fellow pupils in Latin (*Jóns saga helga*, chap. 27, in *Byskupa sögur*, ed. Guðni Jónsson [Reykjavík, 1948; 2nd ed. Akureyri, 1953], 2:43, 153.

difference that at the level of the body knows only the male and at the level of social behavior, only the effeminate, or emasculate, or impotent. The case could be made, particularly on the basis of the mythic narratives, that Norse femaleness was a more complicated business than Laqueur's model would have it,[80] but the general notion, that sexual difference used to be less a wall than a permeable membrane, has a great deal of explanatory force in a world in which a physical woman could become a social man, a physical man could (and sooner or later did) become a social woman, and the originary god, Óðinn himself, played both sides of the street.

[80] Especially important in this connection is the work of Clunies Ross, especially "An Interpretation of the Myth of Þórr's Encounter with Geirrøðr and His Daughters." See also Borovsky, "Male Fears, Female Threats." That the bodies in question are female (e.g., menstruating giantesses) is clear. What is less clear is what femaleness means in a world in which (at least in the learned tradition) the female body and its fluids were regarded as deformations of male ones (e.g., in which menstrual fluid was construed as cooled-down semen); see Laqueur, *Making Sex*, esp. pp. 35–43.

Carol J. Clover is Professor of Scandinavian and Rhetoric at the University of California, Berkeley, CA 94720.

Genders, Bodies, Borders:
Technologies of the Visible

By Kathleen Biddick

HISTORY AS A PROBLEM OF WOMEN'S HISTORY

As the senses of sight and touch separated with the industrial mapping of the body in the nineteenth century, the visible and the visualized aligned themselves in medical, scientific, and sexological discourses; even history claimed to make the past "visible." The criteria of the visible came to mark modernity. Cultural studies of visualization technologies help us to understand history itself as sign of the modern and to join its desires for the visible to those desires for spectacle produced among observers of visualizing media (such as the diorama, photography, moving pictures) in the late nineteenth and early twentieth centuries.[1]

Over the past twenty years women's history has proclaimed its desire to render historical women visible. If women's history acknowledges (as I believe a discursive critique of history requires us to) that such a desire is implicated in the knowledge-power of visualization technologies, then it produces a dilemma for itself. The rich interest in writing a history of medieval women mystics can serve as an example of this. Much recent work in medieval women's history has focused on women mystics in an avowed effort to rewrite a traditional historiography whose contempt and fear of these women's bodily practices had rendered them "invisible." Such studies have tended to take for granted its organizing category "medieval women mystics" without questioning how its terms came to be generated and concatenated. An understanding of how the word "mystic" emerged in usage from the adjective "mystical" suggests, in fact, a contest over the very engendering of what counts as visible at different historical moments.[2] The engendering of the visible thus becomes a historical problem for women's history.

This essay accepts the dilemma that the desire to make historical women visible is both an effect of modern visualizing technologies and also a possibility for

---

[1] This first citation gestures towards an abundant and discursive literature on modernity and its visualizations. My practice here and throughout is to cite those works which have been most important in guiding my thoughts for this essay. For a critique of history as a sign of the modern see Nicholas B. Dirks, "History as a Sign of the Modern," *Public Culture* 2 (1990), 25–32; also Jonathan Crary, *Techniques of the Observer: On Vision and Modernity in the Nineteenth Century* (Cambridge, Mass., 1990); Barbara Duden, *The Woman beneath the Skin: A Doctor's Patients in Eighteenth-Century Germany* (Cambridge, Mass., 1991); Bruno Latour, "Visualization and Cognition," in *Knowledge and Society* 6 (1986), 1–40; Michel Foucault, "The Political Technology of Individuals," in *Technologies of the Self: A Seminar with Michel Foucault*, ed. L. Martin, H. Gutman, and P. Hutton (London, 1988); Jane Gallop, *Thinking through the Body* (New York, 1988); Barbara Maria Stafford, *Body Criticism: Imagining the Unseen in Enlightenment Art and Medicine* (Cambridge, Mass., 1991).

[2] Michel de Certeau, "The New Science," in his *Mystic Fable*, trans. Michael B. Smith (Chicago, 1992), pp. 79–112.

their resignification. It works with the dilemma by articulating it through a reading of an important book that has become emblematic both within and beyond medieval studies, *Holy Feast and Holy Fast: The Religious Significance of Food to Medieval Women* by Caroline Walker Bynum.[3] My reading is an "infra-reflexive" one, meaning that it seeks to display the work of achieving a narrative of visibility at the same time that it dislocates that work to other locations: the past into the present and contemporary academic authority into the past. Such a reading distributes itself discursively—in this case—across medieval history, contemporary critical theories, especially feminist and postcolonial, and cultural studies of visualization.[4]

Since its publication in 1987 *Holy Feast and Holy Fast* has become a required text in courses on medieval women's history and often appears as the one medieval selection in surveys of gender studies. This book, about "woman as body and as food," can be read for problems concerning the production of gendered knowledge in history today. How can we write these histories such that in making women "visible" we do not blind ourselves to the historical processes that defined, redefined, and engendered the status of the visible and the invisible?

The rhetoric of the text can provide clues to its own engendering, to the historical processes it renders invisible in order to make some category visible. I argue that in making medieval women mystics visible, the rhetoric of *Holy Feast and Holy Fast* renders invisible the problems of engendering the medieval category of *Christianitas*. The engendering of both categories was fearfully connected, and that connection needs to be rearticulated; otherwise, making medieval women mystics visible simply reproduces Europe as a category in its medieval guise of *Christianitas*: "No Europeanist should ignore the once and future global production of 'Europe'."[5]

---

[3] The book is the first in the series The New Historicism: Studies in Cultural Poetics (Berkeley, Los Angeles, and London, 1987). (I will refer to *Holy Feast and Holy Fast* as *HFHF* in parenthetical citations.) Readers should please note that I occasionally use the word "gender" in the plural in this article. This intended inconsistency invites us to think of gender as both a performed and a historically constrained construction exceeding the binary of sexual difference as it has been dominantly defined. If we allow for only two genders, we displace sexual difference into a discussion of gender. My reading in this essay concentrates on an engendering of historiography. A future reading is needed to untangle the sexualizing of historiography. The two fields are not commensurate; the ways they intersect cannot be known in advance.

[4] My ways of reading are influenced by Homi K. Bhabha, "Postcolonial Authority and Postmodern Guilt," in *Cultural Studies*, ed. Lawrence Grossberg, Cary Nelson, and Paula Treichler (New York, 1992), pp. 56–68; Jonathan Dollimore, *Sexual Dissidence: Augustine to Wilde, Freud to Foucault* (Oxford, 1991); Donna Haraway, "Reading Buchi Emecheta: Contests for 'Women's Experience' in Women's Studies," in her *Simians, Cyborgs, and Women: The Reinvention of Nature* (New York, 1991), pp. 109–26; Bruno Latour, "The Politics of Explanation: An Alternative," in *Knowledge and Reflexivity: New Frontiers in the Sociology of Knowledge*, ed. Steve Woolgar (Beverly Hills, Calif., 1988), pp. 155–77; Gayatri Chakravorty Spivak, "A Literary Representation of the Subaltern: A Woman's Text from the Third World," in her *In Other Worlds: Essays in Cultural Politics* (New York, 1987), pp. 241–68.

[5] Gayatri Chakravorty Spivak, "French Feminism Revisited: Ethics and Politics," in *Feminists Theorize the Political*, ed. Judith Butler and Joan W. Scott (New York, 1992), p. 58. Medieval historians

CULTURAL CONCEPTS AND THE GENDER OF NARRATIVES

Bynum elaborates an anthropology of symbol and ritual and a social psychology of sexual development in order to explore the bodily practices, especially food practices, of medieval women mystics.[6] Only a single reference to works critical of ahistorical and essentialist aspects of social-psychological theories of sexual development gives a hint of the contest over gender in *Holy Feast and Holy Fast*.[7] Bynum largely dismisses feminist scholarship in the first chapter as "presentist" and evades a feminist concern (already in evidence by the mid-1980s) that the humanities have produced gendered forms of knowledge. Bynum claims instead a methodology with guaranteed access to medieval women's experience: "the women themselves . . . generate questions as well as answers" (*HFHF*, p. 30).[8] There is now increasing question—and not only among fem-

---

have also urged feminist historians to beware of another metanarrative of European history: "progress"; see Susan Mosher Stuard, "The Chase after Theory: Considering Medieval Women," *Gender and History* 4 (1992), 135–46; Judith M. Bennett, "Medieval Women, Modern Women: Across the Great Divide," in *Culture and History, 1350–1600: Essays on English Communities, Identities and Writing*, ed. David Aers (London, 1992), pp. 147–75. For a discussion of the difficulties of writing history without Europe as a referent see Dipesh Chakrabarty, "Postcoloniality and the Artifice of History: Who Speaks for 'Indian' Pasts?" *Representations* 37 (Winter 1992), 1–26. For a series of suggestive contemporary studies that intertwine the imagination of Europe with norms of bodily and sexual behavior see *Nationalisms and Sexualities*, ed. Andrew Parker, Mary Russo, Doris Sommer, and Patricia Yaeger (New York, 1992). "Postoriental" and "postcolonial" theory are not monolithic and are also subject to critique; see a recent issue of *Social Text*, 31–32 (1992), and an exchange in *Comparative Studies in Society and History* 34/1 (1992).

[6] Bynum relies on the following works in social psychology: Nancy Chodorow, *The Reproduction of Mothering: Psychoanalysis and the Sociology of Gender* (Berkeley, 1978), and Carol Gilligan, *In a Different Voice: Psychological Theory and Women's Development* (Cambridge, Mass., 1982).

[7] Bynum notes an article by Joan W. Scott, "Gender: A Useful Category of Historical Analysis," *American Historical Review* 91 (1986), in n. 29 to chap. 10, p. 416. The debate over essentialism in critical feminist theory of the 1980s cannot be reduced to any simple description, since readings of essentialism are historicized not only by gender but by race, class, and the construction of homosexuality. Teresa de Lauretis wisely notes that the debate itself within feminism articulates "difference in the feminist conception of woman, women, world." See her essay "The Essence of the Triangle, or Taking the Risk of Essentialism Seriously: Feminist Theory in Italy, the U.S., and Britain," *differences* 1 (1989), 3–58, citation from p. 3. Essentialist and antiessentialist positions coconstruct each other, as Dollimore shows in *Sexual Dissidence*. The African-American theorist bell hooks joins a critique of essentialism and race in *Yearning: Race, Gender and Cultural Politics* (Boston, 1990); Donna Haraway usefully summarizes different historical positions in the essentialism debate in her essay " 'Gender' for a Marxist Dictionary: The Sexual Politics of a Word," in her collection *Simians, Cyborgs and Women*, pp. 127–48.

[8] Bynum does mention the theoretical work of Luce Irigaray and Julia Kristeva sympathetically in nn. 35 and 41, pp. 416–17, after prefacing her remarks that "French feminist writing has been determinedly atheistical. . . ." For a study that brings Bynum and Kristeva together and extends them critically, see Karma Lochrie, *Margery Kempe and Translations of the Flesh* (Philadelphia, 1991). Important work criticizing the gendered production of knowledge was available when Bynum wrote *Holy Feast and Holy Fast*. She cites Scott's article "Gender," in which Scott cautioned historians that the production of historical knowledge was itself gendered and calls for an alliance between women's history and critical theory to begin to question how rhetorical practices in history used gender as a resource and produced gender as an effect: "it requires analysis not only of the relations between male and female experience in the past but also the connection between past history and current

inists—about whether it is possible to capture the experience of people of the past in this way.[9] Concern over the use of experience as well as the use of gender and race to organize disciplinary knowledge has only heightened since the mid-1980s.

Over the past two decades feminists have worked to formulate critical ways of understanding both historical and contemporary constructions of gender; such tools facilitate insights into ways in which notions of gender implicit in *Holy Feast and Holy Fast* rhetorically organize the text.[10] Such tools also create possibilities for writing histories of medieval gender capable of historicizing gender in *relation* to other engendered categories given as "natural" in medieval discourses and hitherto taken for granted by historians. Critical studies of medieval gender would use these tools to work simultaneously as histories of other foundational categories imagined in the invention of Europe, especially "Christendom" (*Christianitas*), Corpus Christi, and the Jew (as an anti-Semitic category), as they defined and redefined relations of the masculine and feminine.[11]

---

historical practice.... How does gender give meaning to the organization and perception of historical knowledge?" (p. 1055). Perhaps the most famous and widely known critique of the gendered production of knowledge dating to the period of the writing and publication of *Holy Feast and Holy Fast* would be Evelyn Fox Keller, *Reflections on Gender and Science* (New Haven, 1985).

[9] For different aspects of this debate see recent issues (1991) of *Critical Inquiry*; especially relevant is Joan W. Scott, "The Evidence of Experience," *Critical Inquiry* 17 (Summer 1991), 773–97. Dominick LaCapra comments on the problem of "voices"—past and present—in essays collected in his *History and Criticism* (Ithaca, N.Y., 1985); I have found these words of caution very helpful: "The archive as fetish is a literal substitute for the 'reality' of the past which is 'always already' lost for the historian. When it is fetishized, the archive is more than the repository of traces of the past which may be used in its inferential reconstruction. It is a stand-in for the past that brings the mystified experience of the thing itself—an experience that is always open to question when one deals with writing and other inscriptions" (p. 92). Recent critical work on postorientalist history deeply troubles conventional uses of "experience" as a historical category: Gyan Prakash, "Can the 'Subaltern' Ride? A Reply to O'Hanlon and Washbrook," *Comparative Studies in Society and History* 34 (1992), 168–84; Gayatri Chakravorty Spivak, "The Rani of Sirmur: An Essay in Reading the Archives," *History and Theory* 24 (1985), 247–72; Michel de Certeau, *The Writing of History* (New York, 1988).

[10] During the mid-1980s scholars of color and gay scholars called upon academic feminism to grapple with its differences (racial, sexual, class). The citations can only gesture toward the literature that challenged academic feminism and women's history in the mid-1980s as *Holy Feast and Holy Fast* went to press. For historical crosshatching of the debates see Jane Gallop, *Around 1981: Academic Feminist Literary Theory* (New York, 1992). My citations are selective, since this essay is not intended as a review of medieval women's history or of critical feminist theory. For an example of the growing critique of academic feminism for its racism see *This Bridge Called My Back: Writings by Radical Women of Color*, ed. Cherríe Moraga and Gloria Anzaldúa (New York, 1983)—awarded the Before Columbus Foundation American Book award in 1986; for an articulation of feminist theory in an internationalist frame, another pressing concern of the 1980s, see Spivak, *In Other Worlds* (for a recent criticism of a widely read essay in the Spivak anthology see Silvia Tandeciarz, "Reading Gayatri Spivak's 'French Feminism in an International Frame': A Problem of Theory," *Genders* 10 [Spring 1991], 75–91). The critique of the presumption of heterosexuality's organization of theories of sexual difference grew more vocal in the mid-1980s; for example, see Teresa de Lauretis, "Feminist Studies/Critical Studies: Issues, Terms and Contexts," *Feminist Studies/Critical Studies*, ed. de Lauretis (Bloomington, 1986), pp. 1–19; see also de Lauretis, "The Female Body and Heterosexual Presumption," *Semiotica* 67 (1987), 257–59.

[11] In spite of complex and subtle debates over medieval Christendom, scholars have not questioned

To neglect the intersections of gender and ethnic identities with the historical formation of other medieval foundational categories is to run the risk of continuing to write histories of gender that inadvertently use gender and ethnic identities as a resource for producing "Europe" as the referent of history.

At this juncture I need to elaborate upon my understanding of gender as it will come into play in my reading of *Holy Feast and Holy Fast*. I use gender as a theory of borders that enables us to talk about the historical construction and maintenance of sexual boundaries, both intra- and intercorporeal, through powerful historical processes of repetition and containment. Gendered notions of both the topography and the sex of corporeal interiority and exteriority have varied historically (we need only think of the variations of medieval Galenism), as have the ways in which genders are distributed across discourses, institutions, cultures, or any such unitary, bounded categories invented by historical subjects to contain gender and naturalize it. Theories of gender, therefore, need to be histories simultaneously of corporeal interiority and of exteriority: sex, flesh, body, race, nature, discourse, and culture. It is not possible to write a history of gender that takes any of these categories as given in advance, assumed as "natural"; otherwise the study would end up reinscribing the asymmetries and/ or hierarchies of historical genders rather than understanding how gender is a historically variable effect of maintaining unitary categories for the purposes of "naturalizing" sexual difference. To subject the body and sex to critique does not negate them; rather it opens them up as sites of historical and political debate.[12]

Such a critical understanding of gender can help us to understand how foundational categories implicit in *Holy Feast and Holy Fast*, especially "culture" and "Christendom," work to prevent the text both from rhetorically articulating identity and difference, especially with regard to its metaphor of the maternal, and from acknowledging the interplay of transference and empathy between

---

the coconstruction of this category with medieval genders. For a synthetic discussion of how medieval Europeans used the word "Christendom" (*Christianitas*) see John Van Engen, "The Christian Middle Ages as an Historiographical Problem," *American Historical Review* 91 (1986), 519–52. Van Engen notes that the scholar Raoul Manselli traced the origin of the concept to a "self-conscious, defensive reaction to Islam" (p. 539), but he drops the issue of the mutual construction of Islam, Judaism, and Christendom in the article. The failure to look at these contructions *relationally* in an article self-conscious of complexity within Christendom shows the abiding cultural domination of a unitary notion of this category. We can look to theoretical tools developed by African-American feminist theorists, notably Hortense Spillers, to help us to understand the historical ways in which cultural wholes are engendered through the exclusion and exteriorizing of the "other(s)" which exist outside, but in relation to, a political and cultural interior. Through her study of the historical construction of gender in the juridical world of American slavery, Spillers has conceptualized the problem of discontinuous genders, that is, genders exterior to, but in relation with, dominant juridical-kinship systems. Such systems typically conserve a notion of interiority, which is a notion of purity, by constructing a racial exterior. That exterior is also the cultural space where other excluded cultural "others" get located. Medievalists can usefully learn from this work and begin studying the problem of discontinuities of European genders produced juridically by medieval societies: Hortense J. Spillers, "Mama's Baby, Papa's Maybe: An American Grammar Book," *Diacritics* 17 (1987).

[12] Judith Butler, "Contingent Foundations: Feminism and the Question of the 'Postmodern,' " in *Feminists Theorize the Political*, pp. 3–21.

historian, historical subjects, and feminist theory.[13] Bynum questions and revises the cultural anthropology of Victor Turner in her study, but she takes for granted his structurally inspired and implicitly foundational conception of culture.[14] A history of the structuralist influence on the conception of culture in anthropology is a long and complex one; here suffice it to say that this conception, which is both historical and gendered, has come to mean something natural: "a coherent *body* that lives and dies. Culture is enduring, traditional, structural (rather than contingent, syncretic, historical). Culture is a process of ordering, not of disruption."[15]

Such a theory of culture assumes boundaries rather than questions their historical formation. It tends to posit culture as an organic plenitude and to analyze it as a bounded object, thereby reinforcing unexamined notions of inside and outside. The constitution of such a bounded object of study (whatever its internal complexity) then requires a complementary conception of liminality (developed by Turner) as a process for mediating the inside and outside. Conceived as such, this notion of culture has avoided the study of the visualization processes historically at work in the production of the conception of culture as well as analysis of historical relations *between* the imaginary wholes of such posited cultures. The theory of liminality thus works to mystify the problems of the historical construction of interiority and exteriority. In a close reading of Turner's famous essay on Ndembu shamans, Michael Taussig has shown how its rhetoric engages liminality, not only in the narrative description of shamanistic practices, but in the overall flow of argument as well. Such liminal rhetoric, rather than marking a gap or tension between the magic under study and the act of writing, appropriates Ndembu magic in the service of the European observer.[16] Turner thus writes as a shaman, and his ethnography becomes a form of magic.

[13] For a discussion of the problems of "empathy" and "transference" see LaCapra, "Is Everyone a *Mentalité* Case? Transference and the 'Culture' Concept," in *History and Criticism*, pp. 71–94: "Transference implies that the considerations at issue in the object of study are always repeated with variations—or find their displaced analogues—in one's account of it, and transference is as much denied by an assertion of the total difference of the past as by its total identification with one's own 'self' or 'culture' " (p. 72).

[14] In *Holy Feast and Holy Fast*, p. 229, Bynum cites Victor Turner and her earlier article on his work, "Women's Stories, Women's Symbols: A Critique of Victor Turner's Theory of Liminality," in *Anthropology and the Study of Religion*, ed. Frank Reynolds and Robert Moore (Chicago, 1984); reprinted in her *Fragmentation and Redemption: Essays on Gender and the Human Body in Medieval Religion* (New York, 1991), pp. 27–51. The work of Victor Turner has come in for some criticism in recent literature on ethnographic writing and dominant/dominating Western modes of representation. For some mild criticism, see James Clifford, *The Predicament of Culture: Twentieth Century Ethnography, Literature and Art* (Cambridge, Mass., 1990), pp. 48–49, 52, 94. Michael Taussig is more critical of Turner as a proponent of a romantic notion of the symbol; see his "Homesickness & Dada," in *Nervous System* (New York, 1992), pp. 149–82; and his *Shamanism, Colonialism, and the Wild Man: A Study in Terror and Healing* (Chicago, 1987), pp. 441–42.

[15] See Clifford, *The Predicament of Culture*, p. 235. This historical conception of culture is, of course, under critique. Such criticism is the purpose of *The Predicament of Culture*; also important is Edward W. Said, "Representing the Colonized: Anthropology's Interlocutors," *Critical Inquiry* 15 (Winter 1989), 205–25.

[16] Taussig, "Homesickness," p. 151: "there is thus an intentional or unintentional usage of Frazer's

Once an anthropologist writes himself as a shaman, Taussig has observed, a rhetorical collapse usually occurs between the participant-observer (the anthropologist) and the subject-informant (the shaman): "the subject addressed and the addressing of the subject become one."[17] This textual conflation of anthropologist and shaman punctuates a problem of marking difference in ethnographies informed by a bounded, unitary conception of culture. These ethnographies have promoted a kind of autocannibalism, in which representation consumes difference rather than producing it, in order to conserve the "primitive," grounded usually on the body of the female "primitive" (for the anthropologist) or the past (for the historian) as an imaginary, bounded, coherent entity.[18] "Synchronous, bounded but contiguous, and representational"—this string of adjectives, coupled with the metaphor of culture as a body, can be exchanged, uncannily, with dominant representations of the maternal today.[19]

Law of Sympathy, a magical usage, not only in the actual rite itself, but in its representations, by the anthropologist-writer mimetically engaging the flow of events described with the flow of his theoretical argument, to the benefit and empowerment of the latter. Not the least impressive about this magical mimesis is that instead of obviously magicalizing the connectedness that holds the argument together, it naturalizes those connections." This critique by Taussig is not a "modernist" one which denies an aspect of play or carnival in writing; rather it insists that such play, carnival, rely on the marking of the gap.

[17] Taussig, "Homesickness," p. 151.

[18] In an analysis of the rhetoric of a famous essay on symbols by Lévi-Strauss, in which he writes, among other things, that "the shaman provides the sick woman with a *language*, by means of which unexpressed and otherwise inexpressible psychic states can be immediately expressed," Taussig has demonstrated how the *anthropologist* provides the shaman with a language in order to give birth to a structure which authorizes the anthropologist: Claude Lévi-Strauss, "The Effectiveness of Symbols," in his *Structural Anthropology*, trans. Claire Jacobson and Brooke Grundfest Schoepf (New York, 1963), p. 198. This essay, dedicated to Raymond de Saussure, first appeared in 1949 in *Revue de l'histoire des religions* 135 (1949), 5–27. Taussig uses this citation in "Homesickness," p. 168. My analysis follows Taussig closely here. My criticisms of the cultural concept are situated in an extended literature of the postorientalist critique of culture, which views culture as a historically essentialized notion and would encourage instead a refiguring of the concept: "thus to see Others not as ontologically given but as historically constituted would be to erode the exclusivist biases we so often ascribe to cultures, our own not the least. Cultures may then be represented as zones of control or abandonment, of recollection and forgetting, of force of dependence, of exclusiveness of sharing . . . ," cited from Said, "Representing the Colonized," p. 255. This criticism of the conception of culture is also influenced by the following works: de Certeau, *The Writing of History*; Robert Young, *White Mythologies: Writing History and the West* (New York, 1990); Homi Bhabha, ed., *Nation and Narration* (New York, 1990); Dirks, "History as a Sign of the Modern," pp. 25–32; Timothy Mitchell, "Everyday Metaphors of Power," *Theory and Society* 19 (1990), 545–77, and his *Colonising Egypt* (New York, 1988).

[19] I can cite no synthetic reference for the recent history of the critical studies of representations of fantasies of the maternal and theories of such fantasies. Judith Butler, *Gender Trouble: Feminism and the Subversion of Identity* (New York, 1990), and Drucilla Cornell, *Beyond Accommodation: Ethical Feminism, Deconstruction, and the Law* (New York, 1991), both provide useful critiques of some chief theorists of the maternal, ranging from the social psychology school (Chodorow) to Lacanian-influenced theory (Kristeva). Kaja Silverman offers a study of how fantasies of the maternal are staged in films in her *Acoustic Mirror: The Female Voice in Psychoanalysis and Cinema* (Bloomington, 1988); see also Mary Ann Doane, "Technophilia: Technology, Representation, and the Feminine," in *Body/Politics: Women and the Discourse of Science*, ed. Mary Jacobus, Evelyn Fox Keller, and Sally Shuttleworth (New York, 1990), pp. 163–76. The politics of rethinking the maternal is urgent, since

The rhetorical problems attached to such structuralist conceptions of culture trouble *Holy Feast and Holy Fast*. Bynum transfers Turner's anthropology to history, and in so doing, challenges his neglect of gender. She corrects Turner by adding women to his theory of liminality but fails to question the ahistorical frame of a cultural theory that could neglect gender so easily in the first place. By simply adding on to the frame without questioning it, Bynum encounters rhetorical problems similar to those already discussed for Turner. Just as in Turner's work, readers of *Holy Feast and Holy Fast* encounter the rhetorical collapse of the subject addressed and the addressing of the subject. The collapse occurs most dramatically in Bynum's staging of the voices of female medieval mystics. The cultural unity in her study is not the "primitive," such as Turner's Ndembu, but a "past," that is, medieval Christendom. To maintain this conception of cultural unity, a typical symptom of structuralism, Bynum must be careful to distance that past from the present. She attacks "presentism" (*HFHF*, p. 30; the statement of historical problems in terms of issues of pressing modern concerns) both in the introduction to the book and within its chapters.

The "subject addressed and the addressing of the subject" collapses most markedly in chapter 5, which is devoted to food in the writings of women mystics. This chapter first strikes a distance from "modern sensibilities" (*HFHF*, p. 152) that would read erotic metaphors in the writings of women mystics. According to Bynum, readers must listen to the "voices" (*HFHF*, p. 152) of these medieval women and not to their own voices. Once Bynum has established this distance in the opening pages of the chapter, she then shifts to "we," a we of historian and reader. The prose preserves the "we" even when it stages the threat of a "modern" interpretation: "Her [Hadewijch's] account of this meeting with God reads like a description of sexual orgasm (and it is only our modern sensibility that makes the suggestion a shocking one)" (*HFHF*, p. 156). As the chapter progresses, the "we" comes to include the historical subjects as well. Prose circumscribes the historian, the reader, and the mystic as a "we": "Thus, to Hadewijch, the soul should strive not so much to rest in satiety as to suffer a deeper hunger beyond filling. For the truest satiety is the pain of desire; the truest repose is the horror of God's power. And all we attain—fullness or hunger—is the gift of Love" (*HFHF*, p. 159).

Similar rhetorical devices are used to craft the story of Catherine of Genoa in the same chapter. Bynum chastises scholars who would wish to organize her biography "around turning points and into neat stages" (*HFHF*, p. 181), that is, according to stereotyped tropes of masculine moral development. Bynum then relates this important methodological issue in reading women's biographies to a critique of "presentism." By attaching a methodological concern to a critique of presentism, Bynum overdetermines it, but in so doing she manages to strike the distance needed between past and present. The distance, once taken, enables the "we" of the historian and reader to reassert itself. Collapse into the historical subject ensues: "Desire for God is hunger—insatiable hunger. The

_____

fantasies of the maternal produce specific historical bodies as sites of struggle: World Health Organization, *Maternal Mortality Rates: A Tabulation of Available Information* (Geneva, 1986).

food that is God and the food that is neighbor are thus the nourishment we crave, inebriated yet unfilled" (*HFHF*, p. 183).

The sharp divisions of past and present required by the structuralist rhetoric of *Holy Feast and Holy Fast* confront Bynum with the conundrum of establishing some means of relating to historical materials. A structuralist-like approach solves the dilemma by essentializing some human essence, in the case of *Holy Feast and Holy Fast*, "women" and "experience." Because a structuralist rhetoric has precluded any historical connection of the present to the past, Bynum uses the maternal as the essence to forge a "natural" link. The requirements of the foundational categories implicit in the text thus reduce women to the maternal. The model of gender in *Holy Feast and Holy Fast* assumes that gender is an essence that appears prior to other categories and informs them, that the feminine mirrors, indeed reduces to, the female reproductive function, that the female body is the originary, foundational site of gender. Just as Taussig noted that the ordering of a structuralist anthropology often occurs on the body of the female "primitive," the ordering of a structural history in *Holy Feast and Holy Fast* occurs on an ahistorical, imagined body of the maternal.

READING THROUGH THE MATERNAL

Reading through that essential, ahistorical maternal of *Holy Feast and Holy Fast* posed challenges to its reviewers.[20] Many expressed uneasiness about the gendering of knowledge in the text without being able to articulate critically the rhetorical reasons for their confusion.[21] John Boswell, who wrote one of the earliest reviews, uncannily raised the question of shamanism. He asked how a reader could read the difference between a shaman and a saint, a distinction that he would use to separate Bynum's book from a companion volume under his review, Rudolph M. Bell's *Holy Anorexia*. According to Boswell, shamans are

[20] My thoughts here are inspired by Jane Gallop, who has emphasized the political importance of a postmodern engagement with "the anxiety produced by the absence of any certain access to the referent." My argument here is that Bynum forestalls that form of anxiety by using the maternal as a natural referent for the history of medieval women. This move creates anxieties of its own, but, I would argue, they are reductive rather than transformative anxieties: Jane Gallop, "The Body Politic," in her *Thinking through the Body*, p. 96.

[21] Any material in quotation marks in discussion of the reviews are citations from the reviews. Early reviews of *Holy Feast and Holy Fast* by John Freccero (Stanford University), John Boswell (Yale University), and Maurice Keen (Oxford) appeared in the *New York Times Book Review*, April 5, 1987; the *New Republic*, August 24, 1987; and in the *New York Review of Books*, October 8, 1987, respectively. The following reviews appeared in major journals of church history and religious studies: Retha M. Warnicke, *Journal of the American Academy of Religion* 66 (1988), 563–64; Glenn W. Olsen, *Church History* 57 (1988), 225–27; John Howe, *Catholic History Review* 74 (1988), 456–58; Bernard McGinn, *History of Religions* 28 (1988), 90–92; George Holmes, *Journal of Ecclesiastical History* 40 (1989), 274–75; Amanda Porterfield, *Religion* 20 (April 1990), 187–88; reviews in history journals considered for this essay include the following: Lester K. Little, *Journal of Social History* 21 (Spring 1988), 597–99; Ann G. Carmichael, *Journal of Interdisciplinary History* 19 (Spring 1989), 635–44; Judith C. Brown, *American Historical Review* 94 (June 1989), 735–37; Rita Copeland, *Speculum* 64 (1989), 143–47; Jack Goody, *English Historical Review* 105 (1990), 429–31. Also mentioned in this section is the review by Hester Goodenough Gelber, *Modern Language Quarterly* 48 (1987), 281–85.

"natural"; they are sacred by virtue of innate characters that make them "different" from their surroundings. Saints, he contended, are holy through acts of will; by nature they are "not different." Boswell's struggle to distinguish shamanism can be read as an effort to disentangle the rhetorical collapse of saint, historian, and reader in *Holy Feast and Holy Fast*.

Other reviewers read anxiously, seemingly unable or unwilling to analyze its sources, whether from some unexamined revulsion towards the subject matter or from the compounded effects of a structuralist rhetoric that involves the reader in a kind of autocannibalism, a "consumption of otherness," or both.[22] Maurice Keen anxiously asked how the reader can digest the myriad descriptions of women mystics fasting or feasting on noxious substances. He then listed eight examples of the very descriptions that for him "can be testing to the strength of the stomach." His ambivalence seemed, however, to be anticipated by Bynum, who alerts her readers to the contradictions they will encounter in reading her text: "If readers leave this book simply condemning the past as peculiar, I shall have failed" (*HFHF*, p. 9). Or, does her rhetoric succeed, since she claims that one reason she "repeatedly break[s] the flow by citing examples" is to "convince modern readers of the decidedly bizarre behavior of some medieval women" (*HFHF*, p. xv)?

The use of medieval Christendom as a unitary, bounded category in *Holy Feast and Holy Fast* also evoked anxiety. Some reviewers expressed their uneasiness indirectly by simply mentioning other cultures in a comparative vein. John Freccero interrupted his review to mention others outside the Christian tradition, namely, Simone Weil and Gandhi. Boswell noted more directly that Bynum never addresses the "interaction of food, gender, ethic and culture at the level of whole religious systems," namely, medieval Islam and Judaism. His comments inspire the reader to wonder about historical and contemporary fantasies of medieval Christendom. How did the cultural construct of *Christianitas* establish its sense of unity, and, crucially, what does *Christianitas* have to do with the construction of gender?

A review by Jack Goody most directly articulated a criticism of the structuralist categories of the text. Goody pointed out that although Bynum writes with great insight about the polysemous nature of symbols in the past, she has little sympathy for their potential richness in the present. She and many of her sympathetic reviewers, who implicitly defend the structuralism of the book, regard the present as "impoverished." Goody claims that such a judgment "represents only a partial view of the climate of opinion." Goody also suggested that "culture" as used by Bynum is an *effect* of her structuralist approach and its effort to search for structures of thought that underlie not only "divergent expressions

---

[22] Bynum offers protocols of reading. Metaphors of food preparation tempt me to suggest that her book is like food. She describes herself as holding a sieve and "sifting medieval experience," like flour, through a "fine mesh" (*HFHF*, p. xv). Her book is also corporeal; it has a "heart" (*HFHF*, p. 279). I would argue that these reading protocols, suggestive of reading as eating, can also be traced to the structuralist frame of the book. We have seen (above, p. 93) how a structuralist notion of culture can result in a kind of "autocannibalism," the consumption of otherness. These images also raise interesting questions about distinguishing cannibalism from communion.

of individuals, groups and societies, but humanity itself.'' He cautioned that ''doubts must remain about the universality of such an analysis, even within a culture, let alone among all the varied internal and national cultures and sub-cultures, *even* [emphasis mine] of Western Europe.'' Goody's comments invite us to pause. Although he does not go so far as to question the disciplinary frame of knowledge that produces such a foundational notion of culture, he at least introduces the notion of divided cultures, which can be extended to gender divided between the masculine and the feminine, to the past and present divided within itself, even to the divided empathy of the historian.[23]

No review I read directly questioned the ways in which *Holy Feast and Holy Fast* reduces women to the maternal function or challenged the historicity of such a reduction. The uneasiness of the reviewers about this central issue of the book translated itself instead into requests for more context. Ann Carmichael wondered how secular contexts of food practices that were not dominated by women, such as secular medical advice on eating and purging in dietetic treatises, related to the gendering of food practices central to the book's thesis. Judith Brown found that the book failed to address a history of family life and child-rearing practices to justify its reliance on a model of mothering adopted from the work of Nancy Chodorow. This call to historicize maternity and nurture received the most extended attention in a review by Hester Goodenough Gelber in the *Modern Language Quarterly*. Gelber asked to see the arguments linked to changing practices of nursing and wet-nursing in medieval Europe, practices that varied by sex of the child, class, and region. Adding *more* context cannot, however, transform the essentialist move required by the structuralist frame of the text.[24]

The frame itself begs for transformation.[25] As a dominant disciplinary practice, structuralism has historically sought to constrain and conventionalize gender to conform to social practices, especially practices of social reproduction, most notably of kinship. Once we grant anatomy a history, so that it ceases to be a foundational category, then historians and theorists need to think about how gender is performative, meaning that ''there is no gender identity behind the expressions of gender; that identity is performatively constituted by the very 'expressions' that are said to be its results.''[26] The performance of gender,

[23] The notion of a divided empathy suggests that empathy traverses the path of transference.

[24] My comments are restricted to rhetorical problems in *Holy Feast and Holy Fast*; I do not wish to imply here that the history of the construction of motherhood is not crucial. For an important historiographic step with helpful bibliography, see Clarissa W. Atkinson, *The Oldest Vocation: Christian Motherhood in the Middle Ages* (Ithaca, N.Y., 1991).

[25] For a critique of the call for more context see LaCapra, ''Rhetoric and History,'' in his *History and Criticism*, p. 19. My thoughts about framing are inspired by an essay by Jacques Derrida first translated in 1979 and then republished in 1987, the same year in which *Holy Feast and Holy Fast* appeared: Jacques Derrida, ''The Parergon,'' *October* 9 (Summer 1979), 3–41; reissued in his *Truth in Painting* (Chicago, 1987), pp. 34–82: Derrida meditates on how a frame works as an ''objectifying, representational essence, it is inside and outside, the criteria used in definition, the value attributed to the natural, and either secondarily or principally, the privileged position of the human body'' (p. 22 of the *October* version).

[26] Feminists theorize performance as a feminist practice and a way of undoing the ''naturalized'' links between anatomical sex, gender identity, and gender performance. This theorizing offers ways

historical and contemporary, both enacts through repetition and challenges through the very impossibility of perfect repetition ("getting gender right") the rigid boundaries sanctioned between culturally constructed notions of "inside" and "outside" which make "culture" structurally possible. Such imperfect repetition of gender performance also both contains and questions the rigid divides between the real, the imaginary, and the symbolic, the spaces in which much structuralist-inspired theory imagines law, language, and sexual difference.

No foundational category can ever fully frame a text, however. There are always places where the differences within the category interrupt the desires to frame a unity, to argue from an essence. Once again, the reading practices of the reviewers of *Holy Feast and Holy Fast* leave clues to gaps in the text. What do the reviewers overlook? What do they fail to mention? Of the reviews I read, none commented specifically on the thirty plates and frontispiece lavishly illustrating the text. Only Rita Copeland, in her *Speculum* review, praised Bynum for her ability to move "easily into visual discourses as well."[27] Bynum, too, remains strangely silent about many of the plates. Although she deals explicitly with the problems of reading hagiographical material (*HFHF*, p. 5 and chap. 3), she does not discuss her methodology for reading iconographic evidence (*HFHF*, p. 81). She refers to the plates in only three places and reads them conventionally and presentistically for their content, as if visual images did not engender power-charged relations among visual communities, but only reflected them.[28] A demand for a plate-by-plate exegesis, like the desire of some of the reviewers for more context for maternity, would not, however, resolve the problem of the plates in *Holy Feast and Holy Fast*. A reading of the patterns of selection of plates can render visible the foundational category of medieval Christendom invisibly at work in *Holy Feast and Holy Fast*. An infrareflexive reading of this

---

of historicizing the pain of gender performance, where doing "gender right" has been historically subject to political and social coercion. This theory appropriates in a utopian gesture a history of performance among gay and lesbian communities. It also questions gender as a representation: Teresa de Lauretis, "Sexual Indifference and Lesbian Representation," in *Performing Feminisms: Feminist Critical Theory and Theatre*, ed. Sue-Ellen Case (Baltimore, 1990), pp. 17–39. Butler also theorizes gender as performance in *Gender Trouble* and in her article "Performative Acts and Gender Constitution: An Essay in Phenomenology and Feminist Theory," in *Performing Feminisms*, pp. 270–82; see also Cornell, *Beyond Accommodation*. The citation comes from Butler, *Gender Trouble*, p. 25.

[27] Copeland, in *Speculum* 64 (1989), 144.

[28] There is a discussion of iconographic evidence on p. 81 and mention of plates 1, 5, 7, 25, 26, 30: "Iconographic evidence also suggests that medieval people of both sexes associated food and fasting with women." On pp. 268 and 270–72 there is a discussion of the lactating Virgin and reference to plates 13–16 and 20–30. It seems that plates 2–4, 6, 8–12, 17–19 receive no mention. Michael Camille commented on the way the plates of *Holy Feast and Holy Fast* are used simply as illustrations to back up textual arguments, rather than as semiotic objects in their own right that might not only reinforce, but contest and subvert, textual arguments, in a paper delivered at the conference "The Past and Future of Medieval Studies," University of Notre Dame, 1992, forthcoming in a book of that title edited by John Van Engen. In his book *The Gothic Idol: Ideology and Image-making in Medieval Art* (New York, 1989), Camille writes the following about medieval images, but the same could be said for their use as illustrations in current historical texts: "it [his book] also attempts to uncover realms of intervisual and not just intertextual meanings, where images do not just 'reflect' texts innocently but often subvert and alter their meanings" (p. xxvii).

invisibility can begin to articulate the women the text makes visible with the fearful interconnections with invisibility.

ENGENDERING CHRISTENDOM/BLOOD LIBEL

Twenty out of thirty plates and the frontispiece of *Holy Feast and Holy Fast* date from the period between 1450 and 1585. The majority of these late-medieval art works come from German and Netherlandish masters. The earlier illustrations depict works mostly by Italian masters of the fourteenth century. The plates thus mark temporal, regional, and institutional differences (some of the later material is for hospitals, convents, and cathedrals, institutions with different audiences). Rather than hold these contrasting regional, chronological, and institutional contexts in tension with the construction of gender, Bynum collapses such differences into sexual difference: "Indeed, recent scholarship suggests that differences between the sexes over-ride all other factors (such as chronology or social and economic status) in shaping women's piety" (*HFHF*, p. 26). Attention to these differences, Bynum further asserts, has hitherto suppressed the study of correlations of eucharistic devotion with gender.[29]

Bynum calls this sexual difference "gender," but for her gender carries the more restricted sense of "woman." Even though chapter 4, "Food in the Lives of Women Saints," is organized by region (Low Countries, France and Germany, Italy), the essentialized notion of gender reduces discussion of difference to sexual difference: "Despite the suggestion of recent scholars that the nature of female sanctity changed between 1200 and 1500 and displayed different patterns in north and south, the themes found in Low Country spirituality, from Mary of Oignies to Lidwina of Schiedam, echo throughout fourteenth- and fifteenth-century Europe" (*HFHF*, p. 129).

My reading starts with the gaps of regionality and chronology suggested by the assemblage of plates as a way into the breaches within the imaginary whole of Christendom. The blood that flows in the plates serves as the medium of my reading. This blood marks a crisis of exteriority and interiority in the construct of Christendom. The gaps and breaches through which blood could seep and about which Christians expressed great anxiety contest the historical formation of Christendom as a natural structure as well as the rhetorical practices that would perpetuate the study of gender uncritically within Christendom.[30]

[29] "But historians have tended to correlate eucharistic concern with factors other than gender—for example, with religious order (particularly Cistercian or Dominican), with region (particularly the Low Countries or southern Germany), or with type of religious life (particularly monastic or anchoritic)" (*HFHF*, p. 75). Issues of region and audience are complicated by different patronage and distribution patterns in different art markets in the later fifteenth century. To begin exploring this problem see Lynn F. Jacobs, "The Marketing and Standardization of South Netherlandish Carved Altarpieces: Limits on the Role of the Patron," *Art Bulletin* 71 (1989), 208–29.

[30] A historical understanding of medieval European gender requires a study of how gender came to mark as "naturalized" borders of interiority and exteriority of the body, the community, the institutions that institute kinship. The outlines of this complex history, which produced Jews, homosexuals, prostitutes, lepers, and heretics as an exterior to the "natural" European sex-gender system, are delineated by R. I. Moore, *The Formation of a Persecuting Society: Power and Deviance in Western*

Blood was a central food image to the medieval female mystics studied by Bynum, and the bleeding Christ forms the devotional matter of many of the plates.[31] Blood also set the boundaries of marital exchange among medieval Christians; consanguinity measured exogamy and endogamy. Not surprisingly, as a religious symbol blood "was in general a more public and social symbol than bread, as well as a more ambivalent symbol" (*HFHF*, p. 178). Difficult to control because of its fluidity, blood could seep through the boundaries of interiority and exteriority instituted by Christendom. It could mix among Christians and among those others constructed as exterior to Christendom: Jews, homosexuals, and prostitutes.

Anxieties about fluid boundaries began to surface in twelfth- and thirteenth-century Europe, as Europeans invented the unitary construct of Christendom. Christians began to fantasize intensely about blood libel, that is, the ritual murder and bleeding of Christians, usually Christian boys, by Jews, usually male. Christians also began to ascribe acts of ritual cannibalism and host desecration to Jews.[32] By the thirteenth century in certain German territories of northern

---

Europe, 950–1250 (London, 1987). In using the word "homosexuals" here I am not implying anachronistically a gay identity and life-style. For important discussion of how to talk about medieval gay people see the exchanges in the gay and lesbian issue of the *Medieval Feminist Newsletter* 13 (Spring 1992). Historians of gay history tell us that such an identity began to form historically in the nineteenth century; see John Boswell, *Christianity, Social Tolerance, and Homosexuality: Gay People in Western Europe from the Beginning of the Christian Era to the Fourteenth Century* (Chicago, 1980). Eve Kosofsky Sedgwick offers a thoughtful and cogent analysis of the problem of speech acts in discussing histories of sexuality in her *Epistemology of the Closet* (Berkeley, 1990). For a brilliant study of how medical and theological discourses on medieval sexuality are intertwined see Danielle Jacquart and Claude Thomasset, *Sexuality and Medicine in the Middle Ages*, trans. Matthew Adamson (Princeton, 1988).

[31] For discussion of blood in medieval medical treatises, especially menstrual blood, see Jacquart and Thomasset, *Sexuality and Medicine*.

[32] I am anticipating my argument here in two registers. Medieval eucharistic devotion defined cultural boundaries which excluded Jews as Others in medieval society. Accusations of ritual cannibalism against Jews emerged with the formation of an institutionalized orthodox eucharistic theology: Gavin I. Langmuir, *Toward a Definition of Antisemitism* (Berkeley, 1990), pp. 263–82; and that self-fashioning, the mental absorption of others, as a historical and contemporary rhetorical practice deserves critical attention: Maggie Kilgour, *From Communion to Cannibalism: An Anatomy of Metaphors of Incorporation* (Princeton, 1990); see also *The Blood Libel Legend: A Casebook of Anti-Semitic Folklore*, ed. Alan Dundes (Madison, Wis., 1991). See also Langmuir, chap. 14, "From Anti-Judaism to Antisemitism," in his *History, Religion, and Antisemitism* (Berkeley, 1990); Langmuir, *Toward a Definition of Antisemitism*, especially chap. 11, on ritual cannibalism; Jeremy Cohen, *The Friars and the Jews: The Evolution of Medieval Anti-Judaism* (Ithaca, N.Y., 1982); Robert Chazan, *Daggers of Faith: Thirteenth-Century Christian Missionizing and Jewish Response* (Berkeley, 1989); Diane Owen Hughes, "Distinguishing Signs: Ear-rings, Jews and Franciscan Rhetoric in the Italian Renaissance City," *Past and Present* 112 (August 1986), 3–59; Lionel Rothkrug, "Popular Religion and Holy Shrines: Their Influence on the Origins of the German Reformation and Their Role in German Cultural Development," in *Religion and the People (800–1700)*, ed. James Obelkevich (Chapel Hill, N.C., 1979), pp. 20–86, 290–301. References to eucharistic shrines built on the site of Jewish massacres appear in n. 23, p. 292, of *Holy Feast and Holy Fast*; see also Charles Zika, "Hosts, Processions and Pilgrimages: Controlling the Sacred in Fifteenth-Century Germany," *Past and Present* 118 (February 1988), 25–64; and R. Po-chia Hsia, *The Myth of Ritual Murder: Jews and Magic in Reformation Germany* (New Haven, 1988). The following publication links anti-Semitism and the propagation of broadsheets and woodcuts in fifteenth- and early-sixteenth-century Europe: David Kunzle, *History of the*

Europe, eucharistic shrines began to appear at sites where Jews were massacred, and incidences of accusation and prosecution peaked in those areas over the late fifteenth century, the time and the provenance of many of the plates of *Holy Feast and Holy Fast*.

Bynum cites the work of Lionel Rothkrug, who has listed known examples of German shrines erected at sites associated with anti-Semitic incidents, and she also recognizes the connection between eucharistic devotion and anti-Semitism (*HFHF*, p. 64). The word "Jews" and "anti-Semitism" are, however, overlooked in the index of *Holy Feast and Holy Fast*. Does this gap in the index help a reading of the gaps suggested by the pattern of the plates? I want to suggest that it is more than a coincidence that outbreaks of accusations of ritual cannibalism and host desecration peaked in the later fifteenth century in areas of Germany from which many of the plates have been chosen. The time and place of the plates thus mark what *Holy Feast and Holy Fast* cannot, for reasons of its structural frame, fully acknowledge, that is, the implications of the relations of anti-Semitism to eucharistic devotion. The book is thus condemned to repeat and reinscribe a fantastic moment of the European imaginary in its failure to include the excluded others in historical analysis.[33] A historical study of medieval gender interrupts this foundational category of *Christianitas* by asking how a historical construction of gender in medieval Christendom was *simultaneously* a construction of other differences. I can briefly offer here two examples of such discursive conjuncture, where anti-Semitism, anxieties about blood and host desecration, and women mystics, the central subject of *Holy Feast and Holy Fast*, appear to converge. These two illustrations suggest some sense of the trouble of making "medieval women mystics" visible in our histories.

My first example asks us to consider an early accusation of ritual cannibalism made against medieval Jews. In 1235 thirty-four Jews of Fulda were killed for allegedly murdering five young Christian boys for their blood. The incident occurred during troubled political times in the Mainz region. The papacy had organized preaching against heretics and for the Crusades. Conrad of Marburg proved to be one of the most vigorous preachers in the region. Reputedly responsible for burning many heretics between 1231 and 1234, he even began to accuse important nobles of heresy. In a noted papal bull, *Vox in Rama* (June

---

Comic Strip, 1: *The Early Comic Strip, Narrative Strips and Picture Series in the European Broadsheet from c. 1450–1825* (Berkeley, 1973), pp. 11–28; Michael Camille discusses the Jew as image and asks the following question about the medieval church: "Was it only by being on the image offensive that emphasis could be taken away from the questions 'what are *our* images for' and 'what relation does the image bear to its prototype?' and the finger pointed at the false images of the Other" (*The Gothic Idol*, p. 193). I am also indebted to Sander Gilman, *The Jew's Body* (New York, 1991); and Gilman, "The Jewish Body: A 'Footnote,' " *Bulletin of the History of Medicine* 64 (1990), 588–602.

[33] I borrow the term the "imaginary" from Lacanian psychoanalysis, where it has complex meanings. I am using it in this essay in the following sense: "In relation to meaning, the Imaginary is that in which perceptual features like resemblance operate—that is to say, in areas where there is a sort of coalescence of the signifier and the signified, as in traditional symbolism. For Lacan, the Imaginary relationship, of whatever kind, is also that of a lure, a trap. In this sense he is close to the normal usage of the word 'imaginary' to describe something we believe to be something else." From Jacques Lacan, *Speech and Language in Psychoanalysis*, trans. Anthony Wilden (Baltimore, 1968), p. 175.

1233), which heightened tensions, Gregory IX addressed the problem of eucharistic heresies in the Mainz area by drawing upon fantasies of eucharistic
pollution. Conrad was murdered at the end of July 1234, over a year before
the first accusation of ritual cannibalism was made against local Jews. Those
accusations, however, need to be read against several years of powerful crusade
against heresy. Conrad of Marburg also served as the spiritual director of Elizabeth of Hungary, one of the fasting mystics studied in *Holy Feast and Holy Fast*.
Conrad wrote early material on Elizabeth's life, and upon her death (November
17, 1231) he tried to organize her speedy canonization, which took place in
May 1235, approximately one year after Conrad's death. When Conrad of Marburg died, he was buried at his request next to the shrine of Elizabeth. Bynum
writes that the "importance of her stern confessor, Conrad of Marburg, in
inducing her obsession with food is impossible to assess at this distance" (*HFHF*,
p. 135). The staging of the early textual materials of Elizabeth's life and canonization process need to be brought together for their bearing on a complex,
multifocal discourse of purity and pollution involving the Eucharist and the
problems of cannibalism and cannibalizing authority around the Eucharist. Who
is eating whose body, and what or who is engendering problems of visibility and
invisibility around the Eucharist?[34]

The example just cited concentrates on textual conjunctures, local stories of
ritual cannibalism, papal bulls, materials for a canonization process. My second
illustration offers an example of how *visual* discourses joined anxieties over the
circulation of blood in "Western Christendom." It is a predella designed by the
Florentine painter Paolo Uccello for the altar of the Confraternity of Corpus
Domini in Urbino in 1467–68. The predella offers clues to where the trail of
blood depicted in many of the plates of *Holy Feast and Holy Fast* might flow.[35]
Uccello executed the predella just as Urbino, under the influence of Franciscan
preaching, planned the opening of its Monte di Pietà (1468), a lending fund,
to break what was considered to be a Jewish monopoly on credit. Six scenes
from the predella tell a story of the desecration of the host by Jews. The story,
based on a Paris legend, had circulated in Europe since the late thirteenth
century and became a popular source of drama in the fifteenth century. In

---

[34] Many readers of drafts of this essay expected it to turn into my own reading of Elizabeth of
Hungary at this juncture. I have refused that move, because this essay is not about better or different
readings, but about questions of engendering the visible and the invisible in our contemporary
historiography. I wish to keep that problem open in the essay. For historical references to the above
discussion see Gavin Langmuir's excellent essay "Ritual Cannibalism," in his *Toward a Definition of
Antisemitism*, for the Fulda persecutions. The text of *Vox in Rama* appears in MGH Epp. saec. XIII,
1:432–34. For Conrad's writings on Elizabeth of Hungary see Albert Huyskens, *Quellenstudien zur
Geschichte der hl. Elisabeth* (Marburg, 1908).

[35] The motifs of this predella are virtually unique to Italian altarpieces of the period, but the story
it illustrates circulated in popular plays and in northern Europe in broadsheets. Joos Van Ghent
probably began the main panel of the altarpiece, "The Communion of the Apostles," in 1473. The
juxtaposition of a converted Jew (according to Marilyn Lavin's identification) in the Van Ghent
panel with the predella suggests that the tragic scene of the predella is "correctible," but according
to whose perspective? See Marilyn Aronberg Lavin, "The Altar of Corpus Domini in Urbino: Paolo
Uccello, Joos Van Ghent, Piero della Francesca," *Art Bulletin* 49 (March 1967), 1–24; and John
Pope-Hennessy, *Paolo Uccello* (New York, 1969), p. 156, plates 87–100.

Uccello's version, a Christian woman exchanges a host with a Jewish pawnbroker for some coins, although in the written versions she does this to redeem a cloak. The pawnbroker heats the host in a pan, as his wife and two children look on. In miraculous authentication of itself, blood runs from the host all over the tiled floor of the room and out onto the street. Alerted by this bloody rivulet, soldiers appear at the house of the Jewish family. The pope and other clerics restore the host to the altar in a liturgical procession. The woman who exchanged the host repents before her hanging. The Jewish family, husband, wife, and two children, are burned alive, a punishment usually reserved for heretics and witches. In the last panel, angels and devils dispute over the soul of the Christian woman.

The predella narrates a story of pollution which brings together a construction of the feminine and religious difference at the very altar table where priests celebrated the Eucharist. A woman initiates the exchange, the media of which, in most versions of the story, are finery and the host, although the predella depicts coins.[36] The host bleeds miraculously over the floor and into the street in a fantasy of excess that echoes the Scholastic fear of excess in usury. Male members of the community, including soldiers and clerics, work to restore order and purity. The final status of purity and pollution remains in suspension to the viewer of the predella. The debate between the angels and the devils for the soul of the repentant Christian woman invites viewers to project their own ending to this customary debate and opens up the anxious possibility that the process of pollution could be set in motion again.

The Uccello predella visually narrates anti-Semitic stories which coincided with the intensification of persecution of Jews in Germany and Italy.[37] Recent work on ritual murder trials in Germany by Po-chia Hsia (cited above, n. 32) demonstrates how the more virulent accusations of blood libel began to fuse with stories of host desecration to create a discourse of blood and sacramental pollution. The incidences of ritual murder accusations, compiled by Po-chia Hsia, correlate in interesting ways with the growth and geographical expansion of female piety in Europe.

The popular media of broadsheets and printed ballads, which had begun to circulate in the later fifteenth century, spectacularized stories of ritual murder and host desecration at the same time as they advertised Christian pilgrimage

---

[36] Franciscan preachers condemned Italian women for their appetite for finery and claimed that this avariciousness made them partners to the Jews; see Hughes, "Distinguishing Signs," p. 28. For a discussion of Franciscan involvement in the establishment of *montes pietatis* throughout Italy (there were over eighty *montes* in Italian cities at the end of the fifteenth century) see John T. Noonan, *The Scholastic Use of Usury* (Cambridge, Mass., 1957), p. 295. Note that many of the northern Italian cities ordered that Jews wear distinguishing signs just a generation before the predella was executed: Padua, 1430; Perugia, 1432; Florence and Siena, 1439 (Hughes, p. 20).

[37] We need comparative regional histories of the expulsion of Jews in medieval Europe. Such a history would help to pose comparative questions of how anti-Semitism and anxieties about pollution maintained themselves discursively where Jews were present or absent. King Edward I ordered the first permanent expulsion of Jews from England in 1290; Philip IV expelled Jews from France in 1306; Jews in southern Italian communities were subject to the Inquisition in the late thirteenth century, and many migrated to northern Italy or converted. In the 1420s and 1430s many of the imperial cities of the Rhineland expelled their Jewish communities.

Paolo Uccello, Profanation of the Host (predella panels)
Urbino, Palazzo Ducale

(Photographs: Alinari/Art Resource, New York)

centers, such as Wilsnack in Germany, dedicated to the Holy Blood.[38] The ef-
fusions of blood from the Suffering Christ, a holy excess of blood which repeats
itself frequently in the plates of *Holy Feast and Holy Fast*, needs to be read with
other coexistent iconography that depicted desecrated hosts bleeding excessively
at sites of pollution. An anxiety about blood, consanguinity, and pollution expressed itself in the later fifteenth century in certain areas of Germany and
consolidated itself in Italy with the preaching of Bernardino of Siena (1380–
1444). The majority of the plates in *Holy Feast and Holy Fast* date from this
period of intense, popular propagandizing about sacred and polluted blood.

In the medieval Christian economy of exteriority, prostitutes and homosexuals
shared affinities with Jews. The image of Jews as draining blood and devouring
flesh became blurred with images of prostitutes, who were considered parasites
on cities and their food supplies. Prostitutes thus make an exception to the
universal association of medieval women with food preparation argued by
Bynum.[39] Even within medieval Christendom not all women could be reduced
to the maternal function; in fact, those regarded as parasites marked instead
an antimaternal function. Prostitutes were also commonly assumed to be sterile,
and this fantasy linked them with discourses about the sterility of homosexuality.
The trope of sterility linked them further to discourses about usury. Scholastics
regarded money as fruitless, and its sterility came to be associated with homosexual intercourse.[40] The blood of eucharistic devotion thus negotiated complicated borders in which the sacred fluid could seep into an exteriority composed of Jews, prostitutes, homosexuals, and a symbolic economy of usury and
parasitism.[41] In the midst of such anxieties it is not surprising that the chalice,
containing the blood of Christ, disappeared from the communion service to the
medieval laity.[42]

[38] See Kunzle, *Early Comic Strip*, pp. 11–28.

[39] Hughes, "Distinguishing Signs," p. 28.

[40] For the associations of Thomas Aquinas and the sterility of prostitutes see Jacquart and Thomasset, *Sexuality and Medicine*, p. 156; for the well-established antipathy to homoeroticism see
Boswell, *Christianity, Social Tolerance and Homosexuality*; Michael J. Rocke, "Sodomites in Fifteenth-
Century Tuscany: The Views of Bernardino of Siena," in *The Pursuit of Sodomy: Male Homosexuality
in Renaissance and Enlightenment Europe*, ed. Kerit Gerard and Gert Helima (New York, 1989), pp.
7–31; John W. Baldwin, "Five Discourses on Desire: Sexuality and Gender in Northern France
around 1200," *Speculum* 66 (1991), 797–819.

[41] It is the historically charged nature of these boundaries which undoubtedly accounts for the
fact, according to Camille, that "the Host can be described as the single most important image to
Christians from the middle of the thirteenth century onward, perhaps even overtaking veneration
of the cross," Camille, *Gothic Idol*, p. 215; or as Miri Rubin has brilliantly traced the many ways in
which medieval Europeans used the host to think with: "The eucharist was constructed to bear
these meanings as a symbol which still retained an enormous space between signifier and signified
to allow such a broad array of articulations. But it was becoming increasingly overdetermined,"
Miri Rubin, *Corpus Christ: The Eucharist in Late Medieval Culture* (New York, 1991), p. 344. I regret
that the following two essays, which have so much bearing on the argument of this essay, only
became available to me as this essay was going to press: Miri Rubin, "The Eucharist and the Construction of Medieval Identities," and Sarah Beckwith, "Ritual, Church and Theatre: Medieval
Dramas of the Sacramental Body," in *Culture and History, 1350–1600* (above, n. 5), pp. 43–64 and
65–90, respectively.

[42] Rubin, *Corpus Christi*, pp. 70–71. Rubin quotes from *De sacramentis* by James of Vitry, who
wrote: "Because of possible danger the eucharist is not given to the laity under the species of wine"
(p. 71).

The flow of blood across juridical and iconographic spaces has blurred the boundaries between Christendom and the Others of its exterior. We now need to consider how such a reading renders problematic any unitary notions of bodies within medieval Christendom, especially the body of Christ and the bodies of medieval women mystics. The symbolic expulsion of the Jews by members of Christendom produced in the Christian imaginary a fantastic excluded body of the Jew. The fantasy of exclusion and the boundary it creates, however, can only be a fantasy. The excluded body of the Other returns to haunt the pure body of the "interior." The host, the "most important image of Gothic Europe," served as the site of haunting by the excluded body of the Other, the Jew. The haunting came to perform itself in the fantastical grotesque hybrid body of Christ in the Christian imaginary.[43]

Popular rituals that grew up around the medieval celebrations of Corpus Christi enacted an awareness of the hybridity that haunted the host. The carnival processions of monsters and giants that preceded the liturgical procession on the feast of Corpus Christi recognized the problem of body doubles, the differences within dominant European constructions of kinship, and theological constructions of sacred bodies. Before considering some of the problems in constructing mystical gender in such a complicated, contested corporeal world, it is worth reviewing some thoughts of Mikhail Bakhtin's regarding grotesque bodies:

> all these convexities and orifices have a common characteristic; it is within them that the confines between bodies and between body and the world are overcome: there is an exchange and an interorientation. This is why the main events of the life of the grotesque body, the acts of the bodily drama, take place in this sphere. Eating, drinking, defecation, and other elimination . . . as well as copulation, pregnancy, dismemberment, swallowing up by another body—all these acts are performed on the confines of the body and the outer world, or on the confines of the old and new body.[44]

---

[43] Peter Stallybrass and Allon White, in *The Politics and Poetics of Transgression* (Ithaca, N.Y., 1986), make this important point about exclusion and differentiation of the grotesque: "we have to avoid conflating the two different forms of the grotesque. If the two are confused [grotesque as excluded Other; hybrid grotesque as a boundary phenomena of hybridization and inmixing], it becomes impossible to see that a fundamental mechanism of identity formation *produces* the second, hybrid grotesque at the level of the political unconscious *by the very struggle to exclude the first grotesque*" (p. 193). I think their theory could be related to the work of Homi Bhabha in postcolonial theory of "doubling": Homi Bhabha, "Interrogating Identity," in *The Real Me: Postmodernism and the Question of Identity*, ICA Documents 6, ed. Lisa Appignanesi (London, 1987), pp. 5–11; and "Postcolonial Authority and Postmodern Guilt," in *Cultural Studies* (above, n. 4). Dollimore's use of the notion of "proximate other," in his *Sexual Dissidence* (p. 135), which I came across after completing the draft of this essay, could be fruitfully developed here.

[44] I am trying to negotiate and mark the tensions of constructing differences within and differences between in medieval European eucharistic culture: see Mikhail Bakhtin, *Rabelais and His World*, trans. Helene Iswolsky (Bloomington, 1984), citation from p. 317; references to Corpus Christi procession, pp. 229–30. See also Rubin, *Corpus Christi*, pp. 213–86. Bynum cites Bakhtin in *Holy Feast and Holy Fast* for references to folk literature and the pleasures of eating, but she does not use his thoughts on the grotesque body in her analysis. For critical studies that question, among other things, Bakhtin's nostalgia and failure to address political questions of gendering the grotesque body see Mary Russo, "Female Grotesques: Carnival and Theory," in *Feminist Studies/Critical Studies* (above, n. 10), pp. 213–29; Stallybrass and White, *The Politics and Poetics of Transgression*, passim, especially pp. 1–26; Dominick LaCapra, "Bakhtin, Marxism and the Carnivalesque," in his *Rethinking Intellectual History: Texts, Contexts, Language* (Ithaca, N.Y., 1983), pp. 291–324.

The host can be regarded as a hybrid sacred object that served as a relay point between religion and magic, purity and pollution, theological and popular devotion, clergy and layperson, urban and rural, rich and poor, the masculine and the feminine, the insider and the outsider, Christian and Jew. As medievalists study the regulation of its hybridity through gender relations, they will contribute to a history of hybridity and its different modalities and in so doing build an important historical bridge with current postcolonial theories of hybridity.[45]

The Eucharist was good to think with, and it guaranteed the symbolic order of medieval Europe.[46] It was both a "classical" body in the Bakhtinian sense, elevated, static, and monumental, and a "grotesque" body, broken, bleeding, excessive, maternal, paternal, a body which upset any fixed gender binary, a fluid body that troubled any container. It was a body that was distributed across different—and noncommensurate—textual, material, and visual realms. Christians fantasized intensely about both the pollution and the purification of the Eucharist because of its ambivalent position as a border phenomenon.

The host gave occasion to symbolic cannibalism as the church incorporated the host into its own body. With the promulgation of the doctrine of transubstantiation important switches in naming bodies began to occur. The host had been known as "corpus mysticum," and the church as "corpus verum." The church cannibalized the Eucharist, and the host became "corpus verum"; the church, "corpus mysticum." The signified had become the signifier.[47]

How to authenticate the signified that had become signifer during the twelfth century? Notions of visibility and invisibility came to be redefined and reengendered. Relics and the Eucharist came to be presented in new ways. Beginning in the early thirteenth century, ostensories, crystal cylinders in which a relic rested, began to appear, marking a shift away from the presentation of relics

---

[45] Ella Shohat has called for study of the diverse modalities of hybridity: "forced assimilation, internalized self-rejection, political cooption, social conformism, cultural mimicry, and creative transcendence," in her article "Notes on the 'Post-Colonial,' " *Social Text* 31–32 (1992), 110.

[46] It is as if the host functioned in the way in which the "phallus" does today in contemporary psychoanalytic debate. The Eucharist as the guarantee of the symbolic in medieval Europe helps us to historicize the symbolic as a foundational category and to understand power-charged aspects of its work without insisting that medieval Europeans describe their symbolic in terms of penis/phallus. Brian Stock makes the point that the Eucharist was good to think with: "The eucharistic debate in particular opened up two broad subjects to systematic study by medieval thinkers. One was the status of symbol and ritual in a theory of religion that was increasingly preoccupied with explanation in literate terms. The other was the beginning of reflection on observable nature, or, more precisely, on the relation of phenomenal appearances to an inner reality whose logical properties coincided with those of texts," p. 241, in his *Implications of Literacy: Written Language and Models of Interpretation in the Eleventh and Twelfth Centuries* (Princeton, 1983); Rubin, *Corpus Christi*: "The eucharist emerged as a unifying symbol for a complex world. . . . it possessed universal meaning" (p. 348). The symbolic guaranteed by the phallus brings us into psychoanalytic discourse of the twentieth century; for an introduction see *Feminine Sexuality: Jacques Lacan and the Ecole freudienne*, ed. Juliet Mitchell and Jacqueline Rose (New York, 1985). Feminist critiques of the Lacanian model abound; see most recently *differences* 4/1 (1992), an issue of essays dedicated to critical theory and deconstruction of the phallus.

[47] For a suggestive study of the host and Christian cannibalism, see Kilgour, *From Communion to Cannibalism*, passim, esp. pp. 79–139. In my final revisions a copy of Michel de Certeau's *Mystic Fable* (above, n. 2) became available to me. His is a much more detailed argument than Kilgour's.

in reliquaries of the type which mimicked by their design the physical form of the body part they housed, such as a head or a hand, for instance. The older reliquaries are called "talking reliquaries," and the very contrast of the generic names for the two types of reliquaries—talking reliquaries and ostensories—marks a shift toward visibility: the contents of the reliquary must be visible to guarantee its existence.[48]

Hans Belting has argued that the reliquary became the image of the relic and that images could become relics in the thirteenth century, an important time for the revaluation of images and issues of visibility in medieval Europe.[49] If the Eucharist came to signify the church, if the hybrid grotesque body of the host unstably marked the boundary phenomenon of exclusion and incorporation that produced the fantastic identity of Western Christendom, if relic and image were exchangeable, who/what could guarantee signification? New solutions to problems of authenticity and questions about originals and copies emerged in the discourse of relics in the late twelfth and early thirteenth century: "The imagination becomes inspired by material proofs which existed in the East linking the reality of the relic with the evidence of the photograph."[50] Belting argues for this startling and suggestive statement on the basis of controversy over the authenticity of Veronica's veil. First a relic, it assumed the status of an image, an image-relic. The image was that of Christ imprinted on the veil of Veronica.

This reading of Christian bodies, especially Corpus Christi, grows more complicated. The issues raised so far cannot be resolved in an essay of this type (itself a hybrid by virtue of its reading practice). Suffice it to note that the changing status of relics and their presentation makes it clear that the metaphoric nature of the body as referent was undergoing change. What guarantees the imaginary body of Christendom as a referent, and how would that body be gendered? The problem of the body seems to lie in the space in between this metonymic "image-relic," a space which poses problems of intervisuality in Western Christendom. Who could be the "photograph" of the host, as Belting provocatively puts it; who could be its authenticator? What possibilities of gender and mimesis does the image-relic pose?

That set of questions bears on the historiographical problems concerning

---

[48] My arguments in this section are based on Hans Belting, *The Image and Its Public in the Middle Ages: Form and Function in the Early Paintings of the Passion*, trans. Mark Bartusis and Raymond Meyer (New Rochelle, N.Y., 1990), p. 82. My colleague Dianne Phillips pointed out the need for a study of the coexistence and coconstruction of talking reliquaries and ostensories. It is too simplistic to say that one replaced the other.

[49] Belting, *The Image and Its Public*, pp. 212–14; also Camille, *Gothic Idol*, p. 9, who comments that the "very fabrication of a thing" became the cause of concern in thirteenth-century society. Belting also argues against any simple division between public cult and private devotion; he shows how each informed the other and how viewer and image were related mimetically. His work inspired me to question the gendering of mimesis and to wonder how mystics performed mimetically, whether their mimesis could be a kind of countermimesis that marked the gaps between object-illusionism and the depicted subject's mimetic power (Belting, p. 53). In a seminar conducted at the Medieval Institute at the University of Notre Dame (23 March 1993) Brigitte Bedos-Rezak raised complementary questions about complex issues regarding visibility and authentication in the changing culture of charters in France, 1000–1200.

[50] Belting, *The Image and Its Public*, p. 219.

medieval women mystics broached in the introduction to this essay. If we have only the textual effects of their practices, distributed across a range of genres with complicated authorship, how can we read these texts? The work of Bynum has already cautioned us not to embody the texts metaphorically in the form of historical female hysterics or anorectics. My reading of *Holy Feast and Holy Fast* also urges us not to embody the textual effects of the practices of female mystics as a maternal function, as Bynum does. We can, however, figure these textual effects as performances of gender, that the access to the body as referent occurs only imperfectly in the performance, that there is no mystical body prior to the performance.[51]

PERFORMING VERONICA'S VEIL

The problem of authentication, most immediately discernible in the changing status of relics and images, impinged on fundamental epistemological questions regarding the power-charged relations of the visible to the invisible, the masculine to the feminine. The shifting status of the real and the imaginary in visual images occurring over the twelfth century began to reorganize vision around the text, so that the text gave rise to an invisible inner life. *Mere* or "real" physicality became equated with the "oral, the popular, the inauthentic, the disreputable."[52] Brian Stock has succinctly described this epistemological shift: "physicality, therefore, is ambivalent; popular culture utilizes physical symbolism without an interpretative context; sacramental theology places the same tangible objects in a framework of learned culture."[53] Relics could become images, images could become relics in an exchange that required physicality to become a resource for textuality, and textuality produced physicality as an effect. The proliferation of texts about and, much less often, authored by holy women in Western Europe at this time may be usefully considered within the epistemological shifts clustering around authentication, ambivalent physicality, and discursive realignments of visibility and invisibility. This proliferation correlates with the gendering of the oral and popular as feminine, a feminine with positive *and* negative valences. As this composite of communication, physicality, and value came to be gendered feminine, learned culture began to recontain and reframe the feminine textually. The number of hagiographical texts devoted to female saints increased. Thus what textual culture produced as an effect, it also recontained.[54]

[51] This argument then questions the category of "medieval female mystic." My reading here complements that of Karma Lochrie: "We must begin looking at the body itself as an historical construction," *Translations of the Flesh* (above, n. 18), p. 15. Note also her emphasis on the point that the two terms, body and sexuality, are not coterminous in medieval mental maps of corporeality.

[52] Stock, *Implications of Literacy*, p. 250.

[53] Stock, *Implications of Literacy*, p. 249.

[54] Could we think of this as a *historical* moment of the simulacrum, in spite of the many problems posed by Jean Baudrillard's work? The feminine thus became a simulacrum, "never exchanging for what is real, but exchanging itself." This discussion of the circulation of the sign of the feminine derives from a critique of Jean Baudrillard, *Simulations* (New York, 1983), and represents an effort to question further his work by theorizing relations between what he calls hyperreality and what he ignores, embodiment.

The dispersion of holy women across hagiographical texts, mostly male au-thored, then makes more historical sense given the construction and relations of the visible and the invisible, the physical and the textual. As Miri Rubin has aptly remarked of thirteenth-century mystics in her excellent study of the politics of the formation of the feast of Corpus Christi: "we know little that comes directly from these women, and yet the material is rich; we should, therefore, talk not of experience but of the relation between representations of such experience."[55]

Authenticity relied on this relay between physicality and textuality, yet it was a highly ambivalent relay. In such ambivalent conditions, the authenticator of the host—"the photograph" to use Belting's image—has to have aura, which is the sign of the unique value of an authentic object. Aura was difficult to con-struct in a time known for its "crisis of overproduction" of images.[56] There can be no replica of aura; aura is tied to the body.[57] At this juncture in the crisis of representation and authentication, certain pious women began to perform within this gap of physicality and textuality, authentic and photograph, and their performance worked as a complicated visual system. They began to produce aura for the Corpus Christi.

Just as learned theologians produced physicality as an effect of textuality, pious women could produce textuality as an effect of physicality. Their perfor-mance provided a crucial hinge that could join object with interpretation and the tangible with the intangible. The performance of this hinge function was gendered feminine, not because of anatomy or maternity, but because of the gendering effects of dominant learned culture in this period that conflated the oral and popular with the feminine.[58]

The bodily practices of holy women, especially their food practices, may be read as both brilliant and violent glosses on this crisis of representation in

[55] Rubin, *Corpus Christi*, p. 169. For some selected references to important new work on gender and the problems of textual authority and authentication see Lynn Staley Johnson, "The Trope of the Scribe and the Question of Literary Authority in the Works of Julian of Norwich and Margery Kempe," *Speculum* 66 (1991), 820–38; Sarah Beckwith, "Problems of Authority in Late Medieval English Mysticism: Language, Agency, and Authority in the *Book of Margery Kempe*," *Exemplaria* 4 (1992), 171–200; Maureen Quilligan, "The Name of the Author: Self-Representation in Christine de Pizan's *Livre de la cité des dames*," ibid., pp. 201–28.

[56] Camille, *Gothic Idol*, p. 224. Camille talks about a "crisis of overproduction" in reference to Marian images, and his subsequent comments are relevant here: "this would seem to be a response to what I have termed a 'crisis of overproduction,' a kind of relic inflation in which the proliferation of the image of the Virgin meant that she was to some extent fragmented and diminished."

[57] My reflections on aura may seem anachronistic, but the medieval crisis of authentication pro-vided interesting comparative terms for the problems of aura discussed by Walter Benjamin in his famous essay, "The Work of Art in the Age of Mechanical Reproduction," in *Illuminations*, ed. Hannah Arendt (New York, 1968), pp. 217–52. Jeffrey F. Hamburger works with similar ideas in his discussion of the mystic Heinrich Suso; his model of gender comes closer to that of Bynum: "The Use of Images in the Pastoral Care of Nuns: The Case of Heinrich Suso and the Dominicans," *Art Bulletin* 61 (March 1989), 42.

[58] The feminine need not always be constructed negatively; for the positive, nevertheless gendered as feminine, valuation of the oral see Sharon Farmer, "Persuasive Voices: Clerical Images of Medieval Wives," *Speculum* 61 (1986), 517–43.

medieval Christendom.[59] These women produced a kind of textual tattoo on the surface of their bodies; the surface of their bodies produced imprints.[60] At the same time their bodily interiors became the site of intense physicality. In so reversing interiority and exteriority, the two different "bodies" in the medieval model of corporeality, they marked them as relational terms. The many incidents of postmortem investigations of the body cavities of such women, referred to in *Holy Feast and Holy Fast*, testify to the impact of this reversal. Paradoxically, through their food practices holy women produced an exteriorized interior: the "invisible," interior, feminine appeared on the exterior or "masculine" surface according to medieval typologies of the body. By rendering visible the feminine interior through the signs of bodily practices, such performances could make "aura" visible, thus producing the "photograph" necessary to authenticate the host. The invisible feminine body transformed itself into a utilizable textual form: "the oral element thus survived the utilization of writing and was itself transformed."[61] Within this historical dynamic of gender, the host functions as a relic, and the exteriorized "body" of the holy feminine performance serves as devotional image. Together they performed as an image-relic of medieval visual communities. Their performance reminds us to consider medieval textual communities as coconstructed and in tension with medieval visual communities.

The exteriorization of the feminine on the surface of the holy woman guaranteed the host a visual identity. In this material performance of Veronica's veil, the host served as veil, and the exteriorized feminine of the body served as the imprint, and the hagiographical framing of this performance by the clerics who authored the many lives of these holy women served as the "being imprinted on the imprint."[62] Just as devotional images of the thirteenth century depicted in tension object-illusionism (the naturalism or unnaturalism of an object) and the subject's expressive power, the performance of these holy women marked disjunctures, discontinuities, tensions in textual exchanges. Only gradually would these "two demands of mimesis"—"naturalism" and "expression"—be aligned with the emergence of new optical laws of painting in the fifteenth century.[63] The accounts of such holy women enacted problems of mimesis and a crisis of representation.

[59] For an interesting contemporary reading of female anorectics that raises issues about the politics of judgment of their practices see Gillian Brown, "Anorexia, Humanism, and Feminism," *Yale Journal of Criticism* 5 (1991), 189–215.

[60] I deliberately risk anachronism here again to point to meditations on the body and tattoos by a contemporary performance artist and writer: Kathy Acker, *Hannibal Lecter, My Father* (New York, 1991).

[61] Stock, *Implications of Literacy*, p. 252.

[62] I found help in imagining this complicated textualizing process in Jacques Derrida, *On Grammatology* (Baltimore, 1976); see esp. pp. 27–73.

[63] Belting, *The Image and Its Public*, p. 53, for discussion and illustrations. The issues raised here can help us to historicize the practices of female mystics more fully and to ask whether it is advisable to view these practices on a continuum from the twelfth century to the seventeenth century. I would argue for ruptures in these practices and suggest that the brilliant work of Michel de Certeau on mystics, especially mystics of the seventeenth century, requires modification for the study of medieval mystics: see his "Mystic Speech," in his *Heterologies: Discourse on the Other* (Minneapolis, 1986), pp.

It is important for historians not to judge these performances. Since the more severe forms of bodily practices, especially fasting, actually resulted in death, they tempt us to identify ourselves with issues of violence and victimization or with romantic tropes of female heroines. Contemporary feminist theory of performance can help us to think about these historical practices in other ways. This complex body of theory regards gender performance as a political, ethical means of disrupting normative, ontological discourses of sexual difference. A feminist mimesis affirms the feminine as performance, as a role that can be restyled, played differently, but never reduced to or identified with the lives of actual women. Feminist performance (in theory and practice), perhaps better called *counter*-mimesis to distance it from notions of imitation, enacts the non-identity of anatomical sex and gender identity. A feminist performance theory questions the conventionalized notions of corporeal interiority and exteriority:

> such acts, gestures, enactments, generally construed, are *performative* in the sense that the essence or identity that they otherwise purport to express are *fabrications* manufactured and sustained through corporeal signs and other discursive means. That the gendered body is performative suggests that it has no ontological status apart from the various acts which constitute its reality. This also suggests that if that reality is fabricated as an interior essence, that very interiority is an effect and function of a decidely public and social discourse, the public regulation of fantasy through the surface politics of the body, the gender border control that differentiates inner from outer, and so institutes the "integrity" of the subject.[64]

The kind of feminist performance I am speaking of here puts into question the very notion of original and natural identity and also helps to historicize the violence involved in conflating anatomy, gender identity, and gender performance. The brilliant performances of these "hunger artists" disrupted cultural notions of interiority and exteriority and marked the discontinuities in textual exchange *in the service of authenticating the fantasy of an original and a natural identity*, the Corpus Christi. Their performance helped to guarantee the "classic" host, to guarantee the fantasy of an "original," an authentication that helped to contain the contradictions of the identity of Western Christendom. These performances engaged the grotesque hybrid body of the Eucharist, and in that engagement they profoundly challenged dominant representations of learned culture and kept relations of the oral, physical, and local in tension for the learned culture. That learned culture could also recontain these performances to cannibalize their aura, and their writings are riddled by the intertexuality of the complicated textual exchange at work to contain the crisis of representation. This historical performance reminds us today of the high stakes of gender as

---

80–100. Sarah Beckwith makes the same point, that "to posit mysticism then as a natural source of resistance to orthodoxy is dangerously a-historical, both because the function of mysticism varies with the social and historical conditions in which it is produced and reproduced and because, over and above this, the very quality of mysticism which can empower its by-passing of official structure . . . removes both God and the human soul from history": "A Very Material Mysticism: The Medieval Mysticism of Margery Kempe," in *Medieval Literature*, ed. David Aers (London, 1986), p. 40.

[64] Butler, *Gender Trouble*, p. 136; see also Cornell, *Beyond Accommodation*.

performance. In the service of some naturalized notion of original, medieval, modern, or postmodern, performance can kill.[65]

PERFORMANCE/FUSION AND MEDIEVAL HISTORY

> The metaphor of the mother does not complete her.
> —Drucilla Cornell[66]

Aura locates itself in the presence of the body. It also paradoxically requires distance, "however close it may be," and the contemplation of that distance.[67] Medieval holy women could produce aura through their bodily practices to embody the fact that there can be no replica; thus they guaranteed the host. This concluding section asks whether medieval historians and their audiences cannibalize this historical aura to guarantee the visibility of medieval Christendom as a moment of plenitude, a moment to which our allegedly impoverished present cannot measure.

To think about this problem I will return to issues raised at the opening of this essay regarding the collapse of historian, reader, and historical subject at critical moments of *Holy Feast and Holy Fast*. To return to this rhetorical problem could seem gratuitous if it did not help us with some fundamental problems of historical representation germane to the writing of women's history and studies of historical gender. The rhetoric molds the text into the narrative power of history as *dérèlection*. *Dérèlection*, like essentialism, is a term with multifold meanings and charges in contemporary feminist theory. For the purposes of this discussion, I define it as the inability to write about the feminine as other than an imagined unity of the maternal function and the mother-daughter relation.[68] Bynum frames *Holy Feast and Holy Fast* in terms of mothers and daughters, and her prose embodies that relation as fusion. Historian, reader, and historical subject fuse rhetorically in the prose. Bynum's rhetorical practices, which reinscribe a historical fantasy of the feminine as maternal, cannot allow for the historical or contemporary problem of studying *both* separation and connection of daughters and mothers or, in the metaphor of this paper, of studying their fluctuating visibility. Such studies belie the oft-repeated fantasy of the maternal function as a form of symbiosis and a paradise.

Holy Feast and Holy Fast thus cannot escape its own presentism as much as it distances itself from it: "Thus recent work on medieval women has tended to

[65] The kind of performance discussed here interrogates a basic epistemological assumption of Western representation, in urgent need of critical historicization, that a cultural text somehow has a separate nature distinct from a particular articulation or performance. For a provocative discussion of abiding, seemingly naturalized dualism in current conceptions of power, see Mitchell, "Everyday Metaphors of Power" (above, n. 18). I am grateful to Lisa Rofel for drawing my attention to this reference.

[66] Cornell, *Beyond Accommodation*, p. 78.

[67] Benjamin, "The Work of Art," p. 222.

[68] Drucilla Cornell's extended meditation on *dérèlection* inspires my comments; see Cornell, *Beyond Accommodation*. For some further thoughts on the maternal function and its problems in contemporary technology see Kathleen Biddick, "Stranded Histories: Feminist Allegories of Artificial Life," forthcoming in *Research in Philosophy and Technology* 13 (1993).

have either presentist issues or male issues built in" (*HFHF*, p. 30). How could the entanglement of this book in presentism be otherwise, unless the practices of history as representation are questioned? History writing collaborates rhetorically in preserving the process of *dérèlection* by moralizing its rhetorical practices as the authority of experience:

> experience is at once always already an interpretation *and* something that needs to be interpreted. What counts as experience is neither self-evident nor straightforward; it is always contested, and always therefore political. The study of experience, therefore, must call into question its originary status in historical explanation. This will happen when historians take as their project *not* the reproduction and transmission of knowledge said to be arrived at 'through experience, but the analysis of the production of that knowledge itself. Such an analysis would constitute a genuinely nonfoundational history, one which retains its explanatory power and its interest in change but does not stand on or reproduce naturalized categories.[69]

My pause at the collapse of historian, reader, and historical subject can also guide us to problems encountered in the pedagogy of teaching *Holy Feast and Holy Fast*. This book has galvanized and polarized my undergraduates and graduate students in a way that few books have in my gender studies courses. Discussions have often led to charged quarrels in seminar. I interpret those quarrels as enacting political problems in contemporary academic culture (still predominantly coded as white, heterosexual, middle-class, and male) in engaging the politics of identification as they relate historically to positioning the maternal function in the cultural work of reading, writing, teaching. Depending on popular, but often unacknowledged, attitudes toward fusion (and much theory echoes these popular attitudes), readers may regard the collapse of writer, reader, historical subject as good—a celebration of the maternal and a return to paradise lost; or they may experience the rhetorical entanglements as bad, a sign of disorder, a failure to differentiate, a form of psychosis (as Julia Kristeva would argue). The quarrels go unresolved and repetitively flare up because *Holy Feast and Holy Fast* enacts a process of fusion rhetorically without consciously opening a space in the text where the political and historical problem of fusion could be redescribed and replayed in political and ethical ways.

My reading of blood prompted by the "invisibility" of the plates of *Holy Feast and Holy Fast* has sought to open up a space in between the text and its frame and to intimate that the subject addressed and the addressing subject are not one, that these subjects are divided between themselves. By tracing the flow of blood across historically constructed categories I have striven to displace the overdetermined aspects of the book's structuralism and its reinscription of the very exclusions in relation to which medieval genders were maintained. The fact that the plates were uncannily invisible to reviewers suggests to me that they do the dream work of *Holy Feast and Holy Fast* and in so doing warn us of the dangers of the ongoing project of dreaming the Middle Ages and reengendering

---

[69] Scott, "The Category of Experience," p. 797.

Genders, Bodies, Borders

Europe as a foundational category, nostalgically and romantically, as our tropes for reading the Middle Ages are wont to instruct us.[70]

Where the invisibility of the plates comes into contact with the historiographical project of making medieval female mystics visible, there emerges the space where those things that were divided, often violently—the exterior Jew, the interior Christian, the visible and the invisible, the authentic and the copy, the masculine and the feminine—fearfully connect. The joining of those things divided, as urged in this article, does not have as its goal the repair of the past or the fabrication of some new synthesis. This fearful interconnectedness disconnects the space of autocannibalism, both historical and historiographical. Such interconnectedness can help us to appreciate the need for a transformative ethic for medieval gender studies of the sort which Toni Morrison has figured so magnificently and performatively in her novel *Beloved*: "It was not a story to pass on."[71]

---

[70] For a postcolonial critique of the problem of dreaming the Middle Ages, an image compellingly evoked by Umberto Eco in his essay "Dreaming the Middle Ages," in his collection of essays, *Travels in Hyperreality*, trans. William Weaver (San Diego, 1986), pp. 66–85, see Kathleen Biddick, "Bede's Blush," forthcoming in *The Past and Future of Medieval Studies*, ed. Van Engen (above, n. 28).

[71] Toni Morrison, *Beloved* (New York, 1987), p. 274.

I am grateful to the History Department and the Medieval Institute of the University of Notre Dame for permission to teach a graduate seminar (autumn 1991) in preparation for writing this article. The students of the seminar inspired me in their moments of resistance and insight: Stephen A. Allen, Jennifer Blatchford, Carolyn Edwards, Angela Gugliotta, Ann Hirschman, Elizabeth Jensen, Lezlie Knox, Tom Luongo, Dianne Phillips, Martin Tracy, Robert Vega, Lisa Wolverton. The encouragement of Judith Bennett, Michael Camille, Marilyn Desmond, Robert Franklin, Madonna Hettinger, Sandra Joshel, Karma Lochrie, Peggy McCracken, Joan W. Scott, Susan St. Ville, Susan Simonaitis, John Van Engen, and the members of a writing group, Ted Cachey, Julia Douthwaite, Barbara Green, were crucial. To Nancy Partner I owe a special debt of gratitude for her editorial advice and support.

Kathleen Biddick is Associate Professor of History at the University of Notre Dame, Notre Dame, IN 46556.

No Sex, No Gender

By Nancy F. Partner

1. MAN OR WOMAN? AND HOW DO WE KNOW WHAT WE THINK
WE MEAN BY WHAT WE MEAN BY THIS QUESTION?

Then we Bishops appeared and took our seats on the tribunal of the cathedral. Clotild was called before us. She showered abuse on her Abbess and made a number of accusations against her. She maintained that the Abbess kept a man in the nunnery, dressed in woman's clothing and looking like a woman, although in effect there was no doubt that he was a man. His job was to sleep with the Abbess whenever she wanted it. "Why! There's the fellow!" cried Clotild, pointing with her finger. Thereupon a man stepped forward, dressed in woman's clothing as I have told you. Everyone stared at him. He said that he was impotent and that that was the reason why he dressed himself up in this way. He maintained that he had never set eyes on the Abbess, although, of course, he knew her by name. He had never spoken to her in his life, and, in any case, he lived more than forty miles out of Poitiers. Clotild failed to prove her Abbess guilty on this count.[1]

Like a little mass of compacted ambiguity dropped into one's attention, this episode from Gregory of Tours's detailed account of the rebellion in St. Radegund's nunnery at Poitiers in 590 c.e. starts circle after circle of questions, doubts, puzzles, simple and complex inquiry—and all the possible answers open out to more questions. Some of the more obvious matters an ideologically uncommitted pre-postmodern curiosity might like to know about are:

—If the man allegedly living in the nunnery *looked* like a woman, as Clotild claimed ("dressed . . . and looking like a woman"; "indutus vestimenta muliebria pro femina haberetur"), why should there have been no doubt in her mind that he was a man ("vir manifestissime")?

—Bishop Gregory, here reporting as an eyewitness, at once saw and described the person who stepped forward as a *man*, "a man . . . dressed in woman's clothing" ("Qui cum in veste . . . muliebri"). This person apparently was not looking very much like a woman, nor, in his own terse reported comments, did he deny that he was a man. So why would this man cross-dress if he couldn't pass even cursory inspection?

---

[1] Gregory of Tours, *The History of the Franks*, trans. Lewis Thorpe (Middlesex, Eng., 1974), p. 570 (10.15). The episode comes from the culmination of the revolt at St. Radegund's nunnery at Poitiers, after internal rebellion led by Clotild had caused disorder and finally violence and King Childebert had appointed a commission of bishops, including Gregory, to investigate and reimpose discipline and order to the convent.

The crucial passage in the original reads as follows: ". . . eam virum habere in monasterium, qui indutus vestimenta muliebria pro femina haberetur, cum esset vir manifestissime declaratus, atque ipsi abbatissae famularetur assiduae, indicans eum digito: 'En ipsum.' Qui cum in veste, ut diximus, muliebri coram omnibus adstetisset, dixit, se nihil opus posse virile agere ideoque sibi hoc indumentum mutasse," MGH SSrerMerov, 1/1 (new ed. 1951), p. 504.

—Did he, for instance, have a beard? Had he tried to alter his appearance at all beyond changing his clothes?[2]

—And what exactly did he mean by "impotent" ("dixit, se nihil opus posse virile agere")? Was this specifically a chronic failure to achieve erection, or was some wider area of powerless behavior involved in his inability at the *opus virile*?

—Why would he signal a private sexual failure in such a public way? Or had this impotence been made public: involving a marriage perhaps, divorce, exposure before kin and neighbors?

—Even on the premise of great public shame, what sort of logic led from male sexual inadequacy to public adoption of the dress of the other sex in a village in sub-Roman, Christian Gaul?

A different tangent of thought leads one to wonder just what he was doing so conveniently in the cathedral at Poitiers on the day of the trial, when he lived a long country distance away. The entertainment value of the trial was compelling, obviously, but could even the ruthless Clotild have suborned and bribed some ordinary man into playing this part? If so, he certainly panicked and went to pieces at the crucial moment. But even on the hypothesis of Clotild's attempting wild dirty tricks in her vendetta against her abbess, that does not clarify the personal and social meaning of the man in the dress. We are still left contemplating a person who seems to agree that he is a man, standing in the cathedral before at least six startled bishops and many interested strangers (and possibly neighbors) and offering his "impotence" as "the reason" ("ideoque") for going about dressed as a woman. A world of mystery is condensed into the banal logic of that connective: "ideoque"—"therefore, and so. . . ." Really?

The sangfroid of Gregory's account is breathtaking, and even more breathtaking is the implication one might begin to draw about the sexual sophistication of Merovingian village society, presented as too imperturbably blasé to do more than blink at a man solving his sexual problems by changing his sex role, or at least his clothing. As is the case with so many of Gregory's episodes, he tells us just enough to let us know how much more he is not telling. With respect to Gregory as historian, this can be read plausibly enough, following Walter Goffart's interpretation, as another instance of his stern disregard of all the trivial concerns of the temporal world, his deep indifference to the meaningless miscellany of carnal life, over too soon and too pointless while it lasts to be worth the effort of narrative satisfactions.[3] For Gregory, the only point worth making

---

[2] Surely no bearded man could remain smooth shaven all the time with sixth-century barbering techniques, unless his self-description as "impotent" imprecisely points to a castration before puberty (in which case he should have looked much more convincingly like a woman at first sight), or this might be a hermaphroditic female with a nonfunctioning penis (in which case the general female appearance would be even stronger). Neither of these speculations strikes me as likely.

[3] Walter Goffart, *The Narrators of Barbarian History (A.D. 550–800: Jordanes, Gregory of Tours, Bede, and Paul the Deacon* (Princeton, N.J., 1988), offers an empathetic and cunningly argued case for Gregory's conscious intentions in his history; see esp. the section "Miracula: A Christian Historian's Answer to Philosophy," pp. 127–53.

(or at least the only one he makes) is that Abbess Leubovera, custodian of the convent St. Radegund personally founded, is innocent and worthy of her office.[4]

But profound *contemptus mundi* is a rare and uncommon thing. The unspecified "everyone" gathered in the cathedral were there for the vulgar pleasures of hearing the scandals of St. Radegund's nuns rehearsed in all their dreadful detail, and I strongly suspect that Gregory's celebrated narrative deadpan covers an uproar of crude double takes with the laconic "Everyone stared at him." Indeed. Even for Gregory of Tours this is heroic understatement. And for the modern scholarly reader, the sum reaction comes down in the end to a better-articulated version of much the same thing—inwardly, we all do stare.

Yet the questions I posed are inevitable and commonsensical; that is, they request answers that will fit what we know of late Roman/early-medieval social institutions and sexual attitudes. The man in the cathedral offering an aspect (however inadequate) of his genital maleness as the logic for appearing in public as a woman does force us, however reluctantly, toward questions about what we mean by being a man, and being a woman, in private and in public. This reticent little mystery presses us to ask ourselves exactly what we are half-consciously including as necessary and sufficient conditions for male or female human identity, and where we assume this identity is founded—in the self or in society?

We might be thinking about some ineradicable core identity, the namelessly named "Him" in this case, a man who has suffered such massive affront to his sexual and social integrity that he resorted to a mimetic behavioral self-punishment, or had it imposed on him: a sexually powerless man = (i.e., might as well be) a woman. He altered his outer appearance to conform to the nonvirile reality underneath. This approach requires some acceptance of the idea that biological sexual identity (male or female) can stand in very troubled and problematic relation to gender identity (living as man or woman in one's society), and that these aspects require different kinds of understanding. Thinking about "Him" as an essentially male person whom we glimpse for a moment in a painful and distorted way of life means recognizing the need of a depth psychology, because we need a systematic way of discussing core identity, the self, and the centrality of sexual drives and sexual identity to the formation of character. Otherwise, we have no way of discussing what "He" is doing to *himself* by dressing as a woman.

On the other hand, it is possible to weight the discussion almost entirely on the side of exterior social forces. We might consider the possibility that, hidden in the social repertory of sub-Roman Gaulic life, there was an intergendered social role to accommodate males who could not or would not satisfy masculine standards. Perhaps this cross-dressed man went quietly home to his "woman's work" in the village, to a few crude insults but no violence or ostracism, to

---

[4] Cross-dressing itself does not seem to concern Gregory, perhaps because it was not done to assist an otherwise sinful purpose. According to James Brundage, in *Law, Sex, and Christian Society in Medieval Europe* (Chicago, 1987), cross-dressing, although certainly forbidden by canonists of every period in accord with the prohibition in Deut. 22.5, was always treated perfunctorily and without comment or specified penalty; see pp. 57, 213, 251, 314, 473, 537, 571.

occupy some understood place at the social margin of kin and neighbors: a
social facsimile of a woman. At the very least, we have to concede him or "her"
some sort of life before and after that day at the cathedral in Poitiers. Anthropology can offer us some examples of socially condoned transvestism in tribal
societies with a strong warrior ethos.[5] Perhaps there was something about the
Germans that Tacitus forgot to tell us.

Readers of Gregory's *History* know that there is more to add to the discussion,
namely, the next paragraph. Clotild had no sooner "failed to prove her Abbess
guilty on this count" of keeping a disguised lover in the convent when, apparently caught up in an association of ideas, she proceeded to accuse the abbess
of keeping yet another impotent man about her, this one purposely castrated
so that the abbess might imitate the customs of the imperial court at Constantinople. Clotild gave the name of one of the servants "who was a eunuch."[6]
This person was not present, but his physician, Reovalis, was:

> "When this servant was a young lad" (lit.: "Puer iste, parvolus cum esset"), he said,
> "he had terrible pains in the groin. Nobody could do anything for him. His mother
> went to Saint Radegund and asked her to have the case looked into. I was called in
> and she told me to do what I could. I cut out the lad's testicles, an operation I had
> once seen performed by a surgeon in the town of Constantinople. Then I handed him
> back to his mother."

Reovalis's testimony cleared the abbess of the second charge, and it offers a
little more information about sexual identity and social roles among the Mer-
ovingians. A boy who was surgically castrated while he was very young ("par-
volus"), before puberty, would have grown up looking much more feminine
than any recognizable male who classifies himself as "unable to perform the
virile act," which suggests that, being anatomically normal, he had expected or
hoped to be normally potent. If impotence were a customary Merovingian reason for cross-dressing, then it would surely obtain here. And yet we have no
reason to think that the castrated youth was dressed as a woman, and his work,
as one of the servants of the convent quite unknown to the abbess, was an
ordinary male occupation.[7] He is known as a "eunuch," which is a male category,[8] referred to with masculine grammatical gender, and allowed to live a
man's life in his society, at least with regard to livelihood and dress. This allows
one to argue that male identity based on anatomical identification at birth and
reinforced throughout infancy by a mother who knew she had a son could
establish a gender identity strong enough to persist through disabling alteration

[5] The work of the psychoanalytic anthropologist George Devereux is of interest on this subject;
see nn. 26 and 53 below for references.

[6] Gregory of Tours, *History*, pp. 570–71 (10.15).

[7] The "servants" employed by the convent, or by individual nuns, are usually referred to as men
and have no religious functions, as: "While the servants of the Abbess were trying to put down an
affray organized by Clotild's gang, they struck one of Basina's servants and the man fell down dead,"
History, p. 569.

[8] Even if Abbess Leubovera had been guilty of Byzantine grandiosity and had wanted a retinue
of eunuchs, the eunuchs associated with the imperial court of Constantinople did not dress as
women; they were men whose known impairment constituted a legal impediment to the imperial
office (thus making them safe in the imperial household, always nervous about coups d'état).

of the genitals, permanent impotence, and absence of masculine characteristics such as beard, lowered voice, and so forth. Alternatively, it might still be argued that "eunuch" is itself an alternative social/sexual role, specific only to certain times and places, intergendered, defined and reinforced by forces exterior to the self which, following this logic, might not exist at all in our sense.

* * *

This may seem an odd beginning to an essay about studying medieval women, but I wanted to open some fundamental questions about sexual identity, the conventions of gender, and the continuity of human psychology in ways that are historically specific and inevitable-feeling, relatively free of ideological commitments. These are issues that cannot, in the politically and intellectually overwrought climate that prevails, remain long innocent, but it is worth reminding ourselves that unhinging gender identity from sexual identity is not a frivolous abstraction recently invented by oversubtle feminists but the appropriate and inevitable way of discussing central and sometimes overwhelming aspects of the lives of human beings at all times and places.

It is the historical study of women that has opened and defined these curious questions about sexual identity, sexuality, and the sex-linked protocols of social life, matters that never seemed to be questions at all so long as history was chiefly a matter of men studying men. Only the most temperate of feminist criticism was necessary to recognize that biological femaleness did not automatically or "naturally" entail femininity when the "Feminine" turned out to be every society's catchall category for transparent male fears, biological fantasies, and crude excuses for systematic domination. Separation of sexual identity from social identity has been and continues to be a central premise of women's history as well as the related field of the history of sexuality. In theory at least, sexuality as an interiorized defining structure of the integral self, and sexual belief and behavior as semiotic expressions of a culture's preoccupations are now radically separate and incommensurate ways of thinking.

In far too many ways the women whom medieval historians have to study are the imaginative constructions of men: the theoretical women of medical, philosophic, legal, and religious literature; the women seen as the property of masters, fathers, husbands; the women fantasized by poets, romancers, preachers, hagiographers. And yet, historians, men and women alike, have no choice but to do that same sort of work: imagine the women of the past. For this reason, for the sake of a heightened sense of the incorrigibleness of the human mind, and to remind us that the sexes are fated to struggle together, I chose the man in a dress as the emblem for the problems this essay addresses.

2. SEXUALITY AND SOCIAL CONSTRUCTION

Fundamental notions of sexuality, identity, and our estimate of how deeply the cultural conventions of gender impinge on individual character not only affect the *way* we think about medieval women but unavoidably determine whether the "women" we think about are human beings or cultural ideograms.

Our intellectual allegiances concerning such matters are being actively courted these days by enthusiastic adherents of a social constructionist theory of human formation and behavior which flatly denies all concepts of the mind and sexuality which proceed from psychoanalytic theory. In its most consistent and dogmatic versions, this view denies any innate endowment of mind universal to human beings, ignores or denies the psychosexual dynamics which culminate in individual character, and concedes only some minimal biologic substratum as shared among all of our species over time. Psychoanalysis assumes that manifest patterns of behavior, speech, and conscious desire all variously reflect the organization of an individual mind, both conscious and unconscious, which must continually adjust its wishes to the demands of a real exterior world. In the constructivist vision, "mind," in this sense, disappears, and the body and its behaviors are a metaphor map shaped solely by the unavoidable and ubiquitous pressures of social processes determined by power relations: social teleology crushes out human ontology.

The topic of homosexuality in the setting of the ancient world has been the major focus of constructivist scholarship, with studies concerned with feminine gender (as conceived by men) a second favorite topic. One of the most active and adamant proponents of this project[9] is David Halperin, whose *One Hundred Years of Homosexuality* is the best introduction to the subject because it combines Halperin's detailed arguments for the constructivist position, a candid transcribed interview with a challenging questioner, and three essays on scholarly subjects, including his clever and searching "Why Is Diotima a Woman?"[10] Diotima, the name of the learned woman who purportedly taught Socrates the lessons on erotic love he expounds to the company in Plato's *Symposium*, turns out to be not merely the female-gendered fiction she seems ("she," after all, is only a name mentioned by Socrates), but, more complicatedly, she is not even a *feminine* fiction at all. "She" is so wholly appropriated by the male discourse of Plato's philosophy as to be a "reinscribed male identity"; "she is an alternate

---

[9] I find it difficult to settle on an appropriate term for "social constructivism"; I resist calling it a theory because I think constructivism has far too many logical gaps, inconsistencies, and contradictions to qualify for the term even in the loose usage of the humanities, but "view," "project," "idea," "school," etc., are not entirely right either. I follow writers of this persuasion in using the terms "constructivist" and "constructionist" interchangeably.

[10] David Halperin, *One Hundred Years of Homosexuality* (New York and London, 1990), pp. 113—51 for the Diotima essay. The provocative title of the book is a reminder of the central argument: that "sexuality" as an interior psychic organization of the unconscious and conscious mind is an invention dating only from the nineteenth century, and homosexuality as a particular kind of psychic organization is also an invention of recent provenance. Another introduction to the subject could be the anthology *Forms of Desire: Sexual Orientation and the Social Constructionist Controversy*, ed. Edward Stein (New York and London, 1990). This book is entirely focused on the meanings and causes of homosexuality conceived as a rather abstract category term, and the essays are all relentlessly theoretical, but Stein has thoughtfully included a crucial essay by Michel Foucault, several points of view, a bibliography, and a valiant attempt to summarize the controversy, in chap. 12: "Conclusion: The Essentials of Constructionism and the Construction of Essentialism," pp. 325—53. Readers who wonder at these citations to an essay which is not particularly about homosexuality are asked to be patient and remember that theories of sexuality must be adequate for all object choices and erotic modes, for men and women both, or fail a serious test of adequacy.

male identity," a metaphor of masculine discourse: " 'Woman' and 'man' are figures of male speech. Gender—no less than sexuality—is an irreducible fiction."[11]

The social constructivist view goes much further than this radical separation of the "fiction" of gender from biological sex. Sexuality in the complexly extended modern sense, the kernel of individual personality which leaves its signature on other, nonsexual behavior, is also a fiction. In this view there is no psychologically organized individual sexuality at all, and an infant's anatomical status (male or female) does not seem to entail anything about its sexual development aside from being the site for the lessons its society imposes. Directly and heavily derived from Michel Foucault's work in general and his *History of Sexuality* in particular, the constructivist view asserts, with Foucault, that the humanist concept of "the subject," the coherently individuated human being which we also indicate by the concept of the "self," is a myth perpetuated within modern discourses of power to impose and conceal the imprisoning designs of social authority. The complex notions of sexuality as a central and universal expression of the self, offered by psychoanalysis, are regarded by Foucault as a specifically modern invention (as opposed to a discovery or an explanation of human reality), another of the malign and subtle modern instruments for imposing an intimate and totalitarian discipline over all of society by means of knowledge, or perhaps "knowledge."

The leading ideas which have been largely accepted by scholars who wish to work out the detailed history of sexual life along lines suggested by Foucault are (1) that history is characterized by disjuncture, discontinuity, rupture; (2) that the self, a self-existent, coherent being persisting through all change until death, is a naive illusion dating only from the eighteenth century; (3) that sexuality as the interior organization of libidinal drives into wishes, repressions, and sublimations is also an illusion, of yet more modern date (related vaguely and variously to capitalism, science, industrialization, the bourgeoisie, etc., the usual suspects). It does seem to be assumed that humans have some general urge to genital pleasure but that only systems of discourse derived from specific patterns of social authority give this urge any special meaning or form. Ideas that were needling, provocative, and brilliantly wrongheaded as interesting aspects of an interesting mind when offered by their originator are now leadenly reduced to the dogmas of a new orthodoxy. The body and its pleasures, Foucault's program for a true history of sexuality, invariably turn out to be metaphors for society and power.[12]

Scholarship collected under this rubric tends to focus on the sexual behaviors, erotic art and language of premodern societies that most sharply differ from

[11] Halperin, *One Hundred Years*, pp. 150, 151. The essay is subtle and beautifully argued, and quite convincing because it deals solely with a literary text deeply embedded in an exclusive male pursuit of philosophy. The general course of argument, however, and the general tone of the conclusions are never confined to masculine literature alone but are assumed to apply to humans generally in actual social and sexual life.

[12] The excerpt from the introduction to Michel Foucault's *History of Sexuality*, 1, selected by Stein as a locus classicus for constructionist theory, is very explicit on the subject of power and excitement; "The Perverse Implantation," in Stein, *Forms of Desire*, pp. 11–23.

modern practice; a well-chosen selection can be found in the anthology edited by Halperin with John Winkler and Froma Zeitlin, *Before Sexuality: The Construction of Erotic Experience in the Ancient Greek World*, a companion volume to his *One Hundred Years*.[13] The tendency of sexual behavior to incorporate and reinforce social hierarchies, class distinctions, masculine competitions, purity and contamination anxieties is subtly and fascinatingly anatomized by scholars attuned to these frequencies, but for all the luxuriant documentation of erotic cum political and social detail that makes these essays enthralling, there is a certain predictability here. "Surfaces" of behavior, language, and image invariably dissolve away to reveal all of hierarchical society pressing its commands and protocols onto human actors—and nothing else. Constructionist scholarship informed by Foucault's sensibilities adopts his signature correlation of sex with power, and attempts his virtuoso ability to parse all eroticism into elements of (disbursed and displaced) sadism.[14] Power *is* pleasure in this vision, and thus all attention is directed to the configurations of social authority which then serve to "explain" human sexuality: that is the formula underlying the surface variety of constructionist work. As in one of John Winkler's essays: ". . . the energy of sex is conceived [in *Daphnis and Chloe*] not as something that relates friend to friend or equal to equal but more as a dynamic that clarifies a relation between enemies, opposites, unequals."[15] "The social body precedes the sexual body": a circular premise and self-proof.[16]

The best work in this mode produces detailed cultural portraits in which sexual players (interchangeably human and literary) reenact in stylized erotic mime the class, gender, and economic hierarchies of the larger society.[17] The often-

---

[13] *Before Sexuality: The Construction of Erotic Experience in the Ancient Greek World*, ed. David M. Halperin, John J. Winkler, and Froma Zeitlin (Princeton, N.J., 1990). A collection of essays of very high quality, not all of the authors are equally committed to the strongest version of the argument that "sexuality . . . is a specifically modern production," p. 5. In particular, the last essay in the collection, "Bodies and Minds: Sexuality and Renunciation in Early Christianity," by Peter Brown (pp. 479–93), so effectively contradicts Halperin's theory that it sets up a very interesting argument with the entire book, a point I discuss further below.

Another work of great finesse in cultural explication based on dubious large-scale premises about human life is John Winkler's *Constraints of Desire: The Anthropology of Sex and Gender in Ancient Greece* (New York and London, 1990). From the introduction: "The key Foucauldian thesis is that 'sexuality' is a distinctively modern construction, a new nineteenth- and twentieth-century way of speaking about the self as organized around well-defined (and therefore catalogable) sexual characters and desires," p. 4. The trap of cultural relativism (things are only what contemporaries say they are, and any other frame of reference is anachronistic and therefore unsuitable) is strongly present in constructivist thought.

[14] "The medical examination, the psychiatric investigation, the pedagogical report, and family controls . . . function as mechanisms with a double impetus: pleasure and power, the pleasure that comes from exercising a power that questions, monitors, watches, spies, searches out, palpates, brings to light; . . . capture and seduction, confrontation and mutual reinforcement: . . . *perpetual spirals of power and pleasure*." It is a shame to truncate the wonderful spiraling quality of the longer passage; Foucault in Stein, *Forms of Desire*, p. 19.

[15] Winkler, *Constraints of Desire*, p. 117.

[16] Halperin, *One Hundred Years*, p. 38.

[17] *Before Sexuality*; see particularly good examples in the essays by Nicole Loraux, "Herakles: The Super-Male and the Feminine"; Anne Carson, "Putting Her in Her Place: Woman, Dirt, and Desire"; John Winkler, "Laying down the Law: The Oversight of Men's Sexual Behavior in Classical Athens."

startling sexual mores of long-distant societies, when read in this way, as condensed tropes of the structured society, become intelligible and meaningful. The opaque and mysterious quality that clings to human sexuality is exorcised and replaced by the simpler cruelties of privilege and domination. "It begins to look as if the entire procedure [public scrutiny of sexual behavior of Athenian citizens] had very little to do with sex and everything to do with political ambitions and alliances . . ."[18]—this, from John Winkler's essay on the sexual protocol demanded of Athenian men, is a typical sort of interpretation, and typically convincing within its frame of reference. The fixed concentration on social hierarchy and the analogue patterns of sex/status domination which are typical of all traditional societies obscures both individual and cultural variation. Using the constructionist optic, Athens and Sparta are indistinguishable.

Work that conveys the feeling of a genuine "historical anthropology" is the signal achievement of constructionist scholarship, but the philosophic or meta-historical claims made on the basis of these social readings of sexual life are stretched and exaggerated far beyond what the evidence can support. There is something intellectually stifled and rigid underlying the modishly sophisticated language that characterizes this approach: social meaning exhausts all meaning. Once some fragment of a specific cultural pattern (invariably an aspect of dominance: males over females, free over slave, citizens over noncitizens, etc.) can be shown to make a plausible fit with some form of sexual behavior (who can be a penetrator, who a submissive receptor, etc.), the meaning of that behavior is considered complete and nothing more is to be sought. This one-way interpretive move, from experience *outward only* to the group or collective culture, denies by ignoring the other, complementary move from the surface to the personal interior, from public to private, from the historically local to the universal, to the psyche. The interpretive move *outward only* is what Halperin calls a "cultural poetics":

> Cultural poetics refers to the process whereby a society and its subgroups construct widely shared meanings—. . . These meanings are jointly produced, distributed, enforced, and subverted by human communities. . . . We assume the interdependence in culture of social practices and subjective experiences. The erotic experiences of individual human beings are thus, in our view, artifacts that reflect, in part, the larger cultural poetics of the societies in which those individuals live.[19]

This "constructionist thesis," in Halperin's term,[20] here given its most flexible and generous statement, turns out to offer no concept or premise that could plausibly explain how anyone could possibly begin to "subvert" any of the "widely shared meanings" whose production, distribution, and enforcement have constructed the human thing which has no self and no personal sexuality. In fact, the "subjective experiences" glancingly conceded by Halperin are never really acknowledged or explored by him or any of the constructionist scholars, and quite rightly—there are no individuals with subjectivity in any profound

---

[18] Winkler, "Laying down the Law," p. 193.
[19] Halperin, *Before Sexuality*, p. 4.
[20] Halperin, *One Hundred Years*, p. 44. See also above, n. 9.

sense in their conceptual world to have experiences. "Subjective experiences" are, by definition, miniature replicas of "social practices." There is nothing else they can be. He is certainly right in noting that, in modern thought, ". . . sexuality is intrinsic to the concept and set of practices focused on 'the self,' " but is oddly disengenuous when he goes on to define the self as "the blank individual who is the subject of the modern social sciences."[21] There is nothing "blank" about the modern concept of the self—that dense locus of conscious and unconscious mental processes in continual negotiation with the social world. If experience is something more than the passive registration of sensory impact, then only the self can have experience.

Halperin's candid attempts to explain how a constructionist being comes to be constructed lead nowhere, and his discussion of how (or why) the modern social processes, which according to him are monomaniacally intent on creating exclusive heterosexuals, should have carelessly produced so many homosexuals is convoluted beyond comprehension. The constructionist thesis holds that "our intuitions about the world and about ourselves are no doubt constituted at the same time as our sexuality itself," that is, very early in life, and the process of social construction is therefore beyond the reach of intuition or observation.[22] Aside from the slight paranoid style of this theory, it offers no clue as to why there should exist any individual deviation at all (much less, subversion!) after helpless infants are subjected to a social processing so relentlessly immanent and enveloping as to resemble processing in a waffle iron.

The problem here is that constructionists insist on being at war with what they call "essentialism" (briefly, any theory that seeks "culture-independent, objective and intrinsic properties" in human experience),[23] although, as one anticonstructionist, John Boswell, ironically points out, nobody will admit to being an "essentialist" in the constructionists' version.[24] It seems to be assumed that the ground being fought over, human sexuality, has to be taken and wholly occupied by one explanatory force only. This is a reductive and polemical ap-

---

[21] Halperin, *Before Sexuality*, p. 6.

[22] Halperin, *One Hundred Years*, pp. 44–45 for the quotations; the hard questions are attempted in the interview section with Richard Schneider. One of the more annoying characteristics of constructionist polemics is a marked tendency to create unusually stupid straw men as opponents: thus, Halperin proposes that nonconstructionists believe in "such a thing as a 'natural' sexuality, something we are simply born into" (p. 44), when he has to know that sexuality is a complex organization of drives, desires, and sublimations developed over a period of many years. No one, at least no one among the audience for his book, believes that we are "simply born into" our mature sexual identities. The concept of "nature" also comes in for straw-man treatment, with nonconstructionist opinion defined as belief in some very simple, untenable ideas about "natural" behavior, which are then shot down with declarations like the following: " 'Nature' is not exhausted by these two possibilities of sexual object-choice" (i.e., same or opposite sex). Did anyone ever think it was? Similarly, Halperin's definition of modern heterosexuality is found in no psychological theory (nor is it held by any person I know): "a population of human males who are (supposedly) incapable of being sexually excited by a person of their own sex *under any circumstances* [his emphasis]." Since nobody thinks this is what a heterosexual person is (most emphatically not Freud), and no one argues for it, it does make the work of constructionist argument rather easier.

[23] Stein, *Forms of Desire*, p. 338.

[24] John Boswell's essay is cogent and generous-minded, "Categories, Experience and Sexuality," in Stein's *Forms of Desire*, pp. 133–73.

proach to a deeply complex matter. All explanations are instances of some mode of comprehension (in philosopher Louis Mink's phrase) operating with its own concepts and aims, which do implicitly assert epistemological primacy. However, there is no single, all-encompassing mode which satisfies all the aims of understanding:

> But one cannot argue for the primacy of any of the modes except by reference to criteria which themselves are derivative from that mode's aim of comprehension. Hence each mode is self-justifying; critical analysis and intellectual advance are possible within but only within each mode.[25]

This general principle of the nature of explanation, quoted here from Mink's austerely compressed essay, "Modes of Comprehension and the Unity of Knowledge," may seem rather abstract for the subjects under discussion in this essay, but since I am arguing for what is considered an "essentialist" theory as a *contributing* interpretation of complex human behavior in the distant past, I feel I ought to expose the grounds of my position as clearly as I am capable of understanding them.

Rigorous guidance through the intellectual vanity fair of academic theorizing about self and society is offered by George Devereux in some forty years of work as both psychoanalyst and cultural anthropologist. Like Louis Mink, Devereux saw clearly that modes of comprehension appropriate to human behavior proceed from their particular premises toward their intellectual aims; different modes cannot be forced into a single slurred-together unity, nor are they in conflict for ideological dominion over the totality of experience. In "The Argument," introduction to *Ethnopsychoanalysis: Psychoanalysis and Anthropology as Complementary Frames of Reference*, Devereux sets out the principle of "complementarity" as his methodological principle of explanation, which he also calls the "double discourse"—the explanation of human behavior by (at least) two discourses, one addressed outward to society, and one inward to the psychodynamics of the individual:

> [I]n the study of Man (but not only in the study of Man) it is not only possible but mandatory to explain a behavior, already explained in one way, also in another way—i.e., within another frame of reference.[26]

[25] Louis O. Mink, *Historical Understanding*, ed. Brian Fay, Eugene Golob, and Richard Vann (Ithaca, N.Y., 1987), p. 40. It is important to note that Mink does not envision endless modes of comprehension. He identifies three fundamentally different irreducible modes: theoretical or law-forming, configurational, categorial. Each generates its own form of discourse and appropriate concepts.

[26] George Devereux, *Ethnopsychoanalysis: Psychoanalysis and Anthropology as Complementary Frames of Reference* (Berkeley, Calif., 1978), p. 1. Over his long career Devereux published clinical/theoretical studies in psychoanalysis as well as studies based on his fieldwork in anthropology; he is often cited for his work among American Plains Indians. Devereux's writing is fastidious and terse, and his thought is crystalline sharp and unforgiving of muddle and confusion. He is especially noted for his development of the concept of "ethnic disorder," an explanation of the way mental illness follows cultural patterns while retaining a core of structural similarity across cultures. Devereux was emphatic about refusing to combine or elide psychological and anthropological forms of explanation since each proceeds from its own frame of reference. His methodological principle was complementarity, in which two kinds of explanation, each appropriate and complete in its own terms, could construct a double discourse about human experience in specific societies. His work

We may forgive Devereux his use of the out-of-favor collective noun, for the sake of the breadth of mind and logical clarity which see that "a given human act can be made to seem inevitable in terms of either sociocultural or psychological-psychoanalytic explanations of it."[27]

The constructionist argument is too multifaceted and shifts its ground too often for more detailed analysis here,[28] but what is very clear is that in a world in which the sexuality, self-consciousness, intuitions, and desires of young, psycheless humans are simultaneously "constituted," subject to "acculturation [which] consists precisely in learning to accept as natural, normal, and inevitable what is in fact conventional and arbitrary,"[29] incidents such as the following could not, by definition, happen:

> A young girl at Oxford, the daughter of one of the burgesses, and already wedded to a certain youth of the same town, was inflamed by a stronger love for another youth, and deserting her husband, actually lived with him as his wife. Her husband accused her and proved the charge, and the bishop [Hugh of Lincoln] earnestly admonished her to return without delay to him. She, however, was dissuaded by her mother . . . and declared defiantly that she would rather die than live with him. The man of God [Bishop Hugh] then took her husband by his right hand, and combining persuasion with threats said, "If you desire to be my daughter, obey me and give your husband the kiss of peace with God's blessing. If you do not, I shall not spare you and your evil counsellors." He also ordered her husband to give her the kiss of peace, which he would willingly have done, but the wretched girl impudently spat in his face, although he was near the altar and the bishop himself was present in the church. . . . Everyone was deeply shocked. . . .[30]

---

is not always easy or perfectly inviting (and, of course, it uses politically unreconstructed terms like "normal," " abnormal," "high" and "low" culture), but it offers the strongest directives I have yet found for acknowledging both the inner and outer, the universal and contingent aspects of historical experience. Many of his essays are readily available: in addition to the collection of basic theoretical studies cited above, special studies are collected in *Basic Problems of Ethnopsychiatry*, trans. Basia Miller Gulati and George Devereux (Chicago and London, 1980), with full bibliography of his work.

[27] Devereux, *Basic Problems*, p. 157.

[28] Although convinced constructionists like Halperin and Winkler profess to believe that no one who lived before the past two centuries is correctly approached via concepts of self or sexuality, they poach in analytic territory for ideas whose force they find irresistible, like projection. Most of the studies dealing with gender, especially male attitudes toward females, rest heavily on the conceptual ground of projection, as in Halperin's "Diotima" essay: "That Diotima's 'femininity' is illusory—a projection of male fantasy, a symbolic language employed by men in order to explain themselves and their desires to one another . . . ," *One Hundred Years*, p. 147 (also reprinted in *Before Sexuality*). Concepts of stereotyping, displacement, and denial also figure largely, if not always by name, in gender studies. The point to note is that although these ideas are widely popularized and superficially used in all kinds of cultural analysis, these are psychoanalytic concepts which do not "work" except in the context of a psychoanalytic structure of mind, and of the pressing interchanges between unconscious and conscious mind. Projection is a psychic maneuver involving ego ideal, repression, reaction formation, strategies of paranoia and displacement; in the bluntest terms, projection requires a psyche—the interior self with its sexuality. For a detailed explanation of the psychic dynamics underlying projection, a good source is the introductory section of Sander Gilman's *Difference and Pathology: Stereotypes of Sexuality, Race, and Madness* (Ithaca, N.Y., 1985).

[29] Halperin, *One Hundred Years*, p. 44.

[30] Adam of Eynsham, *The Life of St Hugh of Lincoln*, ed. Decima L. Douie and Hugh Farmer, 2 (London, 1962), pp. 31–32. To finish the story, the bishop excommunicated the girl, who remained defiant even after thinking it over for several days; Adam, among the most censorious of the "shocked," insists rather vaguely that she was soon strangled by the devil.

And everyone should have been shocked! Nothing in the ruling systems of twelfth-century English gender, morality, marital and religious authority would seem to have constructed that willful young woman, who had apparently slipped loose from whole epistemes of discursive processing. But there she *and* her mother are—rejecting husbands, choosing lovers, shrugging off the bishop, and spitting in church. The "run but you can't hide" constructionist thesis has nothing to tell us about this incident, while cultural history with a depth psychology at its heart welcomes and recognizes a self-willed bourgeoise who plainly understood that social disciplines emanate from sources exterior to *herself*, and that, with a little luck (and the support of a strong-willed mother), even women can have erotic projects of their own.

The constructionists of ancient history simply ignore the work of E. R. Dodds with its deftly incorporated psychological insights, but their contemporary Peter Brown, who enters into intricate conversation with ancient and medieval sources with a deep and assured command (and who is around to defend his work), is not so easily ignored. Although he is one of the contributors to the *Before Sexuality* anthology, Brown's essay, "Bodies and Minds: Sexuality and Renunciation in Early Christianity," a summary of the major themes of his brilliant book, *The Body and Society*, so contradicts and disproves central constructionist dogmas as to require some response from the editor:[31]

> To be sure, a certain degree of identification of the self with the sexual self can be noticed in late antiquity and was strengthened by the Christian confessional; however, it did not become complete, explicit, and authoritative until the eighteenth- and nineteenth-century scientific construction of sexuality as a separate field of positivistic study.[32]

This slighting acknowledgment ("To be sure, a certain degree . . .") precedes a weak and evasive dismissal, which is nothing more than a reassertion of Foucaultian dogma. In any case, I have not noticed constructionists limiting themselves to "complete, explicit, and authoritative" evidence to support their own arguments, and since when has Christianity not been culturally "authoritative"? Brown assembles and analyzes complex masses of difficult materials before arriving at his well-grounded and powerful interpretations:

> As on an X-ray photograph, therefore, a patch of disquieting opacity lay at the center of the human heart. What is distinctive is the speed and the tenacity with which that dark spot came to be identified, in Christian circles, with specifically sexual desires, with unavowed sexual stratagems, and, as we shall see, with the lingering power of sexual fantasy. . . .
>
> Body and mind, now sensed as mysteriously interconnected through sexuality, had sunk together since the time of Galen, receding into the depths of the half-charted and, from now onward, ever-fascinating unity of the self.[33]

Attentive readers of *The Body and Society* know that the persuasive power of

---

[31] Peter Brown's essay in *Before Sexuality*, pp. 479–93, summarizes central aspects of his *Body and Society: Men, Women, and Sexual Renunciation in Early Christianity* (New York, 1988).

[32] Halperin, introduction to *Before Sexuality*, p. 6.

[33] Brown, "Bodies and Minds," in *Before Sexuality*, pp. 481, 492.

Brown's readings lies in the open secret that he greets all the historical dead as once-complete persons, fully interiorized men and women with, implicitly, the same drives and psychosexual organization as ourselves, who yet freely regarded the world and analyzed themselves with values and concepts radically different from our own. The deep and subtly calibrated balance Brown finds between an unstated psychological premise of human universality and an explicit historical sense acutely sensitive to local cultural pressures accounts for his ability to make the most austerely removed desert ascetic seem to turn and show us a human face. The presence of a successful "double discourse" (whether or not the author worked it out with conscious intent) is signaled by the reader's sense of richly expanded insights: the sense of recognizable human lives adapted to, yet in tension with, the requirements of the social world. Brown's work is offered in the pre-postmodern (alias, traditional) theory-free manner, and in an entirely personal style of evocative, almost painterly metaphor. A generational audience who no longer read Freud or any of his successors might easily not even recognize that this is psychoanalytically informed history.[34]

The structure of human *experience* of the body and desire from the second century C.E. to the death of Augustine traced so sensitively throughout this study is "an encounter of mind with world, neither of these ever simple or wholly perspicuous," in Peter Gay's elegantly plain-language psychoanalytic definition.[35] Every human being brings an innate endowment of psychological organization, mind, to encounter the social structures and belief systems of the surrounding society, world. Human experience emerges from the ensuing negotiations, frustrations, and reconciliations of this endless traffic. Culture and social pressures are one great dimension, but only one dimension, of human experience. We never seem to encounter any people in constructivist studies, just bundles of behaviors or collective thought patterns linked to names. In Peter Brown's writing, the most attenuated sun-dried hermit is a man:

> [S]exual fantasies highlighted the areas of intractability in the human person. But this intractability was not simply physical. It pointed into the very depths of the soul. Sexual

---

[34] And, of course, the author may not even agree with me, but just as men and women have unavowed stratagems, so can books. Peter Brown is exceptionally concerned that we not impose inappropriate modern preconceptions on the conscious and almost-conscious preoccupations of people in ancient societies; for example, he warns us not to be misled by the medical metaphors used by Cassian "to express his sense of psychic powers that burned like subcutaneous fevers within the unconscious self. . . . Cassian, however, was a loyal follower of the Desert Fathers on this issue. Sexuality, for him, was not what it has become in the lay imagination of a post-Freudian age," *Body and Society*, p. 421. The reader should note that we are being offered meticulous distinctions between what *Cassian* did not intend or mean and the author's firm and clear use of terms like "psychic powers" and "unconscious self" to describe persons of the fourth century.

[35] Peter Gay, *The Bourgois Experience*, 1: *Education of the Senses* (New York and Oxford, 1984), p. 11; the general introduction, pp. 3–16, offers the author's historically sensitive project for bringing the insights of psychoanalysis to history and should allay any fears about often-alleged reductionist or "essentialist" tendencies as inevitable to psychohistory. "For all the intricate and energetic activity of the unconscious, the historical interpretation of experience must be sensitive to its conscious no less than to its unconscious dimensions, to the work of culture on mind—the world, in a word, in which the historian is most at home," p. 13. "For the psychoanalyst's individual is a social individual," p. 16.

desire revealed the knot of unsurrendered privacy that lay at the very heart of fallen man. Thus, in the new language of the desert, sexuality became, as it were, an ideogram of the unopened heart.[36]

Explicitly realized intuitions into sexuality as the unified connector of body and mind were fully developed by the time of Augustine, and Brown notes that this insight was established "from now onwards." Medievalists should accept this conclusion at its full weight. There are endless consequences for the discipline of history in its entirety of a choice between the social constructionist vision of human life and a history based on humans with complex psychosexual organization. The specific consequences for the history of women are crucial. The question for feminist scholars should *not* be whether everything psychoanalysis has to say about women is perfectly flattering, but which body of assumptions helps us to the richest, most complex and generous understanding of women—especially the women of frankly misogynist societies. Which set of assumptions offers them humanity, and which reduces them to passive anthropological exhibits?

3. AMBITIONS OF THE SELF: HELOISE ON HER OWN

> No one having skill in medicine judges an inward disease by inspection of the outward appearance.
>
> —Heloise to Peter Abelard[37]

Heloise, more than any other female voice, can tell us something important about what it was to be a woman in the twelfth century. She does us the great service of candidly anatomizing the full resources available to the conscious mind: rational argument, acquired knowledge, wishes, fears, memories, self-conscious reflections, waking fantasies, dreams. Her logic is Augustinian (the mind is self-divided, and the will is incorrigibly willful), her style a classical/patristic pastiche, but her voice is her own. If we ask unprejudiced questions about her life, and are willing to remember Devereux's principle that "a given human act can be made to seem inevitable in terms of either sociocultural or psychological-psychoanalytic explanations of it,"[38] she offers us generous and candid answers which are both culturally patterned and specific to her alone. This is a point that can too easily be lost. Because Heloise was not ordinary and did not live an ordinary life, we should never lapse into regarding her as a sport or marginal deviant of her society. For all her striking talent and education, and through all the dramatic plot of her life, she was fully intelligible to those who knew her; she attracted sympathy, trust, and respect from very discerning friends. And she was profoundly known to herself.

---

[36] Brown, *Body and Society*, p. 230.

[37] Heloise, second letter to Peter Abelard, in *The Letters of Abelard and Heloise*, trans. C. K. Scott Moncrieff (New York, 1942), p. 83; Latin text in J. T. Muckle, "The Personal Letters between Abelard and Heloise," *Mediaeval Studies* 15 (1953), 82.

[38] Devereux, *Basic Problems*, p. 157. This is a restatement of his basic principle of complementarity, or multiple explanation through different frames of reference.

Her bizarre postmortem career as an honorary man in literary drag has been recently analyzed by Barbara Newman in an extraordinarily fine essay, "Authority, Authenticity, and the Repression of Heloise,"[39] whose frank title tells us its plot. One hopes that after this meticulously argued exposé, Heloise's literary gender will be permanently attached to her literal sex, and that both, reunited in her historical self, will finally be allowed undisputed ownership of her letters.[40] Newman's own analysis of Heloise, grounded in the idea that complex personalities must incorporate conflicts and self-contradictions, is sensitive, generous, and real. This view of Heloise takes her seriously. It makes her intensely developed intellectual life the central source of the multiplied feminine (and often misogynist) paradigms Heloise enacted for and to her one love: "she enacted each of these roles vis-à-vis a single beloved other who became in turn her Ovidian seducer, her Pompey, her Aeneas, her Jerome; she could be his Corinna or Cornelia, his Dido, or his Paula."[41] All I wish to add here are a few emphases in tone and nuance to point up the advantages of a psychologically grounded approach in dealing with the Heloise themes of feminine abjection and sublimation.

The historically specific, culturally constructed nature of Heloise's experiences, from her classical/patristic Latin education to her office as abbess, is apparent to us. What has to be thought about through another optic is exactly *who* was having those experiences. Peter Gay's explication of mind and world is acute and sympathetic: "The human mind hungers for reality; except for the largely encapsulated id, which is the depository of the raw drives and of deeply repressed material, the other institutions of the mind, the ego and the superego, draw continuously and liberally on the culture in which they subsist, develop, succeed, and fail. While the mind presents the world with its needs, the world gives the mind its grammar, wishes their vocabulary, anxieties their object."[42] The openness of the mind to its world, its conformity and its ability to push back—the reality principle, so central to psychoanalytic thought—is the bridge between the double discourses of mind and culture. My remarks about Heloise are my own attempt at an interpretation built on complementary frames of reference.

Heloise's letters do not sustain a psychohistorical inquiry because she was neurotic; quite the contrary. Heloise displays what a strong and well-adapted female personality looks like in the cultural world she shared with everyone else of her time, in the personal crisis she faced alone, and under the most poignant and unremitting disappointments. She was not happy, admittedly, but consistent good luck has never been a necessary condition for any serious conception of psychic health. The keynote of the letters is her refusal to sacrifice her person-

[39] Barbara Newman, "Authority, Authenticity, and the Repression of Heloise," *Journal of Medieval and Renaissance Studies* 22 (1992), 121–57.

[40] Barbara Newman actually undertakes to read Heloise's first two letters *as if* they were written by Abelard; the reading which follows this premise self-destructs, of course, on every ground, which is exactly her argument; see "Authority, Authenticity," pp. 123–44.

[41] Newman, "Authority, Authenticity," p. 151.

[42] Peter Gay, *Bourgeois Experience*, pp. 13–14.

ality and history to embittered shame disguised as religious compunction (Abelard's strategy). She never cultivated emotional numbness as an antidote to reality:

> For what repentance of sins is that, however great the mortification of the body, when the mind still retains the same will to sin, and burns with its old desire? Easy is it indeed for anyone by confessing his sins to accuse himself, or even in outward satisfaction to mortify his body. But it is most difficult to tear away the heart from the desire of the greatest pleasures. . . .[43]

The mind seeks its pleasures—and so it follows perfectly from the logic of this vigorous mind, open to experience and strongly reality-principled, that Heloise *would* naturally have sought the alternative gratifications offered to her in the religious life she perforce led: the respect, honors, and daily sense of achievement earned by her work as abbess of the Paraclete.[43a] There is no contradiction here between her frank longings for past delights and her exemplary life in the convent: just as she refused to suppress memory and desire, so she also acknowledged the claims of external reality in the present. With all her longings and frustrations, her anger and regrets, Heloise never fails to meet a psychoanalytic standard of psychic health: strong reality principle, the capacity to adjust and readjust to changing circumstance without self-destroying conformity, a correct appreciation of the difference between her own wishes and the external pressures imposed by her society.

Heloise had arrived at a deep understanding of the divide between inner and outer lives, between the pressure of wishes and the frustrations of reality. Every configuration of her life had accentuated that division between what she would demand of reality and what reality instead demanded of her. She rebuked Abelard for his slack and convenient willingness to accept her outward role, The Abbess, as the totality of her identity: "No one having skill in medicine judges an inward disease by inspection of the outward appearance." She was not speaking here literally about disease or herself as a diseased person. The metaphor of medical examination expresses her scorn of superficiality and literalness, with Abelard cast as the stupid doctor unable to diagnose an affliction of the heart. Provoked beyond the self-suppressing decorums of medieval literary convention by Abelard's dismissive and banal reply to her first letter, Heloise let herself speak from her self.

Her second letter is an insistent, multiply argued demonstration of the truth that she had not become merely the sum total of her manifest daily behavior. "They preach that I am chaste who have not discovered the hypocrite in me. They make the purity of the flesh into a virtue, when it is a virtue not of the body but of the mind."[44] The "outward appearance" is not all. Although she had conformed her speech and her actions to the demands of her office, she

---

[43] Heloise, second letter, in Moncrieff, trans., p. 80; Muckle, ed., p. 80.

[43a] In *Speculum* 68 (1993), 435, I mistakenly placed Heloise as abbess of Argenteuil when the setting of the letters and her career as an abbess was the Paraclete; my thanks to Mary Martin McLaughlin, author of *Heloise and the Paraclete: Ductrix et Magistra* (Toronto, 1993), for bringing this error to my attention in time to correct it.

[44] Heloise, second letter, in Moncrieff, trans., pp. 81–82; Muckle, ed., p. 81.

had not surrendered her mind. Her deepest and most intransigent assertion is *not* of a continuing sexual urge (that is the fiercely defiant evidence: fantasies during mass, dreams at night, unsuppressed memories), but of her continuing *identity*: "I *am*." I desire and thus prove that I persist as my self, not as my role as The Abbess, or The Penitent, or even The Victim. If there is any shock value in Heloise's second letter, it is not found in a shocking eroticism, but in the shock of recognition we feel at being addressed so directly by a mind that speaks to us from the interior of the self.

The first and overwhelming fact about Heloise is that she never attempted to obliterate or neutralize the reality and force of her original and enduring desires. She seemed to locate and ground her identity in precisely those desires, body and mind "mysteriously interconnected through sexuality," as Peter Brown put it. This is crucial to any assessment of Heloise and encourages us to think about the permanent qualities of human life over time. In the first place, no epistemic system or discursive pressures we can discern in medieval culture seem to suggest, much less support and justify, the strategy of mind and will Heloise allows us to witness. Secondly, her revealed personality points directly to developed interiority, to unusual possibilities of autonomous maneuver under great pressure to conform, to an astute understanding of social forces as distinct from the self, to an emotional decision to support the unique "I" even at the cost of great pain and inner turmoil.[45] In short, Heloise is only understandable as a self, a psyche compounded of the drives we all share, developed in a particular time, place, and culture—a person negotiating her life between wishes and denials, internal pressures and external stresses.

She never acceded to the massively overdetermined pressures of religious and social authority, even when Abelard added his personal influence to them, to attempt the desire-erasing process of repentance and atonement. By her own account, she recognized that her thoughts were sinful, but she never repented and never atoned. She never turned herself against herself; she preferred the inner triumph of the intact "I" of her *own* history, her own desires, her own identity. All her words and reported behavior point to a recognition on her part that the obliteration of her deepest wishes would be a disorganizing assault on her identity. Her love for Abelard had focused and condensed all her powerful intellect and heroic emotions onto one object. This complicated love carried her ambitions (highly developed with very little outlet), her full ego ideal, her powers of sublimation, and her defiance/compliance with the society that constrained her, as a woman, to channel all her wishes "through him," through some Him.

Sublimation is easily misunderstood; it does not mean the vaporizing of libido,

---

[45] In speculative answer to Newman's speculation: "We do not know, of course, whether or how far Heloise succeeded in this second repression [Abelard's demand that she obey him and give up her inner loyalty to her original love for him]" (p. 155), I want to argue that she declined even to attempt it. As I read the assertive passion of the first two letters, too much of her identity, her sense of existence as a coherent individual, was defined through her passion for her to undertake this self-obliteration; she was never really self-destructive. Her "silence" or acquiescence in a proper religious discourse may be read according to her own dictum about judging "an inward disease by inspection of the outward appearance."

or an ethereal or ascetic turning away from worldly pursuits, nor does successful sublimation require giving up all sexual pleasures. In a classically simple statement: "This capacity to exchange its originally sexual aim for another one, which is no longer sexual but which is psychically related to the first aim, is called the capacity for sublimation."[46] Sublimation is the routine work of civilization, and its projects are found in and suggested by the world. Chief among these is the pursuit of knowledge. Heloise is a perfect instance of the close and energizing connection between well-developed sexual curiosities arising in early childhood and the intense intellectual interests of adulthood; Freud noted that sexual excitement is often aroused by concentration on intellectual work.[47] Heloise and Abelard (like Paolo and Francesca) knew the erotic power of books. Freud also acutely remarked that the systematic punishment and suppression of sexual curiosity in small girls undoubtedly inhibited and depressed their intellectual development: "In this way they are scared away from *any* form of thinking, and knowledge loses its value for them." This "special application of [the] proposition that sexual life lays down the pattern for the exercise of other functions"[48] is shown at its exuberant opposite by Heloise's passionate learning and learned passion. These mirrored and mutually reinforcing sexual and intellectual drives *were* her achieved sublimation, not the enforced discipline of monastic life.

She did not learn from Abelard her ideal of "the philosopher"—pinnacle of human achievement and object of reverence and renown; that was her own fantasy/ideal, one wholly denied to her by every convention and institution she knew. Heloise's interior style was to turn exterior suppression inside out: she internalized the self-suppression and social limitations imposed on her and remained so heroically resolute in this discipline that she exasperated and frightened Abelard and her uncle, who were always prepared to compromise much

---

[46] Sigmund Freud, " 'Civilized' Sexual Morality and Modern Nervous Illness," *Standard Edition* . . . , ed. and trans. James Strachey et al., 24 vols. (London, 1953–74), 9:187. He goes on to note that extending the displacement of sexual aims indefinitely seems impossible for nearly all people (acknowledging that intercourse with another person is only one of a multitude of possible sexual activities).

[47] Freud's explanation of the deep connection between earliest sexual interests and the full development of the intellect in children is found in *Three Essays on Infantile Sexuality* (1905), specifically part 5, "The Sexual Researches of Childhood," of the second essay, in vol. 7 of *Standard Edition*. These essays admittedly contain some of the theories of female development that feminists find offensive, and which have been largely amended by later psychoanalysts; but it is a serious loss if readers ostracize these indispensable classics.

[48] This passage from the essay " 'Civilized Sexual Morality' " (passages quoted from pp. 198–99) deserves fuller quotation: "A special application of this proposition that sexual life lays down the pattern for the exercise of other functions can easily be recognized in the female sex as a whole. Their upbringing forbids their concerning themselves intellectually with sexual problems though they nevertheless feel extremely curious about them, and frightens them by condemning such curiosity as unwomanly and a sign of a sinful disposition. In this way they are scared away from *any* form of thinking, and knowledge loses its value for them. The prohibition of thought extends beyond the sexual field. . . . I do not believe that women's 'physiological feeble-mindedness' [quoting P. J. Moebius's book on female physiology] is to be explained by a biological opposition between intellectual work and sexual activity. . . . I think that the undoubted intellectual inferiority of so many women can rather be traced back to the inhibition of thought necessitated by sexual suppression." Please note that the inferiority Freud mentions is specifically *not* innate, but socially enforced.

more easily. Since she could not become a famous philosopher herself, she would do nothing *except* what furthered and protected Abelard's career even if it meant refusing to marry after she had a child and Abelard wished to marry her. Once she was coerced into the marriage, she steadfastly refused to acknowledge it, although her uncle had broken his own promise of secrecy, and disaster threatened from the confusion her denials caused. For all of Abelard's notorious ambition and touchy vanity, Heloise was the one who had the clearest and most ambitious conception of what a "philosopher's" life must be, and she *insisted* on sacrificing herself to that ideal. It was her own fierce ambition, suppressed and channeled through Abelard.

Her love for Abelard was masochistically tinged (and unsurprisingly, he describes his for her with sadistic callousness.) She cultivated, rapturously exaggerated, her erotically charged idea of Abelard as father/teacher/lord/autocrat of love. Patriarchy has never been rendered so exciting. Her acknowledgment of sin, her understanding of sin, was, unremarkably, what she had learned from patristic and contemporary Christianity. Yet fervently self-critical as she was, and only too eager to share in the blame for the calamities of Abelard's life, she never apologized for the feelings and acts for which she had no honest regrets:

> I call God to witness, if Augustus, ruling over the whole world, were to deem me worthy of the honour of marriage, and to confirm the whole world to me, to be ruled by me for ever, dearer to me and of greater dignity would it seem to be thy strumpet than his empress.[49]

It does not require any deep commitment to feminism to find this peculiarly energetic self-abasement a little unnerving (although we should also note that her fantasy is of being emperor, not mere consort). "No reward for this [monastic life] may I expect from God, for the love of whom it is well known that I did not anything. . . . I have forbidden myself all pleasures that I might obey thy will. I have reserved nothing for myself, save this, to be now entirely thine."[50] It is hardly surprising that Abelard begins his cautiously distanced reply, "To Heloise his dearly beloved sister *in Christ*, Abelard her brother *in the Same* [my emphasis]," by bringing in a third party as witness and chaperon. Heloise had managed to turn the conventional submissiveness of women into a weapon.

Her style of love is more abject than anyone, man or woman, now admires: she cultivated a passionate abjection, an unreserved inside-out aggression of total surrender to one solitary exalted object (who may have been as oppressed by this gift as any modern man would be). This strain of overrefined masochism, with its secret core of control and manipulation never perfectly hidden, was not entirely unfamiliar to her contemporaries. If the chosen lover's name were Jesus, the rhetoric of cultivated pain, languishing, and total erotic submission could be recategorized into respectability.[51] This erotic style fit Heloise's requirements,

[49] Heloise, first letter, in Moncrieff, trans., p. 57; Muckle, ed., p. 71.

[50] Heloise, first letter, in Moncrieff, trans., p. 60; Muckle, ed., p. 73.

[51] Again, Barbara Newman's comparison of Heloise's erotic style with that of later female mystics is very nicely drawn; "Authority, Authenticity," pp. 152–53.

but it was also culture-specific, endlessly exploited and elaborated in monastic and mystical practice, and in women it seems to build on a deep structure of unresolved lack and sense of need (I am nothing/you are everything), a deep psychic base externalized and given massive cultural endorsement by the near total male dominance in society. In another time and place she might have pursued her vision of intellectual and moral distinction by a less indirect route. In twelfth-century Paris she had little choice but to pursue all her aims, sexual, intellectual, her exalted ego ideal, through *Him*.

Offered Abelard's account of his life with Heloise, and the intimate confidences of Heloise's letters, we should feel no need to apologize or equivocate over ascribing to her a psychic structure of drives, internalized strictures of conscience, and a complex, reality-connected conscious ego. Nor is there any reason to hesitate before our sense that Heloise's sexuality was the living core from which the full expression of her personality radiated; she clearly felt it to be so. She assures us that there is a human mind, intelligible to us in its structure and dynamic, which variously adapts to culture's changing repertory of patterns over time. Heloise's complex sexuality speaks to us intelligibly and powerfully: sexuality speaks to our common humanity. Her femininity, her particular twelfth-century European way of being a woman, living a woman's life, is what disconcerts us: gender speaks of distance and difference. Sexuality may be cruel, but gender can be mean.

4. THE MAN IN THE DRESS: ONCE MORE

When Abelard retreated to the Monastery of St. Denis after being castrated, he was doing, in a more sophisticated mode, something analogous to the cross-dressing of the man in the cathedral at Poitiers. He was putting the dress of public and institutional celibacy onto private sexual incapacity: ". . . with what face would I appear in public, to be pointed out by every finger, scarified by every tongue, doomed to be a monstrous spectacle to all; . . . it was the confusion of shame . . . that drove me to the retirement of a monastic cloister."[52] There was always something lurking in medieval culture ready to see monks as unmanly. But no one has ever thought that Abelard's gender had slipped loose from his sexual identity; he remained permanently and unproblematically a man in identity, and indeed so conventionally masculine in his feelings that he could not bear the prospect of life in the world where everyone "knew." Without recourse to any special insight or theory, everyone can recognize that Abelard's masculine sensibility, his male pride, was, if anything, intensified by his genital loss. He did not become a social facsimile of a woman in anyone's eyes.

The man at Poitiers, following a simpler logic of desperation and gender calculation, put on the dress of male failure, of effeminated maleness: "might as well be a woman" is not the same as being a woman. Gender is not so easily parted from sex. This is not to deny that gender *roles*, under certain special circumstances, may be available to individuals who do not qualify for them in

---

[52] Abelard, *Calamities*, in Moncrieff, trans., p. 21.

biological sex but who "earn" them through other attributes of personality and behavior; one of these instances in Old Norse law which allowed a daughter to substitute for a son is discussed by Carol Clover; another is the "berdache" transvestites of the Plains Indians studied by analyst-anthropologist George Devereux.[53] But these cross-sex gender roles are quite restricted, infrequent, and marginal, very different matters from the allegedly shattering discoveries that social constructivists typically announce when they find evidence that gender and sex are separable in some people's minds some of the time.[54]

A certain kind of hypersophisticated and cavalier talk about the liberating separation of sex from gender has become fashionable in self-consciously "postmodern" scholarship. It is strange how easily subjects like these can become unreal and abstract; we all can benefit from a reality check. For those willing to learn what it is like for an actual human being to experience the total disjuncture of anatomical sex from psychological gender identity, there are the lucid and humane accounts by Robert Stoller, an analyst who worked with transsexuals over many years. Stoller's detailed, candid, and self-critical accounts of his twenty-five years of clinical work are an ideal entry for humanist scholars into the complex configurations that sex and gender can form in real human lives, not textual abstractions. The clinical work was the basis for Stoller's theoretical interest in gender identity: "my ongoing search to understand the origins, development, dynamics, and pathology of gender identity—masculinity and femininity. . . . From the start, my purpose was to find nonbiologic roots of gender behavior. . . ."[55] His clinical work was with people suffering severe

---

[53] Devereux's main work on this subject is *Reality and Dream: The Psychotherapy of a Plains Indian*, 2nd rev. ed. (New York, 1969).

[54] As, for example, David Halperin's use of a letter from prisoner Jack Abbott to Norman Mailer (*One Hundred Years*, pp. 38–39), explaining the gender system in prison where some men counted as "women" and others as "men" in the sexual transactions of a single-sex institution. Halperin quotes Abbott's letter at length ("it was years before I realized that they were not women, but men . . ."), compares prison society with classical Athens, interprets it all into appropriate "discourse" discourse ("desire is sparked only when it arcs across the political divide, when it traverses the boundary that marks out the limits of intramural competition among the elite and that thereby distinguishes subjects from objects of sexual desire"), and proclaims Abbott an excellent illustration of poststructuralist doctrine "that when meaning is not fixed by reference but is determined solely by the play of differences within a system of signification . . ." etc., etc.

Abbott's sexual attitudes are accepted at face value and given so much respectful attention because they seem to Halperin to support his larger contention that "we need to de-center *sexuality* from the focus of the interpretation of sexual experience—and not only ancient varieties of sexual experience. Just because modern bourgeois Westerners are so obsessed with sexuality, . . . we ought not therefore to conclude that everyone has always considered sexuality a basic and irreducible element in, or a central feature of, human life." It seems impolite but necessary to bring into the discussion the fact (ignored by Halperin) that on his parole Jack Abbott killed a man he had met minutes before, in an act of almost wholly unmotivated macho rage, following a slight encounter with women in a restaurant. His ideas about sexuality, sexual identity, and the meaning of gender are the thoughts of a mind most deeply disordered, self-ignorant and self-deceiving precisely on these issues of sexuality.

[55] The passage quoted is from Robert J. Stoller, *Presentations of Gender* (New Haven, Conn., and London, 1985), p. vii. His work, both clinical and theoretical, has been published as it proceeded: *Sex and Gender*, 1 (New York, 1968); *Sex and Gender*, 2 (London, 1975); *Splitting* (New York, 1973); *Perversion: The Erotic Form of Hatred* (New York, 1975); *Sexual Excitement: Dynamics of Erotic Life*

identity disorders, but the information leads to an understanding of the normal processes of identity development.

Interestingly, Stoller's psychoanalytic premises (a Freudian model with important modifications) agree entirely with the constructivists in that "sex and gender are by no means related. In most instances in humans, postnatal experiences can modify and sometimes overpower already present biologic tendencies."[56] The psychoanalytic thesis, however, explains the particular circumstances in which this disjuncture can occur in individual lives and offers us a useful way of thinking about sex and gender, about *how* they are related, how the individual works out the terms of mature character in its society. Stoller offers a conceptual model of the earliest stages of infant development, which establish "core gender identity": "a conviction that the assignment of one's sex was anatomically, and ultimately psychologically, correct."[57] This conviction is successfully established in the vast majority of children during the very first year or so of life; it is not easily dislodged by later influences, and forms "the nexus around which masculinity and femininity gradually accrete."[58] In most people (excluding the richly informative but relatively rare cases of those with identity disorders) anatomical sex is the basis for a corresponding core gender identity, which is the central psychic structure for the elaborated, psychologically motivated gender of later life, incorporating sexuality and cultural patterning. This model of gender development offers historians a sensible approach to understanding *both* individual sexuality and culturally patterned gender traits in appropriate balance and tension. Stoller's chapter "A Primer for Gender Identity" is a clear summary of basic information on sex and gender from a medical and psychoanalytic viewpoint, including some widely accepted modifications of Freud's thoughts on female development.[59] Gender as a cultural poetics of power is fascinating, but it needs a human corrective.

The two polar terms of sex and gender (alias: body vs. society; nature vs. culture; biology vs. artifice) offered us in current discussions are just not enough conceptual equipment to address the complex issues of psychosexual identity and collective culture. There is no *mind*, the source of variety, the negotiator between private wishes and public requirements, in this too rigid opposition. Asking endless variations on the question of whether fully elaborated, historically

---

(New York, 1979); *Observing the Erotic Imagination* (New Haven, Conn., 1985). Readers interested in sex/gender issues should note that Stoller's ideas changed as his experience with patients accumulated, and therefore the later book, *Presentations*, must be read with the earliest works.

[56] Stoller, *Presentations*, p. 6 and n. 3.

[57] Stoller, *Presentations*, p. 11.

[58] Stoller, *Presentations*, p. 11; it should be noted that core gender identity does not, by itself, determine later sexual behavior with respect to object choice or gender roles: "That later gender identity is not so uncomplicated has been more than amply demonstrated in innumerable psychoanalytic studies. . . . But it may not be recognized that the earliest and, as it turns out, unalterable, part of gender identity—the core gender identity—does develop smoothly, silently, and without conflict," *Sex and Gender*, 2:33.

[59] Stoller, *Presentations*, chap. 2 (pp. 10–24); this exceptionally lucid explanation of how biology, psychology, and social beliefs act and react in the formation of human character can be very usefully read by historians.

variable sets of femininity and masculinity are *necessarily* attached to anatomic females and males distorts the discussion. The answer is too obviously no. But if sex is nothing, then gender, the field of social constructs and pressures, is everything, and this concept just cannot bear such forced overelaboration and yield persuasive answers about human behavior. Sex and gender offer an inadequate conceptual framework. A middle or third term is always needed—"self" or "sexuality" will do quite well—to acknowledge the developmental negotiations of mind with world which produce men and women who do tend to be recognizably like others of their same sex (and class, society, etc.) when regarded collectively, but yet are quite distinct and individual seen "close up." Gender, as a concept carrying all the explanatory weight for human behavior, thins out and dehumanizes the individual while never accounting for the deviance, rebellion, and simple idiosyncrasy which happily fill the historical record. The currently missing middle term of psychosexual development would restore the reality that human beings actively negotiate their way into their worlds; they are not passively processed by them.

The unfortunate cross-dressed man in the church at Poitiers, trapped between the failure of sex and the punishment of gender, was still a man and not a socially constructed woman. If this is the solitary thing we can justifiably say about him, it is at least an important thing. His only offered reason for his behavior—his impotence—points to a core gender identity of maleness, an identity paradoxically strong enough to react with self-punishing exaggeration to its own failure to pass the minimum test of adult masculinity. That his "solution" to his problem (and it was a solution in that it removed him from the threat of heterosexual relations) was improvised and idiosyncratic (though simply constructed from prevailing attitudes) is suggested by the ordinary male life being led by his contemporary, the eunuch servant of the nunnery. The man in the dress gave up even his prima facie claim to a man's social identity. In the absence of a distinct Merovingian social construct to govern the lives of all "unmanly men," only a sexually organized male self in furious revulsion against itself would have arrived at this simple improvisation on gender.

The detailed, anthropological registration of all the varieties of sexual behavior and the minutiae of gender stereotyping in past societies being done by constructivist scholars is obviously important and needs no defense. My objections to the constructivist project are entirely directed to its unbalanced weighting of evidence and its overwrought claims and dehumanizing insistence on the socially constructed, desexualized automaton with which it replaces the self. It is one thing to document exactly how socially generated standards made perfect masculinity and femininity nearly impossible for ordinary males and females to attain. It is quite another to make dogmatic assertions about social construction on the basis of repeatedly "discovering" what everyone knows already: that genital anatomy has never been a sufficent passport to the status and privileges that are routinely monopolized by the elite males (and females to a certain degree) of any society.

It is rewarding to feel that informed, scrupulous, and open-minded attention to the specific preoccupations of past societies can open a kind of secret entry to past life, in its own terms. But the price for carrying this effort too far is a dogmatic cultural relativism, a blinkered perspective in which all behaviors, customs, meanings are exactly what the people most directly involved in them said they were, and nothing else, and nothing more. Writing history can then only be an effort of paraphrase, with no translation or serious interpretation allowed.

The worse limitation that comes packaged with this exteriorized theory of meaning is its devastating consequences for the human being whose image stands at the center of all historical study. The pervasive, inescapable processes of social conditioning impress their lessons *onto* the human object, who is thereby formed, molded, constituted, constructed with inert plastic receptivity. The political implications of such views should not be ignored: with the autonomous self as bearer of inalienable rights removed from the polity, the way is expressly open to utopian projects for constructing ideal citizen-subjects.[60] This theoretical world opens no intelligible space for resistance, refusals to conform, or even skepticism of the limited cultural menu presented in place of human possibility. If men, in this view, are incessantly occupied in playing out their stylized social theater of dominance and submission, women have nothing to do at all, except passively display whatever imprint the patriarchal discourses have directed to their specific class, race, status (e.g., flute dancer or matron). Whatever insults psychoanalysis is accused of inflicting on women, they fade to nothing when compared with complete evisceration of the psychic interior. The young woman in Oxford who spat at her husband and stalked defiantly out of church to return to her lover would have found a more sympathetic confidant in Freud than in Foucault.

[60] Men as different as psychoanalytic anthropologist George Devereux and linguist Noam Chomsky have seen the political consequences quite clearly. Devereux: "The *total* disorganization that some advocate as the very essence of freedom is also a technique of enslavement, for the technique that deprives man of all organization is the first condition of his slavehood," *Basic Problems*, p. 320. Chomsky: "A vision of a future social order is in turn based on a concept of human nature. If in fact man is an indefinitely malleable, completely plastic being, with no innate structures of mind . . . then he is a fit subject for the 'shaping of behavior' by the state authority . . . ," quoted in Philip Pomper, *The Structure of Mind in History: Five Major Figures in Psychohistory* (New York, 1985), p. 8. It remains true that constructivist scholars are almost invariably political progressives, often activists on behalf of gay rights, feminism, etc., and do not see the political implications of their theory as I do.

Nancy F. Partner is Associate Professor of History at McGill University, 855 Sherbrooke St. W., Montreal, PQ H3A 2T7, Canada.

When Women Aren't Enough

By Allen J. Frantzen

1. WHY WOMEN AREN'T ENOUGH

If writing about women was once an innovation, it is now an imperative. Very rare only two short decades ago, feminist scholarship today pervades the disciplines of art, history, law, literature, and religion. This volume, as probably every reader will have observed, is another sign that feminist studies, if not the norm, are now so regular an exception to it that they have redefined the norm. This volume is a sign of something else, which is that feminism has made a place for men. I was invited to participate because my recent work argues for theoretical self-examination and revision in the disciplines of medieval studies. A traditionalist eager to see tradition challenged and revitalized, I believe that scholarship ought to represent a joining of our public and private selves. This is a kind of self-awareness on which feminist scholars insist, but that view does not make me a feminist. When I chose the title for this essay, I did not know that I was to be the volume's only male contributor. As the token man, with no desire to speak for all men (many of whom would not choose me for the role in any case), I fear that I speak for them nevertheless. If women aren't enough, for this volume or for feminist criticism, one essay by one man isn't enough to explain why.[1]

Feminist criticism has put traditionalists, men and women alike, on the defensive. Traditionalists should be on the defensive: that's what being a traditionalist means. But being a traditionalist often means being anxious about (rather than anxious for) innovation, especially an innovation like gender theory, which is likely to last. Traditionalists who put gender theory to use will find that they put some feminists on the defensive. As defenders of innovations and improvements in women's status, feminists should be on the defensive too. And, increasingly, they are.

Recently a number of feminists have become anxious about what Elaine Showalter calls "the rise of gender."[2] Gender is a tool for reconceptualizing male as well as female roles, reconfiguring the power struggles between the sexes, and merging sexual distinctions founded on reproductive difference. Gender studies, where those reconceptualizations are carried out, examine how males and females choose to think and act in reference to the conventions expected of the men and women of their ages. In this essay I hope to show how gender serves both traditional and innovative scholarship; by analyzing some examples of the "manly man" and the "manly woman," I want to balance new gender

---

[1] In writing about this topic, which seemed both too new and too much for me, I have been greatly assisted by James W. Earl, Gillian R. Overing, Nancy Partner, and George R. Paterson; I owe an especially large debt to Clare A. Lees, who generously shared her forthcoming work on grammatical gender in Old English and on women saints' lives.

[2] Elaine Showalter, ed., *Speaking of Gender* (New York, 1989), pp. 1–13.

anxiety against the old defensiveness that gender has long prompted in traditionalists. In my view, contemporary critical theory, whether deconstruction or
New Historicism, is not the private reserve of modernists in literature, language,
or history departments; and neither is gender exclusively the territory of feminists. Feminists who work in medieval subjects need to account for the dates
and material details of manuscripts, and traditionalists need to account for the
social logic of sex that gender ideologies express in the Middle Ages. Think of
the political commitments of feminism what one will, it is impossible to dismiss
the revaluation of medieval evidence that feminist scholarship and gender theory
have already produced. Think of traditional scholarship what feminists will, they
would have no case to make, no place to begin, without it.

It is curious to see how quickly, in academic circles, "gender" has replaced
"sex," a word people of my generation were always uncomfortable saying any-
way. Recently a colleague, describing the discussion that followed a guest lecture,
noted that the response was "split along the lines of gender." For her, sex and
gender were the same. What "gender" makes plain, and what is concealed by
"sex," is the relation of sexual identity to power; gender is a more powerful
analytical concept than sex. Gender can explain why some men are less powerful
than others, why some women are more powerful than some men, and other
imbalances that the physical equipment of sex does not account for. Discussion
of such imbalances, which complicate the social logic of sex as biology seems
to decree it, is not always welcome even among feminists, for the imbalances
expose the inadequacy of assessments in which women are always oppressed
and men always oppressive: women can be oppressive, men can be oppressed.

Gender also challenges the assumption that heterosexual relations, since socially normative, are also natural: gender defines the spaces between heterosexual roles and refigures the old opposition between male and female. Just as
woman was "naturally" secondary, the homosexual was "unnatural" and so
secondary to the "natural" phenomenon of heterosexuality. Gender exposes
the dependence of such first principles on other assumptions. That is why,
understood as something other than biological sex, gender has been resisted as
an idea even though it is accepted as a word.

Gender anxiety arises out of the success of feminism, which, as measured by
curricular reform alone, has been enormous. Barrie Ruth Straus, editor of a
recent collection of feminist essays (in which all the contributors, I note, are
women), warns readers that "Feminisms' inclusion should be questioned as much
as its exclusion has been." The grammar is revealing: "Feminisms," the subject,
strives to include all forms of feminism, but "its," the adjective, disagrees,
anxiously suggesting that at some level these many operations are one after all.
We should be wary of the idea that "feminism's theories have arrived," the
editor continues, and also be wary of "a phallocentric system that will always
accomodate [*sic*]—often through co-opting—critical dissent."[3] Discord, if not
dissent, proves difficult to suppress.

These cautions notwithstanding, and without furthering a liberal illusion that

___

[3] Barrie Ruth Straus, "Skirting the Texts: Feminisms' Re-Readings of Medieval and Renaissance
Texts," *Exemplaria* 4 (1992), 1–4, quotations from p. 4.

greater equity between men and women in the curriculum (or the academy) translates into greater social equity, I regard feminism as triumphant. Like many others, I see distinct stages in the feminist transformation of the academy. In the early phase scholars debated the legitimacy of women's perspectives. Did women and men see, understand, perceive, live, speak, and write in ways sufficiently different to justify the use of "her" alongside the previously universal "his"? The answer was clearly that they did. The significance of the difference between women and men was not, of course, new. For centuries women historians, critics, and linguists protested the exclusion of their point of view, but to little effect. Only in the last twenty years have scholars in significant numbers agreed that the perceptions of women, previously assumed to be identical with those of men, had been grossly neglected. Now, for at least a decade, feminists have been cataloguing the phases of their revolution, ranging from "Womanless History," the first of Peggy McIntosh's five phases, to "Women in History" (the second), "Women as a Problem, Anomaly, or Absence in History" (the third), and "Woman as History" (the fourth).[4]

The phase I call the "women in" phase, which corresponds to McIntosh's second, was marked by flourishing courses and conference sessions about "Women in the Middle Ages," "Women in Medieval Literature," and so forth. It was first in these forums, now so abundant, that scholars examined political and social contexts in which women had previously and uncritically been either lumped together with men or left out because there was little evidence of their activities. An example of the older "womanless" approach is Dorothy Whitelock's superb discussion in *The Beginnings of English Society*. Having written about "The Nobleman," she then observed, "We are less well-informed about the activities of the women of this class," whose duties were constituted by a mere handful of household tasks.[5] (Whitelock might have added that both men and women of other classes were equally obscure.)[6] In contrast, the new "women in" approach claimed that the activities of women were plain to those armed with the right theoretical tools. Texts great and small were reexamined in order to discover "the woman's" point of view. Jane Chance drew attention to the limits of this monolithic approach by concentrating on aristocratic and heroic women.[7] But quite often "the woman's" point of view was the only view in question, and it was reexamined merely to assert that women had been overlooked and undervalued as a group (which was easy to see), and simultaneously

---

[4] Peggy McIntosh, "Interactive Phases of Curricular Re-Vision," *Towards a Balanced Curriculum: A Sourcebook for Initiating Gender Integration Projects*, ed. Bonnie Spanier, Alexander Bloom, and Darlene Borovink (Cambridge, Mass., 1984), p. 26. McIntosh's fifth phase is a "utopian" reconstruction. I thank Gillian Overing for directing me to this essay.

[5] Dorothy Whitelock, *The Beginnings of English Society*, The Pelican History of England 2 (Harmondsworth, Middlesex, 1952; rev. 1972), p. 92.

[6] See G. N. Garmonsway's comment that Ælfric's *Colloquy* is "chiefly of interest for the picture it presents of the life and activities of the middle and lower classes of Anglo-Saxon society, concerning which Old English literature is, in the main, silent," in *Ælfric's Colloquy*, ed. Garmonsway, 2nd ed. (London, 1947; repr. 1967), p. 1.

[7] Jane Chance, *Woman as Hero in Old English Literature* (Syracuse, N.Y., 1986), pp. xiii–xiv.

to demonstrate that men in these texts had been getting away with rape, murder, and other kinds of physical and psychological abuse (which was not).

As women were added to literary and historical research, the universal categories of "man" and the "male" or "masculine" survived intact and were even affirmed by them. Strangely enough, criticism of the patriarchy seemed to renew its power. "Woman in History," McIntosh wrote, was something like a "patronizing affirmative action program which assumes that the discipline, like the institution, is perfect as constructed" and that the excluded could want little more than to be included in it.[8] It was not enough, as Joan Wallach Scott wrote, to expand the categories to include women when the categories themselves ignored or proscribed the evidence most pertinent to the revisionist project.[9] As one such category, sexual identity had been masked as natural and, as such, seen as beyond (or beneath) scholarly analysis.

The shortcomings of the "women in" approach soon became obvious. "New readings" of the "women in" sort were seen as mere reinterpretations and reversals of old themes, bound by the same paradigms as the old readings they sought to revise and no less dedicated to thematic coherence and artistic originality, for example, than previous formalist literary interpretations. Old-style "women in" scholarship was seen as theoretically impoverished and excessively pragmatic, even empirical (where are the women in this text? here's one; there's another, etc.). Indeed, "women in," despite its value in cataloguing and listing hitherto dismissed data, ultimately differed little from the approaches it augmented. However revisionist their aspirations, such readings were contained by traditional hermeneutics that were male-centered not only in their content but also in their founding principles.

As the "women in" phase expanded, feminists began to see that the problem involved more than including women. Women were not enough because traditional approaches to history and literature were not enough. An early (1979) anthology of bibliographical essays about women frankly differentiated "old" women's history from the "new" and identified theoretical self-consciousness as the factor that distinguished the two.[10] But theoretical self-consciousness and poststructural methodologies proved even more difficult to introduce into the scholarly mix than women's views had been. Ten years later (1989) another anthology, this one concentrating on women in Anglo-Saxon England, showed how little effect the earlier call for theoretical self-consciousness had had. This anthology was called (significantly) *New Readings on Women in Old English Literature*.[11] One might expect a book on "new readings" to be about the "feminist readings" that the editors refer to throughout the introduction, but the collection lacked a single theoretical discussion of the problem. The collection's

[8] McIntosh, "Interactive Phases," p. 26.

[9] Joan Wallach Scott, *Gender and the Politics of History* (New York, 1988).

[10] Barbara Kanner, ed., *The Women of England from Anglo-Saxon Times to the Present* (Hamden, Conn., 1979), pp. 10–11. See comments by Lenore Davidoff and Joan Kelly, especially Davidoff's claim that "the lack of an explicit framework can narrow, even cripple, historical analysis" (p. 24).

[11] Helen Damico and Alexandra Hennessey Olsen, eds., *New Readings on Women in Old English Literature* (Bloomington, Ind., 1989).

title is ambiguous: "new readings" are "new things to read," as in "new reading material," but also "new readings" in the sense of "new interpretations." The latter would seem to have been the intended meaning, in theory if not in fact, even though—despite the use of "new" in the title and "feminist" in the introduction—over half the essays (eleven of eighteen contributions) are reprints from 1943, 1959, 1981, and 1986, which, in 1989, were not "new." Some of the reprints are designated not only as "new readings" and "feminist," but also as "classic" studies ("classic feminism"?). This anomaly is conveniently obscure, since the copyright date of only one of the essays is given.[12] The last section is coyly entitled "The 'Deconstructed' Stereotype." Given the title, it is astonishing to find no reference to deconstruction in the essays themselves; in the title, reprinted over thirty times in the running head to the verso pages, "deconstructed" means merely "rethought" or perhaps "inverted." It is the most superficial acknowledgment possible that the concept (at least the word) is important. The collection demonstrates how recently medieval scholarship that sustained the "women in" approach was content to fit women into existing categories and to valorize those categories as "classic." This representation of scholarship readily and reassuringly incorporates traditional approaches, giving new value to traditional data and disciplinary assumptions while suggesting that poststructuralist thinking can be safely contained by quotations-within-quotations if by nothing else (hence the " 'deconstructed' " stereotype).

The "women in" approach won relatively easy acceptance, for it extended and refined rather than challenged the basic operating procedures of historians, literary critics, archaeologists, and others who worked with medieval textual and material culture. Feminist scholarship of the "women in" sort also replicated one of the least desirable features of the scholarship that it attacked: it joined sex to women in a construct nearly as monolithic as that which had traditionally joined everything else to men. But early feminism did not create an "Everywoman" as the equivalent of "Everyman," the one speaking for all. Rather, "Everywoman" was superior to "Everyman," for she claimed sex as a subject of her own. "Sex," Virginia Woolf wrote in *A Room of One's Own*, "woman, that is to say."[13] Early in the century though her remarks were made, they suited academic conditions quite near its end. If one were to write about sexual identity, one had to write about women; to write about men was unnecessary, for everything already written was written about them.

But the polyphony of poststructuralism demonstrated that there had to be more than "woman" to "women in." Feminism needed to avoid constructing a universalized female paradigm corresponding to the universalized male paradigm created by Freud. Thanks to the transhistorical and unexamined category

---

[12] Damico and Olsen, *New Readings*, p. viii (for the reprint date), p. 16 (on "classic"), and p. 18.

[13] Virginia Woolf, *A Room of One's Own* (London, 1929; repr. New York, 1957), p. 27. Woolf is describing her reaction to discovering the range of books about women catalogued by the British Museum. "Sex and its nature might well attract doctors and biologists; but what was surprising and difficult of explanation was the fact that sex—woman, that is to say—also attracts agreeable essayists, light-fingered novelists, young men who have taken the M. A. degree; men who have taken no degree; men who have no apparent qualification save that they are not women."

of "male," men had not needed to be theorized beyond Freud, who had taken the male as the norm in the analysis of all human sexual experience. But eventually it became clear that men's writing had to be approached as multiple and varied sexualized discourse—as gendered discourse—that contained tensions and material divisions among men, including, for example, that between the homosexual and heterosexual, the rich and the poor, and the black and white. The poststructuralist rereading of Freud, led by Luce Irigaray, turned from the neglect of women to the limitations of men. "Masculine language," she wrote in something of an understatement, "is not understood with any precision."

> So long as men claim to say everything and define everything, how can anyone know what the language of the male sex might be? So long as the logic of discourse is modeled on sexual indifference, on the submission of one sex to the other, how can anything be known about the "masculine"?[14]

Finally, from a poststructuralist feminist, came a challenge to the assumption that, after Freud, men did not need to be theorized. A better understanding of women and their language required a better explanation than Freud had offered of men and theirs. It was not enough to include women; instead, the idea of women had to be reexamined, and this reexamination required, of all things, a new look at men.

The political clout of writing about women could not be denied, and as such writing became more widespread, so did the impression that feminism had overtaken its first objective, which was to include women. As texts and courses about women multiplied, a certain ennui born of success set in. Writing about women was a necessary remedy to generations of academic and political neglect of women's careers. But writing about women was also naively equated with political action, and curricular change was naively equated with social change. More courses in "women's literature" raised the consciousness of women, but raising consciousness did not necessarily lead to action that improved their status or shifted the balance of power.

Those who had asked for little soon achieved it: the triumph of feminism was academic. Feminism required merely that everybody talk about women, which, it seems, everybody was willing to do, in particular a host of guilty men eager to be identified with an undeniably powerful trend. As a result, the word "women" by itself no longer signaled revisionist claims, since "women" were everywhere. And from this abundance, and the introspection of poststructuralist thinking, it became clear that "women" were not enough and that new terms and ideas would have to be developed. Feminists searched for theoretically sophisticated positions that debated the premises of inclusive feminism and began dividing into various camps, including academic feminists, political feminists, lesbian feminists, and many others. Out of this surfeit of feminisms, I believe, "gender" arose as the term of preference for a new kind of writing and thinking that would include all men and women, appropriate poststructuralist thinking, and still pursue a progressive political agenda.

[14] Luce Irigaray, *This Sex Which Is Not One*, trans. Catherine Porter, with Carolyn Burke (Ithaca, N.Y., 1985), p. 128.

It became obvious that feminism was concerned with gender instead of—or as well as—with women when men began practicing feminist criticism.[15] This development was marked by *The Making of Masculinities* and *Men in Feminism* (both published in 1987).[16] Because gender made possible the extension of feminist critical practice to men, it began to alter the shape of feminist criticism and to produce anxiety about its relation to the politics of equality for women. With gender in the calculation, feminist criticism could no longer be either about women or by women only: women were no longer enough, for men began to borrow feminist practices and to apply critical scrutiny to the male as a gendered subject.

Now that the study of the "masculine" has become as crucial as the study of the "feminine," we find that gender not only threatens sex as a subject but severs the supposedly "natural" connection between the subject of sex and women; gender also creates new ways of viewing oppressive social relations in historical contexts. First, gender theory redefines the positions from which one can write about sexual difference; it allows men equal opportunity to assume the positions of feminist critics. Second, gender theory also redefines the positions of power in medieval texts and institutions (and in others, of course). Those positions, traditionally seen in the fixed binary terms of sexual oppression, can be recast in fluid terms, not to deny oppression, but to redefine its relation to sexual identity. The roles of victimizer and victim can be occupied by men and women alike, and the same men and women can occupy different roles at different times. These positions are clearest in those gender studies which focus on the phenomena of performance, choice, and role-playing, gestures which complicate the binary division of the sexes and create multiple possibilities both for tracing the play of signs within medieval cultures and for exploring those signs in our own interpretive responses. New positions are available both for historians who study the behavior of the sexes and for the historical male and female subjects they study. In both cases, what is new with gender studies is the inclusion of men in the feminist project.

The shift from "women in" to "gender" criticism is part of a shift from "sex" to "gender." The former had been understood to refer objectively to males and females who could be distinguished biologically and simply. The latter referred to interpretive distinctions that described both the behavior expected of men and women and the behavior not expected of them: it allowed for men who "acted like men" and for those who did not (leaving open the possibility that they therefore "acted like women"), and for women who "acted like women" and those who did not (leaving open the possibility that *they* therefore "acted like men"). Gender admitted the force of the social into sexual identity

[15] See the discussion of the role of men in feminism in Elaine Showalter, *Speaking of Gender*, pp. 6–8. For a particularly tortured example of "men in feminist" criticism, see Gerald M. MacLean, "Citing the Subject," in Linda Kauffman, ed., *Gender and Theory: Dialogues on Feminist Criticism* (New York, 1989), pp. 121–39; better on several counts is Joseph A. Boone, "Of Me(n) and Feminism: Who(se) Is the Sex That Writes," and the response by Toril Moi, "Men against Patriarchy," in Kauffman, *Gender*, pp. 158–80 and 181–90.

[16] Alice Jardine and Paul Smith, eds., *Men in Feminism* (London and New York, 1987); Harry Brod, ed., *The Making of Masculinities: The New Men's Studies* (Boston, 1987).

that, biologically seen as sex, had been much less complicated. But gender is not just a constructed human identity opposed to an unconstructed human nature. Gender theory unmasks various constructions of identity that have been confused with the natural reality: to talk about gender is to talk about how identity has been shaped by custom and institutionalized social possibilities that exclude certain forms of behavior. The benefit of discussing gender is not only that gender constructions are examined, but that their basis in nature, the ground on which "natural" sexual identities rest, is also scrutinized. One cannot, of course, dispute the existence of "male" and "female" bodies, but one can debate—and revise—the cultural interpretations those bodies have been made to bear and the social possibilities that contain them.

As gender has been theorized as "culture," biology (the "natural") has not escaped scrutiny as a construction of its own. Thomas Laqueur's analysis of "one-sex" biology in *Making Sex* argues that biological sexual difference, the "two-sex" theory, is a "cultural construction." Laqueur uses pre-Enlightenment texts to demonstrate a reversal of the usual relationship of sex to gender, in which "*sex*, or the body, must be understood as the epiphenomenon, while *gender*, what we would take to be a cultural category, was primary or 'real.' "[17] But he admits that no matter how predominant the one-sex model was in the premodern period, it was never a hegemonic ideal. For, amidst "other discourses, other political demands, other social relations, even other medical ways of speaking," it was nevertheless "deeply at odds with rigid gender boundaries and the social body's imperative to ensure reproductive mating." Laqueur suggests that the one-sex body was "the more or less stable sign for an intensely gendered social order" (and, in his analysis, also gendered as "intensely" heterosexual), with the one-sex body representing the hierarchy of the cosmos, the male doing so more fully than the female, and that hierarchy being most fully approximated when male and female join to perpetuate "macrocosmic order."[18]

But the distinction between male and female cannot be said to be prediscursive (that is, existing before the language that refers to it) even on the biological level, at least for the periods Laqueur writes about. The complementary distinction between heterosexual and homosexual must also be seen as at least partly produced by discourse rather than preexisting it. Gender means, in the first instance, rethinking the absolute categories of male and female, of women and men, of homosexual and heterosexual. This is an exciting prospect for any medievalist, whether feminist or not, simply because it requires a reassessment of the flow of power in and around medieval texts of all kinds. Traditional scholars have been slow to see the merits of gender studies, and that is no surprise. What is unexpected is that the shift from "women" to "gender" has created uneasiness at the most sophisticated levels of the disciplines engaged with women's studies.

---

[17] Thomas Laqueur, *Making Sex: Body and Gender from the Greeks to Freud* (Cambridge, Mass., 1990), p. 8.

[18] Laqueur, *Making Sex*, pp. 114–16.

2. GENDER ANXIETIES OLD AND NEW

In a recent review of two collections of essays about gender, Mary Poovey describes gender as a "positional term" that links the "feminine" not to women but "to something else within a signifying system of differences," namely, the "masculine." As more men share in feminist criticism, the "feminine" becomes an assumable position rather than a biologically dictated one, a "position of otherness" available to both male and female critics.[19] Poovey describes the emergence of gender as a displacement of sex that threatens to overwhelm the "relation between women and feminism" and asks if "the substitution of gender for sex" has the potential to "destroy the basis for feminism." Poovey heralds "the new age of gender," but she worries that gender has the potential to undo the force of feminism as a means of overcoming the political oppression of women.[20] Since male critics can become feminist critics, *real* feminist criticism, it seems, will have to move to another position in which the female is again protected territory available only to women. Gender studies allow critics to take positions, to be "positional," as Poovey says, but this idea of "positionality," like the performative phenomena mentioned earlier, can be easily and, I think, irresponsibly used to suggest that gender is something one can put on and off like a costume. This facility is not equally available to those on either side of the homosexual and heterosexual divide; cross-dressing is neither as necessary nor as effective on one side as it is on the other.

For gender theorists like Poovey, feminist discourse must have a unique, oppositional character. For them, "gender" challenges purely feminist formulations in accounting for women's place. Here we should recall Scott's comment about "the difficulty that contemporary feminists have had incorporating the term 'gender' into existing bodies of theory and of convincing adherents of one or another theoretical school that gender belongs in their vocabulary."[21] Scott wants to fit gender into the discussion; Poovey is afraid that gender fits in all too well. We can see that the debate about "gender" is another sign of the fear that, once more, "women" will be left out.

A similar anxiety appears in an essay by Elaine Showalter that introduced one of the collections Poovey reviewed. Gender, Showalter writes, means "talking about both women and men." As she sees it, feminists hoped to win acceptance for women's studies by including men in the concept of gender, and by doing so to transform traditional disciplines more radically than the study of women alone had been able to do. In her version of feminist history (the opposite of mine on this point), feminists thought up gender as a way to ensure that feminism would not be "ghettoized" within traditional disciplines.[22] Showalter suggests that feminists sought to avoid the old-style expansion of accepted categories— or, in this case, a brand new category, "women"—that proved so limiting to the "women in" phase. But like Poovey, Showalter worries that talking about gender

---

[19] Mary Poovey, "Recent Studies of Gender," *Modern Philology* 88 (1991), 415–20; see p. 415.
[20] Poovey, "Recent Studies," p. 420.
[21] Scott, *Gender and the Politics of History*, p. 41.
[22] Showalter, *Speaking of Gender*, pp. 1–2.

is a way to avoid "the political commitment of feminism" or to isolate gender from race and class. To debate gender without "a commitment to dismantling sexism, racism, and homophobia," she warns, "can degenerate into nothing more than a talk show, with men trying to monopolize the [post]feminist conversation" (her brackets). Showalter describes the fear that gender studies could be "a pallid assimilation of feminist criticism into the mainstream (or male stream), of English studies, a return to the old priorities and binary oppositions that will reinstate familiar male canons while crowding hard-won courses on women writers out of the curriculum."[23] Showalter's vision of regression strikes me as inconceivable; a return to a prefeminist curriculum is as likely in most universities as a resurgence of the electric typewriter. Gender theory may balance some of the traditional concerns of feminist politics against new concerns about masculinist politics; but with academic departments giving preference to women in hiring and universities appointing more women to senior administrative posts, it is difficult to see how "familiar male canons" or prefeminist and nonaffirmative hiring criteria will return.

This is not to say that everybody who writes about women is a feminist. Showalter's anxiety about the "male stream" brings to mind Camille Paglia, a writer who celebrates the "male stream" in *Sexual Personae: Art and Decadence from Nefertiti to Emily Dickinson* and who boldly reasserts the primacy of men in the production of culture. The Allan Bloom of feminism, Paglia does not bother with gender or manifest gender anxieties. "The male projection of erection and ejaculation," she writes in a characteristic moment of oracular absolutism, "is the paradigm for all cultural projection and conceptualization—from art and philosophy to fantasy, hallucination, and obsession." She adds:

> Concentration and projection are remarkably demonstrated by urination, one of male anatomy's most efficient compartmentalizations. Freud thinks primitive man preened himself on his ability to put out a fire with a stream of urine. A strange thing to be proud of but certainly beyond the scope of a woman, who would scorch her hams in the process. Male urination really *is* a kind of accomplishment, an arc of transcendence. A woman merely waters the ground she stands on. Male urination is a form of commentary. . . . This is one genre of self-expression women will never master.[24]

Almost everything that is both wonderful and dubious in Paglia's romp through thousands of years of cultural history is evident in this passage: her insistence on the undeniable biological difference between men and women; her assertion that men are more creative (at least, in some ways more expressive) than women; her depressing assessment of the cost of the male "compartmentalization" behind this creativity; her correlation of physical functions with expressive, creative acts (the stream of urine serving as an analogy for the projected male gaze and even the projection of film in a movie theater);[25] her thesis that the sexes, although they can and must be politically equal, are irreconcilably

[23] Showalter, *Speaking of Gender*, p. 10.

[24] Camille Paglia, *Sexual Personae: Art and Decadence from Nefertiti to Emily Dickinson* (New York, 1990), pp. 20–21.

[25] Paglia, *Sexual Personae*, p. 31.

different and indeed at war. Paglia's use of "projection" suggests that she disregards the traditional understanding of projection of an inner, unknown hostility attributed to an external other,[26] and this is but one of a number of claims that, modified, would have greatly improved the acceptance of her book among feminists. "Hurricane Camille" would have done better to engage some of the feminist theory that she dismisses with antifeminist verve.[27] Her argument about the relation between sexuality and the production of culture is not the restatement of traditional assumptions that Paglia presents it as. In her unrepentant enthusiasm for the chaos at the heart of human existence, Paglia does not so much push through as explode the limitations of politically correct feminist politics, and many readers will enjoy her performance even as they reject her thesis that the patriarchy is not an exercise in sexual oppression only but a necessary and inevitable struggle against the "chthonic" in woman.

Quite at the opposite end of the discussion from Paglia, who is readable and exuberant, stands Judith Butler, who is the sort of elaborate and arcane theorist Paglia deplores. Butler begins *Gender Trouble* by remarking that "Contemporary feminist debates over the meanings of gender lead time and again to a certain sense of trouble, as if the indeterminacy of gender might eventually culminate in the failure of feminism." Butler notes a "dialectical reversal of power" in which the "radical dependency of the masculine subject on the female 'Other' suddenly expose[d] his autonomy as illusory." Today, as feminists warily regard the emergence of men's studies alongside women's studies, one might respond that we now see the radical dependency of women's studies on a universalized, if not untheorized, conception of the masculine. It is as if, to revert again to Butler's paradigm, the masculine now refuses to be the object of the feminine gaze, and "reverses the gaze, and contests the place and authority" of feminine positions.[28] Butler argues that gender is a performative concept that disrupts fixed notions of the masculine and feminine and exposes the heterosexual exclusivity of gender constructions. She sees gender as "an activity, a becoming" and believes that sexed bodies can be the occasion for a number of different genders:

> Consider the further consequence that if gender is something that one becomes—*but can never be*—then gender itself is a kind of becoming or activity, and that gender ought not to be conceived as a noun or a substantial thing or a static cultural marker, but rather as an incessant and repeated action of some sort.[29] (My emphasis)

Butler argues that too much feminist theory and politics incorporates notions of fixed, specific sexuality as stable points of reference. These notions reverse the oppositions of patriarchal discourse without exposing the contingencies outside and alongside those oppositions. Butler believes that fixed notions of gender conceal gender's performative character. By performance she does not

---

[26] Sigmund Freud, "Taboo and the Ambivalence of Emotions," in *The Basic Writings of Sigmund Freud*, ed. and trans. A. A. Brill (New York, 1938), pp. 855–56.

[27] I refer to the profile of Paglia, "Woman Warrior," in *New York* (4 March 1991), pp. 23–30.

[28] Judith Butler, *Gender Trouble: Feminism and the Subversion of Identity* (New York, 1990), p. ix.

[29] Butler, *Gender Trouble*, p. 112.

mean role-playing—although playing roles is involved—but instead identity that
is not essential but fabricated:

> In other words, acts and gestures, articulated and enacted desires create the illusion
> of an interior and organizing gender core, an illusion discursively maintained for the
> purposes of the regulation of sexuality within the obligatory frame of reproductive
> heterosexuality.[30]

There is no psychological "core" of gender identity, she argues. Rather, "true
gender is a fantasy instituted and inscribed on the surface of bodies," and
genders themselves are "produced as the truth effects of a discourse of primary
and stable identity." Butler maintains that identity is an "effect" that is produced
and that opens up new possibilities of agency.

Butler has said explicitly that "taking on a gender *role* as a choice" is explicitly
what she does not mean by performative gender; rather she means that "the
notion of 'choice' or 'self' is produced as an effect of a certain compulsory
repetition" and that "gender presentations produce the appearance of self-
identity as well as an inner 'truth' that they are said to express" (although gender
theory does not, as I see it, confuse the play of signs with playfulness). The
theatrical idea of performance implicit in Butler's work is nonetheless apparent
and a good deal more accessible than some of her more philosophically framed
statements. (Butler claims to be "somewhat dismayed" at "popular misappro-
priations" of her argument; if so, she might try communicating with her public
with some of Paglia's punch.)[31]

It remains unclear what kind of politics of gender Butler envisions. Her many,
many questions—piled up, five, six, and more in a row—play off against very
sharply reasoned arguments that both define and deny definition. (Butler takes
this Irigaray-esque tic to extremes; she even ends her book with a question
mark.)[32] Vague assertions of a new, as-yet-unthought world order are traditional
gestures in discourse that seeks empowerment. Given the radical intent of so
much that she professes, and the deliberately undecided rhetoric of so much
that she writes, it is reassuring to find that Butler, like Poovey, wants to point
the way to new territory, even though none of us knows what it is as we are
urged towards it.

Yet Butler's work with gender as performance has great value. Butler un-
dercuts the traditional anthropological hierarchy in which "culture" is seen as
a construct imposed on a prediscursive "nature," and, correspondingly, "gender" is seen as a construct imposed on "sex" (that is, in which sex, like nature,
is "raw," while gender, like culture, is "cooked"). Her poststructural account
of culture, which draws on Clifford Geertz's challenges to the "universal logic"
of Claude Lévi-Strauss's kinship systems, recasts old concepts of fixed oppression
in the new, slippery, and seemingly apolitical semiotic language. Butler argues

[30] Butler, *Gender Trouble*, p. 136, for this and the following quotations.

[31] "Judith Butler: Singing the Body," an interview with Margaret Nash, in *The Bookpress* 2 (March
1992), 5, 12. I thank John Ruffing for bringing this interview to my attention. Butler claims to have
based her position on Jacques Derrida's essay "Signature, Event, Context," a work that I have not
been able to find cited in her book.

[32] See Butler, *Gender Trouble*, pp. 5–7, for examples.

that only by dislodging biological oppression from its unchallenged place as a founding tyranny, as "sex nature before the law" which gender identity allows one to escape, can the potential of gender as more than "unnatural and non-necessary" be understood.[33] Suggesting that cultural configurations of sex and gender will proliferate in the postfeminist era, she writes, "What other local strategies for engaging the 'unnatural' might lead to the denaturalization of gender as such?"[34]

Butler's contribution is twofold. First, she complicates the simplistic distinction between sex and gender as natural and "produced," showing that gender, defined by repeated and exclusionary patterns of behavior, has come to be seen as expressive of an inner, genuinely personal core that is difficult to distinguish from natural sex. Second, although she resists the implications of her thesis for discussions of role-playing in texts, her idea of performance suggests processes important for understanding medieval texts in which gender identity is put into play. Her ideas are useful in examining grammatical gender in Old English and for rereading Old English saints' lives.

3. GENDER IDENTITY AND MEDIEVAL TEXTS

Butler's concept of gender is slippery and, in her own description, trouble-making. The slipperiness of gender conceived less radically—as a grammatical category—has long made trouble for traditionalists. In the hallowed orders of grammar, gender is murky when sex is not. In his analysis of grammatical gender in Old English, Bruce Mitchell notes that nouns may have "more than one gender" or show "change of gender." He observes that some changes involve the "replacement of gender-categories (masculine, feminine, and neuter) by those of sex (male, female, asexual)," but that other changes simply reflect the use of more distinctive phonological forms (for example, strong endings to adjectives) to indicate case, regardless of gender. Mitchell refers to those examples in which attributes of a noun do not agree with the noun's grammatical gender, but rather agree with its natural gender, as "triumphs of sex over gender." Such cases occur when neuter nouns that refer to males or females take masculine or feminine pronouns (*he* or *heo*) rather than neuter forms (*hit*), or when masculine nouns that refer to females take feminine pronouns. On the other hand, when masculine or feminine nouns referring to "asexuals" take masculine or feminine forms, Mitchell writes, "gender triumphs over sex."[35] It

[33] Butler, *Gender Trouble*, p. 37; on Lévi-Strauss see pp. 37–43.

[34] Irigaray's questions are designed to introduce "a plurality of voices," to examine "a priori concepts," without insisting on answers, according to her publisher; see *This Sex*, p. 221. For Butler's final question, see *Gender Trouble*, p. 148. It is encouraging to find a book opening with Butler's concluding rhetoric: describing the developing state of feminism in musicology, Susan McClary writes, "What would a feminist criticism of music look like? What issues would it raise, and how would it ground its arguments theoretically?" Susan McClary, *Feminine Endings: Music, Gender, and Sexuality* (Minneapolis, 1991), pp. 6–7.

[35] Bruce Mitchell, *Old English Syntax*, 2 vols. (Oxford, 1985), 1:33–37. See p. 33, par. 68, and, for examples of noun-pronoun agreement, p. 37, par. 71. See Charles Jones, "The Functional Motivation of Linguistic Change: A Study of the Development of the Grammatical Category of Gender in the Late Old English Period," *English Studies* 48 (1967), 91–111.

is the discourse of battle in this discussion, as Clare A. Lees observes, that is revealing: gender is ambiguous and unsettled, while sex is the determinant that the grammarians trust. "That is to say," Lees writes, "either biological sex has everything or nothing to do with grammar." Mitchell's discussion, as she points out, "is perhaps representative in that examples of miscongruence between nouns and attributive words are treated as exceptions to the conventional rule governing concord in Old English."[36] When nouns are sexed as male or female, the "natural" condition of grammatical gender favors congruence that clarifies identity, not contradictory data that confuse the identity of one sex with attributes of the other.

An early manifestation of gender anxiety is found in the strangely neglected writing of Thomas Jefferson on the Anglo-Saxon language. Jefferson wrote not only as an inveterate amateur scholar but also as a formidable authority in the early-nineteenth-century debate concerning the formation and regulation of American English as distinct from British English. Already at this point, gender was regarded as a potentially confusing sexual terrain that had to be ordered to make the masculine clearly superior to the feminine. Such figures as Noah Webster, Horne Tooke, and others in addition to Jefferson stressed the "Saxon" origins of the English language and sought to place the "common man" at the center of correct language usage. David Simpson describes their efforts to "speak out for the linguistic (and wider) authority of the common man and against the learned class and, perhaps, their patrons."[37] Although the framers of language wished to make the speech of the "common man" the standard, they also felt compelled to reject "rude" or barbaric precedents. Simpson states that they ultimately institutionalized the speech of "the American yeoman," who was nothing but "a translation of the English country squire, minus the loyalty of his retainers."[38] When "rhetoric of the common man" met the "ideal of national language," the result proved to be dependent on upper-class, if not aristocratic, precedent. The "yeomen" about whom Webster and others wrote were in fact wealthy landowners, said Webster in *Dissertations on the English Language*, "masters of their own persons and lords of their own soil. These men have considerable education."[39] Simpson notes that Webster omits reference to the speech of "real" common men, the peasant class, since the development of such a class was not anticipated in the United States. It is equally obvious that Webster does not need to consider the speech of women, even women "of considerable education" (although the education of the gentry household's females was not neglected). The dependence on tradition, which Simpson shows to have been obsessively important to Samuel Johnson, Edmund Burke, and other authorities on language use in the eighteenth century, ensured that wom-

---

[36] I quote Clare A. Lees from "Anglo-Saxon Studies: Gender and Power: Feminism and Old English Studies," coauthored with Helen T. Bennett and Gillian R. Overing, *Medieval Feminist Newsletter* 10 (1990), 15–23; on p. 15 Lees is identified as the author of the section on Old English language, pp. 19–20. See also Lees's forthcoming "Grammatical Gender in Old English."

[37] David Simpson, *The Politics of American English, 1776–1850* (New York, 1986), p. 83.

[38] Simpson, *The Politics*, p. 90.

[39] Noah Webster, *Dissertations on the English Language, with an Essay on a Reformed Mode of Spelling* (Boston, 1789), p. 289. Quoted in Simpson, *The Politics*, p. 70.

en's language would not become an issue as the speech of the "common man" was regulated. Public oratory, equally traditional and neoclassical, intensified the male domination of linguistic culture. Speakers evoked classical rhetorical ideals as a means of stressing the importance of masculine custody for the new nation's security.[40]

Jefferson's grammar of Old English asserts the superiority of the male by proscribing gender and reinstalling the clear distinctions of biological sex, which are safely ordered in other discourses in a pattern of male dominance. Jefferson's discussion of gender has been considered in the context of his unfinished "Essay on the Anglo-Saxon Language" in an article by Stanley Hauer and in an important book by Reginald Horsman.[41] Jefferson rejected classical languages as models for modern English and proposed sweeping revisions of method for the presentation and teaching of the Anglo-Saxon language. He protested that those who had written earlier grammars had given the language "too much of a learned form" and had endeavored "to mount it on all the scaffolding of the Greek and Latin, to load it with their genders, numbers, cases, declensions, conjugations, etc." He regarded these features as "embarrassments" that impeded understanding of the Anglo-Saxon language, much as Norman institutions, added to the Saxon heritage, had obscured its inherent purity.[42] Just as Jefferson sought to make Old English look as much like modern English as possible by reforming its orthography, and to recover obsolete words and restore some of the Anglo-Saxon vocabulary to popular speech, he sought to eliminate gender as a category from English grammar. Gender was among the distinctions between the classical languages and English for Jefferson:

> The word gender is, in nature, synonymous with sex. To all the subjects of the animal kingdom nature has given sex, and that is twofold only, male or female, masculine or feminine. Vegetable and mineral subjects have no distinction of sex, consequently are of no gender. Words, like other inanimate things, have no sex, are of no gender. . . . [G]ender makes no part of the character of the noun. We may safely therefore dismiss the learning of genders from our language, whether in its ancient or modern form.[43]

Jon Edgar Grant has pointed out that Jefferson's theory regarding gender is based on a misinterpretation of Elizabeth Elstob's *Rudiments of Grammar for the English-Saxon Tongue*, which reports that all nouns have gender.[44] His attempt,

---

[40] In the period from 1830 to 1860, Steven A. Wartofsky writes, "it is quite clear that at least in the American context, oratory and male power, male identity, are mutually reinforcing": "Critique of the Upright Self: Everett, Webster, Calhoun and the Logic of Oratory," *Massachusetts Review* 33 (1992), 401–26.

[41] The text has yet to be edited in complete form; for the currently available edition, see Thomas Jefferson, "Essay on the Anglo-Saxon Language," *The Writings of Thomas Jefferson*, ed. Andrew Lipscomb et al., 20 vols. (Washington, D.C., 1903–4), 18:365–411; quotation from p. 378. Stanley R. Hauer, "Thomas Jefferson and the Anglo-Saxon Language," *PMLA* 98 (1983), 879–98. Reginald Horsman, *Race and Manifest Destiny: The Origins of American Racial Anglo-Saxonism* (Cambridge, Mass., 1981; repr. 1986).

[42] See Jefferson's letter to J. Evelyn Denison, M.P., in *Writings*, 16:131.

[43] Jefferson, "Essay," pp. 376–78.

[44] Elizabeth Elstob, *Rudiments of Grammar for the English-Saxon Tongue* (London, 1715; repr. 1968), p. 8.

as Grant shows, is particularly important because Jefferson equates gender identity with sexual identity: that is, words that have gender are those marked "by
nature" as having sex: "priest, priestess." "Gender, for Jefferson, is equivalent
to sex: men are masculine, women are feminine."[45]

Jefferson desired a manly language to be spoken by the manly class. He and
Webster had no great admiration for one another, but their views on language
share some important points.[46] Just as Webster defined the yeoman as a land-
owning, educated country squire, Jefferson defined the language in which that
man's speech originated as manly. The elimination of gender confusion is not
simply an attempt to make gender confusion or neutrality in language an impossibility; it is also an attempt to define the language as manly by eliminating
any possibility for confusion between men and women. If the language clearly
demarcates the sexes, all will be well, for nature already shows that they are
different and that one is superior to the other. Elstob's interest in language is
an attempt to demonstrate that the language is democratic in a sense Jefferson
cannot admit: that is, that it is feminine at its root, that language is mothering
(the mother tongue). Jefferson's dismissal of gender is, therefore, a suppression
of ambiguity.[47] To insist that there is no gender is, in effect, to insist that the
sexes exist only in the form they naturally have, which is, also naturally, dominated by the male.

The gender anxieties of Jefferson and Mitchell suggest that gender, even
before its link to critical feminism, made traditional readers of Old English texts
somewhat nervous. By suppressing issues of gender identity and absorbing them
into traditional disciplinary paradigms—a comforting reassertion of "women in
history"—such readers miss opportunities to examine gender as performance,
as an identity element put into play in the Old English texts whose grammatical
norms are in question. Switches of gender identity are opportunities to explore
the meaning of gender itself as a performative category that interrogates the
natural positions of male and female that are opposed centers of gender anxiety.
I look for this middle ground in Old English figures who seem to define it, in
"manly women," a name for transvestite saints, women whose gender identities
must change before they can achieve the sanctity they desire.

I begin not with a manly woman but with a manly man in *Beowulf*. When
Hrothgar has rewarded the hero's victory over Grendel, the narrator says

> Swa manlice   mære þeoden
> hordweard hæleþa   heaþoræsas geald
> mearum ond madmum,   swa hy næfre man lyhð.
>
> (1046–48)

[45] I quote Jon Edgar Grant's unpublished paper, "Jefferson, Gender, and *Judith*: The Politics of
Reception," read at the 1988 meeting of the South Atlantic Modern Language Association, Washington, D.C.

[46] See Simpson, *The Politics*, p. 78, regarding Webster's contempt for Jefferson's ideas about
language and for their political disagreements.

[47] For a reading of Elstob in the context of gender and Old English poetry, see Gillian R. Overing,
"On Reading Eve: *Genesis B* and the Readers' Desire," in *Speaking Two Languages: Traditional
Disciplines and Contemporary Theory in Medieval Studies*, ed. Allen J. Frantzen (Albany, N.Y., 1991),
pp. 35–63; see pp. 35–36. See also comments in Frantzen, *Desire for Origins: New Language, Old
English, and Teaching the Tradition* (New Brunswick, N.J., 1990), pp. 52–53 and 60–61, and, for
comments on Jefferson's Anglo-Saxonism, pp. 15–19 and 203–7.

So manfully did the glorious prince, hoard-guard of heroes, repay the battle-rush with steeds and treasure that no man will ever find fault with them. (My translation; Fr. Klaeber's text)

"Manlice" is translated as "manfully, nobly" (Klaeber) or "generously" (E. Talbot Donaldson), choices that come as no surprise to anyone familiar with the ways in which Anglo-Saxonist editors have used glossaries to shape translations produced from their editions, and used translations to shape readers' ideas of the culture.[48] But is it the poet or the editors or translators who valorize "manly" as that which is "generous" and "noble" in this passage? Hrothgar seems to define the word "manfully" rather than to be described by it: the word need not mean "generous" or "noble" here, but instead "that which belongs to human nature as opposed to another"—for example, the nature of God or of the devil. This is not the only example of a word that acquires a specific sense because of an overdetermined poetic context, of course, but it is a good example of what it means to "gender" (as a verb) a text. The poet would seem to be referring to a kind of generosity appropriate to human nature such as no one (no "man") could fault. The word is not gendered by excluding the female from "manly," for Hrothgar's sex is plainly male; rather, the word need not be gendered but can be marked by reference to class.

A famous Middle English example is Chaucer's Monk, "a manly man, to been an abbot able" (General Prologue A167).[49] In this case, obviously, there is supposed to be some confusion between the sexuality—not the sex—of the character and his social role. The place of the "manly" man is well understood in the Middle English lexicon, where "manly" as an adjective has four senses: "human" (1); "masculine, male" (2); "brave" or "reliable" (3); and "noble, worthy" (4).[50] What is the point of saying that a monk is manly enough to be an abbot if abbots are supposed to be manly? The joke is that abbots are not supposed to be manly, meaning sexually identified as male; rather, they are supposed to be sexless in the sense that their sexuality is firmly under control. The Monk is presented as a sexualized—that is, gendered—male so that Chaucer can satirize him for being inappropriately worldly in this sense as well as in others (e.g., in having a fine horse), and simultaneously satirize the clergy for being less than manly—that is, claiming to idealize the sexless, when in fact sexless is what they are not.

The sexualized holy man helps us understand the manly woman. In the Old English saints' lives I examine, manliness is clearly marked by gender rather than by class. Three striking and related examples of the desexed holy woman

[48] Fr. Klaeber, ed., *Beowulf and the Fight at Finnsburg*, 3rd ed. with supplements (Lexington, Mass., 1953), p. 372. E. Talbot Donaldson, trans., *Beowulf: A New Prose Translation* (New York, 1966), p. 19. Donaldson's translation is reprinted in the *Norton Anthology of English Literature*, 1, ed. M. H. Abrams et al., 5th ed. (New York, 1986); see p. 47.

[49] I quote the General Prologue to *The Canterbury Tales* from Larry D. Benson, ed., *The Riverside Chaucer* (New York, 1987), p. 26.

[50] The adverb is equally rich: "in the human way" or "in a masculine way" (1); "like a good fighting man" (2); "with religious courage or determination" (3); or "with proper manners, courteously" (4). See *The Middle English Dictionary*, ed. Hans Kurath et al. (Ann Arbor, Mich., 1954–).

are Agatha, Eugenia, and Euphrosyne; the last two are transvestites, and all three are found in Ælfric's *Lives of Saints*. The audience of this vernacular collection was not monastic, as Ælfric suggests by noting that his patrons, Æthelerd and Æthelmær, are laymen. His previous collections, Ælfric says, concerned saints honored by the "English nation" generally; this collection, in contrast, deals with saints honored by the monks themselves.[51] If we allow that Ælfric's lay audience held monastic communities in high regard, this reference to an intended lay audience gives reference to gender and monastic life particular importance.

Like many other early saints, Agatha is the daughter of a wealthy family. She is desired by the cruel minion of the emperor, a governor named Quintianus. His attempts to corrupt her fail, for the "faith in her breast" cannot be "extinguished."[52] Quintianus subjects her to various tortures, finally putting her on the rack and cutting off her breast. Undaunted, Agatha replies, "Oh, you most merciless, are you not ashamed to cut off that which you yourself sucked? But I have my breast safe in my soul, with which I shall feed my understanding entirely" (1:202.124–26). The governor's punishment of her refusal to sin disfigures her womanhood but leaves her spiritual identity untouched. The true nature of her faith does not reside in her outer breast but in her inner breast, her soul—that is, not in her identity as a woman (which the pagan falsely assumes to be essential) but in her dedication to the true faith.

When her breast is miraculously restored by God's messenger (1:204.145), the furious governor throws Agatha onto burning coals. In the midst of the fire she cries out to God, "who created her in human form" ("to menn gesceope," 1:206.185), and dies. At her funeral, an angel of God, another creature "walking like a man" ("gangende swa swa mann," 1:206.199), bears a stone to her tomb. The pagan has failed to corrupt her by making her *his* woman: she is no woman if she is not a man's, and since she will not be a man's, she must be breastless, and in this like a man. When the breast is restored, Agatha is no longer manlike. Her identity crisis is a switch of gender brought about by the performative demands of her conversion. And the results are unmistakable. When she is restored to womanhood, we supposedly see that sexual identity is irrelevant to sanctity: breasted or unbreasted, Agatha is true to the faith. But sexual identity is in fact central to her story, for she has transcended the female body and become, however briefly, like a man. Thereafter she can once again be a woman, for now female secondariness is replaced by male secondariness—human secondariness—in the obliteration of human identity and the achievement of true holiness, as the manly angel at her funeral reminds us.

The transvestite saints illustrate this process of transcendence more clearly.

---

[51] Walter W. Skeat, ed., *Ælfric's Lives of Saints*, EETS OS 76, 82, 94, 114 (London, 1881–1900; repr., in 2 vols., 1966). "National" saints are those honored by "angel-cynn mid freols-dagum," while monastic saints are for "mynster-menn mid heora þenungum betwux him" (1:4). For a recent bibliography, see Gopa Roy, "Female Saints in Male Disguises: The Old English *Lives* of St Eugenia and St Euphrosyne: A Bibliographical Guide," *Medieval Sermon Studies* 31 (1993), 47–53.

[52] Skeat, *Lives*, 1:196, line 31. Further references to this collection are given by volume, page, and line number. Translations are mine.

Eugenia is the daughter of the governor of Alexandria and has been sent to school with her brothers; even her servants, Protus and Jacinctus (both eunuchs, significantly), are educated in Greek philosophy and Latin rhetoric (1:26.20–21). But she also hears about St. Paul and the Gospels, and with her servants seeks instruction in Christianity. She calls the eunuchs her "brothers," cuts her hair "after the fashion of men" ("on wæpmonna wysan"), and dresses as if she were a boy ("swylce heo cniht wære," 1:28.50–51); in this disguise, she presents herself to a bishop named "Helenus" (as if a masculine "Helen"?), who says that he has already learned in a vision that "she is no man" ("heo man ne wæs," 1:28.78), even though manly is what she wishes to be.[53] He warns that she will suffer terribly when her virginity is tested but that she will triumph. Thereafter Eugenia lives with a man's mind, although she is a woman ("mid wærlicum mode, þeah þe heo mæden wære," 1:30.93), and is elected abbot of the monastery (1:32.116–20).

Eugenia works many miracles and becomes a famous healer. A widow named Melantia is cured by her and falls in love with her, thinking that the beautiful maiden is really a young man (she comes to "þam wlytegan mædene," thinking that "heo cniht wære," 1:32.146). Melantia embraces Eugenia and offers her money, and, when this seduction fails, reports to Eugenia's father, Philip, that Eugenia, disguised as a physician, tried to rape her. Philip imprisons Eugenia, the daughter he does not recognize, along with her servants, whom he does not recognize either (of course). About to be tortured, Eugenia bares her breast to her father (1:38.234), who, with the rest of the family, converts and is subsequently punished by the emperor for treason. Like Agatha, Eugenia uses the disguise of a man to transcend a woman's body; she can bare her breast because she has used her manly status to become holy. Once she is returned to a woman's appearance, however, Eugenia—formerly the "abbot" of a monastery—founds a female monastery ("mynecena mynster," 1:42.311). She and her mother convert other women (for example, the widow Basilla, actually converted at Eugenia's direction by her eunuchs, 1:44.326–46), while the eunuchs convert young men (1:44.347–48). Eugenia's powers are, after her refeminization, contained within a woman's world.

Similar conditions obtain in the life of Euphrosyne (not written by Ælfric).[54] Euphrosyne's father, a prominent benefactor of the monastery where he and his wife pray, teaches the young girl and has her baptized. When she is going to be married, he decides that she must be educated in wifely behavior and takes her to the monastery for special instruction (2:336.36). Enamored of the faith, she plots to escape her marriage; a visiting monk reminds her that "Whoever will not forsake father and mother and all his kindred, and moreover

---

[53] Clare A. Lees's discussion of this language is forthcoming. See "Spirituality and Sex in Late Old English Prose Hagiography," a paper delivered to the Medieval Studies Center of Fordham University (February 1991); I thank Professor Lees for the opportunity to see this paper in prepublication form.

[54] The life is incorrectly titled by Skeat "Euphrasia or Euphrosyne," but the text refers only to Euphrosyne. For a discussion of authorship and for a fine introduction to these lives, see Paul E. Szarmach, "Ælfric's Women Saints: Eugenia," in Damico and Olsen, *New Readings*, pp. 146–57, at p. 156, n. 3.

his own soul, he cannot be my disciple" (2:342.112–14). Euphrosyne knows
that if she goes to a woman's monastery she will be found; she therefore changes
into a man's clothes, cuts her hair, and presents herself as a eunuch from the
king's household (2:344.140–42).

The abbot welcomes the newcomer, who says his name is Smaragdus, and
assigns him (her) to a senior monk for instruction. But there is a catch, for
Smaragdus is a great beauty:

> Because this same Smaragdus was beautiful in appearance, the cursed spirit sent many
> thoughts into the brothers' minds as often as they came to church, and they were very
> tempted by his fairness. And eventually the brothers became angry with the abbot
> because he had brought such a beautiful man into their monastery. And the abbot
> called Smaragdus to him and said, "My son, your face is beautiful, and great destruction
> is befalling the brothers because of their weakness. Now I want you to sit by yourself
> in your cell and sing the hours there, and eat there; and I do not want you to go
> anywhere else." (2:344.159–69)

Her father Paphnutius, distraught at Euphrosyne's disappearance, asks "both
slaves and freemen if they know what had been done to his daughter" ("[he]
ongan axian æt eallum ge þeowum ge frigum [hwæt] be his dohtor eufrosinan
gedon wære," 2:346.178–79). At the monastery the brothers are distressed and
pray that he will find her; Euphrosyne, alone in her cell, prays that he will not
(2:348.214–15). The abbot assures Paphnutius that no harm will have come to
her, and Paphnutius is temporarily consoled. On another visit he is sent to see
the holiest of the brothers, who is of course Smaragdus (Euphrosyne); Smaragdus recognizes her father, but he does not know her (she is much changed
by penitence). She teaches him, among other things, that "a man should not
love father and mother and other worldly things before God," thus invoking
the scriptural idea of leaving one's family to join the family of God (2:350.241–
43). Her father is so pleased that he tells the abbot he is as happy *as if* he had
found his daughter (2:350.258). Thirty-eight years pass. Paphnutius, now nearing death, returns to the monastery and spends three days with Smaragdus, and
at the end of that time she reveals herself to him as his daughter (2:352.290–
92). She dies; he inhabits her cell as she could not inhabit his house. Her teacher
asks that through her powers the other brothers will come manfully to safe
harbor ("werlice becuman to hælo hyðe," 2:354.316).

These lives detail the temporary obliteration of female identity in the male
for the purposes of conversion and the holy life. They show that the one-sex
model, in which the female is assumed to be included with the male, is doubly
hierarchical. The model subordinates women to men and the conflates male and
(secondary) female in another hierarchy under God, the force above the
"manly." The secondariness of the female is reinforced since the women can
be saved only by becoming like men. This transformation was, evidently, an
article of faith. Concerning the "apparent exclusion of women from the five
thousand fed by Christ," Ælfric wrote in a mid-Lent homily included in another
collection, known as *The Catholic Homilies*, "if a woman is manly by nature and
strong to God's will, she will be counted among the men who sit at the table

of God."[55] That is, the woman earns salvation by acquiring a man's nature; that is why, in these saints' lives, the woman first acquires *the appearance of* a man's nature: when the natural transformation is accomplished, the way for the supernatural transformation is prepared.

Theorizing about cross-dressing is, expectedly, kept to a minimum in the Old English texts. Ælfric's Latin source, Paul E. Szarmach observes, is more forthcoming. There Eugenia elaborates on the cross-dressing herself. "So great indeed is the power of [Christ's] name that even a women standing in fear of it may obtain a manly dignity (*virilem dignitatem*)," she says, "nor can a difference in sex be considered superiority in faith, when blessed Paul the Apostle, the master of all Christians, says that before God there will be no distinction between masculine and feminine."[56] This comment, as Szarmach notes, echoes St. Paul's to the Galatians, which itself concerns transformation since it deals with the need of Gentiles to become Jews before they can be saved. "There is neither Jew nor Greek; there is neither slave nor free [man or woman]; there is neither male nor female. For you are all one in Christ Jesus," Paul wrote (3.28).[57] Paul's letter argues that faith is the ground of one's true identity—as Agatha has demonstrated—and that, like ritual observances dividing sects, gender roles are secondary. This is Butler's performativity: gender is merely the *appearance* of self or identity that is constituted when repeated "performance" defines the possibilities for any man or woman at any point in history.

Cross-dressing and, more generally, gender are not theorized much more fully in current Old English scholarship than they are in Old English texts.[58] Lavishly praising Ælfric's narrative economy and coherence (a standard apology for Ælfric's apparent editing of source material), Szarmach suggests that Ælfric left out Eugenia's Latin explanation because it would have been too complex a doctrine to include. But he admits that "a purely literary explanation may not be as compelling in this case."[59] Indeed it is not compelling, and neither is the idea that Ælfric, in preparing a collection specifically for an educated audience, wanted to avoid theological complications. Eugenia's short speech in the vernacular version states the idea plainly enough: woman's chastity, her chief virtue and her ideal state in the world, is best protected—and is most holy—when she does the womanly thing and becomes a man.

Just as gender goes untheorized, relations between gender and other social factors go unobserved. Commenting on the use of transvestitism as a narrative

[55] Benjamin Thorpe, ed., *The Sermones Catholici or Homilies of Ælfric*, 2 vols. (London, 1844–46), 1:188. This text is quoted by Janet Bately, "Old English Prose," in Malcolm Godden and Michael Lapidge, eds., *The Cambridge Companion to Old English Literature* (Cambridge, Eng., 1991), p. 79.

[56] The Latin text and a translation are given by Szarmach, "Ælfric's Women Saints," p. 153.

[57] I quote *The Oxford Annotated Bible*, Revised Standard Version (New York, 1962), p. 1411. This edition claims that the letter to the Galatians is "often called the Magna Charta of Christian liberty" (!). See also the text quoted by Szarmach, p. 157, n. 21.

[58] For a full discussion of cross-dressing, see Marjorie Garber, *Vested Interests: Cross-Dressing and Cultural Anxiety* (New York, 1991). For important criticisms of Garber's methodology and assumptions, see the review by Anne Hollander, "Dragtime: The Professor, the Transvestite, and the Meaning of Clothes," *New Republic* (31 August 1992), pp. 34–41.

[59] Szarmach, "Ælfric's Women Saints," p. 154.

motif, Szarmach cites Vern L. Bullough's view that cross-dressing is "generally acceptable" in Christian narratives because "such a change is a healthy desire, as Bullough puts it, 'a normal longing not unlike the desire of a peasant to become a noble'."[60] But is it equally "normal" for a male to want to dress as a woman? Evidently not, although there are many examples in romance of knights who "cross-dress" in class terms and dress down as squires—usually to gain access to a beautiful woman.[61]

We can see that one compelling reason to look closely at transvestitism is that it links gender to class. Another is that it exposes the homosexual subtext of the hagiographic text. Female sexual aggression is mocked in Eugenia's life, in which the saint's beauty as an abbot incites another woman's lust. This test of the saint's virtue is presumably safe and perhaps no test at all, since the idea of a woman's sexual attraction to another woman is not seriously entertained. Melantia's lying servants are also ridiculed for claiming that a woman (i.e., Eugenia) tried to rape another woman. No *man*'s status is compromised by Melantia's advances: the widow's sexuality is out of control, but the man she would tempt commands powers of resistance.

In a similar vein, the monks in the monastery Euphrosyne joins first seem to be mocked as homosexual but, in the end, demonstrate their power to resist temptation. Smaragdus's beauty seriously disturbs the monks and threatens their damnation, a direct reference to homosexuality in the monastery, which was a serious problem, medieval handbooks of penance and other sources tell us, and not, one imagines, suitable for the monks' sacred reading.[62] But the narrative curbs the risk, since the source of the temptation to the homosexually vulnerable men (all of them, apparently) is a beautiful woman. Male beauty is represented to them in a transvestite form, just as it is to Melantia in the life of Eugenia. The manly men may be tempted by beautiful men or beautiful women, but the source of temptation is subordinate to their determination to resist it. However beautiful, Euphrosyne is above all holy and therefore wholly above the discourse of sex.

Two consequences of these women saints' lives as men must be clarified if we are to see the value of gender *as* performance. First is the role of female sexual aggression; second is the role of male sexual identity. Eugenia and Euphrosyne must disguise themselves as men in order to escape men—their fathers; Agatha annihilates her womanhood more effectively than her torturers when she disowns the breast she has lost in favor of the true faith in the breast of her soul. In each case womanhood must be denied because men necessitate the denial. Second, manhood itself, and in particular the eunuchs in each life, is also complexly represented. In these lives, women perform gender roles that are, for the men—the father, the abbot, the brothers, the eunuchs, the servants—

[60] Szarmach, "Ælfric's Women Saints," p. 148.

[61] I discuss the case of Arcite in the Knight's Tale in "Documents and Monuments: Difference and Interdisciplinarity in the Study of Medieval Culture," in *Speaking Two Languages*, ed. Frantzen, pp. 14–15. Another famous example from Middle English romance is King Horn.

[62] Male homosexual intercourse was severely punished in the penitentials. See Pierre J. Payer, *Sex and the Penitentials: The Development of a Sexual Code, 550–1150* (Toronto, 1984), pp. 135–39.

fixed.[63] Gender roles are performed by women in disguise; gender switching is seen as enabling. For a man to be holy is to act like a man; for a woman to be holy is also to act like a man. That is why these women must disguise themselves as men and deny their womanhood in order to be saved. Men, in other words, do not need to perform in order to acquire new gender identity.

Or so it seems, for the holy role models are all men, including abbots, bishops, and teachers. But it is also clear that *their* gender identity is harshly suppressed: indeed, they are sexless. That is why the brothers cause scandal by having sexual responses to Smaragdus as a beautiful man. The holiest men are manly— "wærlice," "manlice," "on wæpmonna wysan," and so forth—but not sexually male. Thus the women who, in order to become holy, cannot remain women are not alone. They are "manly" in giving up their sex, for that is what the *real* men, idealized in the eunuchs with Eugenia and the eunuch Euphrosyne claims to be, have already done. Real men finally transcend the body altogether, a performative gesture of their own, a repeated and ceaseless denial of the male body. As the first step in that process, their female counterparts must escape the female body by becoming manly; only then are they holy enough to die as women. All gender roles, therefore, are performative, and the hierarchy that relates them is likewise performative and never seen as naturally favoring the male.

Reading the saints' lives as demonstrations of gender performance runs counter to the traditional scholarly paradigm that sees these lives in a typological rather than a sociological context. As if writing in response to claims for "literary merit" in the saints' lives, such as those espoused by Szarmach, Michael Lapidge concludes a recent discussion of hagiography in the Old English period by reminding us that he has been "concerned principally with the function of hagiography in general, rather than with the literary merits of individual saints' lives." Although he would not "wish to deny that individual lives may have such merits," it is a violation of "hagiographical intentions" to see anything individual in the narratives, for it is in their collectivity that their representational power lies:

> Certainly Ælfric regarded himself as the apologist of the universal church: and it would have been no compliment to him to tell him that his hagiography had imparted individual characteristics to individual saints. . . . The saint's power of intercession was the hagiographer's uppermost concern, and hence it did not matter whether the saint was tall or short, fair or bald, fat or thin, blond or brunette.[64]

Despite what Lapidge says, physical beauty or fairness, always the property of the saint, matters greatly. Likewise, when Szarmach concludes that Ælfric gives us "an erotic story with no erotic content,"[65] he downplays the sexuality, homosexual and heterosexual, that bubbles beneath the surface of the text and that represents the complexity of medieval gender ideologies.

---

[63] I explore the implications of literacy and gender for performative identity in these saints' lives, in the early Middle English poem "The Love Rune," and in "Cleanness" in a forthcoming essay.

[64] Michael Lapidge, "The Saintly Life in Anglo-Saxon England," in Godden and Lapidge, *The Cambridge Companion*, p. 261.

[65] Szarmach, "Ælfric's Women Saints," p. 155.

4. WHEN NOTHING IS ENOUGH

My discussion of gender is nested within Old English saints' lives, within the narrow confines of Old English grammar, within contemporary criticism, and within professional academic life and its extraordinary (if recent) concern with class status. I have so situated it because my aim has been to show that gender theory frees up discursive space for both the scholar and the male and female subjects of medieval texts. Gender theory is, as I said at the outset, feminism's latest way of putting traditionalists on the defensive. Traditionalists should enjoy occupying both positions that gender theory puts them in: the newly powerful position of gender-conscious reader and the familiar position of defender of tradition. Now that traditionalists, especially men like me, are talking about gender, gender theorists have a new defensive position, too; their worry that feminism is losing its political edge is added reason to pursue their goals with new vigor.

Gender functions within the categories of tradition and innovation in the discussion of contemporary theory in medieval studies (greatly boosted by the 1990 issue of *Speculum* devoted to the topic), although gender is articulated rather imprecisely with them, often at their edges. Gender functions within other, more recently defined categories, including the hallowed entities of race and class, nationalism and professionalism, and other forms of identity, and within very old categories, such as grammar. True, if one positions his or her discourse at the edges where these categories meet, rather than clearly within one category or another, he or she risks being accused of indifference. For example, in a review of *Desire for Origins*, Alexandra Hennessey Olsen takes me to task for failing to acknowledge either gender or sexual identity as I examined the histories of Anglo-Saxon and medieval studies. I quote:

> The true value of the [first] chapter lies in its statement of Frantzen's own critical bias, his desire "to teach the cultural dimensions of Anglo-Saxon studies—connections to *race, expansionism, and class status*" (20; italics mine). As a woman, I immediately note Frantzen's omission of *gender* (which he briefly discusses on 106 and 170–71). I suspect that others might note his omission of *sexual preference*.[66] (Olsen's emphasis throughout)

Now the thesis of my book, stressed in every chapter, is that the pretense of bias-free scholarship is damaging to the integrity and integration of Anglo-Saxon studies. Indeed, the involvement of scholars in scholarship is fundamental to my argument. Here is my sentence in context:

> One who wishes to teach the paradigms of grammar can remain outside the material, much as a police officer can direct traffic without moving in it. One who wishes to teach the cultural dimensions of Anglo-Saxon studies—connections to race, expansionism, and class status—is immediately inside a discussion of values and beliefs, a web of lived experience into which and around which Anglo-Saxon texts and *all their teachers, readers, editors, and hearers are woven*. (P. 20, emphasis mine)

---

[66] Alexandra Hennessey Olsen, review of Frantzen, *Desire for Origins*, in *In Geardagum* 12 (1991), 63–66; quotation from p. 63.

Olsen assumes that gender is a sensitive subject for women only ("As a woman"); at the same time, while affiliating herself with that group, she makes sure that readers will not associate her with another ("others might note") covered by "sexual preference." Olsen here flaunts what Eve Kosofsky Sedgwick describes as a woman's "privilege as a presumptive heterosexual" who suffers one set of oppressions ("as a woman") but is enabled by others ("others might note").[67] I am held to be insensitive to both groups, but only because the reviewer suppresses the context and quotes only fifteen words from a forty-nine–word sentence (without bothering with ellipses). My inclusiveness is misrepresented as exclusive: because I did not single out women as a special group, the reviewer claims that I left them out. This is the "women in" approach with a vengeance. In an age in which many critics are anxious not to be seen as old-fashioned feminists, a few are anxious not to be seen as anything else.

Gender anxiety manifests itself in various kinds of defensiveness, of course, including my own. In both cases I have described, that of feminists (Poovey, Showalter, Butler, and others) and that of traditionalists (Jefferson, Mitchell, and other Anglo-Saxonists like me), those in power fear the loss of power; those at the center of attention fear that attention spans are short. Such fears are justified, particularly if the performance in question is an academic one, for scholarly fads fade. But the social questions that play mere supporting roles in these scholarly performances do not disappear. What is disturbing about old-style gender anxieties is that they claim to be free of any political commitments whatsoever. What is disturbing about new-style gender anxieties is the depressing frequency with which they confirm Showalter's warning that it is possible to talk about gender without any kind of political commitment except to the advancement of one's own career. Scholars, expensively dressed and well fed, gather at conferences of the most explicitly political sort to talk to their own kind, lament the encroachments of students on research time, and deplore the profanations of conscious neglect that their departments and universities visit upon them. The conversations at traditional conferences are exactly the same, and at both meetings there are additional complaints about the critical opposition. The political work of such meetings, in either camp, has little to do with the social problems of race, class, and gender that is not, to use Poovey's language, "positional." Whether scholars assume positions that are ostensibly political or apolitical, they are, in both cases, safely isolated from the larger social world. I believe that the isolation in either case is a serious failing, particularly to be lamented in those who see themselves as forces for change in the status of women or other groups. We have heard many times that it is false to assume that scholarship is above politics. Let us now see some demonstration of the difference between writing about oppression and doing something about it.

Of all the kinds of political discourse that the traditional academic disciplines have suppressed, sexuality, male as well as female, heterosexual as well as homosexual, has surely been suppressed most effectively. Whether seen as a subject of scholarship or as a personal attribute of the scholar, sexuality has been passed

---

[67] Eve Kosofsky Sedgwick, "Across Gender, Across Sexuality: Willa Cather and Others," *South Atlantic Quarterly* 88 (1989), 53–72; see p. 54.

over in favor of national identity and class solidarity, and those institutions were hardly recognizable as "race" and "class" because we were so used to seeing them in only one form. Now that sexuality (female sexuality, that is) and gender have risen to prominence, other political subjects, including race and class, risk being left out.

The chief value of gender studies to medieval studies is its power to join educational levels and lives that academic organization divides, not just the disciplines within any single level but institutions across many levels. Medievalists in the university fear that they are a vanishing breed. But few of them take seriously the power of medieval studies to link universities to other academic forums, such as high schools. Indeed, "secondary" education is a term that reveals too clearly how medievalists see the wider world and that suggests why they are reluctant to perform within it.

The 1991 meeting of the Medieval Academy concluded with a session discussing the importance of teaching medieval studies and the link of the Academy's work to high schools. But one had the feeling that the effort was itself secondary, just as teaching is so often secondary to research. The major paper in that session described the university as "the only semblance" of monastic "refuge" left to us and invoked a Gregorian balance between *saeculum* and *monasterium* that a call for more effective teaching would seem unavoidably to upset.[68] Although I prize peace and quiet as much as anybody else, and although I have deep respect for the need to reflect on our work as well as to carry it out, I resist the vision of the university as a monastic refuge. Instead, I advocate gender studies because gender is a good way to find out what happens when we set our scholarly concerns into the communities outside the academy. And just as we need to make men an object of study as prominent as women, we need to interrogate the relationships between academic privilege and social class, not as academic subjects but as extensions into the world outside offices and classrooms.

In a recent essay, Americanist Frederick Crews takes a stand between the theory-laden left with which much gender criticism is allied and the anti-theory right that regards theory as the onset of disciplinary decline. It is a mistake to view the academic left as a radical unity, Crews writes, for critiques of the left usually come "from segments of the left itself that continually deflate fashionable theories for their failures of social inclusiveness, concreteness, and practical utility."[69] By "practical utility" Crews probably means application in the classroom, as in the application of deconstruction to *Beowulf*. But practical utility has other connotations as well, in particular the application of insights gained from our work to the wider world.

There is much for professionals to do outside the academy to change the

---

[68] See Milton McC. Gatch, "The Medievalist and Cultural Literacy," *Speculum* 66 (1991), 591–604, especially pp. 603–4. Gatch appeals to medievalists to pay more attention to their teaching, and this I applaud; I make several arguments urging the same in *Desire for Origins*, pp. 201–26 especially.

[69] Frederick Crews, "The New Americanists," *New York Review of Books* 39/15 (24 September 1992), 32–34; quotation from p. 32.

social conditions that they discuss so enthusiastically inside it: community adult literacy, AIDS and HIV education, women's shelters, recordings for the blind, and dozens of other programs need skilled volunteers. Those activities relate directly to the social issues that are, at scholarly conferences, so frequently explored exclusively in their medieval forms (pestilence, sexuality, reading, literacy, orality, and others). The lead in bridging the academic and nonacademic worlds, and the various levels of the academy (and the Academy), should be taken by those who derive their professional capital from debating social issues in academic discourse, Marxists and feminists in particular, but not only them.

I realize that these comments resemble an old-fashioned polemic, an odd note on which to conclude a new-fashioned essay collection. Alone among scholars, *perhaps*, I do not regard polemic as inappropriate, and I welcome the debate that polemic seeks to provoke. There is, of course, special danger in polemic about gender. McIntosh, in a short essay that casts a long shadow over mine, writes that whose who "use their anger in a way that gives them pleasure" are "real to themselves."[70] Anger I leave to others; my focus has been the gender anxieties that make us "real to ourselves." We cannot all be gender theorists, obviously, but everyone should examine gender critically—not only those who think about it all the time but also those who never seem to think about it at all.

[70] McIntosh, "Interactive Phases," p. 33.

Allen J. Frantzen is Professor of English at Loyola University Chicago, 6525 N. Sheridan Rd., Chicago, IL 60626.

Bibliographies

Medievalism and Feminism
Judith M. Bennett

Feminist scholarship, because of its phenomenal growth and interdisciplinary range, has never been amenable to the static and controlled format of a printed bibliography. To be sure, bibliographies are regularly published, but by the time they are actually available in libraries or bookstores, they are already seriously out-of-date. As a result, trying to keep up with trends in feminist scholarship is an ongoing and never-ending task. I have found that one of the best strategies for following developments in the field is to peruse and read feminist journals on a regular basis. Apart from the obvious value to be derived from journal articles, I also learn a lot about feminist scholarship by reading the tables of contents of feminist journals, their book reviews, their bibliographies, and their other research aids. In the diverse and changing field of women's studies, journals are perhaps the best media for keeping up-to-date on developments. I hope, therefore, that readers will find useful the following list of *some* of the major journals for feminist scholarship.

FEMINIST JOURNALS AND REVIEWS

Feminist Periodicals: A Current Listing of Contents.
   I have placed this first and out of alphabetical order because, although not a "real" journal at all, *Feminist Periodicals* is perhaps the most important resource for keeping abreast of the periodical literature. Each issue reprints the tables of contents of dozens of feminist journals and also supplies information for subscribing to all of them (including most of those I've listed below). To subscribe to *Feminist Periodicals*, contact Phyllis Holman Weisbard, UW-System Women's Studies Librarian, 430 Memorial Library, 728 State St., Madison, WI 53706 (608-263-5754). The cost for out-of-state individuals in the United States is currently $25, and this includes two other useful publications: the quarterly *Feminist Collections*, which generally surveys library resources in women's studies (oriented towards librarians and bibliographers), and the twice-yearly *New Books on Women and Feminism*. *Feminist Periodicals* has been published four times a year since 1981.

differences: A Journal of Feminist Cultural Studies.
   As suggested by both its subtitle and its affiliation with the Pembroke Center for Teaching and Research on Women at Brown University, the editors of *differences* encourage and publish scholarship that combines postmodernism and feminism. Most (but not all) of its issues focus on a particular topic, e.g., "The Essential Difference: Another Look at Essentialism" (vol. 1, no. 2); "Sexuality in Greek and Roman Society" (vol. 2, no. 1); and "Queer Theory: Lesbian and Gay Sexualities" (vol. 3, no. 2). It

comes out three times a year and publishes no reviews. First published in 1989, this journal is already established as a major forum for cutting-edge theoretical work in feminist scholarship.

Feminist Issues: A Journal of Feminist Social and Political Theory.

Published since 1980, *Feminist Issues* comes out twice a year. Each issue is comparatively short (less than 100 pages) and may include as few as two articles. For medievalists, the chief value of this journal lies in its efforts to emphasize international and theoretical perspectives. Most issues include translated works by feminists from other countries. Book reviews are occasionally included, and one regular section of considerable human interest is the "*Feminist Issues* Sociological Interview," which chronicles the lives and thoughts of ordinary women.

Feminist Review.

Started in 1979, this London-based journal comes out three times a year. Like the U.S.-based *Feminist Studies*, it is strongly grounded in contemporary feminist politics and theory, and it publishes creative as well as academic work. Each issue includes a few book reviews as well as scholarly articles. Although *Feminist Review* has published only a few items on premodern women, it is an excellent vehicle for keeping up-to-date on feminist activities and feminist scholarship in Great Britain and Northern Ireland.

Feminist Studies.

Beginning publication in 1972, *Feminist Studies* is one of the first and best journals of feminist scholarship. Originally published in New York City, it has long been produced by an editorial collective headed by Claire Moses at the University of Maryland–College Park. The journal's offerings are eclectic, including creative works as well as articles and review essays. It comes out three times a year. Compared with *Signs* (the other premier U.S.-based journal for feminist scholarship), *Feminist Studies* might seem slightly less scholarly and slightly less historical, but it often presents research that is very hard-hitting in its feminism and very cutting-edge in its approach. As the editors emphasize in their statement of purpose, they "wish not just to interpret women's experiences but to change women's condition."

Gender and History.

First published in 1989, this is a transatlantic venture, edited in both England and the United States. The journal includes a very strong section of book reviews as well as articles on empirical topics, theory, and historiography. Of English-language journals in feminist history, *Gender and History* is the most strongly connected to the work and interests of European scholars. It is published three times per year, and about one issue annually is devoted to a special topic. In its short history, *Gender and History* has published a few articles on premodern women, and I understand that featured topics for the future include an ancient and medieval issue as well as an issue on witchcraft in early-modern Europe.

Genders.

Running underneath the title of this journal are four words that summarize its focus: "Art, Literature, Film, History." The order is important, for this is primarily a journal for scholarship on the creative arts. First published in 1988, *Genders* does not offer book reviews and comes out three times a year. Most articles focus on specific works or authors (a few, but only a few, premodern).

History Workshop: A Journal of Socialist and Feminist Historians.

Founded in 1976 as a journal for socialist historians, *History Workshop* has always included some feminist work, and in 1982 it officially took the subtitle "a journal of socialist and feminist historians." It is published twice a year, in the spring and autumn. Each issue includes articles and book reviews as well as a "Noticeboard" about forthcoming events and a "Report Back" section on conferences just past. In recent years, both Janet Nelson and Lyndal Roper have joined the editorial collective, and the coverage of premodern topics has expanded considerably. Almost every issue now contains material of interest to feminist medievalists, and issue 33 (Spring 1992) included a special section entitled "Europe's Medieval Origins?"

Journal of Feminist Studies in Religion.

Offering two issues per year since 1985, this journal is edited by Judith Plaskow and Elisabeth Schüssler Fiorenza. It sees itself as drawn from "two parents: the academy, in which it is situated, and the feminist movement, from which it draws its nourishment and vision." The *Journal of Feminist Studies in Religion* does not carry book reviews, but almost every volume includes articles of interest to medievalists.

Journal of Women's History.

First published in 1989 and coming out in three issues per year, this journal is especially valuable for its up-to-date coverage of developments in the practice of women's history in the United States (often via the publication of papers delivered at conferences). In addition to research articles, many issues include a "dialogue" on an issue of theoretical importance in the field. Including thematic reviews, abstracts of books, and a bibliography section (devoted to a specific topic each time), the *Journal of Women's History* also provides readers with an easy way to keep up with current literature. The bibliographies, however, cover only journals (thereby excluding the many articles published in edited books), and they tend to overlook or miscategorize entries on medieval topics. See vol. 2, no. 2, for a list of the journals included in the bibliographies. Although I certainly use these bibliographies, I never treat them as definitive. In 1992 the bibliographies already published in the journal were updated and published as *The Journal of Women's History Guide to Periodical Literature* (Indiana University Press). I consider the *Journal of Women's History* and *Gender and History* to be the essential journals in women's history. Of the two, *Gender and History* currently seems to be more accommodating to the interests of feminist medievalists.

Medieval Feminist Newsletter.

Begun in 1986, this newsletter is now essential reading for every feminist medievalist. It provides commentaries, book reviews, bibliographies and syllabi, announcements, and short articles (usually organized into a forum on, e.g., "Feminism and Medieval Art History" or "Gay and Lesbian Concerns in Medieval Studies"). Published twice a year, it is always a delight to read.

NWSA Journal.

This is the official journal of the National Women's Studies Association, published since 1988 on a quarterly basis. It offers articles, review essays, reviews of single books, and various reports and announcements. Although the *NWSA Journal* rarely includes information of direct interest to medievalists, it is very good for keeping up with the interdisciplinary field of women's studies. And some of its articles—especially those in its section "On Learning and Teaching"—are of broad interest to all feminist scholars.

Signs: Journal of Women in Culture and Society.

First published in 1975, *Signs* is one of the two top-rank journals for feminist scholarship in the United States (the other is *Feminist Studies*). It comes out quarterly. In addition to research articles, *Signs* publishes viewpoints, reviews (usually of a collection of books, not single volumes), archives (a section that prints transcripts of primary sources), and a series of invaluable review essays that offer quick introductions to the current state of feminist research in specific disciplines or topics. Since the editorship of *Signs* rotates to a new setting every five years, the character of the journal changes as well, but it has always remained a distinguished scholarly journal that regularly includes material on medieval or early-modern topics. In 1989 *Signs* devoted a special issue to scholarship on medieval women (vol. 14, no. 2). The articles in that special issue were combined with similar articles from earlier issues of *Signs* and published by the University of Chicago Press in *Sisters and Workers in the Middle Ages* (1989).

Women's History Review.

First published in 1992, this journal is still getting established. It is jointly edited from England and the United States, and it now offers four issues per year. It includes book reviews and viewpoints as well as articles. To date, it has not published any material on medieval women.

The Women's Review of Books.

Like *Feminist Periodicals*, *The Women's Review of Books* is not strictly a journal, but it is an invaluable resource for tracking developments in feminist scholarship. Since 1983 it has provided monthly (except for August) reviews of a wide range of books (scholarly as well as popular, nonfiction as well as fiction) of interest to feminist scholars. I find *The Women's Review of Books* an essential tool for following developments in the field, not only for its informative reviews but also for its bibliographic value; I keep up on the publication of new feminist books via its extensive advertisements from publishers and its extensive listings of books received for review. In addition to being informative, *The Women's Review of Books* is both amusing and stimulating. Issues often include reports on various subjects of current feminist concern (e.g., the circumstances of women's writers or women's reactions to the Gulf War) and very lively exchanges in the letters column.

Women's Studies.

Since its inception in 1972 this journal has enjoyed the continuous attention of one main editor, Wendy Martin. Under her guidance, *Women's Studies* has provided an important forum, particularly for literary scholars. It is published four times a year, and most of its articles focus on a specific work or author. Book reviews, although published, are few and far between. In 1984 *Women's Studies* devoted two numbers to an excellent special issue on medieval women (vol. 11, nos. 1 and 2).

Women's Studies International Forum.

First published in 1978, this journal seeks "to publish exciting, challenging, intellectually rigorous, women-centred radical feminist scholarship from all over the world." With editors covering all the continents (except Antarctica), *Women's Studies International Forum* is probably the most international of all feminist journals. It also offers many more issues per year (six) than other journals. In addition to articles, most issues also include a section for comments and/or reports on women's studies per se, as well as a few book reviews. This journal is very useful for keeping up-to-date with international developments, but it is not always reliable in terms of the quality of its articles. Yet some of the work published in *Women's Studies International Forum* is first-rate, and it is a place where articles are published with exceptional speed.

Patron or Matron? A Capetian Bride and a Vade Mecum for Her Marriage Bed
Madeline H. Caviness

Art history lagged behind in developing new theoretical frames comparable to those that transformed text studies or social sciences in recent decades. Art criticism, on the other hand, has developed theories in relation to recent and contemporary works: feminist critiques have especially contributed to a questioning of the canon of modern art and of the notion of the artist, and to identification of the male gaze within the general context of viewer reception; key contributions are included below. The challenge presented by a case study of the Hours of Jeanne d'Evreux as a contribution to feminist studies was to build on this new framework while maintaining a historical/new historicist perspective. To this end, I read extremely broadly, and encourage students in my courses to do likewise. It is not always predictable what area of new thinking will yield most for the medievalist. Useful as they are, I have decided not to list the several recent historical accounts of "women in the Middle Ages." The following bibliography, arranged topically and chronologically, attests to the general breakdown of disciplinary boundaries that is occurring all around us. It includes the readings that most challenged me during the interrogation of Jeanne's Hours, including points of departure in deconstruction and in the purported role of the unconscious that assisted me in constituting the role of the reader.

SELF-CONSCIOUS READING

Richard Wollheim. "Freud and the Understanding of Art." In his *On Art and the Mind: Essays and Lectures*, pp. 202–19. London, 1973.
  Encoding and decoding of unconscious elements in visual art.

Jonathan D. Culler. *On Deconstruction: Theory and Criticism after Structuralism.* Ithaca, N.Y., 1982. Especially pp. 42–64.
  On constituting the woman reading, especially resistance to patriarchal readings.

Jeffrey T. Nealon. "The Discipline of Deconstruction." *Publications of the Modern Language Association of America* 107 (1992), 1266–79.
  Critique of the simplification and codification of Derrida's philosophy, leading to deconstructions without a base in ethical praxis.

FEMINISM—GENERAL STUDIES OF SPECIAL IMPORT

Julia Kristeva. "Women's Time." Translated by Alice Jardine and Harry Blake. And Hélène Cixous. "Castration or Decapitation?" Translated by Annette Kuhn. *Signs* 7/1 (Autumn 1981), 13–35 and 41–55.

Toril Moi. *Sexual/Textual Politics: Feminist Literary Theory*. London, 1985.
> Critical analysis of the major feminist writers in the French and Anglo-American intellectual traditions (including Cixous and Kristeva), especially in relation to the politics of their writings.

Linda Alcoff. "Cultural Feminism versus Poststructuralism: The Identity Crisis in Feminist Theory." *Signs* 13/3 (Spring 1988), 405–36. And Karen Offen. "Defining Feminism: A Comparative Historical Approach." *Signs* 14/1 (Autumn 1988), 119–57.
> The relevance of history of/to feminism.

Josephine Donovan. *Feminist Theory: The Intellectual Traditions of American Feminism*. New York, 1985.
> Lucid account of the history of feminist ideas, especially in the U.S. The suggested dichotomy between cultural and radical feminism provides a useful fulcrum for discussion. A more nuanced view is that of Alcoff, 1988.

Jane Flax. *Thinking Fragments: Psychoanalysis, Feminism, and Postmodernism in the Contemporary West*. Berkeley, 1990.
> A practicing therapist examines the intersections between psychoanalytic theories, feminist theories, and postmodern philosophies.

Christine Di Stefano. *Configurations of Masculinity: A Feminist Perspective on Modern Political Theory*. Ithaca, N.Y., and London, 1991.
> Uses psychoanalytic object relations theory in a lively analysis of the writings of Hobbes, Marx, and Mill.

FEMINIST CRITIQUES OF ART HISTORY/ART CRITICISM

Linda Nochlin. "Why Are There No Great Women Artists?" In *Woman in Sexist Society: Studies in Power and Powerlessness*, edited by Vivian Gornick and Barbara K. Moran, pp. 344–66. New York and London, 1971.
> First resounding statement to the effect that "artistic genius" is socially constructed in ways that exclude women artists.

Laura Mulvey. "Visual Pleasure and Narrative Cinema." In *Art after Modernism: Rethinking Representation*, edited by Brian Wallis, pp. 361–73. New York, 1984. Reprinted in *Feminism and Film Theory*, edited by Constance Penley, pp. 57–79. New York, 1988.
> Reprints of her important 1975 study of the male gaze which objectifies women on film.

E. Ann Kaplan. "Is the Gaze Male?" In *Powers of Desire: The Politics of Sexuality*, edited by Ann Snitow, Christine Stansell, and Sharon Thompson, pp. 309–27. New York, 1983.

> Male domination of filmmaking and the cinema has erased the female, so that women have to identify as male viewers. Postulates the development of a female gaze.

Thalia Gouma-Peterson and Patricia Mathews. "The Feminist Critique of Art History." *Art Bulletin* 69 (1987), 326–57.

> Useful overview of contributions to the field.

Griselda Pollock. *Vision and Difference: Femininity, Feminism and Histories of Art.* London and New York, 1988.

> The paradigm shift called for by Nochlin: a series of essays on nineteenth-century and modern art explore issues such as the relation between ("Marxist") social histories or psychoanalysis and histories of art.

Carol J. Clover. "Her Body, Himself: Gender in the Slasher Film." In *Misogyny, Misandry, and Misanthropy*, edited by R. Howard Bloch and Frances Ferguson, pp. 187–228. Berkeley, Los Angeles, and London, 1989. Reprinted in her book, *Men, Women, and Chain Saws: Gender in the Modern Horror Film*, pp. 21–64. Princeton, 1992.

> Postulates the role of the male gaze in the creation of sado-erotic imagery.

Margaret R. Miles. *Carnal Knowing: Female Nakedness and Religious Meaning in the Christian West.* Boston, 1989.

> Biblical and early Christian texts, and a variety of medieval images, examined in relation to the politics of the female body.

Edward Snow. "Theorizing the Male Gaze: Some Problems." *Representations* 25 (Winter 1989), 30–41.

> Does not argue his case persuasively enough to free masculine vision from the charge that it is pervasively "patriarchal, ideological, and phallocentric." Instead, he turns the gaze back into the picture by analyzing the use of mirrors.

Joanna Frueh and Arlene Raven, eds. "Feminist Art Criticism." *Art Journal* 50/ 2 (Summer 1991).

> Contains several contributions that articulate the state of the question.

Kimberle Crenshaw. "Beyond Racism and Misogyny: Black Feminism and 2 LiveCrew." *Boston Review* 16/6 (December 1991), 6, 30–33.

> Contests Henry Louis Gates's defense of violent rap lyrics.

Nanette Salomon. "The Art Historical Canon: Sins of Omission." In *(En)Gendering Knowledge: Feminists in Academe*, edited by Joan E. Hartman and Ellen Messer-Davidow, pp. 222–36. Knoxville, 1991.

> Argues a link between the omission of women artists from the canon and masculinist constructions of the past: both are driven by the concepts of genius and influence that reenact father/son relationships.

Pamela Sheingorn. "The Medieval Feminist Art History Project." *Medieval Feminist Newsletter* 12 (Fall 1991), 5–10.

> Review of prior contributions; the introductory paper in the session in which I gave the first version of the case study printed here.

Norma Broude and Mary D. Garrard. *The Expanding Discourse: Feminism and Art History*. New York, 1992.

> Reprints of a number of articles on art of the Renaissance and later, demonstrating the sobering lack of such writings in the medieval field.

SOURCES OF "MEDIEVAL MISOGYNY" OR GYNEPHOBIA

In addition to the above, several authors have specifically treated this topic in relation to ancient philosophers, the Bible, and church fathers; a few such studies are listed here. In my view, "misogyny" is a misleading term, since it concentrates on only one of the manifestations of men's pervasive fear of women (gynephobia); another manifestation is anxiety, including doubts about paternity that give rise to genealogies and histories.

Mary Douglas. *Purity and Danger: An Analysis of Concepts of Pollution and Taboo*. London, 1966. Chapters 3 and 9.

> Comparative anthropology as a base for understanding commonly occurring phobias, such as menstrual pollution.

Karen Horney. "The Dread of Woman." In her *Feminine Psychology*, pp. 133–46. New York, 1967.

> Classic statement of the psychoanalytic view of the fear of women.

Wolfgang Lederer. *The Fear of Women*. New York, 1968.

> Broad treatment of psychoanalytic theory.

Rosemary Radford Ruether. "Misogynism and Virginal Feminism in the Fathers of the Church." In *Religion and Sexism: Images of Woman in the Jewish and Christian Traditions*, edited by Ruether, pp. 150–83. New York, 1974.

Prudence Allen. *The Concept of Woman: The Aristotelian Revolution, 750 B.C.–A.D. 1250*. Montreal, 1985. Especially chapter 4.

> Includes the ways female thinkers, such as Hildegard of Bingen, dealt with Aristotelian views on sexual difference.

Sharon Farmer. "Persuasive Voices: Clerical Images of Medieval Wives." *Speculum* 61 (1986), 517–43.

> Clerical views of the weaknesses and strengths of women.

R. Howard Bloch. "Medieval Misogyny." In *Misogyny, Misandry, and Misanthropy*, edited by Bloch and Frances Ferguson, pp. 1–24. Berkeley, Los Angeles, and London, 1989.

———. *Medieval Misogyny and the Invention of Western Romantic Love*. Chicago, 1991.

> Both deal with the many utterances against women as literary topoi.

Elizabeth A. Clark et al. "Commentary" on Bloch, "Medieval Misogyny." Bloch's response and "Editors' Note." *Medieval Feminist Newsletter* 6 (Fall 1988), 2–12; 7 (Spring 1989), 6–10.

> The critiques emphasize the varieties of woman-hating that have existed and contest that they are "only" a literary topos.

Elaine H. Pagels. *Adam, Eve and the Serpent*. New York, 1988.
A very useful survey of the exegeses of Genesis.

FEMINIST CRITIQUES OF HISTORY, PHILOSOPHY, ANTHROPOLOGY

Rayna R. Reiter, ed. *Towards an Anthropology of Women*. New York, 1975.
Includes a reconsideration of matriarchy.

Lillian S. Robinson with Lise Vogel. "Modernism and History." In *Sex, Class, and Culture*, edited by Robinson, pp. 22–46. Bloomington and London, 1978. Reprinted New York, 1986.
First formulation of the "new historicism" whereby the historian is acknowledged to be subject to historical processes.

Judith Lowder Newton. "History as Usual? Feminism and the 'New Historicism.'" In *The New Historicism*, edited by H. Aram Veeser, pp. 152–67. New York, 1988.

Andrea Nye. *Words of Power: A Feminist Reading of the History of Logic*. New York and London, 1990.
Critique of the privileging of logic in the history of philosophy (e.g., Abelard and Ockham).

Peggy Reeves Sanday and Ruth Gallagher Goodenough, eds. *Beyond the Second Sex: New Directions in the Anthropology of Gender*. Philadelphia, 1990.

POSTMODERN AND FEMINIST CRITIQUES OF BAKHTIN

Mikhail Bakhtin. *Rabelais and His World*. Translated with an introduction by Helene Iswolsky. Cambridge, Mass., 1968.
The translator situates Bakhtin's historical theories in his own immediate political and cultural environment.

Wayne C. Booth. "Freedom of Interpretation: Bakhtin and the Challenge of Feminist Criticism." In *The Politics of Interpretation*, edited by W. J. T. Mitchell, pp. 51–82. Chicago and London, 1983.
Notices Bakhtin's omission of women from pluralistic concepts such as "heteroglossia" that potentially should serve all participants.

Dominick LaCapra. "Bakhtin, Marxism, and the Carnivalesque." In *Rethinking Intellectual History: Texts, Contexts, Language*, pp. 291–324. Ithaca, N.Y., and London, 1983.
The role of "dialogization" as a tool for cultural studies.

Dale M. Bauer and Susan Jaret McKinstry, eds. *Feminism, Bakhtin, and the Dialogic*. Albany, 1991.
Opening chapters by Diana Herndl, Suzanne Kehde, Patrick Murphy, and Gail Schwab discuss the theoretical implications of "a feminine dialogic"; postmedieval case studies follow.

SEXUALITY/GENDER

Thorkil Vanggaard. *Phallòs: A Symbol and Its History in the Male World*. New York, 1972.

> Phallic cults in Europe from antiquity on; chapters 14–16 cover the Middle Ages.

Bruno Roy, ed. *L'erotisme au moyen âge: Etudes présentées au troisième colloque de l'Institut d'études médiévales*. Montreal, 1977.

> Several very useful essays, as cited in the footnotes to my article.

Michel Foucault. *Histoire de la sexualité*. 3 vols. Paris, 1976. Translated by Robert Hurley. *The History of Sexuality*. Harmondsworth, 1985.

> I relied especially on his notions of discourse, of plotting the experience of sexuality, and of an archaeology of problematization, as outlined in the first two chapters of volume 2, *The Use of Pleasure*. Arguments against his claim that there was no discourse of sexuality until the modern period were made in prior versions of my paper, but reduced to a passing reference (p. 53) in the final version.

Henri Rey-Flaud. *Le charivari: Les rituels fondamentaux de la sexualité*. Paris, 1985.

> Structuralist analysis of the varieties of mocking rituals in Europe, known from vestiges or descriptions.

Joan W. Scott. "Gender: A Useful Category of Historical Analysis." *American Historical Review* 91 (1986), 1053–75.

Teresa de Lauretis. "The Technology of Gender." In her *Technologies of Gender: Essays on Theory, Film, and Fiction*, pp. 1–30. Bloomington and Indianapolis, 1987.

> Theoretization of "women" and "men" as gender terms.

Irene Diamond and Lee Quinby, eds. *Feminism and Foucault: Reflections on Resistance*. Boston, 1988.

> Several useful reassessments, grouped under the headings of "Discipline and the Female Subject" and "The Uses of Foucault for Feminist Praxis."

Jill K. Conway, Susan C. Bourque, and Joan W. Scott. "Introduction: The Concept of Gender." In *Learning about Women: Gender, Politics, and Power*, edited by Conway, Bourque, and Scott, pp. xxi–xxx. Ann Arbor, 1989.

> History of the concept; its impact in various branches of investigation.

Monica H. Green. "Female Sexuality in the Medieval West." *Trends in History* 4 (1990), 127–58.

> Critical review of research on medieval texts dealing with female sexuality.

Thomas Laqueur. *Making Sex: Body and Gender from the Greeks to Freud*. Cambridge, Mass., 1990.

> Explores the history and politics of "scientific" views of sexuality and procreation.

Pseudo-Albertus Magnus. Translated by Helen Rodnite Lemay. In *Women's Secrets: A Translation of Pseudo-Albertus Magnus's De Secretis Mulierum with Commentaries*. Albany, 1992.

> Finally! A usable translation of this "seminal" thirteenth-century text on female sexuality.

SEXUAL HUMOR, JOKING, AND SLANG

Frederick Charles Forberg. *Manual of Classical Erotology (De figuris Veneris)*. 2 vols. Manchester, Eng., 1884.
> Indispensable reference for Latin vocabulary and excerpts; hard to find because librarians hide it away.

Sigmund Freud. *Jokes and Their Relation to the Unconscious*. Edited and translated by James Strachey. London, 1960.

Gershon Legman. *Rationale of the Dirty Joke: An Analysis of Sexual Humor*. New York, 1971.
> Modern jokes as expressions of male aggression and anxiety.

Thomas D. Cooke and Benjamin L. Honeycutt, eds. *The Humor of the Fabliaux: A Collection of Critical Essays*. Columbia, Mo., 1974.
> Useful analyses of pornographic and obscene elements in these vernacular tales by Cooke and by Roy J. Pearcy.

Barbara Westbrook Eakins and R. Gene Eakins, eds. *Sex Differences in Human Communication*. Boston, 1978.
> Includes a gendered analysis of modern slang by Julia Stanley.

R. Howard Bloch. "The Fabliaux, Fetishism, and Freud's Jewish Jokes." *Representations* 4 (Fall 1983), 1–26.
> Reflections on the world—and language—turned upside down, and the roles of displacement, obfuscation, and scotomization in the "humor" of the fabliaux.

Genders, Bodies, Borders:
Technologies of the Visible
Kathleen Biddick

Nancy Partner, the guest editor of *Speculum* for this special issue, has asked the contributors to produce an annotated bibliography of works from critical contemporary theories that inspired our essays. Such lists always run the unfortunate risk of looking like a canon, something whole, coherent, authoritative. I have tried to counter such a tendency by organizing the list around problems and debates in order to suggest the fluctuations and productive political disorder in critical debate today. In using the list readers are invited to imagine theoretical practices that continue to trouble the political spaces of theory suggested here.

PROBLEMS WITH REPRESENTATION, KNOWLEDGE, HISTORY

Our historical and theoretical work takes place within historically formed technologies of representation, recognition, specularity, visibility. The readings in this section gesture toward an abundant and discursive literature critical of the effects of modernity and its visualizations.

Jane Gallop. "Where to Begin?" In her *Reading Lacan*, pp. 74–92. Ithaca, N.Y., and London, 1985.

> Does looking into the mirror really organize the disordered body? Can theory help to fracture the organization of history?

Joan W. Scott. "The Evidence of Experience." *Critical Inquiry* 17 (Summer 1991), 773–97. Reprinted under the title "Experience" in *Feminists Theorize the Political*, edited by Judith Butler and Scott, pp. 22–40. New York and London, 1992.

> Does "experience" ground the identity of the subject? How can we call into question the originary status of experience in historical explanation?

Christina Crosby. *The Ends of History: Victorians and "the Woman Question."* New York, 1991.

Michel de Certeau. *The Writing of History*. Translated by Tom Conley. New York, 1988.

Nicholas B. Dirks. "History as a Sign of the Modern." *Public Culture* 2/2 (Spring 1990), 25–32.

> Crosby, de Certeau, and Dirks ask how history constituted itself as an epistemology and ontology during the nineteenth century. As a technology of the self how did history produce (and how does it continue to produce) foundational categories of time, space, gender, experience, and tradition as its effects?

James Clifford. *The Predicament of Culture: Twentieth Century Ethnography, Literature, and Art*. Cambridge, Mass., 1988.

Michael Taussig. *Shamanism, Colonialism, and the Wild Man: A Study in Terror and Healing*. Chicago, 1987.

―――. *The Nervous System*. New York, 1992.

> The mirror into which hegemonic history has gazed is shaped by culture. The participation of culture in the specular regime of history also needs to be considered. The Clifford volume provides a critical way into deconstructive ethnographic criticisms. Taussig is also engaged in a historical critique of the anthropological enterprise. His work radically questions abiding questions of time and memory that still dominate the practice of history today in the academy.

Trinh T. Minh-ha. *Woman, Native, Other: Writing Postcoloniality and Feminism*. Bloomington, 1989.

> Trinh's work may be productively read as a postspecular way of thinking about history, identity, and difference.

Bruno Latour. "Visualization and Cognition: Thinking with Eyes and Hands." *Knowledge and Society: Studies in the Sociology of Culture Past and Present* 6 (1986), 1–40.

> How do technologies produce power through visualization practices? Latour's work is an invaluable starting point for thinking about the materiality of specular, representational regimes of knowledge.

Jonathan Crary. *Techniques of the Observer: On Vision and Modernity in the Nineteenth Century*. Cambridge, Mass., 1990.

> A historical complement to Latour, Crary asks how the seeing body got made into the observer, an autonomous producer of visual experience. Crary's material genealogy alerts us to complexities of forms of control and the standardization of the gaze.

Rosalind E. Krauss. *The Optical Unconscious*. Cambridge, Mass., 1993.

Michel Foucault. *Discipline and Punish: The Birth of the Prison*. Translated by Alan Sheridan. New York, 1977.

———. *The History of Sexuality*, 1: *An Introduction*. Translated by Robert Hurley. New York, 1978.

> Where to begin with Michel Foucault, much of whose work involves a critique of technologies of the visible. Every reader has his or her own answer. These two books draw me back to rereadings.

READING AND WRITING PRACTICES:
EFFECTIVE HISTORIES AND NEW ARCHIVISTS

How can we read and write such that our reading and writing disrupt the circularity of specularity, a circle that produces knowledge of the already known and recognized? What if categories such as "Europe" or "man" are no longer the referents for history? Writers of color, postcolonialists, feminists, and queer theorists are grappling with this question in powerful ways. Effective histories can be thought of as counterdiscursive history-telling, which neither fashions a new coherence nor provides "better" readings of contradictions.

Gloria Anzaldúa. "La conciencia de la mestiza: Towards a New Consciousness." Reprinted in *Making Face, Making Soul/Haciendo Caras: Creative and Critical Perspectives by Women of Color*, edited by Anzaldúa, pp. 377–89. San Francisco, 1990.

Homi Bhabha. "Postcolonial Authority and Postmodern Guilt." In *Cultural Studies*, edited by Lawrence Grossberg, Cary Nelson, and Paula A. Treichler, pp. 56–68. New York, 1991.

Dipesh Chakrabarty. "Postcoloniality and the Artifice of History: Who Speaks for 'Indian' Pasts?" *Representations* 37 (Winter 1992), 1–26.

Donna J. Haraway. "Reading Buchi Emecheta: Contests for 'Women's Experience' in Women's Studies." In her *Simians, Cyborgs, and Women: The Reinvention of Nature*, pp. 109–24. New York, 1991.

Dominick LaCapra. "Rhetoric and History." In his *History and Criticism*, pp. 15–44. Ithaca, N.Y., 1985.

Bruno Latour. "The Politics of Explanation: An Alternative." In *Knowledge and Reflexivity: New Frontiers in the Sociology of Knowledge*, edited by Steve Woolgar, pp. 155–76. London, 1988.

Toni Morrison. "Unspeakable Things Unspoken: The Afro-American Presence in American Literature." *Michigan Quarterly Review* 28 (1989), 1–34.

Eve Kosofsky Sedgwick. "Privilege of Unknowing." *Genders* 1 (Spring 1988), 102–24.

Social Text 31–32 (1992).
A special volume devoted to criticism of "postcolonial" theories.

Gayatri Chakravorty Spivak. "The Rani of Sirmur: An Essay in Reading the Archives." *History and Theory* 24 (1985), 247–72.

Jennifer Terry. "Theorizing Deviant Historiography." *differences* 3 (Summer 1991), 55–74.

Patricia J. Williams. *The Alchemy of Race and Rights: Diary of a Law Professor.* Cambridge, Mass., 1991.

TROUBLING THE EFFECTS OF REPRESENTATION

1. FEMINIST THEORIES

It is possible to read the history of critical feminist theories in North America since the 1960s as a struggle with writing "effective histories," that is, histories that do not take for granted the production of knowledge as a reflection of the already known.

Jane Gallop. *Around 1981: Academic Feminist Literary Theory.* New York, 1992.

During the mid-1980s scholars of color and gay scholars called upon academic feminism to grapple with its differences (racial, sexual, class). The citations can only gesture toward the literature that challenged academic feminism and women's history in the mid-1980s. For historical cross-hatching of the debates see:

Cherríe Moraga and Gloria Anzaldúa, eds. *This Bridge Called My Back: Writings by Radical Women of Color.* 2nd ed. New York, 1983.
An example of the growing critique of academic feminism for its racism (awarded the Before Columbus Foundation American Book Award in 1986).

Gayatri Chakravorty Spivak. *In Other Worlds: Essays in Cultural Politics.* London, 1987.
An articulation of feminist theory in an international frame, another pressing concern of the 1980s.

Silvia Tandeciarz. "Reading Gayatri Spivak's 'French Feminism in an International Frame': A Problem for Theory." *Genders* 10 (Spring 1991), 75–90.
A recent criticism of a widely read essay in the Spivak anthology.

Teresa de Lauretis. "Feminist Studies/Critical Studies: Issues, Terms, and Contexts." In *Feminist Studies/Critical Studies*, edited by de Lauretis, pp. 1–19. Bloomington, 1986.

————. "The Female Body and Heterosexual Presumption." *Semiotica* 67 (1987), 259–79.

> De Lauretis strongly criticized the collapsing of sexual differences into gender and warned of the dangers of the occulted heterosexual contract operating in discussion of gender.

2. THE DEBATE OVER ESSENTIALISM

The debate over essentialism in critical feminist theory of the 1980s cannot be reduced to any simple description, since readings of essentialism are historicized not only by gender but by race, class, and the construction of homosexuality. Recent work in queer theory, in particular, is remapping the debate of the essentialists and the constructionists. The article by Katie King is a strong example of this refiguring. Scott's article is also important, since it articulated a strong constructionist position in a "mainstream" disciplinary journal. Donna Haraway usefully summarizes different historical positions in the essentialism debate in her essay. De Lauretis makes the important point that the debate needs to be read as a critical performance that articulates differences within feminism. Essentialist and anti-essentialist positions coconstruct each other, as Dollimore shows in *Sexual Dissidence*. The African-American theorist bell hooks joins a critique of essentialism and race. Eve Kosofsky Sedgwick remaps the essentialist-constructivist in her work in antihomophobic theory and has developed the terms "minoritizing" and "universalizing" to help us rethink this debate. Her work contains interesting critiques of both Michel Foucault and David Halperin.

Teresa de Lauretis. "The Essence of the Triangle, or Taking the Risk of Essentialism Seriously: Feminist Theory in Italy, the U.S., and Britain." *differences* 1 (Summer 1989), 3–58.

Jonathan Dollimore. *Sexual Dissidence: Augustine to Wilde, Freud to Foucault.* Oxford, 1991.

Donna J. Haraway. " 'Gender' for a Marxist Dictionary: The Sexual Politics of a Word." In her *Simians, Cyborgs, and Women: The Reinvention of Nature*, pp. 127–48. New York, 1991.

bell hooks. *Yearning: Race, Gender and Cultural Politics.* Boston, 1990.

Katie King. "Producing Sex, Theory, and Culture: Gay/Straight Remappings in Contemporary Feminism." In *Conflicts in Feminism*, edited by Marianne Hirsch and Evelyn Fox Keller, pp. 82–101. New York and London, 1990.

Joan W. Scott. "Gender: A Useful Category of Historical Analysis." *American Historical Review* 91 (1986), 1053–75.

Eve Kosofsky Sedgwick. *Epistemology of the Closet.* Berkeley, 1990.

3. UNPREDICTABLE INTERSECTIONS:
RETHINKING THE MATERNAL/QUEER THEORIES OF PERFORMANCE

In the 1980s feminist theorists struggled to rethink the maternal as a way of fracturing the essentialist debates. Criticisms questioning psychoanalytically based theories of the maternal (Freud, Lacan, Kristeva) began to intersect in unpredictable and often unacknowledged ways with queer theories of performance. In a move intended to remind us of the problems of the unpredictable intersections of feminist and queer theories, I have listed together here critiques of the maternal and theories of gender performance that have influenced my work. The crisis of psychoanalytic authority grows acute at these unpredictable intersections and needs more overt articulation in the late 1990s. Also in need of further work are Eve Kosofsky Sedgwick's arguments about the construction of the "women who can't know" as part of a discourse of both gay and homophobic constructions. The intersection of that historical construction with historical constructions of the maternal is much needed.

Judith Butler. *Gender Trouble: Feminism and the Subversion of Identity*. New York, 1990.

———. "Performative Acts and Gender Constitution: An Essay in Phenomenology and Feminist Theory." In *Performing Feminisms: Feminist Critical Theory and Theatre*, edited by Sue-Ellen Case, pp. 270–82. Baltimore and London, 1990.

Drucilla Cornell. *Beyond Accommodation: Ethical Feminism, Deconstruction, and the Law*. New York and London, 1991.

Teresa de Lauretis. "Sexual Indifference and Lesbian Representation." In *Performing Feminisms: Feminist Critical Theory and Theatre*, edited by Sue-Ellen Case, pp. 17–39. Baltimore and London, 1990.

Mary Ann Doane. "Technophilia: Technology, Representation, and the Feminine." In *Body/Politics: Women and the Discourses of Science*, edited by Mary Jacobus, Evelyn Fox Keller, and Sally Shuttleworth, pp. 163–76. New York and London, 1990.

Jane Gallop. *Thinking through the Body*. New York, 1988.

Ruth Leys. "The Real Miss Beauchamp: Gender and the Subject of Imitation." In *Feminists Theorize the Political*, edited by Judith Butler and Joan W. Scott, pp. 167–214. New York and London, 1992.

Eve Kosofsky Sedgwick. *Epistemology of the Closet*. Berkeley, 1990.

Kaja Silverman. *Acoustic Mirror: The Female Voice in Psychoanalysis and Cinema*. Bloomington, 1988.

4. Critiques of Interiority/Exteriority: Antihomophobic Discourses

The binary of interiority/exteriority is a powerful one that founds dominant representational practices. Recent work in feminist and queer theory is challenging how these notions function as the very figure for signification.

Diana Fuss, ed. *Inside/Out: Lesbian Theories, Gay Theories*. New York and London, 1991.

How Do I Look? Queer Film and Video. Edited by the Bad Object Choices. Seattle, 1991.

differences 3 (Summer 1991).

A special issue on queer theory.

Jonathan Goldberg. *Sadometries: Renaissance Texts, Modern Sexualities*. Stanford, Calif., 1992.

CRITICAL PEDAGOGY: THE BORDERS OF DESIRE,
IGNORANCE, KNOWLEDGE IN THE CLASSROOM

My essay ends by recalling the classroom and teaching. The following entries have inspired my work as a teacher.

Gloria Anzaldúa. "La conciencia de la mestiza: Towards a New Consciousness." Reprinted in *Making Face, Making Soul/Haciendo Caras: Creative and Critical Perspectives by Women of Color*, edited by Anzaldúa, pp. 377–89. San Francisco, 1990.

Walter Benjamin. "Theses on the Philosophy of History." In *Illuminations*, translated by Harry Zohn, pp. 255–66. New York, 1968.

Leo Bersani. "Pedagogy and Pederasty." *Raritan* 5/1 (Summer 1985), 14–21.

Jacques Derrida. "Violence and Metaphysics: An Essay on the Thought of Emmanuel Levinas." In his *Writing and Difference*, pp. 79–153. Translated by Alan Bass. Chicago, 1978.

Jonathan Dollimore. "Desire and Difference." In his *Sexual Dissidence: Augustine to Wilde, Freud to Foucault*, pp. 329–56. Oxford, 1991.

Shoshana Felman. "Psychoanalysis and Education: Teaching Terminable and Interminable." In her *Jacques Lacan and the Adventure of Insight: Psychoanalysis in Contemporary Culture*, pp. 69–97. Cambridge, Mass., 1987.

Henry A. Giroux and Roger I. Simon. "Popular Culture as a Pedagogy of Pleasure and Meaning." In *Popular Culture, Schooling, and Everyday Life*, edited by Giroux and Simon, pp. 1–29. Granby, Mass., 1989.

Chandra Talpade Mohanty. "On Race and Voice: Challenges for Liberal Education in the 1990s." *Cultural Critique* 14 (Winter 1989–90), 179–208.

Chantal Mouffe. "Feminism, Citizenship and Radical Democratic Politics." In *Feminists Theorize the Political*, edited by Judith Butler and Joan W. Scott, pp. 369–84. New York and London, 1992.

Eve Kosofsky Sedgwick. "Privilege of Unknowing." *Genders* 1 (Spring 1988), 102–24.

Ronald Strickland. "Confrontational Pedagogy and Traditional Literary Studies." *College English* 52 (1990), 291–300.

Simon Watney. "School's Out." In *Inside/Out: Lesbian Theories, Gay Theories*, edited by Diana Fuss, pp. 387–401. New York and London, 1991.

Lynn Worsham. "Emotion and Pedagogic Violence." *Discourse* 15/2 (Winter 1992–93), 119–48.

No Sex, No Gender
Nancy F. Partner

In looking outside of historical/contextual modes of analysis to other disciplines, I try to keep scrupulously in mind the lesson offered so cogently by philosopher Louis Mink and analyst-anthropologist George Devereux: that every form of explanation works within a frame of reference that implicitly suppresses other, alternative, frames of reference. No single-frame explanation of complex human behavior can possibly be adequate. Individual subjectivity exists only in a social world; cultural patterning meets the resistances of private ambitions.

DEPTH PSYCHOLOGY FOR HISTORIANS

My argument with the social constructionists is that their approach offers, in effect, only half an interpretation, especially given the complex matters of sexuality and social presentation they prefer to discuss. In exaggerating and wildly overstating the implications of cultural variation and of social conditioning on the individual, they reduce men and women to social puppets or embodied discourses and leave a great deal of life unacknowledged and unexamined. Given current academic fashions, it is the psychological aspect that needs renewed attention.

I can't help but suspect (mistakenly, I hope) that students are reading Foucault and perhaps some Lacan on sexuality while ignorant of the modern origins and classic texts of this field of inquiry; indicating a few indispensable works may be of use, and some others I have found most helpful.

Josef Breuer and Sigmund Freud. *Studies on Hysteria.* 1895. Reprinted in *The Standard Edition of the Complete Psychological Works of Sigmund Freud.* Translated under the general editorship of James Strachey. 24 vols. London, 1953–74. (Henceforth cited as *SE.*) Vol. 2. London, 1955. Also reprinted New York, 1957.

> Here is where it begins: the first understanding of the tension-filled intersection of sexual drives, social demands, and language. This crucial, fascinating book, the collaborative effort of Breuer and Freud, is the autobiography of the birth of psychoanalysis from the "talking cure" Josef Breuer learned from his brilliant patient, Anna O., through Freud's earliest case histories, with his explanation of the development of therapeutic method and theory of hysteria, and the relation of psychoanalysis to language and narrative structure. This book is notable for its candid self-exposure of false starts and failures as well as the principal author's respect for his patients.

Sigmund Freud. Explanations of the syndrome of hysteria: "Hysteria," *SE*, vol. 1, pp. 41–59; "The Aetiology of Hysteria," *SE*, vol. 3, pp. 191–221; "On the Psychical Mechanism of Hysterical Phenomena," *SE*, vol. 3, pp. 27–39.

> Hysteria was the first neurotic illness to be studied by Freud as well as by many contemporaries (including Charcot and Janet in France), and analyses of hysteria yielded the basic principles of psychic structure and conflict. It is very unfortunate that the mere word "hysteria" should have become a casual emblem of insult to women in the minds of many feminists including medievalist students of mysticism, but even worse is that the term is used by scholars in its colloquial, popular, wholly incorrect usage. Scholars should at least insist on knowing the correct analytic meaning (which is not derogatory to women). In addition to the well-known case histories, some of Freud's discussions include those cited above.

———. *The Interpretation of Dreams*. 1900. Reprinted in *SE*, vols. 4–5, and widely available elsewhere.

> One of *the books* of modern culture, this is also a work curiously and especially accessible to medieval scholars who will recognize immediately the universal deep stratagems of mind which inform the allegorical tropes of biblical exegesis and medieval language theology, here analyzed at work in dreams.

———. "Three Essays on the Theory of Sexuality." 1905. Reprinted in *SE*, vol. 7, pp. 135–243, and widely reprinted.

> Another of the indispensable core statements of analytic theory; feminists who insist on rejecting Freud should at least read him first.

———. "Five Lectures on Psycho-analysis." 1910. Reprinted in *SE*, vol. 11, pp. 8–55.

> The lectures delivered at Clark University in Worcester, Mass., 1909; one of Freud's most cogent and lucid summaries of the basic principles and terminology of psychoanalysis, excellent for teaching.

———. "Obsessive Actions and Religious Practices," *SE*, vol. 9, pp. 117–27; "Character and Anal Eroticism," *SE*, vol. 9, pp. 169–75; " 'Civilized' Sexual Morality and Modern Nervous Illness," *SE*, vol. 9, pp. 181–204; "Family Romances," *SE*, vol. 9, pp. 237–41.

> Dating from the years 1906–9, these short essays are of great interest to historians.

Peter Gay. *Freud: A Life for Our Time*. New York and London, 1988.

> As much intellectual history as biography; see especially Gay's clear and informative discussion of Freud's thoughts about women, pp. 501–22.

———. *Freud for Historians*. New York and Oxford, 1985.

> Gay argues for his project of psychoanalytically informed history and against the most common objections.

Sander Gilman, ed. *Introducing Psychoanalytic Theory*. New York, 1982.

> This is the book Gilman recommends to readers of his very popular *Difference and Pathology* for understanding the premises of his argument. A useful set of essays based on a lecture series at Cornell University on psychoanalytic theory for undergraduates, part 1 expounds basic elements of psychoanalysis; part 2 relates psychoanalysis to other disciplines.

Alan Krohn. *Hysteria: The Elusive Neurosis*. New York, 1978.
> A historical and clinical treatment of this contentious subject by an analyst, combining an excellent survey of the history of diagnosis and treatment, structural analysis of the syndrome, and case histories bringing this most protean and socially impressionable of syndromes into near contemporary times. This book is far more useful for a historian's understanding than the widely read but poor work by Ilza Veith.

Many readers share my deep respect and enthusiasm for Robert Stoller's work; it combines his many years of clinical experience with gender-disorder patients, a flexible, self-questioning, acute interpretive ability, and a generous, accessible, engaging writing style. Stoller is a Freudian analyst who accepts important modifications of the theory with respect to female identity and development; his concept of the "core gender identity" genuinely helps one to think about this politically charged subject in intelligible human terms. The development of gender identity in relation to sexual and social behavior was the focus of all Stoller's clinical and theoretical work.

Robert J. Stoller. *Sex and Gender*. 2 vols. Vol. 1: New York, 1968. Vol. 2: London, 1975.

————. *Splitting: A Case of Female Masculinity*. New York, 1973.

————. *Perversion: The Erotic Form of Hatred*. New York, 1975.

————. *Sexual Excitement: Dynamics of Erotic Life*. New York, 1979.
> Both this book and *Perversion* seem to me necessary reading for anyone interested in current trends in scholarship on sexuality. The bland acceptance, via some strangely mild and evasive readings of Foucault, of domination and submission as the core of normal human erotic life which marks so much current writing should invite critical inspection. Knowledge of the psychic role of hostility in sexual excitement is a good place to start.

————. *Observing the Erotic Imagination*. New Haven, Conn., 1985.

————. *Presentations of Gender*. New Haven, Conn., and London, 1985.
> To judge from what I have read, sophisticated scholars are actually capable of forgetting that sex assignment and gender identity involve more than visible anatomy and social performances. There are some biological facts concerning hormone production and balance, brain chemistry, etc., that are not susceptible to alteration by discourse. Stoller's summary of the biological, psychological, and social factors involved in producing a mature female or male person is exceptionally clear and well organized.

ANTHROPOLOGY

Historians read anthropology these days quite routinely, and these books are only some that I have found very compelling and which I think are less known than the work of Clifford Geertz, say, or Victor Turner. Discovering the work of George Devereux, both a psychoanalyst and anthropologist, and his strict protocol for using approaches that draw on psychic and social life respectively, was exhilarating.

George Devereux. *Basic Problems of Ethnopsychiatry*. Chicago and London, 1980.

> The particular value of Devereux's work for historians is his understanding of the universal structures and resources of mental life combined (but never confused) with his fieldwork-based knowledge of the great variations produced by cultural patterning. He introduced the concept of the "ethnic disorder": a psychopathology that conforms to cultural expectation in its expression, a concept of great value to historians. See especially chapter 1: "Normal and Abnormal." This book contains a bibliography of Devereux's writings from 1933 to 1978.

―――. *Ethnopsychoanalysis: Psychoanalysis and Anthropology as Complementary Frames of Reference*. Berkeley, Los Angeles, and London, 1978.

> The title sets the theme; the severely condensed first chapter, "The Argument," deserves close study for the rigor with which it expounds the principles of "double discourse," in which forms of explanation are to be pursued thoroughly in their own terms, never blurred or fused into self-contradictory hybrids. The essays in this book all carry out Devereux's project of understanding behavior as both personal and collective.

Gilbert Herdt. *The Sambia: Ritual and Gender in New Guinea*. Fort Worth, Tex., and Chicago, 1987.

> Herdt's work is fairly often cited by constructionist scholars because he studied New Guinea tribes which forced all boys to live in active homosexual, male-only groups until marriage, when they were expected to be exclusively heterosexual husbands and warriors. These studies are cited disingenuously as modern evidence of the plasticity and ease with which humans can live according to social/sexual models wholly different from our own, and as proof of the constructedness of all norms of sexual and social behavior. The fieldwork should be read for information about the massive coercion, suffering, and violence required to enforce this social behavior on successive generations, and the resulting endemic hatred and dysfunctional relations between men and women. Herdt's work is illuminating, and he is not responsible for its misuse. His discovery of a classic Oedipal origins myth invented independently by isolated New Guinea tribes is very interesting.

Gilbert Herdt and Robert J. Stoller. *Intimate Communications: Erotics and the Study of a Culture*. New York, 1990.

> Extraordinary and original collaboration, undertaken in New Guinea, on the possibilities of psychoanalytic investigation in fieldwork; both authors comment in dialogue form.

I. M. Lewis. *Ecstatic Religion: An Anthropological Study of Spirit Possession and Shamanism*. Middlesex, Eng.; New York; etc., 1971.

> Rather well known, this nondogmatic, sensible, and sensitive work covers a great deal of information across cultures on mystics and the social functions of mysticism; of considerable use to medievalists, it allows for a double discourse between social function and psychic meaning.

BOOKS WITH A DIFFERENCE

This brief miscellany consists of books that have shown me the many ways in which historical studies can acknowledge the mind, the self, the private wish and rebellion, within the confines of culture and the movement of event.

Peter Brown. *The Body and Society: Men, Women, and Sexual Renunciation in Early Christianity.* New York, 1988.

> In addition to the comments in my essay, I should stress that while Brown obviously appreciates Foucault's insights into ancient protocols of sexuality, this is emphatically not a Foucauldian study. Attention to the language, structure of metaphor, and presiding assumptions ought to show any reader that this is a beautifully achieved "double discourse," balancing psychological insight with historical/cultural sensitivity.

E. R. Dodds. *Pagan and Christian in an Age of Anxiety.* Cambridge, Eng., 1965.

> Study of attitudes toward life, mortality, the body, and the world from about the second century B.C.E. through the first two centuries of the Christian era; deftly incorporates psychological insights with deep knowledge of the ancient world.

————. *The Greeks and the Irrational.* Berkeley, 1951.

Kenneth Dover. *Greek Homosexuality.* London, 1978.

> Constructionist scholarship stands very heavily on the shoulders of this work, which carefully documents the sexual practices, attitudes, and patterns of approved behavior among upper-class Greek men, based on extensive use of vase paintings to supplement the literary and legal evidence. An urbane and fastidious scholar with no ideological agenda, Dover does not at all argue toward a constructionist view of human nature although his work has been more or less appropriated for the constructionist thesis; unsurprisingly, his findings work well with other points of view.

David Kunzle. *Fashion and Fetishism: A Social History of the Corset, Tight-Lacing and Other Forms of Body-Sculpture in the West.* Totowa, N.J., 1982.

> This is a surprising book. The subject indicated by the title is surveyed from antiquity to the twentieth century, with most material on the nineteenth century; the approach is cultural, sociological, and, in a nondoctrinal, implicit way, psychoanalytic. The salutary surprise consists in the entirely persuasive demonstration that what would appear, by a too-obvious sort of feminist interpretation, to be the perfect emblem of patriarchal domination of the female body was really a female-controlled device of personal gratification and social defiance. Many of the themes (discipline and pleasure, medical and scientific discourse, social patterning and private wishes) will be familiar to readers of Foucault, but the tone is quite different and this book's world is filled with women. This study constantly reminds me that meaning is rarely read off the surfaces of things.

Jonathan Lear. *Love and Its Place in Nature: A Philosophical Interpretation of Freudian Psychoanalysis.* New York, 1990.

> Another surprising book, this one by a classicist, author of two books on Aristotle. In this original essay, carefully and lucidly constructed, Lear's deep knowledge of classical philosophy and psychoanalytic theory are logically combined in his discussion of the crucial, central role of love in the psychic economy: the structure of the self and its basic stance towards the world. In an academic world apparently infatuated with the explanatory force of concepts of power, domination, control, and discursive processing, it is very satisfying to read this study of self-reflection, rationality, freedom, and love.

When Women Aren't Enough
Allen J. Frantzen

Gregory W. Bredbeck. *Sodomy and Interpretation: Marlowe to Milton*. Ithaca, N.Y., 1991.

This book typifies some notable trends in gender theory, in particular the intersection of writing about gender with the developing area of "queer theory." Bredbeck is a Renaissance literary scholar whose readings of plays and poems by Shakespeare, Marlowe, and Milton are not going to make medievalists regret their choice of specialization. His survey of Renaissance writing about sodomy includes little-known nonliterary texts (although they are read with literary interpretation in mind). Sodomy, Bredbeck notes, involved both women and men, although (pace several asides regarding the lesbian community) he focuses almost exclusively on sodomy and men. Sodomy was sexually nonspecific and was applied to a range of unorthodox acts; it included several acts (not only sexual) that transgressed social boundaries, gender boundaries included. Bredbeck writes in an academic atmosphere that plainly privileges his kind of scholarship, but you'd never know this. His last chapter, grim and gratuitous, struggles to portray the author as an outcast. Another young scholar victimized by an Ivy League education (Pennsylvania), a good job (California at Riverside), and first book with a major university press!

Judith Butler. *Gender Trouble: Feminism and the Subversion of Identity*. New York, 1990.

This is an important, but badly written and poorly edited, book that does not serve introductory purposes well. Butler claims that gender is not a cultural idea "written on" sexual bodies (a widespread belief) but that gender is instead a way of producing sexual identity through performance and repetition. Butler's view of gender as performative has won quick acceptance, but her idea of the performative is based on poststructuralist language theory and is much more philosophical—and much less merely theatrical—than some of her followers seem to think. Butler's critique of another popular topic—the exchange value of women—is a stimulating and much-needed reworking of Claude Lévi-Strauss's often-invoked, but rarely examined, model.

Caroline Walker Bynum. *Fragmentation and Redemption: Essays on Gender and the Human Body in Medieval Religion*. New York, 1992.

This collection of Bynum's essays engages current research in a variety of disciplines. Several essays address the fluidity of gender boundaries in the Middle Ages and the tendency of medieval writers to use such terms as "male" and "female" without regard for physiological constraints ("The Body of Christ in the Later Middle Ages" and other examples). Bynum asserts the difference between sexuality and genitality and stresses that the sexual content of medieval art should not be understood only (or at all?) in terms of modern sexual conduct. Like other books by Bynum, this one pointedly refrains from engaging the contemporary theoretical ideas that would seem to be closest to her subjects (e.g., gender theory or feminist theory of any stripe; Foucault is mentioned but twice). *Fragmentation and Redemption* takes no pains to identify its own assumptions as theoretical, but the essays are nonetheless rich and rigorous in their assessment of work from various disciplines (anthropology, e.g., and Victor

Turner's concept of liminality). Bynum has mastered a laconic style and takes some amusing sidelong glances at contemporary culture; she reprints a tabloid front page announcing "Human Soul Weighs 1/3000th Of An Ounce," for example ("This proves there IS life after death, say top scientists"). Bynum's caption for the illustration reads, "A modern argument for survival after death emphasizes material continuity."

Catherine Clément. *Opera, or the Undoing of Women*. Translated by Betsy Wing. Minneapolis, 1988.

Medievalists sometimes need to explore nonmedieval (i.e., postmedieval) materials in order to learn more about their own periods. Gender theory, a poststructuralist by-product, all but requires us to start in the modern period and work backward to medieval ideas. Gender theory also encourages exploration of other disciplines, and of these, especially for literary and historical scholars, music seems unusually promising. Clément's book (like Koestenbaum's and McClary's, both below) analyzes a number of female stereotypes that opera has taken over from literary forms and calls attention to ways in which operatic form adapts textual modes of encoding gender to its own conventions. As an entry into the gender-rich codes of opera, one of the twentieth century's most innovative and yet tradition-laden forms, Clément's book can scarcely be bettered.

Jonathan Dollimore. *Sexual Dissidence: Augustine to Wilde, Freud to Foucault*. Oxford, 1991.

By "sexual dissidence" Dollimore means the use of gender to undermine the assumed opposition between dominant (heterosexual) and subordinate (homosexual) cultures. Dollimore analyzes various modes of transgression that express resistance to cultural domination. Gender and some of the operational strategies of gender, including cross-dressing, are discussed throughout the book. Dollimore stresses the social and revo-lutionary implications of gender inversion. The reading of Augustine, frankly hostile, is challenging and refreshing. Dollimore's book is wide-ranging, as the title indicates, and annoyingly diffuse when it degenerates into short reviews of writing about homo-sexuality by novelists, playwrights, and others. But his frequent recourse to Renais-sance texts helps to render this book, which is densely theoretical, accessible to me-dievalists.

Michel Feher, ed. *Fragments for a History of the Human Body*. Vol. 3. Zone 5. New York, 1989.

Scholarship about gender benefits from engaging the representational power of the body and the history of the body as a representational device. This is a big, beautiful, lavishly illustrated book about the use of the body as a vehicle for cultural ideas from the classical period to the nineteenth century. Essays by Thomas W. Laqueur, Françoise Héritier-Augé (two each), Giulia Sissa, and Aline Rousselle pertain most directly to medieval issues. The collection is cross-cultural and, given the possibilities, unavoidably eclectic. It contains an extensive annotated bibliography, and it would make a superb textbook.

David F. Greenberg. *The Construction of Homosexuality*. Chicago, 1988.

Gender studies and gay studies are, with the increasing specialization of the latter, now separate territories. This book, traditional in its methodology, was written when the two fields of inquiry seemed closer than they now do, and it is all the better for its synthetic grasp of the subject. Greenberg surveys the history of homosexuality in a wide range of Eastern and Western cultures, from ancient civilizations to the present. He shows how the construction of deviance necessarily involves the construction of the norm; he finds much evidence in earlier cultures for the tolerance of male and female homosexuality, but he resists the compulsions that embarrass some more recent work on the topic. He does not use early evidence to valorize homosexuality as normative, and he does not dwell on indictments of the modern age. Greenberg shows how certain sexual sins—e.g., sodomy—were used in the Middle Ages to attack non-sexual practices also considered excessive. This is not a history of homosexuality but rather a sociology of the subject, focused on patterns and processes rather than on a specific period in time. Not the least of the book's many important contributions are Greenberg's concluding reflections on methodology.

Geoffrey Galt Harpham. *The Ascetic Imperative in Culture and Criticism.* Chicago, 1987.

Harpham's book is another that does not directly take up gender as its subject but that engages gender consistently in several ways. This is a superb discussion of asceticism as portrayed in the temptation of St. Anthony, commentaries on that event, other saints' lives, and related sources. The first chapter is a dense but readable discussion of the relationship between ascesis and linguistic theory, and it benefits from powerful observations on narrative. Harpham is obviously at ease writing at a high level of theoretical sophistication. Subsequent chapters on Augustine's *Confessions* and the Isenheim Altarpiece are closely argued and sharply observed. Harpham is an impressively synthetic thinker who holds together disparate topics, navigates historical detail gracefully, and writes clearly in a contemporary critical idiom. This is a book with the power to change the way one thinks about some revered medieval traditions, including martyrdom and sacrifice. The final section, on criticism and theory, examines interpretation as an act that involves both desire and ascesis. In the end, Harpham puts the critic in St. Anthony's place—a position, one sometimes gets the impression, that medievalists who are asked to read contemporary criticism think they already occupy.

Luce Irigaray. *This Sex Which Is Not One.* Translated by Catherine Porter, with Carolyn Burke. Ithaca, N.Y., 1985.

The poststructuralist feminist rereading of Freud is greatly indebted to this frank and diverse group of essays that reflect on Irigaray's earlier *Speculum of the Other Woman.* The argument is that female sexuality has always been framed within terms of masculine sexuality and that a reconceptualization of female sexuality perforce results in a new view of the sexuality of the male. Chapters on Marx (and the exchange value of women) and on the subversive function of male homosexual relations are especially resonant. This is one of the most readable psychoanalytical books ever written, and its representation of gender theory as that which necessitates a reconceptualization of the masculine is of fundamental importance.

Linda Kauffman, ed. *Gender and Theory: Dialogues on Feminist Criticism.* New York, 1989.

Kauffman asked half of her contributors to write essays and the other half to respond to them, and her collection benefits from this innovative approach, although in some cases the writing is so personal, one would have thought, as to be silly if not unworthy of publication (Jane Tompkins and Gerald M. MacLean are mutually excessive). However, one of the good things about gender theory is that it closes the gap between scholars' personal and professional voices, and this collection makes a real contribution to that venture. A collection of essays by medievalists disciplined along similar lines would have obvious merit. Anybody interested?

Wayne Koestenbaum. *The Queen's Throat: Opera, Homosexuality, and the Mystery of Desire*. New York, 1993.

> This very funny and very "out" book has two subjects: the diva, the opera star whose roles represent the female as powerful, unnatural, and hence doomed; and the diva lover, the other "opera queen," the gay male who performs self-authorizing roles offstage. Koestenbaum enriches his self-exploration with scholarly detail about the development of recorded sound and its early accommodations to mass taste, about early manuals on training the voice, and a number of other topics involved in translating gender ideologies into text, music, performance, and criticism. This is a learned and often moving book that directly addresses gender issues in criticism and culture. "We know that words and music are gendered properties," he writes; "it's a commonplace idea that language is masculine and music is feminine" (p. 177). But opera tries to blur the distinction between these two halves: language can be musical, music has languages of its own, and many operas play with the distinction between male and female ("trouser roles," for example).

Salvatore J. Licata and Robert P. Petersen, eds. *Historical Perspectives on Homosexuality*. New York, 1981. (= *Journal of Homosexuality* 6 [1980–81].)

> This collection of essays explores perceptions of homosexual behavior from the Middle Ages to the modern period. Homosexuality is crucial to gender studies since it displaces traditional understandings of male and female desire; homosexuality is indeed a test of what cultures consider typical and appropriate behavior for men and women. This collection is, within the ever-expanding horizons of gender studies, a dated one, and the politics in some of the essays will strike some readers as hopelessly naive, even counterrevolutionary. But as a medieval-to-modern survey it is hard to beat; indeed, it is exactly this kind of mixing of the historical, the scholarly, and the political that nourishes gender studies. This, too, would make an excellent textbook.

Susan McClary. *Feminine Endings: Music, Gender, and Sexuality*. Minneapolis and Oxford, 1991.

> Musicology is an academic discipline, McClary argues, curiously unresponsive to the importance of gender in its history and development. Medievalists will find the more explicitly historical chapters valuable (the first four); they describe gendered aspects of traditional music theory and discuss gender and the musical construction of characters in operas by Monteverdi, Bizet, Donizetti, and Strauss. The musical ideas discussed in the book are heavily literary and are, in many cases, based on recognized literary works. McClary's book demonstrates the usefulness of gender in exploring the close connection between literary and musical forms and their ways of encoding sexual difference.

Joan Wallach Scott. *Gender and the Politics of History*. New York, 1988.

> Scott's book is a concise and clear summary of the history of gender studies and their importance for revisionist scholarship. Scott is not a "theorist" per se—Butler is, Dollimore is—and her work is therefore particularly accessible to readers who approach the subject of gender with skepticism. The first two chapters are a splendid introduction to the emergence of feminism in history. Since the book largely is a collection of essays about nineteenth-century historiography, readers will have opportunities to observe Scott's traditional historiographical methods as they interact with gender theory. Her focus on labor as a site for the interaction of historiography and gender theories is most welcome.

Victor J. Seidler. *Rediscovering Masculinity: Reason, Language and Sexuality.* London, 1989.

> Seidler's argument about masculinity parallels some aspects of Irigaray's (he doesn't seem to have used Irigaray, however). His subject is the illumination of "men's contradictory relation to an experience and culture supposedly made in their image" (p. 201, n. 1). He maintains that personal experience "must be recognized as opening up ways of locating ourselves within a shared experience of power and subordination" (p. ix). Seidler identifies rationalism as the chief source of difficulties for men in the feminist age; "[i]f it is important to recognize . . . that our identities are historically forged," he writes, "it is also important to retain the substance of our individual experience as a theoretical resource" (p. 1). This admirable, direct, and coherent essay casts doubt not only on the purity of theory as an alternative to experience but on the foundations that contemporary scholarship has built on both Freud and Marx. Many men who read it will be reading about themselves.

Elaine Showalter, ed. *Speaking of Gender.* New York, 1989.

> There are a number of other collections about gender and gender politics. Showalter's has a good mix of essays that focus on the institutions of criticism, on the varieties of gender theory, and on applications (if that isn't too crude a word) of gender theory to texts ranging from the Renaissance to contemporary film. Essays in the sections called "Gender Subtexts" (especially Patrocinio P. Schweickart's) and "Reading Gender" (Susan Stanford Friedman's and Phyllis Rackin's) are useful and informative.